THE SHADOW WAR

Resistance in Europe 1939-1945

By the same author

The Second World War

HENRI MICHEL

THE SHADOW WAR

Resistance in Europe 1939–1945

Translated from the French by
Richard Barry

ANDRE DEUTSCH

First published 1972 by
André Deutsch Limited
105 Great Russell Street London WC1

Copyright © 1970 by Editions Bernard Grasset
Translation copyright © 1972
by André Deutsch Limited
All rights reserved

First published in France under the title
La Guerre de l'Ombre by Henri Michel

Printed in Great Britain by
Ebenezer Baylis and Son Ltd
The Trinity Press, Worcester, and London

ISBN 233 96350 2

Contents

Introduction   7

PART I – *The Occupiers and the Allies*

1   The Occupation and Exploitation of Europe   19
2   The Collaborators   35
3   External Resistance – the Allies and the Exiles   49

PART II – *Origins and Organisation of Clandestine Warfare*

4   First Moves   73
5   Propaganda   87
6   Movements and Circuits   102
7   External Contacts   118

PART III – *Component Forces of Resistance*

8   Classes and Groups of Society   135
9   Political Parties, Trades Unions, Churches   150
10 The Captive Societies   166
11 The Communists   181
    APPENDIX – Women in the Resistance   193

PART IV – *Hundredfold Battle*

12 Passive and Administrative Resistance   197
13 Sabotage, Assassinations and Strikes   207
14 Conspiracies   230
15 The Resister's Calvary   245

PART V – *The Shadow Army*

16 Guerrilla Warfare – *Maquis* and Partisans   267
17 The Clandestine State   292
18 The National Rising   315

19 Seizure of Power – Restoration, Renovation or Revolution?   335

Conclusion   355
Chronology   361
Abbreviations   383
Bibliography   385

Introduction

During the second world war two types of warfare were waged. The first ranged the vast regular armies of the two sides against each other: while hostilities were in progress it monopolised the communiqués; everyone was convinced that its outcome would decide the future of the world. The second was fought in the darkness of the underground: in a desperate effort, apparently doomed to failure by the disparity of forces, the vanquished and occupied peoples rose against their conquerors and oppressors. Not until liberation did the existence of this clash become partially known; even today it is still shrouded in some mystery and is shot through with myth and legend.

On the Allied side these two parts of a single whole were as different as night from day. On occasion, moreover, they followed differing paths, at best running parallel: in China, Chiang Kai-shek's troops looked down on those of Mao Tse-tung; in France the clandestine organisation which sprang from the Armistice Army long kept itself to itself. Sometimes mutual distrust, to some extent inherent in the situation, even produced definite hostility: Rokossovsky's army remained inactive on the banks of the Vistula until the flames of the Warsaw rising were extinguished. In most cases, fortunately, co-ordination was achieved and in some it was of great symbolic significance; in Corsica, for instance, a 'shock battalion' arriving from Algiers combined with the local *maquis* to throw the occupiers into the sea. But integration invariably came late in the day and was an uneasy process. In all countries regular officers showed a certain scorn and no small lack of understanding of the 'little war'; on their side the underground fighters considered that the traditional rules of war did not apply to, indeed were at variance with, the specialised nature of the warfare on which they were engaged.

The fact was that, whatever their numbers, whatever the quantity and efficiency of the weapons they used, whatever the country or régime they served, the regular armies of the second world war were, from the qualitative point of view, waging warfare similar to that of their predecessors. On both sides and in all theatres of war they were directed by staffs receiving directives from the governments they served; they fought without seeking to change the machinery of state, the administration, the economy or diplomatic usage; they merely made use of these things in order to harness every effort towards the attainment of a single goal – victory. Their battles on the ground formed part of broad strategic concepts in which visions of the political future combined with short-term military objectives and were sometimes even the governing factor. Battles were fought on a well-tried pattern: invariably the object was to assemble forces superior to those of the enemy, to engage them wisely at the right place and the most favourable moment in order to annihilate or capture the enemy's forces, to conquer his territory and dictate an armistice to him. Once the play was over, the curtain would fall and an interval of peace ensue.

In this traditional form of warfare every precaution is taken to ensure that the opposing forces can recognise each other. In principle, they fight according to the 'rules of war' which guarantee a minimum of protection to civilians, occupied peoples or prisoners of war. In general terms the opposing units are similarly organised, their dispositions are comparable, they are subject to an identical hierarchy and a major factor in their strength is the discipline of their members. Every man can therefore fight his enemy to the death while at the same time respecting him because he sees in him a counterpart to himself. The average soldier worries little about what his enemy is thinking or the ideology which inspires him – before the Normandy landing Patton told his subordinates that the problems of fascism and democracy were no more important than the electoral battles periodically fought by Republicans and Democrats in the United States. In short, soldiers in regular armies want to be no more than technicians of war pursuing their trade to the best of their ability.

The 'little war', the clandestine war, had its place in the 'big war'. From the 'big war' it drew its strength and its hope; it mirrored the Allied cleavages – the counterpart to the Anglo-American/ Soviet alliance with all its arguments and misunderstandings was the co-operation, sometimes tinged with drama, between communists and nationalists. Yet it was something quite different; its aims were different and its methods were its own. Its troops, for instance, were haphazardly raised; their arms were always inadequate and their training left much to be desired. They could not, therefore, deliver a frontal attack; they could not hope to engage in a decisive battle; they could not have a strategy and they could only embark on tactical operations. In their weakness they were often forced to refuse battle, to vanish when the threat was too great and to reappear at a different place and time when conditions had again become more favourable. When von Paulus' Sixth German Army was surrounded and made prisoner at Stalingrad, its war was over and it departed into captivity; when the guerrillas were crushed at the Vercors or in the Auvergne in July 1944, guerrilla warfare flared up again in August. Clandestine warfare knows no armistice or cessation of hostilities; it lights fires which are never extinguished; its embers may even flare again after the major war is over – as happened in Greece.

The clandestine warrior harbours no great vision that one day he will carry the war into the enemy's country; he is fighting on his own territory, while his country's armies have either been beaten or are fighting far away, perhaps overseas. Of course he is fighting the invader, but he is also fighting those friends whom the invader may have been able to recruit. There are two sides to the war of resistance: it is both a foreign and an internal war; as such it may have to paralyse the administration, sabotage the economy and destroy the communications of its own country to prevent the enemy from using them.

As a result, clandestine warfare does not obey the 'rules' of conventional war: it is not 'chivalrous'; sometimes it must even use 'unfair' methods. It does not, for instance, allow itself the luxury of keeping prisoners; it punishes 'traitors' severely, without trial, sometimes without verifying that treason has been committed. Equally, to fight it, the occupying power makes use less of his regular forces than of specially-trained units formed into an organ of repression whose favourite weapon is merciless cruelty. One side uses assassination, sabotage and surprise attack to which the other replies with torture, shootings, summary executions and the destruction of farms and villages. Both work more or less according to the motto 'If it's not you, it's your brother'; insecurity is answered by terror. Clandestine warfare therefore soon assumes a character of implacability – fires raging, prisoners screaming

1*

under 'questioning', weeping hostages being marched off in chains. It ends only in the pale dawn with the firing squad at work or in the smoke of the concentration camp crematoria; even then the end is only temporary, for 'when a comrade falls, a comrade takes his place', emerging full of resolution from the inexhaustible reservoir provided by an entire population of accomplices. A regular army invariably lives somewhat apart from the population; the men of the *maquis* and the partisans must be immersed in it 'like the fish in water'.

Since he is a volunteer obeying solely his own impulses, the clandestine fighter spurns the ritual associated with professional armies – discipline, external marks of respect, uniform, ranks, unquestioning obedience. He challenges the leader in whom he has no confidence; he insists on his right to demobilise himself at the moment of his choosing. Most important of all, he never separates his actions as a fighter from his views as a citizen. The war he wages is ideological as much as national; it will not necessarily end when the occupying power has been beaten and driven out, because the political aims which he desires must be achieved as well.

These are some of the characteristics peculiar to clandestine warfare; they are to be found in the past in the actions of the Chouans in France, of the Gueux in the Netherlands, the carbonari, the Polish revolts of 1863, the Spanish guerrillas of 1809, the Russian peasants of 1812 and the French francs-tireurs of 1871. None of these earlier stories had really been studied; people knew of them as part of popular mythology, but the lessons to be drawn from them often seemed obscure. Occupied peoples who had apparently resigned themselves to slavery seemed one day to have recovered their freedom without bloodshed – like the Czechs three centuries after they had been crushed at the White Mountain. These memories of the past, often a distant past, provided food for thought and for propaganda, but they hardly produced any direct guidance for action.

If any general rule was deducible, it was that in most cases the revolting peoples had been easily crushed if left to themselves – for instance, Vercingetorix at Alesia, the Spaniards under the Moors or the Italians charging the Austrians with the proud motto *Italia farà da se*. Conversely, the majority of peoples who had recovered their independence had done so with the aid of powerful foreign support: the Irish had been upheld by the large numbers of their fellow countrymen who had emigrated to the United States; the Kingdom of Sardinia had been supported by Napoleon III, the Belgians by Louis-Philippe; it had taken a world war to create or revive the Polish, Finnish, Czechoslovak and Yugoslav states.

But history never deals its cards the same way twice; between 1939 and 1945 occupied Europe was in a situation without parallel or precedent. In the first place the extent of the occupation was unparalleled; it stretched from Finistere to the Volga, from the North Cape to Cape Matapan. Secondly, the occupying power was no mere conqueror and looter; nor was he satisfied with re-drawing the map and departing once his ambitions were fulfilled. He had a doctrine, and a philosophy which he intended to impose; he believed in the superiority of his race and he made no secret of the fact that, because they had been beaten, the occupied peoples would be turned into slaves and a whole hierarchy of enslavement instituted. Any tendency to show pity, generosity or indulgence he regarded as a sign of weakness.

Faced with this terrible enemy resistance could not apply any of the lessons which it might have learnt from the past. It had to think out from the beginning its objectives, its methods of warfare and the weapons it would use. On the other hand, it did have one advantage over its predecessors: it could benefit from a technique born of the progress of science and applicable primarily to communications and liaison. We shall be dealing later with its development and employment. This was to extricate the Resistance from its isolation and give it its niche in the great Allied coalition.

Although 'British resistance' and 'Soviet resistance' are current phrases, we shall obviously not deal with the former – the Channel Islands were the only parts of Great Britain to be occupied. As far as the latter is concerned, we shall not tell the story of the battles fought by the Red Army but only of those fought by the inhabitants of the occupied areas of the USSR. The first characteristic common to resistance throughout Europe is that it was a *patriotic struggle to liberate national territory*; this was as much the overriding object of the Dutch as it was of the Czechs or the Byelorussians; this was the aim which led many Frenchmen or Poles to forget their peacetime differences and co-operate in the same battle on which their freedom and the future of them all depended.

But the second world war was not a repetition of the first. The occupier was not the enemy armed forces alone; he did not manifest his presence solely through the location of his armies. In his baggage train he brought a doctrine and a political régime which he intended to impose and perpetuate, and both had their formidable acolytes, the ss and Gestapo. Mussolini had announced that 'the twentieth century would be fascist' and Hitler had proclaimed that he would construct a 'Thousand-Year Reich'. Experience proved, however, that fascism, and even more nazism, was as fundamental a negation of a western civilisation founded on humanism, Christian morals and the liberalism of an enlightened century as it was of communist democracy, the *raison d'être* of which was the advancement of the working classes. As well as being a patriotic struggle, therefore, the Resistance was also an *ideological struggle for the dignity of man*; on this basis it was possible for Catholics, communists and liberal agnostics all to find themselves in the same camp – something which would have been unthinkable before the war.

If these two axioms be accepted, it is clear that all those who took the side of nazi Germany during the war were by definition enemies of the Resistance; this was clearly so in the case of the 'collaborators' whose existence added a third dimension to the resistance problem, that of *civil war*. At first sight some of the puppet régimes which attempted to sit on the fence, or even to remain neutral, can hardly be included in this category; examples are Admiral Horthy's government in Hungary and, above all, the Vichy régime in unoccupied France. Gradually, however, they lost all freedom of action and were forced either to submit or to resign. Those who submitted became enemies of the Resistance and sometimes its principal targets because they were the easiest to hit.

Having studied the subject for some twenty years, it seemed to me not impossible to grasp, explain and characterise as a whole the historical phenomenon of the 'shadow war'. I make no attempt to tell the whole story, however, as differences between countries and periods are so great that areas of obscurity remain which research cannot unravel and a catalogue of actions of similar type would be both monotonous and pointless.

What first strikes the historian is the extreme variety of the clandestine struggle, its mobility and the fact that it resolves itself into a host of small-scale actions. Each national Resistance had its own peculiar characteristics which depended on the attitude of the occupying power, the nature of the country, the assistance provided by the Allies and the country's strategic importance.

Only in rare cases was the Resistance homogeneous. As with the great coalition of which it was a small segment, the components of European resistance varied, and were sometimes even hostile to each other. The differing motives, groupings, methods and objectives produced a highly complex pattern: within the *Conseil National de la Résistance* [National Resistance Council – CNR] in France, representatives of the communists, the socialists, the Christian democrats, the right-wing parties and the syndicalists were living and working side by side; the French Forces of the Interior were formed by a theoretical merger of the communist *Francs-Tireurs Partisans* with the Secret Army (Gaullist) and the Armistice Army (Vichy). So explosive a mixture inevitably produced clashes, friction and upheavals.

Nevertheless, despite its extreme diversity, its antagonisms and its differing organisations, the Resistance basically acted in unison: it was fighting a common enemy; the weapons it used were the same; its sufferings were similar and its development followed an almost identical pattern. Because of this, I have attempted to survey the general evolution of resistance in Europe; in broad terms it seems to me to be the same in all countries. I shall only be able to make certain cursory allusions, however, to events outside Europe.

In the first place it seemed necessary to place resistance in the context of German or Italian occupation. Resistance had to fight the enemy's friends, in other words the collaborators; though not without misunderstandings it frequently benefited from the support of foreign governments or groups of its fellow countrymen in exile. It had to fit its own struggle into the framework of that of the major Allies, sometimes to its disadvantage and at the price of terrible dramas.

Resistance everywhere arose from a spirit of rejection – rejection of defeat, of the political régimes created or tolerated by the occupying power, of collaboration with the victor. At first it took the form of small gestures – passage of information, malicious humour, acts of solidarity, propaganda. In its early days the Allies were indifferent to it; it suffered from an inherent weakness which made it permanently precarious; it was ineffective owing to lack of weapons, money, cadres, experience and targets with which it could deal. This was the phase of *refusal to submit* as dictated by the conscience of each individual. The various social, political and religious groupings did not all react similarly; as a general rule each man made his own lonely choice, without too much regard for the lessons of the past.

A distinctive development followed, more often than not under the impulse of certain unifying forces such as repressive action on the part of the occupying power, establishment of contact with external forces or the action of political parties, primarily of the communist party. As the overall course of the war led to a rebirth of hope, individual initiatives and the little groups which had sprung from them tended to coalesce: the occasional pamphlet turned into a periodical newspaper; safe houses for prisoners on the run were linked to form escape lines; the collection of intelligence was systematised and channelled into regular 'offices'; official organisations and the various strata of society were penetrated. This was the *organisation* phase.

During this phase, by an expensive process of trial and error, the Resistance worked out its methods. It learnt how to select its objectives and adopt tactics to suit them; it gained experience by demonstrations, strikes, sabotage and assassinations. Then it blossomed into armed groups in town or country, frequently subordinate to a single headquarters; these were the partisans or *maquis* and they constituted a force which ultimately attracted the attention of the major Allies and was given its equipment by them. Thus the Resistance worked out its methods and went into *battle*.

This was a drama of hundreds of different scenes ranging from conspiracy to revolt, from indiscipline to desertion, from the hit-and-run raid to the large-scale battle. Everywhere, however, the goal was the same – a *national rising* in which every inhabitant of the country would participate, each in his appointed place. At this stage the Resistance became a major factor; it was able to attack the occupying power, to make a definite impression on him, even to demoralise him; it was unwilling to be ordered about by the Allies; it acquired both a military doctrine and a political viewpoint and it sometimes even worked out ambitious plans for the post-war period. It became a clandestine state, identifying itself with the nation and preparing itself to gather up the reins of power on liberation. But it did not invariably do so without internecine strife.

These phases did not, of course, develop all over Europe at the same tempo; their duration and intensity varied and they did not necessarily follow each other but often overlapped. Nevertheless, whether fast or slow, whether hindered or assisted by the context in which it took place, in its general form the evolution of resistance throughout occupied Europe was uniform. Chained, gagged and tortured though it was, an identical 'Shadow Army' rose everywhere to wage a constantly changing war and drive the occupier from every country conquered by his armies. This force made its contribution to and played its part in the common victory. Viewed as a whole, this was a truly extraordinary development, in many ways unprecedented. Its importance and its influence, should not be underestimated; it has a lesson to teach, especially to the colonial empires and, more generally, to the 'third world': in the era of 'press-button warfare' and nuclear holocaust there is not a conflict in the world today in which the 'little war' of guerrilla warfare will not assuredly find its place.

PART I

The Occupiers and the Allies

The resistance formed part of the global conflict: its origin cannot be understood, its development followed or its effect estimated in isolation. As the defeat of the Axis became more certain the occupied peoples regained their hope; thanks to the assistance received from the Allies warlike action took the place of mere hostility. Any study of the 'shadow war' must therefore start by placing it in its correct context and dealing with the occupation and exploitation of conquered Europe, the assistance furnished to the enemy by the 'collaborators', the operations of the Allies and the part assigned by them to clandestine warfare.[1]

---

[1] This first part can be no more than a brief summary. For a fuller study I would refer the reader to my book *The Second World War*, London: André Deutsch, 1973.

CHAPTER I

The Occupation and Exploitation of Europe

Nazi Germany, fascist Italy and Japan's military clique divided the world between them before victory was assured. The area destined to fall to Japan was definite – the Far East, the areas reserved to Germany and Italy less clearly established. The cake, of course, was Europe and its appendages in Africa and the Middle East but, although Italy was to be overlord of the Mediterranean basin, the precise boundaries of this geographical expression had never been laid down. In fact Italian troops occupied only parts of France (tiny in June 1940 but extending from the Rhône to the Alps between November 1942 and September 1943), Croatia, the Dalmatian coast and a portion of Greece; in addition Italy controlled French North Africa. The swastika dominated the whole of the rest of conquered Europe.

In principle the German and Italian attitudes were the same. They proclaimed that they owed their victory as much to their doctrine as to their armed forces; they liquidated their ideological enemies, primarily communists and Jews; they disarmed the conquered countries and exploited their resources shamelessly, applying in its most extreme form the motto *Vae victus*; they installed reliable collaborators in the corridors of power; they mercilessly suppressed all opposition; they carried out an intensive propaganda campaign through the press, the cinema, the radio, etc. The growing weakness of Italy, and the fact that the Italian is naturally disinclined to severity, meant that Italian occupation was infinitely less onerous than that of the Germans.

The Italian army did annex certain areas in the territories it occupied – at Mentone and in Istria for example; sometimes it took hostages and made arbitrary arrests – over 800 in Corsica; it attempted to levy the heaviest possible tribute on the subject populations. Frequently, however, it proved itself tolerant: it was lax in the enforcement of anti-semitic measures in France; it was opposed to Ustashi excesses in Croatia; it showed little enthusiasm for fighting the early *maquis* in the Alps, Yugoslavia or Greece. In Corsica, and even more in Nice, its propaganda for the recruitment of collaborators was a failure. As the war developed and Mussolini turned increasingly into a camp follower, the coercion to which the conquered populations were subject became that of Hitler and his nazi régime alone; they were regarded as the real enemies and it was against them that the people rose.

Hitler's Europe

In nazi Germany the Führer ruled, omnipotent and omniscient; nothing of importance could be done which Hitler had not decided or approved. In *Mein Kampf* he had firmly stated his purpose, though leaving the means of its attainment fluid; the great idea which was to govern his reign was the conquest of 'living space', *lebensraum,* and he turned towards eastern Europe along the time-honoured route followed by the Teutonic knights. He had, however, to win the war under the best possible conditions and as quickly as possible, but in order to subjugate and divide his conquered opponents the Führer revealed to each of them only the essential minimum of his plans for the future. Each could, therefore, hope to improve his position by zealous servility to the leader. All of Hitler's great satraps vied with each other in anticipating his wishes – Ribbentrop as minister of Foreign Affairs, Göring in his capacity as the Reich's economic director, Rosenberg as the party theorist with the added responsibility of administering the conquered eastern territories, Himmler as the guardian of racial purity, Goebbels determined to impose on the world the nazi variety of German *kultur*. The Wehrmacht leaders could also make their voice heard on matters concerning the operational theatres, where they were responsible for security and administration.

From this tangle of authorities emerged the first principle of the nazi ideology: the superiority of the Germanic race. On 28 November 1940 at a Gauleiters' meeting Himmler proclaimed: 'I believe in a community of the Germanic peoples in which each will retain his language and his cultural heritage; this does not mean, however, that he will be able to decide his external, economic or military policy.' Speaking of the 'great European Reich' which he was constructing, Hitler traced its origin back to the Germanic Holy Roman Empire.

On 1 July 1943, in one of the endless monologues which were his speciality and in which certain 'overriding ideas' ran through the confused torrent of words, Hitler revealed some of his thinking to certain of his generals. 'Force,' he said, 'is not enough to ensure total domination; admittedly it is still the decisive factor but no less important a factor is that intangible psychological faculty which the lion tamer must have if he is to dominate his animals.' This analogy of the circus is a good indication of Hitler's concept of the relationship between victor and vanquished – the victors would stop at nothing to force through their plans and advance their own interests; the vanquished had merely to submit, agreeing in advance that might governed right and that weakness carried with it obligations only.

For the purposes of this book nazi Europe will be described as it was when at its maximum extent.[1] At its heart lay the *German state,* in other words the Germany of the Versailles treaty but with the additions of Austria, the Sudetenland, the province of Poznan, Upper Silesia, the Polish Corridor and Danzig, Luxemburg, the three departments of France known as Alsace-Lorraine after 1871, and part of Slovenia.[2] All these territories were governed under German law and German administration; they were both germanised and nazified; the 'racially impure' had been driven out, Poles into the 'Government General' and Lorrainers into that part of France known as the 'free zone'. In those territories which had simply been annexed, however, the neo-Germans were not entirely on the same footing as their fellow citizens: they were subject to a certain degree of surveillance as if 'in purgatory'; sometimes whole communities were uprooted in order that they might be more easily assimilated – entire villages of Alsace were moved into Baden, for instance.

Relatively close to the Reich were Norway, Holland and Denmark; their 'Aryan' origin earned them the privilege of administering themselves, in the case of the first two under the control of a German administrator. They were allotted their part to play in the 'colonisation of the eastern territories' planned to

[1] See map on pp. 207-8.
[2] After September 1943 a further addition was the ex-Italian Tyrol, despite agreements concluded with Mussolini and the fact that the latter had set up the Salo Republic which was still fighting on the side of Germany.

start in June 1942, a vast programme entitled 'Master Plan East'. Similar hopes were also held out to the Flemings.

In addition to the 'Protectorate' of Bohemia and the 'Government General' in Poland, the Great German Reich was surrounded by a circle of *satellite states* which had willy-nilly become its allies in the war against the USSR. Vague promises of territorial acquisitions were made to them; when their interests proved to be conflicting, as happened in the case of Rumania and Hungary over Transylvania, other avenues of expansion were indicated to them, such as Transnistria and Odessa for the Rumanians. Fascist régimes were installed in Slovakia and Croatia which wished to sever their connections with the Czechs and Serbs. Rumania, Hungary and Bulgaria managed to preserve their institutions by reinforcing their authoritarian character, though the German ambassadors in these countries were no longer diplomats but assumed the role of protectors and Wehrmacht units were located at points of strategic importance.

Areas of major military importance – occupied France, Belgium, Greece and much of conquered Russian territory – were still administered by the Wehrmacht. Their future was highly uncertain. In this category the Vichy government was the object of special attention, at least until the invasion of the unoccupied zone in November 1942.

Italy, Spain and Finland were regarded as allies of Germany. The only neutrals were Portugal, Switzerland, Ireland, Sweden and Turkey, though economically the two latter were incorporated into the German sphere of influence.

Such was the map of nazi Europe – a coat of many colours composed of bits and pieces. Because of their many different authorities and high-handed attitudes it was difficult to fathom what the Germans had in store for any particular people, though the fate of the Poles, the Russians and the Jews was clear – and terrifying.

Systematisation of terror in eastern Europe

The problem in the ex-Polish territories incorporated into the Reich was to decide who should become German. For this purpose a 'German racial list' was drawn up to include all Germans who had previously been Polish citizens and certain Poles considered worthy of assimilation. The rest – the mass of the people – became 'protected persons', with the exception of Jews and gypsies whose status was 'reserved'. 'Protection' was an oppressive affair – the Germans were in no sense the guardians of the people. Poles had no right to own real estate, to receive more than a primary education, to form associations, to occupy positions of authority or to use cultural institutions (theatres, libraries or museums). Workers and employees were paid at the lowest rate and their food rations were inferior to those of Germans. Movement was restricted by vexatious regulations – Poles had to have a special permit to use a bicycle; they were liable to the death penalty for any gesture of ill will towards a German. German 'colonists' were installed in the administration, the liberal professions, industrial and commercial concerns and the larger farms.

As early as May 1940 Himmler had decided to 'screen the Poles from the racial point of view' with the object of removing the superior elements for the benefit of the Reich and leaving in Poland only 'inferior human material suitable for manual labour'.

Poland was decapitated by the destruction of its upper class. Poles were barred from positions of responsibility, sometimes in favour of Lithuanians; their possessions were gradually looted, their works of art stolen; they were cut off from their Catholic priests who were looked on as possible leaders – in short they were treated as implacable enemies. Instructions distributed to Germans reminded them that they were the 'masters' and that 'the Poles were not their comrades but their inferiors'. Forced labour camps were opened in the very early days. As a result of the occupier's brutality Poland was the country which, of all occupied Europe, suffered the greatest human and material losses in proportion to its population.

German behaviour in the conquered Russian territories was governed by the same principles. Himmler considered that Slavs were backward beings, sub-humans, criminals by nature; in addition, in the USSR they were 'Asiatic communists'; from time immemorial they had threatened Europe and its civilisation. The danger must be eliminated once and for all. Hitler accepted his Reichsführer's ideas enthusiastically. Moreover, both the military and civilian authorities, in the shape of OKW [*Oberkommando der Wehrmacht* – High Command of the Armed Forces] and Rosenberg, agreed that in the conquered territories in rear of the front 'police duties' should be carried out by the ss, and that their object should be to rid the country of the virus of communism and Judaism, thus safeguarding Germany from all contamination.

Consequently make-believe and reality existed side by side in occupied Russia. The make-believe was the territorial division instituted by Rosenberg. He organised the conquered territories into two 'Reich Commissariats', one for the Ukraine and the other, christened 'Ostland', comprising Byelo-Russia, the Baltic areas and Lithuania. This might have indicated some respect for nationality and might have heralded the creation of states in greater or lesser degree vassals of the Reich. Lower level adminis-tration was entrusted to nationals of the countries concerned, though subject of course to strict German control, but, obsessed as he was by the 'Slav peril', Rosenberg did not dare go further: he allocated parts of the Ukraine to the Government General of Poland and to Rumania; he pretended to believe that there was no such thing as an indigenous ruling class and, except in the Baltic States, no national of the occupied territories was appointed to any position of authority, administrative, economic or cultural.

As far as everyday life was concerned, the 'Master Plan East' was partially enforced, the object being, in Himmler's semi-scientific jargon, 'to reconcile the area to be colonised with the available manpower'. On the one hand the inhabitants were sub-jected to innumerable rules and regulations – they had to register with the police, they were only allowed out of their houses by day, their movement was restricted and their work hampered by numerous injunctions. On the other hand, although the occupa-tion authorities thought it worth maintaining the collective orga-nisations, generally under new titles, they introduced capitalist-type companies which the inhabitants knew nothing about, and summoned 'Aryan' technicians to run them. This meant that the Wehrmacht's supply requirements were more easily met, but as no distribution of land took place the rural population could not feel that they had gained anything.

The crowning act of this policy was the issue and enforcement of a series of measures by Himmler. The Red Army's 'political commissars' were not considered as prisoners of war and were automatically liable to the death penalty. Since the ussr had not signed the Geneva Convention, Soviet prisoners of war, whose numbers rose to several millions, were treated with extreme severity, crowded into sub-standard camps where hunger and disease took their toll, or even despatched to concentration camps. All the conquered areas were the scene of coldly-calculated measures of extermination, the main victims being the Jews.

The 'final solution' of the Jewish question

The nazi case for the prosecution against the Jews created an imaginary Jew, the possessor of every known defect, physical, intellectual and moral. Hitler, who was oblivious of the contradictions in his 'thoughts', had said in *Mein Kampf* that 'the Jew has always been able to unite on the international level princes, aristocrats, bourgeois and proletariat'. The Jew was regarded as rootless, the eternal nomad, cleverly making his niche in societies in order to devour them from within like a cancer; in nazi mythology the Jew was a deadly danger which, if not exorcised, would render any lasting German power impossible.

The initial idea had been to expel the Jews from German territory. In a Europe occupied by the Wehrmacht this became impossible; since all exits to the outside world were closed, the problem was to dispose of more than ten million people. At least the raging anti-semitism of the nazis could now operate on a larger scale. Everywhere Jews were forbidden to work in the public services, to follow the liberal professions, to occupy any position of authority in activities where they might 'poison public opinion' such as the cinema, the radio, the press, etc. They were subject to special registration and had to wear a distinctive badge, the yellow star; they might not frequent public places; their identity documents carried a special stamp.

Moreover, all possessions were gradually removed from Jews on the pretext that they had fraudulently extracted them from the countries which had granted them asylum. This was the vast operation known as the 'aryanisation' of factories, firms and real estate from which a whole swarm of shady characters profited, not to mention the occupier himself. These methods of subjection, expropriation and humiliation were supported by a virulent campaign of hatred and contempt using posters, films and exhibitions. The bill for the smallest indiscretion on the part of the occupied peoples was paid by the Jews in the form of fines, confiscations and seizure of hostages. In the countries of long-established freedoms this vile behaviour frequently marked the genesis of popular hostility to the occupying power as a result of the revulsion, condemnation and sense of solidarity which it produced.

In eastern Europe, where they could be sure that there would be no retribution, the nazis' maltreatment of the Jews knew no bounds. Special groups of ss, the '*Einsatzgruppen*', reverted to the well-tried methods of the pogrom; they incited the inhabitants to murder and pillage. Three pogroms carried out by Ukrainian nationalists at Lwow in Poland resulted in 10,000 dead. Even worse crimes were committed in the USSR; groups of Jews were systematically exterminated by gassing with the exhaust from motor lorries. Thus began the 'final solution'.

It is almost inconceivable that human beings should be capable of the cold decision to exterminate, by a sort of metaphysical death sentence, millions of their fellow men without distinction of age or sex. In Poland, Lithuania and Russia the nazis collected the Jews into a number of ghettos, into which they also crowded Jews no longer living there and Jews brought in from other areas. Each ghetto formed a closed Jewish world, an isolated entity from both the human and the economic points of view. This might have been the initiation of a plan of total segregation, but in fact it was only one phase in a monstrous scheme.

In two speeches early in 1942 Hitler announced that the Jews would be annihilated. Technical 'trials' in the USSR had proved the 'inadequacy' of existing methods – mass shootings, cremation of the bodies in furnaces and mobile gas chambers. But the German chemists now had a 'quick and clean' solution: they had produced a deadly gas named Zyklon B which, after encouraging trials, the 'specialists' considered full of promise.

The method adopted was to construct gas chambers camouflaged as shower baths in certain camps in Poland – the main one was at Birkenau; to these were attached giant crematoria in which the bodies were burnt. The number of Jews rounded up all over Europe and carted to the 'death camps' is estimated at six million. At least as many others fell victim to the maltreatment meted out to them in the ghettos, the diseases which raged there and German action in suppressing revolts such as that in Warsaw.

The death of the Jews was in no way necessary to ensure the victory of nazi Germany; this hideous crime was entirely gratuitous. Its gigantic proportions were only realised after the war, though the Polish Resistance had managed to contact certain deportees and pass information to its government in London.

The warnings and threats issuing from the B B C made no difference to the murderers' determination. With hindsight, however, it is clear that in the eyes of European Resistance this massacre more than anything else legitimised, indeed sanctified, their action.

Principles governing the exploitation of Europe

Without waiting for victory the nazi economists had already sketched out the economy of the Thousand-Year Reich. They worked on two principles: first, in exploiting the resources of conquered territories, a system of autarchy must be adopted in order to integrate these resources into the German Four Year Plan.

The second principle stemmed from the racial character of nazism. The superiority of the German people implied that the exploitation of conquered territory must be to the sole advantage of Germany; all power would flow to Germany; other peoples would be entitled to a standard of living proportionate to the services they rendered and the servility they showed. Germany would have the monopoly of heavy industry as it provided armaments; she would control industry, technology and scientific research in the other countries to ensure that they were restricted to prudent and innocuous proportions; the conquered peoples would become providers only of raw materials, agricultural products and labour. The crowning piece of the whole structure was to be an unrivalled expansion of German culture; in the arts, in thought, in fashion and in luxury Berlin would be the capital of Europe.

There was nothing new in this idea. Nazi Germany simply had a 'colonial pact' in store for Europe: victory would perpetuate the slavery of the vanquished. The conquered peoples had no inkling of the scope of the plans designed to enslave them as the nazis used every trick and subterfuge to avoid revealing them. But in the first place Britain continued to resist, and then the war extended into the steppes of Russia at a scope and level of violence which produced unparalleled attrition; the occupier was forced to drop his mask and institute an out-and-out campaign of pillage. He did so with such savagery that not only did he bring ruin in his wake, but he also aroused first discontent, then hostility and finally belligerence among his victims.

Pressures of the war of attrition

The nazi system was caught between two sets of contradictory desiderata. In Holland, for instance, how was the desire to win over to the German cause a people regarded as Germanic in origin to be reconciled with the impoverishment of the country resulting from the diversion of its best products to Germany at cut prices? In France, for reasons of security, the German military wished to turn the 'demarcation line' between the occupied zone and the so-called free zone into a hermetically sealed frontier; separated from each other, however, the two halves of France would wither away, to the detriment of the German economy.

The solution to these problems was dictated by necessity. After the euphoria of the great victories of summer 1941 in Russia there was no more *blitz*, no more overwhelming victories won by a few irresistible panzer divisions supported by an undisputed Luftwaffe. The war bogged down in the cold of Russia, the long winter nights and the spring thaw. The casualties and the exhausted had to be replaced; arms and equipment had to be renewed, increased in quantity and modified. Nazi Germany had to choose between her vast plans for the future and the immediate compelling requirements of the war of attrition and the great bloodbath. There could be no shadow of doubt; everything was sacrificed to ultimate victory. The object now was to ensure that the Wehrmacht regularly received the reinforcements it demanded and that arms production in the factories nevertheless continued to increase. Nazi Germany became an insatiable minotaur.

In a speech to Reich Commissars of the occupied territories and military commanders on 6 August 1942 Göring set out in cynical language this determination to plunder without limit. 'In the old days,' he said with a note of regret in his voice, 'one looted; he who had conquered a country disposed of the riches of that country.' Then, however, having stated that 'things are done more humanely now', he produced the contradiction typical of nazi logic: 'As far as I am concerned I propose to loot all the same, and on a large scale.'

The actual procedure resolved itself into a vast plundering expedition for anything which seemed of interest to the Germans. Göring explained: 'I shall despatch to Belgium, Holland and France a number of special purchasers who will be authorised to buy up practically everything they find in the high class shops and stores; all this I shall put in the shop windows so that the German people can have it.' He advised his audience to 'organise a real round-up' in the territories under their control. 'It must all be done in one swoop – out with the stocks and over to us; the soldiers can buy as much as they want provided that they can carry it away with them.' Would this not lead to inflation, someone asked. Göring was quite happy about that: 'Let that come and let it be a good one; there is no need for the franc to be any more valuable than certain paper normally used for a certain purpose.'

Monetary exploitation

On the monetary side the Germans were clever enough to appear to pay for services rendered or goods provided by the occupied countries, but they did so in a way which cost Germany practically nothing.

In the areas where it was fighting or which it administered the Wehrmacht initially paid for what it got by cash vouchers issued by the various services or in occupation marks, the exchange rate of which it fixed itself. In addition in Russia new taxes were levied – a poll tax, a tax on housing, taxes on dogs and cats, a tax on cattle, etc.

When the military situation had apparently stabilised, the national currencies (French and Belgian francs, Polish zloty, Dutch florin, etc.) were retained but the mark was arbitrarily overvalued in relation to them – in France by nearly 20 per cent. The first result of this was to restrict purchases of German goods, which had obviously become dearer, and so preserve them for the citizens of the Reich; the second, and more important, result was to enable the Germans to supply themselves cheaply on the spot. The occupying forces were the first to take advantage of this and the voracity of both officers and men in rifling the shops was extreme.

To avoid any devaluation of national currencies, which would have reduced the advantage enjoyed by the mark, the occupation authorities assumed a right of supervision over the issue banks. In Holland a staunch Dutch nazi was appointed director of the currency; in France the Germans were justifiably suspicious of the

Treasury civil servants who were energetically defending the franc, so the military authorities attached to the Bank of France a German controller with a right of veto. In the Polish Government General they just took over the Bank of Poland. Any inflation of national currencies was thus prevented; on the other hand the occupied peoples had no means of preventing, or even of knowing about, the vast issues of marks which took place.

Another method of obtaining currency was to fix an exorbitant sum for the maintenance of the occupying forces; the criterion used was not the number of soldiers stationed in any particular country but the estimated capacity of that country to pay. This was tantamount to a compulsory levy, sometimes presented by the Germans as the country's contribution to its own defence against the Allies. In France the rate per day was 400 million francs in July 1940 and this rose to 500 million after the occupation of Southern France in November 1942.[1]

The national authorities of the occupied countries were well aware of the obnoxious and dangerous nature of these procedures. The people themselves were slower to realise them; they were grateful not to be brutally pillaged without compensation and took time to understand that they were being cheated. One of the first consequences from which they suffered was the universal rationing essential to avoid a prices explosion.

Economic plunder

In the combat zone the Germans invariably requisitioned, working on the principle that might was right. This, together with their systematic destruction, turned the occupied areas of eastern Europe into a charnel house in the middle of a desert. Western Europe had more to offer the looters, and cessation of hostilities did not necessarily bring their activities to an end.[2] At least in the West exploitation became ostensibly 'correct' through the financial mechanism for economic pump priming.

As the war of attrition developed other methods had to be used to satisfy the German appetite for war production. German 'experts' were despatched to all occupied or 'allied' countries, and

[1] About 1·2 and 1·5 milliard at today's rates.
[2] Before evacuating Lyon in July 1940 the Germans despatched hundreds of goods wagons full of merchandise of every description.

listed Europe's resources in detail so that they might be diverted to the Reich at prices fixed by Germany. This was the fate of almost all Hungarian grain, Danish butter, Dutch vegetables, Lorraine iron ore, Rumanian oil, Polish coal, Yugoslav copper and Norwegian timber, not forgetting, of course, the agricultural and mineral products of the Ukraine. The so-called French 'free zone' also felt the turn of the screw; the Germans demanded the entire production of bauxite and claimed a share of imports from the French Empire – Ouenza iron ore, Tunisian phosphates and oils, Senegal ground nuts, etc.

There was no bargaining; payment was made through a 'clearing' arrangement, rapaciously used. In each seller country a German debit account was opened and in principle Germany was to provide goods of equivalent value; in fact, apart from certain deliveries of a propaganda nature – a little Danish butter and Dutch cheese to France, for instance – the goods wagons and trucks left for Germany full and either returned empty or did not return at all. Used in this way, the 'clearing arrangement' was no more than a vast racket, the German buyer paying with promissory notes for good solid merchandise received.[1]

To facilitate negotiations and ensure that their 'orders' were met the Germans urged their suppliers to form themselves into groups; moreover this was in line with the corporatist theory of fascism. Such grouping was essential in rural areas because of the wide dispersion and the difficulties of supervision. They encouraged the formation of an 'agricultural corporation' in France, for instance; in the USSR, in order to ensure that they were dealing with responsible people to whom they could dictate, they were even unwise enough to allow the sovkhozes and kolkhozes to continue, though under other titles.

The 'aryanisation' of Jewish businesses and the appointment of German puppets to run them were also sources of vast wealth. Surpluses from the occupation indemnities were also highly profitable. For instance, the Germans used them to buy French shares in concerns located in territories under their control such as Rumanian oil, Czech banks, Hungarian coal, Yugoslav mines, etc. They also took up shares in the major French concerns, attracting sellers by paying more than the stock market price.

[1] As a contrast, Italy had no comparable methods of exerting pressure and so the agreements which she concluded, particularly those with France, were perfectly equitable.

The Germans also stole works of art including even those which, according to the nazi code of aesthetics, showed signs of 'decadence'. Göring's and Rosenberg's scouts hunted out the treasures of museums, rifled art galleries and took possession of private collections. Poland was stripped in six months on the pretext that there was no such thing as Polish art. Witt Stwosz's famous reredos in Cracow was dismantled and taken to Germany; Watteau's *Femme polonaise* was discovered in one of Göring's villas.

The compulsory labour service

Although some people became rich from these measures, they gave rise to much discontent. No head of a firm could be sure that he would retain ownership or even remain in charge; even those who thought that they had concluded good business soon saw that they had relinquished solid assets for worthless money. For the mass of the population the dire consequences of all this were not always perceptible; they could not realise the scale of the disaster or its effects. The compulsory labour service, however, was an entirely different matter; gradually this became an immediate threat to the majority of able-bodied men.

Labour in the occupied territories had come forward voluntarily, as only the occupiers could provide secure employment and frequently offered wages higher than pre-war ones. When the labour supply proved inadequate, forced labour camps were opened, primarily for Jews; the War Crimes Commission counted 435 of these in Poland.

The greatest requirement for labour was in the fields and factories of Germany herself to fill the vacancies left by recruits called into the Wehrmacht to make good its enormous casualties on the Eastern front. The first expedient was to set the prisoners of war to work – and there were several millions of them.

The situation became so acute that even the ss, which ran the concentration camps, was forced to revise its ideas. The original aim of the camps had been purely repressive, but now they provided the majority of German firms (Krupp, I. G. Farben, Hermann Göring, Roechling, etc.) with wretched gangs of slaves. These were protected by no laws – even the Red Cross had no right to concern itself with them. This labour was expendable and uncomplaining but, unfortunately for its employers, being under-nourished and debilitated by maltreatment its output was low.

To meet their requirements the Germans were forced to revert to a modern form of the slave-trader's methods. Gauleiter Sauckel, who was appointed labour dictator, initiated a compulsory labour service covering the whole of Europe. For the sub-humans of the east, who could be pitilessly exploited, there were no half measures: localities ravaged by war were forcibly repopulated; hundreds of thousands of workers were compulsorily moved from one end of their country to another; millions of Poles, Russians, Yugoslavs, Czechoslavaks, Hungarians and Rumanians were sent to work in the Reich.

In western Europe it was at first thought wise to use kid-glove tactics. All sorts of promises were made to attract volunteers – bonuses, high wages, better rations. But compulsion soon became necessary. Classes of conscripts were called up in turn to serve the occupier. Sometimes they were employed on the spot, on major Todt Organisation works or the construction of the Atlantic Wall, for instance. More often they were despatched to Germany – from France, for example, 600,000 were sent.

The first result of this new-style conscription was to turn Germany into a tower of Babel. Some ten million workers of varied extraction flowed into the Reich; most were young and the majority were men but there was a strong female contingent.

The second consequence was that no one in the occupied countries felt himself secure from the demands and extortions of the occupying power. With the institution of the compulsory labour service there was hardly a family which did not feel itself threatened; either it was mourning the failure of a prisoner to return or it was afraid that its members would be carried off. Though theoretically conscripted, many resorted to the only escape open to them; they failed to answer the call-up and hid to escape the man-hunts. The compulsory labour service therefore raised the numbers of recalcitrants, who later became the Resistance fighters.

Throughout occupied Europe inflation and shortages due to paralysis of the economy or to German exactions produced the same disastrous consequences: the population's standard of living fell until eventually even food requirements could not be met. Of course there were profiteers, and some scandalous fortunes were made; the main beneficiaries were the racketeers serving the occupier and, in general, the collaborators. In the midst of the general misery they flaunted their mode of life. But the majority of the population was faced with rationing, artificial substitutes and endless queues in front of empty shops; it suffered from tuberculosis and rickets, diseases of malnutrition; it was short of bread, heating, clothing and transport. In its suffering it turned a deaf ear to the blandishments of the collaborators.

CHAPTER 2

The Collaborators

Fascism in Europe

The nazi party had recruited adherents all over Europe even before the war, although they were not very numerous. Some came from the German minorities outside the Reich; they had been instrumental, for instance, in bringing about the annexation of Austria[1] and the creation of the 'protectorate' of Bohemia. They consisted of millions of people who had more or less retained their national characteristics in a human environment not always sympathetic to them; they were to be found in Brazil, in the Sudetenland, along the Volga, in Transylvania and Bukovina, in the Italian Tyrol, in Hungary and in Slovenia. Italian fascism had also made efforts to arouse national sentiment among its emigrés – in the Argentine, in France, in Algeria and Tunisia, in Egypt and the Middle East, in Slovenia and Dalmatia, etc.[2] Everywhere the same methods were used: consuls gave assistance to the less fortunate members of their communities; they assembled their nationals in cultural societies where the praises of national consciousness were sung; they subsidised schools where the national language was taught; they organised periodical pilgrimages to the home country and leader training courses.

Other supporters of fascism came from circles opposed to democratic régimes and from small groups which hailed the dawn and first successes of the European 'revolution'. They were particularly numerous in states demanding revision of the Treaty of Versailles, such as Austria or Hungary. But even in countries which had emerged through the treaty, the Little Entente for instance, there were internal dissensions and, spurred on by Mussolini's and Hitler's successes, these gave rise to pro-Axis movements – in Croatia, Slovakia and Rumania.

[1] Approved, be it noted, by Cardinal Innitzer and Renner, the socialist.

[2] In general, German and Italian immigrants into the United States had become denationalised, but the policy of the US government nevertheless had to take account of the emotional ties between these American citizens and their country of origin.

Oddly enough, in Yugoslavia the Stoyadinovich government sought Hitler's protection against the ambitions of Mussolini. In Greece, for similar reasons, Metaxas, the Prime Minister, having lost the 1936 elections, dissolved parliament and suppressed political parties. Although the king was basically pro-British, Metaxas modelled his government on that of Berlin; he sent delegates to the Nuremberg Rally and nazi agents arrived in Greece as administrative and police advisers.

In fact there was hardly a country in Europe where fascism did not have its disciples. In some cases these were already in power, in others they were poised to create the opportunity to seize it. Even countries with a high standard of living, long-standing national unity and a general consensus in favour of democratic institutions did not escape the rising flood. Fear of communism was the best recruiting agent.[1] The inefficiency of parliamentary régimes and the economic crisis of the 'thirties swelled the influx of fascist sympathisers. Everywhere there was a feeling that the political institutions inherited from the past, founded on liberalism and positivism and inspired by the principles of the French Revolution of 1789, were increasingly obsolete in the face of the economic problems thrown up by industrialisation, the development of capitalism, the growth of an urban proletariat, the integration of natural economies in international markets, and the difficulties of the rural population and middle classes in adapting themselves to technical progress.

Many industrialists were by no means averse to the prohibition of strikes; the more immature intellectuals were fascinated by the 'dynamism of the future' preached by fascism. The middle classes found in the corporatist theory some hope of arresting the changes which threatened to drag them down into the ranks of the proletariat; nationalists hoped that dictatorship would re-establish social order and the authority of the state; even 'left-wing' politicians like Lloyd George, and many labour leaders, succumbed to Hitler's social demagogy.

In short, between 1934 and 1939 'big chiefs' and 'little chiefs' budded and blossomed all over Europe. In Norway there was Quisling, a believer in the germanic racial community of which Rosenberg was the prophet; in Holland Mussert was ready to be

[1] After a visit to Mussolini in 1927 Churchill, then Chancellor of the Exchequer, had said: 'Had I been Italian, I am sure that I should have been with you . . . in opposition to the bestial appetites and passions of leninism.'

germanism's lieutenant in the Low Countries, helped by the multiplicity and obsolescence of the Dutch political parties; in Belgium
de Clercq and his Flemish movement strove for equality of rights
with the Walloons, rejecting all French influence as foreign
oppression and proclaiming themselves a branch of the great
germanic family. The French or French-speaking movements
were more unexpected – Degrelle and his 'Rexists' in Wallonia,
La Rocque and his 'French Social Party', Doriot and his 'French
Popular Party'; all three made inroads into the conservative Right
which was uneasy over the prevailing political and economic
disorder.

In addition, a whole swarm of professional agents was milling
around in search of pickings: journalists hunting for news
and sensational 'scoops', writers and aesthetes whose political
sense was not their strong point, men-about-town looking for
'kicks'. They all collected in various gatherings typified by the
Comité France-Allemagne [Franco-German Committee]; on the
French side this was run by the journalist de Brinon and on the
German by Otto Abetz, a small-time drawing master married to
a Frenchwoman. Though activated by different, if not contradictory, motives, many ex-servicemen were working in the same
direction; they were determined to prevent a repetition of the
great Franco-German bloodbath of 1914–18. Then there were the
pacifists, convinced that war was the root of all evil, and certain
politicians who thought that a *rapprochement* with Hitler and a
policy of 'appeasement' might save their country from the
German juggernaut.

Even before the war, therefore, there existed a 'fascist international'; everywhere it used the same methods to indoctri-
nate the masses, fought the same enemies and evinced the same
ferocious determination to strike them down; the groups
directly inspired, or even subsidised, from Rome and Berlin were
numerous. Even in Great Britain Mosley had an active little
following.[1]

Nevertheless, although Hitler had his adherents everywhere,
they never constituted a true 'fifth column' advancing on orders
from Berlin, moved about like pawns by the Führer, acting on an
overall plan, or capable of seizing power in preparation for the
Wehrmacht's arrival. Certain fascist sympathisers, moreover, put

---

[1] In passing it should be noted that there were dictatorships, each with their own
peculiar features, under Peron in the Argentine and Vargas in Brazil.

their money on Mussolini rather than Hitler – Prince Starhemberg's Austrian *Heimwehr*, for instance, and Pavelich's Ustashi. Others, either scared by Hitler's ambitions or playing their cards close to their chest, paraded an attitude of germanophobia rooted in nationalist tradition; in France this was the case with La Rocque and even with Doriot, who in 1939 was still saying: 'Neither Berlin nor Moscow.'

New prospects held out by the war

The German victories fundamentally changed the problem. At one fell swoop all those who had been hesitant to take sides swung over to the probable victor – Doriot among them. Moreover, the nazi party now had many more methods of action open to it; its propaganda no longer came openly and solely from Berlin. In all the occupied countries it could now hide behind news agencies, publishing and film-producing firms, the press, the radio and cultural organisations, all ostensibly directed by responsible nationals or even nationalists. So diversified a network could cover every aspect of society, social, professional or regional; unlimited funds were available, furnished at the behest of the occupier by the occupied peoples. With such resources, utilised by Ribbentrop's and Goebbels' organisations, the ranks of the fascist movements were quickly swelled by opportunists, unemployed and by new converts following the German victories; miniature groups turned into parties. In addition new groupings appeared, the result of initiative on the part of new arrivals or created from scratch with directives and subsidies from the occupying power. All this formed a close-knit network designed to embrace the entire population and direct public opinion as a whole.

Hitler's policy towards the collaborators was purely pragmatic. To the nazi leaders the only groups who counted were those which could assist them in specific circumstances towards a definite object. They supported some and abandoned others, according to the efficiency they showed; the Führer's attitude was never governed by the smallest trace of gratitude, as even such faithful disciples as Quisling and Mussert were to discover. The nazis used the collaborators as additional means of gathering the fruits of victory, and counted on them to reduce the hostility of the occupied peoples towards their victors. They hoped, if possible, to turn this hostility into sympathy or at least passive resignation. From the more fanatical or the more compromised they recruited auxiliaries for lower-level police duties; from the more belligerent they raised volunteers whom they incorporated into the Wehrmacht or into special ss units to be used against the Resistance in their own country.

For these purposes everything was grist to the nazi mill. They naturally made full use of the German minorities abroad, the 'racial Germans' [*Volksdeutsche*]; they exploited any abilities they found. They were also astute enough, however, to support certain dubious régimes to which, not without some risk, they allowed a semblance of independence – Vichy France is the most obvious example.

Collaboration, as well as occupation, was thus a factor in moulding the character and action of the Resistance. In the first place it meant that both in the order and importance of resistance activities priority had to be given to counter-propaganda – the battle of the mind had to be won before the battle on the ground. Secondly, collaboration meant that a merciless civil war was added to the war between occupiers and occupied – a new edition of the Spanish Civil War.

The 'racial Germans'

Not all the minorities of German origin or tongue located outside German territory were solidly pro-nazi; a social democrat group in the Sudetenland, for instance, bravely opposed Henlein's pro-nazi majority party. The Germans had frequently had the humiliating feeling, however, that they were treated rather as second-class citizens by the ethnic majority in their adopted country, and the Wehrmacht's victories gave them undreamed-of opportunities for advancement.

In effect the Germans everywhere were granted a measure of autonomy and given additional rights guaranteed by the intimacy of their relations with the Reich. In this way the Germans of Slovakia were allowed a Secretary of State to represent them in the government of the new Slovak state, and they even levied taxes to support their cultural activities. In Croatia the Germans, even including officials of the Ustashi state, took an oath to

Hitler and had their own administration under their local 'führer'. To the 'Saxons' of Transylvania, who had become Rumanians in 1918, General Antonescu granted a special protocol giving them the status of a public corporation with the right to draw up its own rules. Because of the jealous nationalism of the Magyars the Germans were less successful in Hungary but, although given no privileges, they were granted proportionate representation in the administration. Denmark was the only country where Hitler wished to humour the established government; he therefore placed a damper on the claims of the German group in Danish Sleswig, although he still regarded them as fellow-Germans lacking a country.[1]

In all these groupings activity by anti-nazi elements was considerably muted by an understandable acknowledgement of the advantages obtained and a sense of their German heritage; their fellow-Germans would inevitably look upon any opposition as treachery. In those countries, therefore, which had thought it wise to side with Germany, whether militarily or economically, semi-national organisations sprang up, barely recognising any authority other than that of the German Führer. Stalin thought the danger so great that he had the entire colony of Volga Germans deported to Siberia before the Wehrmacht reached the river.

It is more difficult to estimate German achievements in penetrating Alsace, now annexed to Germany. Admittedly they took immense pains to eradicate all French influence; they germanised and nazified unrestrainedly. French-speaking Lorrainers were expelled; Alsatian officials were transferred to Germany and replaced by Reich Germans, thus purging the area of those considered non-assimilable and reinforcing its 'racial purity'. The policy of germanisation was furthered by strict insistence on the use of German laws and language, the regimentation by nazi organisations of the entire population by areas, professions and ages, conscription of young men into the Wehrmacht and the harsh irksome activities of the various forms of police force. Alsatians were divided among themselves; some of the ex-protagonists of autonomy accepted the new state of affairs and

---

[1] The German Ambassador in Washington himself admitted that all similar efforts in the United States were a failure, saying: 'The first precaution must be under no circumstances to appear to be trying to use the German minority to influence public opinion.'

many others resigned themselves to it. On the other hand there were many desertions among the irreconcilables, and a special camp had to be set up at Schirmeck for the internment of recalcitrants.[1] In areas annexed by Germany resistance was obviously a more dangerous affair than in the occupied countries: it was akin to treason and punished as such; it had no hope of help from outside; it was forced to invent its own rules of self-expression and organisation.

Collaborator groupings

For various sections of the occupied populations the nazi 'order' had certain attractions. Collaborator groupings of varying importance developed or were formed in all countries directly occupied by or indirectly subordinate to the nazis. As a general rule the German leaders concentrated them into a single organisation, thereby increasing their impact and making them easier to control. This was the case with the parties led by Quisling in Norway, Clausen in Denmark, Mussert in Holland, Horia Sima in Rumania (the 'Iron Guard'), Szalassy in Hungary (the 'Arrow Cross') and Pavelich in Croatia (the Ustashi); to these may be added the Grand Mufti of Jerusalem who issued calls from Berlin to the nationalists of all Arab countries under colonial régimes. In Belgium account had to be taken of the existence of two nationalities; there De Clercq's Flemish movement and Degrelle's 'Rexists' (Walloons) existed side by side, competing in servility. In France, probably to avoid the formation of an enormous nationalist movement which might in the long run have given trouble or to keep in touch with the whole spectrum of public opinion, the Germans allowed several groupings to develop; they were by no means averse to the resulting rivalries and internecine struggles. The strongest of these groups were Déat's *Rassemblement National Populaire* [National Popular Rally] whose members were 'on the left' and Doriot's *Parti Populaire Français* [French Popular Party] which posed as the defender of the middle classes.

Despite their various titles and certain differences in aims, all these movements were organised on an identical pattern. All were headed by a leader proclaimed as infallible and a gift of Providence,

---

[1] Nothing comparable seems to have occurred in the case of the German populations in Poland or the Baltic States.

a powerful satrap whose word was law; everywhere the population was regimented by areas and corporations; in the newspapers over the radio and at colossal meetings the same slogans were handed out containing identical calls to violence, fanaticism and blind obedience. At their meetings the uniforms, the gestures, the ritual and the language were faithful copies of nazi ceremonial. Ideas were simple and few – unstinted praise of nazi Germany and complete confidence in her victory; hatred of the Jew, the capitalist, the democrat and the marxist; unrelenting war against great Britain, the USSR, the United States and their internal allies, the Resistance; protestations of class solidarity to guarantee economic stability; the 'cult of the chief' as leader and saviour of his people; denunciation of the divisive principles of liberty and equality; faith in the 'construction of Europe' through the victory of Germany.

Though few in numbers the collaborators, whether inspired by fanaticism or by avarice, proved to be valuable assistants to the Germans. Without them the Gestapo, working in a foreign country, not really knowing the language, customs or people, would often have missed its prey. Denunciation was the collaborators' first and primary task. They infiltrated resistance groups or joined the *maquis* posing as fugitives from authority, and thanks to them the Gestapo could strike with certainty and net an important haul every time. Some of them, such as a team of French policemen in Paris, turned torturers. Others became touts for the German organisations which were systematically plundering a country – collaborators were the executive agents for the dispossession of the Jews, for instance. Finally, from the most determined the occupier raised his units armed for civil war; in France, for example, Darnand's 'militia' was sent into action against the *maquis*; it set fire to farms, tried suspects by 'courts martial', used torture and carried out executions in prisons, the most notorious case being at Eysses. For the Resistance these perverted fellow-countrymen were not merely the most formidable of their enemies but also the most hated, being looked upon as traitors. Because of the collaborators the clandestine war took on the ferocity of the wars of religion; all men of the Resistance, however varied their background, felt themselves united against the collaborators.

The satellite states

The nazis were, however, well aware of the unpopularity of these faithful minions, and if they seemed to be discredited the Germans had no hesitation in disowning them. Quisling, Mussert and Horia Sima all had this bitter experience. To achieve their ends the nazis preferred to work through men or régimes which the people held in higher regard and could more easily accept; from these they could expect more on condition, of course, that they were allowed a modicum of resources and were not deprived of all hope. The Germans were careful to keep their own demands secret; on occasions they let the satellites think that they might be allowed to defend themselves against Germany's allies – the Italians for example; they stifled old enmities under a facade of unity against a common foe; they allowed these vassals certain pickings or held out the possibility to them. In certain countries the Germans gained the acquiescence of the population through governments that ostensibly retained a measure of freedom but were actually under strict control.

Thus in Slovakia the loyalty of Mgr Tiso's clerico-fascist régime was guaranteed by the hostility shown by the Slovaks to the Czechs who, they considered, had been their oppressors in the now non-existent Czechoslovakia of Mazaryk and Beneš. In Rumania General Antonescu had contributed thirty divisions to the war against Russia in the hope of recovering Bessarabia and extending Rumanian territory beyond the Dniester to include Odessa. In Hungary Admiral Horthy also joined the anti-bolshevik crusade to ensure that he kept Transylvania, retaken from the Rumanians with German support. In Bulgaria, although King Boris had refused to declare war against the USSR because of the strong Bulgarian sympathies for Russia, Bulgarian troops had taken part in the campaigns against Greece and Yugoslavia and had occupied parts of those countries; they hoped to be recompensed with territory in Macedonia and a 'window' onto the Aegean, both traditional aims of Bulgarian policy. In Athens power was wielded by a handful of generals convinced that Germany had won the war. In Belgrade General Nedich posed as the champion of Greater Serbia against the autonomist pretensions of the Croats and Bosnians. Finally, in France the Vichy régime hoped that, by aligning itself with the victor, it might reduce the severity of his demands and preserve the greater part of France together with her colonial empire.

All these régimes retained certain attributes of sovereignty; they could pass legislation, they administered, they had an army, a police force and diplomatic representation abroad; they accordingly enjoyed the confidence of their citizens to such an extent that the Germans sometimes became suspicious of them – particularly of the French generals. In fact, however, the nazis were well insured against all risk; they still retained methods of pressure which were irresistible. In reserve they held the collaborator groups whom they could always put in power if necessary – as they did in Budapest and Vichy in 1944. In fact, with greater or less good grace, the governments of the satellite states were forced into an attitude of submission, though under the illusion that they had chosen their policy themselves. The fact of their existence, the small forces under their command and the spirit of patriotism which animated some of their leaders were actually factors in creating confusion and division; for the Resistance they were factors of neither strength, clarity nor unity. The Vichy régime provides a convincing illustration.

The Vichy régime

What Hitler wanted from the Vichy régime is known from the disclosures he made to Mussolini just before the grant of an armistice to France in 1940. The Duce wished to satisfy his considerable territorial ambitions immediately, to the great detriment of the defeated country; the Führer, however, counselled moderation, for which he gave convincing reasons. The important thing, he said, was to prevent the French fleet and empire from continuing to fight with the British; secondly, and perhaps more important, the French people would accept administration by the victors only with ill will; they would, however, obey the victor's directives unconsciously if these were passed on through a government ostensibly free to take the decisions itself. This, engineered with Hitler's devilish cunning, was the genesis of the tragic enigma of the Vichy régime.[1]

The armistice admittedly spared France total occupation; the Vichy régime administered rather less than half metropolitan

[1] See the author's *Vichy année 40*, Robert Laffont, Paris 1966.

France and the whole of the empire in Africa; it possessed a rump of an army known as the 'armistice army' together with a fleet undefeated and intact – which it was forced to disarm; in principle it was responsible for administration of the occupied zone. Clearly the cessation of hostilities in June 1940 had saved the French much suffering and destruction. Under the armistice France still existed as an entity with opportunities for ac on or even resurrection. In the occupied zone the Vichy régime could act as the population's protector vis-à-vis the Germans; when peace was concluded it might be able to reduce France's territorial losses at the expense of Great Britain; it could even hope for some protection from Germany against Spanish or even Italian ambitions. The vast majority of the population of the unoccupied zone accordingly placed an almost mystic confidence in the new and universally respected head of state, Marshal Pétain.

In fact Pétain did on many occasions protest against the exactions of the Germans, and tried to get them reduced; he sometimes saved the lives of a few Frenchmen. Basically, however, the Vichy régime was unable to evade the onerous obligations imposed on it by the armistice or even oppose the deliberate violations of its terms which the victor carried out for his own profit. It applied the anti-semitic laws; it could not take a decision or make an appointment of importance without authorisation; it did not publicise its protests against the annexation of Alsace which it could do nothing to prevent; it was regular in its payments of the vast indemnities imposed on it and allowed them to appear as freely negotiated agreements, thereby concealing their gravity from public opinion; it could achieve no more than partial repatriation of prisoners of war and, on the other hand, encouraged Frenchmen to work in Germany; economically it did in fact collaborate and politically proclaimed its will to do so. Although it did not bring France back into the war on Germany's side, prior to November 1942 the only fighting which its troops did was against the British and Americans in the Middle East or in Africa. Finally, and most important, it was Vichy's police who organised the man-hunts after Jews both in unoccupied France and in Paris; it was Vichy's security forces which were first in the field against the *maquis*. Like the other satellite states the Vichy régime was caught on the horns of a dilemma: either Germany would win the war with ease, in which case, having no further need of the satellites' services, she would take no further account of their demands, or, alternatively, if the Wehrmacht got into difficulties the nazis would demand ever more complete collaboration and submission, the probable results of which became increasingly obvious as a German victory became increasingly difficult to envisage. The initial supporters of the régime were ultimately forced to choose between two courses of action: either to refuse to conform and break with it openly, as did Giraud and, with less enthusiasm, Darlan; or to become embroiled in collaboration tantamount to increasingly stringent servitude – summarised by Laval in the notorious phrase that he 'desired the victory of Germany' without which bolshevism would triumph in Europe.

Pending the necessity for each individual to make a specific choice or the course of the war itself providing the answer, for the Resistance the existence of the Vichy régime was a source of complication and equivocation. The majority of the Resistance supporters thought that Britain had lost the war and that there was, therefore, no sense in remaining on her side; this inevitably gave rise to an attitude of passive resignation. Some Frenchmen, though faithful supporters of Vichy, remained anti-German and considered that action, however feeble, should be taken against the occupier, but these were the anglophobes, the anti-communists and the anti-Gaullists. All they could do was to pin their hopes on the Americans – without much conviction; more often they tended towards a French isolationism tantamount to a state of permanent impotence summarised by Maurras in the phrase 'France, France alone'. In any case, the régime, caught between the upper and nether millstones of collaboration and resistance, ended by being suspect both to the occupier and to his enemies; gradually resistance become synonymous with opposition to Vichy. As a result, it was no longer solely a struggle against the foreigner; these 'halfway house' régimes were a factor in accentuating the civil war character of the clandestine struggle. In France the ultimate proof of this was the stern punishment meted out to Darnand's henchmen after the war for the fires they had lit and the murders they had committed.

The defeat of collaboration in Poland and the USSR

In Poland a strain of pro-German sentiment had always existed;

to be more precise, in this country torn between its two powerful neighbours, a section of the leaders – the group known as 'the colonels' with Beck as Foreign Minister – had on several occasions sought a *modus vivendi* with Germany against the common enemy, bolshevist Russia. When the Polish Army had been crushed and the country divided according to the secret clauses of the Russo-German pact, certain high-ranking Polish aristocrats and well-known intellectuals offered their services in order to avoid a worse fate for their fellow-countrymen, in the spirit, in fact, which gave rise to the Vichy régime. But Hitler would have none of them: for him Poland no longer existed, and what remained of it was not worth consideration. As a result of the savage attitude of the occupier the entire political spectrum was united in the Resistance, in spite of the fact that as a nation the Poles were very prone to split into opposing camps.

In Russia the German leaders were divided over what attitude to adopt. In the opinion of Rosenberg, who was in charge of administration of the 'Eastern Territories', the Balts, the White Russians and the Ukrainians should be granted a certain degree of autonomy to align them against the Russians proper and dismember the Muscovite empire in the long term. Some senior officers of the Wehrmacht advocated an even bolder policy. A distinction should be made, they said, between the people and the régime; Germany should declare that she was making war only on the latter, not on the former, and act accordingly; land should be returned to the peasants, looting forbidden, private property respected and a minimum of human rights guaranteed in order to pave the way for a Russo-German rapprochement in the period following the disappearance of the Soviet régime.

The military were accordingly given authority to recruit unarmed auxiliaries from among the prisoners of war, and the success of the campaign exceeded all expectations; rather than die of hunger hundreds of thousands of men agreed to enter the service of the occupier. A further experiment was then tried, the formation of a sort of 'white army' of deserters, half-castes, emigrés and prisoners of war; it was commanded by General Vlassov, a highly qualified Red Army general whom Stalin's savagery had induced to change sides. But Hitler refused to regard these recruits as anything but mercenaries; he allowed them nothing but certain propaganda facilities to increase the number of desertions and so weaken the Red Army; all political activity was forbidden them and Hitler would make no promises about the future status of the USSR. Under these conditions the anti-Stalinists soon lost heart, and by early 1944 some of the Ukrainian nationalists had become as anti-German as they were still anti-Russian.

CHAPTER 3

External Resistance – the Allies and the Exiles

It was hardly surprising that the subject peoples were not content with their lot. There could be no doubt that, wherever nazism was in power, it would impose its mythology of leader, race and people, degrade the intellect and regiment the individual; it would introduce the rites, festivals and symbols of a neo-paganism; its authority would be founded on violence and terror; society would be divided into masters and slaves with the Jews as out-casts. Within its 'civilisation' culture was the servant of propa-ganda; war and rapine were both the aims of its policy and the methods it used. Though it would make no outward change in the structure of capitalist economy, it would control it through a series of measures of nationalisation. It would annihilate its enemies.

Internments, deportations and plunderings soon showed the occupied peoples the fate in store for them – during the war no one had any inkling of the ghastly concentration camp system. Everyone felt himself threatened.

Nazism's victims and its crimes were legion. Its propaganda was both intensive and crude – who was likely to believe the story that liberalism, capitalism, pacificism and communism were the bastard children of the Freemason and the Jew? Its appetite was insatiable – for food, industrial goods, raw materials, labour and even gold. Though it claimed to be the founder of a new-style economy in which gold played no role, it nevertheless rifled the reserves of the issue banks in the conquered countries and forced the doors of private safe deposits.[1]

Nazism, therefore, charged on to the stage of history like an avalanche which sweeps away every feature of a countryside to grind and churn it into a shapeless mass. If one lists all the groups of society affected or threatened, one would have thought that the

---

[1] In France the Germans forced the Vichy government to hand over the gold deposited by the Belgian government in May 1940.

occupying power would at once have found itself faced by unanimous resistance. In fact, however, its enemies were too absorbed in their old quarrels immediately to perceive that the same deadly peril threatened them all; lack of unity was one of the perennial factors in their weakness; until the very end of the war they were still opposing one another, even tearing each other to pieces. When circumstances compelled them to merge, their unity was invariably and inherently fragile. Left to themselves the conquered peoples, weaponless, deceived, exploited, starving, oppressed and divided were tormented by this virtually incurable failing.

The *major Allies and clandestine resistance*

This section will not deal with Chinese resistance, whether communist or nationalist. The vast area of China, the length of its history, the potency of its civilisation and the solidity of its social structures meant that it was an objective out of all proportion to Japanese capabilities, military, administrative or economic.

In Europe there were many obstacles, not least those of a psychological nature, to the essential co-operation between the Allies and the underground. Resistance abroad and resistance at home were in fact two facets of the same struggle but they were as disconnected as the two sides of a page.

Viewed from outside, the Resistance presented itself to the major Allies as a mass of uncertainties, a long list of requirements and a source of anxiety. What would it do with the weapons sent to it? Would it use them wisely? Would it not start by using them for its own internal battles? No one could be sure that it would obey orders – during the Spanish Civil War the anarchists had left their sentry posts to attend a political meeting. The underground remained a vast uncertain shadow. Precisely how strong was it? Militarily what was its quality – in terms of determination, courage, experience and fighting spirit? The professional soldiers of all countries – in the Red Army as much as in the new French Army of Africa – had only distrust, even contempt, for guerrilla warfare, the 'little war'; they placed their hopes of victory in their well-trained, well-equipped and well-commanded units; as they advanced, whether in Poland, Italy or France, it was the security of the rear areas that they were thinking about. Far from giving them appreciable assistance the Resistance, with its internal quarrels, its apparent anarchy and its sectional aims seemed to be a source of manifold dangers. Admittedly, quite apart from its questionable military contribution, the Resistance might be a valuable card in the political game, provided that its own aims and those of the Allies were the same – which was not always the case.

Accordingly, the attitudes of the Allies to the national resistance movements had much in common. As a general rule the Allies were not the instigators of resistance; when they were, they looked upon the movements as barely more than auxiliaries to their secret services, as a thorn in the enemy's flesh or at most as a flank guard. At no time did they dream of allowing them to participate in planning; they did not always tell them of their plans, even when these committed them to operations without much hope of success. In their eyes resistance was no more than a bonus which they could utilise if they thought fit but which in no way represented the country to be liberated. Support of the Resistance entailed no commitment by the Allies to the country concerned; they kept their hands free.

The overall problem of resistance, the concept of an immense Trojan horse behind the enemy lines, was never even raised in Allied strategic discussions. This attitude, common to all the Allies, was pregnant with misunderstandings and dramas. Whenever resistance was tiresome, whenever it threatened to become an apple of discord, the major Allies abandoned without hesitation that section of it which they had temporarily supported; Churchill did it to General de Gaulle and the 'gaullist' Resistance, Churchill and Roosevelt to the Polish government in London and the Home Army, Stalin to the Greek communists.

Nevertheless Great Britain, the Soviet Union and the United States did not view matters through the same spectacles, nor did they pursue an identical policy. Their attitudes varied according to the resistance movement with which they were dealing, circumstances, the stage of the war and their immediate or long-term interests. Equally, the national resistance movements adopted differing or alternating attitudes to the Allies, varying from the closest co-operation to open hostility or even severance of relations.

Great Britain

In everything to do with clandestine resistance Great Britain played the leading role, largely because Churchill advocated a proper Allied policy on the subject. As early as 1939–40 the British were thinking of sabotaging German shipping on the Danube. In August 1941, at his meeting with Roosevelt in Placentia, Churchill included among the five points summarising the principles of Allied strategy 'assistance to resistance groups in all occupied countries'. Yet at this stage resistance was no more than a hypothesis – probable but still no better than a gleam in the eye.

From summer 1940 to autumn 1942 all resistance in Europe drew its support from Great Britain. She alone was still in the war, and she was ready to use any weapon that came to hand. The occupied peoples clung to this last chance, to this supreme beacon of hope – that Britain would remain determined to fight and would not be defeated. In this hour of trial a sense of solidarity was born which never entirely faded though Great Britain, poorly armed, on the defensive and in mortal danger, could only provide occupied Europe with intermittent and inadequate assistance; she was in fact begging at the door of the defeated countries – she made numerous approaches to the Vichy government, for instance.

'sis', the British Intelligence Service, maintained or reconstituted its information circuits in occupied Europe. An entirely new service was also set up, under the Ministry of Economic Warfare: 'soe', the Special Operations Executive. Its task was to train agents to recruit small groups on the Continent to carry out minor sabotage as ordered. Another organisation, the 'Political Warfare Executive', was in charge of propaganda; escape lines were dealt with by Section 9 of the Military Intelligence Directorate in the War Office (mi9). All these organisations were divided into sections, one for each of the occupied countries.

All that the British expected of the Resistance was useful action, geared to the circumstances and their overall plans; they wanted information on German preparations for invasion in 1940, acts of sabotage to upset the enemy's military arrangements, minor actions by small parachute parties to produce a sense of insecurity in the rear areas, the repatriation of valuable personnel such as air force pilots, etc. These were the well-defined aims which led the British to develop a whole technique of clandestine warfare – radio communications with an ingenious system of 'personal messages', clandestine sets transmitting information, production of special explosives (plastic) or equipment (the S-Phone), despatch of suitable arms and ammunition, parachute operations dropping men and containers, operations by patrol boats and submarines, lines for agents through Scandinavia, Hungary, Spain and Portugal, etc. From June 1940 to November 1942 London was the arsenal, the banker and the headquarters of European resistance. London was the destination of all information and agents from central and western Europe. Everything was improvised; there were setbacks (particularly in Holland), there were internecine squabbles (with Free France for instance), but British aid to the Resistance was always on the increase. The main limitation to this action was imposed by geography. Distance, in fact, prohibited major operations in eastern Europe – one of the factors in the Warsaw drama.

Between November 1942 and April 1944 the British still controlled the Resistance in most of occupied Europe, but they no longer had a monopoly; the other two major Allies took a hand in the theatres where they were in command.

Gradually, however, clandestine resistance developed on a major scale and it was not prepared to accept orders so easily, whether these were positive or negative. More important still, it worked out its own plans visualising immediate action and a national politico-military rising when the time was ripe. It produced plans for the seizure of power and categorically declined to be controlled or supervised by foreigners. Churchill was himself somewhat alarmed by the growth of a force which he might not be able to control and by the increasing dissensions within the Resistance, which gave rise to a revolutionary atmosphere, and he seems to have back-tracked. The relationship between Great Britain and the Resistance, therefore, became less intimate and uninhibited. From spring 1944 Great Britain's role vis-à-vis European resistance became less important because she was occupying a smaller place in the war as a whole and her relative weakness was beginning to become obvious. The task of supplying the Resistance then fell to the Americans, with their limitless resources, while Soviet influence grew in eastern Europe. British influence remained predominant, however, in the smaller countries of western Europe – Belgium, Holland and Norway – where British armies were to operate. From this time, too, Churchill's attitude was dictated more by political than by military considerations. He even emerged as an opponent of the Resistance – in Italy and even more in Greece where British armed intervention was approved by the 'collaborators'. When the war ended, therefore, the British did not reap all the benefits to which they might have thought they were entitled as a result of their courage and far-sightedness in 1940. They were even to be found opposing the Resistance and defending a political and social system which it had been their object to destroy.

This reversal of fortune was, to some extent, both dramatic and inequitable; Britain paid a high price for the courage, determination and sacrifice which, for almost a year, had made her the sole defender of freedom. As long as the object was merely the formation and equipment of a sort of clandestine warfare chivalry, of 'circuits' embarking, like commandos, on clearly defined and limited operations, Britain scored indubitable successes and played the leading role. From the time, however, that the Resistance developed into mass movements visualising the formation of peoples' armies and the installation of revolutionary institutions, Britain's difficulties increased and she gradually faded into the background.

There were also political reasons for this semi-defeat of Great Britain. She proposed to the Resistance that Europe should revert to its pre-war state, which the Resistance no longer wanted. As a result of the occupier's exploitation Europe had become an under-developed area; it condemned the pre-war political régimes which it regarded as responsible for its defeat; it was waging civil war as well as a war of liberation. So the Resistance was aiming not only at national independence but also at revolution, both social and political. To this problem the ussr could provide an answer which the victories of the Red Army endowed with an irresistible power of persuasion.

The USSR

The development of the ussr's attitude to resistance followed a course precisely opposite to that of Great Britain. Until 21 June 1941 Russia was at best in a wait-and-see position. Because of her non-aggression pact with Germany she had managed to annex certain territories; for the emergent Resistance she was an enemy equivalent to Germany. The USSR was scrupulous in her observance of the economic and political clauses of the Russo-German pact; diplomatically she was anti-British at a time when Britain alone carried the hopes of all the occupied peoples. On 31 October 1939, in his report on foreign policy to the Fifth Session of the Supreme Soviet, Molotov accused Great Britain and France of wishing to prolong the war when Hitler was striving for peace; he reproached Britain for 'tampering with democratic liberties at home'. The USSR then officially criticised the volunteers still fighting on Britain's side and the Soviet press labelled them 'lackeys of capitalism' – de Gaulle most of all. Following directives from Moscow, the national communist parties approved the Russo-German pact, thus divorcing themselves from the rest of the population.

By all accounts the USSR, despite warnings received from Great Britain and also, apparently, the Czech resistance, was surprised by the German assault in June 1941. Until Stalingrad she was on the defensive and all her efforts were devoted to the avoidance of defeat. Her place in the world conflict changed radically on 21 June 1941: she in her turn was now the victim of nazi aggression and she mobilised all her forces; anyone fighting the aggressor became her friend. The loss of much of her territory meant that she was now partially dependent on foreign aid, like the Resistance in other countries. In her desperate straits she identified the Resistance with her own war. But there was an exceptional feature in the situation: the clandestine groups which formed in occupied Russia were in touch, not with emigrés who must beg everything from an ally and, at whatever damage to their pride, are totally dependent on him, but with a regular national army receiving its orders from a legitimate government, still fighting in its own country and drawing its resources from that country's economy; the entire population concentrated around that army, conscious that it was fighting not merely for a political régime but for the independence and unity of the nation.

Nevertheless, in view of her precarious situation, the USSR could play no role outside her own frontiers; she could furnish no assistance to resistance in other countries, nor had she a right to expect any, in spite of Stalin's appeal to all communist parties to attack the occupier by every means in their power. The only way to bring Russia some relief from the stranglehold of the Wehrmacht was the earliest possible large-scale landing by Allied armies in the west; local diversionary operations were no good.

Unlike Great Britain, therefore, the USSR at this stage organised no parachute drops outside her own territory; she did not form sabotage groups; she did not despatch agents to the occupied countries. The distress of the western communist parties and their pressing requests to the British and Americans for arms and money give one to think that Russia was not financing them either. Russia's own house was on fire and all her national resources were concentrated on extinguishing the conflagration.

The decisive development was the victory of Stalingrad at the turn of the years 1942–43. In the eyes of European resistance the influence and importance of the USSR continually increased after that, as did her position in the Allied coalition. The Soviet government no longer considered only the fate of the country: victory could be foreseen in the longer or shorter term. From this time on Russian policy was dictated by post-war considerations, the defence of her long-term interests and the requirements of her security.

From her role as a German ally up to June 1941, the USSR was by the end of 1944 able to appear as the prime example of the country of resistance. This she owed basically to the Red Army's victories, to the example she had provided of a national Resistance struggling to victory through its own resources, to the casualties and sufferings caused by an occupation unequalled in savagery except perhaps in Poland, and to the importance of the role played in most countries by the communist parties. Viewed against this great canvas, the Russo-German pact was no more than a passing aberration.

The United States

The Americans were the last of the three major Allies to enter the world war and, at least as far as Europe was concerned, they only assumed a leading role towards the end of 1943. Not even belatedly did they co-operate much with the Resistance. The war the Resistance was waging was the very antithesis of the American concept of industrialised warfare, with its emphasis on arms production, the organisation of transportation, continuous modernisation and standardisation of equipment. By contrast the Resistance, lacking everything, seemed like an organisation of beggars in arms, whose only assets were determination and spirit of self-sacrifice.

In the conduct of American policy Roosevelt played a considerable personal role, though he had to keep his eye on public opinion rather more than Churchill and a great deal more than Stalin. The war aims of the two latter were governed by the basic interests of their countries and their attitude to resistance derived from this, while overall American policy was never very clearly defined. For them Europe remained throughout the war an unknown land, full of pitfalls, which they were bent on leaving as soon as victory was won. There were, therefore, no long-standing American traditions, territorial or ideological purposes to act as safeguards against the moods and whims of Roosevelt, who was frequently a disconcerting personality. He refused, for example, to admit the increasing authority of General de Gaulle because he disliked him as a man, in spite of unanimous advice to the contrary from the State Department, the War Department and oss. Conversely, according to Admiral Leahy, he was sympathetic to Darlan because he and the latter's son were sufferers from the same disease.

On the executive level the us military, secret services and even diplomats showed themselves extremely ignorant of political problems and almost afraid to deal with them; us agents or parachute teams lived divorced from the men of the resistance whom they had come to help and had no understanding of the ideas, needs or aims of the men alongside whom they were fighting. Numerous misunderstandings and considerable friction were the result.

Obviously, as leaders of the coalition and the only one of the three major Allies to be fighting simultaneously in Europe and Asia, the Americans were preoccupied with vast problems of industrial mobilisation and the formation of a gigantic army. They were not hankering after territory or any particular economic advantages, but merely wished to ensure that after victory the world would be at peace. Consequently they were miles away from the Resistance, its animosities, its problems and its aims. They never formulated or followed an overall policy in regard to the Resistance; the attitudes they adopted were temporary and local.

By the autumn of 1942 the Americans had barely emerged from

their period of neutrality. Every sort of problem at once crowded in on them. The first was the strategic question: Europe or Asia? They were not totally ignorant of the type of warfare being waged by the Resistance – they had had some experience of it in the Philippines, but only in matters of propaganda and sabotage. In any case, all they had to do in Europe was to prepare themselves to take the offensive, and for this they required information; the time for action had not yet come. While still neutral their natural inclination had been to look to their ambassadors to keep them informed, and their sources were generally senior officials of the occupied countries; they did not change their habits on entering the war.

Consequently, even when they realised the existence of the embryo clandestine movements which were taking the first inept steps at this time, the American judgement of them was faulty; they looked upon them as negligible quantities.[1] Moreover, they made little use of those who had emigrated to the United States; their radio propaganda, broadcast from distant stations and difficult to hear, never equalled the volume or efficiency of that of the BBC; it was neither so well founded nor so adroit.

The next stage began with the landing in North Africa. Lacking the connivance of the Vichy authorities, the Americans were forced to contact the opposition to ensure its success. The first American effort at co-operation with resistance therefore took place with the French; as we shall see later, it was done with astonishing ineptitude. The Americans were subsequently unable to disengage themselves from the labyrinth of the French Resistance and were at a loss to pick their way through the tangle.

Nevertheless, the Americans had both military and political links with the Resistance from this time. In 1942 they set up a central agency, the 'Office of Strategic Services' (OSS), under General Donovan;[2] its Swiss office was its main focus. They were not always discerning in their choice of agents, however, and were prone to accept men whose links with the occupying power had made them suspect to their fellow-countrymen. Gradually they

---

[1] Admiral Leahy, the US Ambassador in Vichy, thought 'the men of the *maquis* odd'.

[2] In contrast to the British organisation, OSS dealt both with information and action; a third section was responsible for 'Research and Analysis'. The system adopted by OSS had the advantage of ensuring central direction.

organised their own information and action circuits in occupied Europe, all with a view to preparing the vast vital landing operation which they were to command.

By 1944 the United States had become the arsenal of the Allied coalition and consequently of the Resistance too. They did arm the Resistance, and the battles it fought demonstrated the support it could provide; yet in western Europe the Americans would admit this only grudgingly and in central and eastern Europe they abandoned the Resistance to its fate. In France, until the very end of the occupation, they were still supporting those who were divorced from, or even opposed to, the Resistance; they even thought of installing in Paris a Chautemps-Herriot government sponsored by Laval. Paradoxically the us military, and particularly Eisenhower, showed greater political sense than the civilians in spite of the fact that the military objectives of the Resistance frequently differed from their own.

In eastern Europe the Americans sacrificed the Resistance in the interests of their overall post-war plans. Once the German menace was dead, their primary object was to avoid planting the seeds of a possible third world war. In effect Roosevelt abandoned eastern Europe to the Russians without even fighting a rearguard action to define spheres of influence.

The absence of a real American policy towards the Resistance was confirmed in the final settlement. No other country was so naturally anti-communist, yet the us complacently accepted Soviet expansion westwards. Neither of the other major Allies made so vast and disinterested an effort or provided the occupied countries with aid on so massive, even philanthropic, a scale – they supplied whole populations which were destitute and starving. Yet the gratitude of the liberated peoples was tinged with resentment. The Americans had fought nazism to the death but, on the way, they had fallen out with some of nazism's enemies and they had sometimes supported men and régimes with suspect political and social beliefs. When the war ended, they possessed power unprecedented in history, but their reward was meagre. They had not grasped the fact that the political structure of post-war Europe was decided in the underground of the Resistance. By turning their back on the Resistance the Americans showed that they were not yet ready to play the leadership role in history which their stature should have enabled them to assume.

The exiles

Midway between the Allies and the clandestine organisations stood certain groups of political exiles. First came the Italian and German anti-fascists, though their will to fight was inevitably affected by the crisis of conscience implicit in hostility to one's own government, carrying with it the risk of injuring one's own country. Between March 1939 and spring 1941 a number of legitimate governments left their respective countries to continue the fight on the Allied side; the destination of them all was London. Their aim was to direct their own clandestine resistance, but they were not invariably successful; the Allies gave them little assistance and they were no exception to the rule that between exiles and their country of origin misunderstandings, animosities and divisions multiply.

Another group of emigrés, however, had taken refuge in Moscow. These were the communist leaders who formed a very solid block, an international assembly faithfully carrying out Stalin's directives and placing itself unreservedly at the service of Soviet policy.[1] Accordingly, like the two camps within the 'strange alliance' formed in answer to the Hitler menace – the USSR on one side and the Anglo-Americans on the other – two sections emerged within the Resistance both inside and outside the occupied countries and the relationship between them became a serious additional factor in the war plans and post-war aims of the Allies. For some time the two sections worked in parallel; in some cases they agreed, particularly in France, Italy and Czechoslovakia; frequently, however, they tore each other to pieces and the resulting internecine struggles were ghastly – as in Poland and, more especially, Yugoslavia.

The Italian anti-fascist opposition

For many years Mussolini's enemies attempted to continue the battle in Italy using the methods permitted them by the régime – parliament, the press and public opinion. The liberals, centred on Benedetto Croce and his periodical 'Critica', made no pretence to be conspirators; they acted within fascist law, denouncing the abuses and perils of fascism in educated circles.

[1] On the subject of these communist emigrés see Chapter 11 below.

It soon became evident, however, that such methods were ineffective and out of date. One after another Mussolini's opponents were detected or denounced, arrested by the police and interned on the Lipari Islands or elsewhere – 'Silvio Pellico prisons' in the tradition of the Risorgimento; many followed another tradition and went into exile abroad – the *fuorisciti*. The majority went to Paris, where they were granted asylum; others went to Geneva, the headquarters of the League of Nations, where they could retain contact with international circles; still others departed for London or the United States. The leaders were not the only people to emigrate; frequently they were followed by lower-level activists. One of the opposition's exploits was the spectacular flight of the veteran socialist leader Turati.

Nevertheless, the Italian political emigrés were a heterogeneous collection little inclined to unite. They included republicans like Count Sforza, radicals like Nitti, Christian democrats like dom Sturzo (who departed for New York) and socialists centred on Pietro Nenni and Giuseppe Saragat; the communists formed a group apart, some remaining in Italy with Gramsci and others taking refuge in Moscow with Togliatti.

They were mostly chieftains without followers, who devoted their efforts primarily to debunking fascism. Tasca recounted the somewhat inglorious circumstances under which it was born; others told of Mussolini's racketeering and sometimes murky existence. These exposures made some impact on Italian working-class circles abroad, but their real object was to influence world public opinion. The emigrés' main hope was that fascism might be outlawed by the community of nations; they were not helped, however, by the policy of Chamberlain and Laval, which was aimed at detaching Italy from Germany, and even less by Mussolini's victory in Abyssinia.

Living under difficult circumstances, embittered by their exile and watched by fascist spies, the emigrés nevertheless attempted to unite, papering over their differences and overcoming their rivalries. Before he died Piero Gobetti launched his 'liberal revolution', holding out some prospect of ideological *rapprochement*; the 'justice and liberty' movement of the Rosselli brothers and Ferrucio Parri was even more hopeful, visualising a marriage between socialism and liberalism and proclaiming that fascism could only be defeated by a national rising. Accordingly an 'antifascist concentration' under the socialist Claudio Treves was formed in 1927 with *La Libertà* as its newspaper. From 1934, when the USSR began urging the formation of 'popular fronts', the communists joined more willingly, but their arrival scared away the Christian democrats and liberals; what anti-fascism gained on the left it lost on the right. Nevertheless, a 'general anti-fascist congress' was held in Brussels in 1935. The Spanish Civil War cemented the growing unity.

In 1927 the fascist régime demonstrated that it took this opposition seriously by having the Roselli brothers assassinated. Unless, however, the anti-fascists could penetrate Italy, they were bound to fade into ineffectiveness. This fact was well understood by the communists; they did not confine themselves to the distribution of newspapers and clandestine pamphlets; they joined fascist organisations and 'infiltrated' them with the object of playing on grievances and provoking demonstrations. The others followed their example, primarily 'Justice and Liberty' which established a regular system of liaison with movement-affiliated groups in the main cities of northern Italy; explosions occurred in buildings occupied by fascist organisations and some of the fascist thugs were murdered.

The régime struck back through its secret police, the OVRA. Those of its enemies whom it had managed to arrest it brought before a 'special tribunal'; it organised spectacular trials in the hope of discrediting them in the eyes of the public as traitors to their country and minions of foreign powers. The desired effect was only partially achieved; the trials produced publicity for the opposition and proved that it had made some impact on worker and intellectual circles. This impact was not, however, great enough to affect the mass of the Italian people, and was entirely without effect in southern Italy.

German opposition to Hitler

The case of the German anti-fascists illustrates the crisis of conscience with which the exiles were faced. They were caught on the horns of a terrible dilemma: the success of the régime they were opposing reduced them to impotence, but on the other hand their cause would be furthered by any setbacks it might suffer. How could they cheerfully hope for setbacks, particularly if they themselves were responsible, when these would be setbacks for their country? Every member of the German resistance, therefore, had to make his choice in the secrecy of his own conscience.

The National-Socialist Party had been swept into power by the economic crisis of the 'thirties – the increase in its vote at successive elections follows closely the rising tide of unemployment. Less directly it had exploited the German people's deep-seated trauma following their defeat in 1918 and the revolutionary upheaval stemming from it. Initially it had been supported by heavy industry and the Wehrmacht and had used violent street agitation as a weapon. There was no doubt, however, that it had come to power by legal means.

But the nazis only retained power by force. Six months later they obtained 93 per cent approval for their policy out of a total vote of 95 per cent, but only because of the fear they inspired and liquidation of their most dangerous opponents. The poll was rigged, but it does give a measure of the number of determined opponents who had the courage to vote against nazism – slightly over two million. Who were they?

Basically they were communists, socialists, Jews and a small hard core of Christians, both Protestant and Catholic. The wrath of the nazis descended on them. Political parties were banned, the trade unions suppressed, the press muzzled and over 200,000 arrests made – 8,000 communists in 1937 and 11,000 in 1938, the only years for which nazi police statistics are known. It was for these anti-nazi Germans that the 'labour camps' were initially opened on the Hanover moors; they were succeeded by 'concentration camps', pictured as innocent 'correction' institutions. Those militants who escaped the man-hunts went into exile – socialists and Christian democrats to the western democracies and communists to Moscow. Over 300,000 Jews also left Germany. Internal opposition to nazism was therefore leaderless. Nevertheless, over a million clandestine leaflets, the majority communist, circulated in Germany in 1936 and 1937; as late as 1939 one hundred militants were executed. But all this caused scarcely a ripple on the surface of public opinion.

In fact, who was there now left in Germany to protest effectively? Admittedly the administration, particularly the Wilhemstrasse diplomats and certain army circles, were uneasy about the excessive risks Hitler was taking. The General Staff at first approved of neither the remilitarisation of the Rhineland nor the annexation of Austria, both of which they thought too dangerous.

But inevitably the intoxication of success won them over. The victories of the Führer were even more brilliant than those of the Duce and were not merely gained at the expense of some African tribe. More important than all, nazi policy had given the Germans an economy ostensibly balanced internally, an end to unemployment and the abrogation of a detested treaty, the *diktat* from without. It was difficult not to rejoice over the return to the great German family of the lost Sudeten Germans and the Austrians. Even the slightest hesitation was equivalent to playing the game of that implacable enemy, France, always on the watch to prevent Germany assuming the role due to her.

Even more than the anti-fascists, the anti-nazis had to work from outside. Well-known names in politics, literature, the arts and science were among the exiles. The fact remains that they barely made an appearance. Statesmen like Dr Wirth, who had fled to Switzerland, hesitated before making one or two fruitless contacts with British government representatives. The German communist leaders in exile remained comparatively inactive, no doubt in obedience to Stalin's policy of caution aimed at averting the nazi threat to the USSR. The only German whom France asked for advice after September 1939 was Thyssen, the industrialist. At first sight the inactivity of the Jews was astounding, but it is explained by their deep-rooted sense of being German, their wish to integrate themselves as best they might into the country offering them asylum to avoid untimely agitation, and by their fear of drawing down the wrath of the nazis on the Jewish community still in Germany. Nevertheless, the fact that well-known personalities such as Thomas Mann and Einstein had chosen exile probably helped to arouse American public opinion. The emigrés were scattered worldwide, however, and nowhere did they form a bloc. The world had to wait for years and for major defeats to be suffered by Hitler's Reich before a true German resistance was born. Many of its permanent and special characteristics can be attributed to the difficulties of its early days.

The Spanish Civil War

In spring 1936 a section of the Spanish army revolted and was supported by a majority of the Catholic Church and many of the aristocracy. The rebellion soon assumed an importance extending beyond the frontiers of Spain. In the first place this was a fresh offensive by international fascism, this time without even a mask of revolution or social reformism. Moreover, both Hitler and Mussolini thought it in their interests to support Franco – for reasons of prestige of course, but also to further more long-term plans. The Wehrmacht wished to put its technique and its new weapons to a live test; Italy wanted to improve her position in the Mediterranean by the establishment of additional naval bases, in the Balearic Islands for instance. The dictators made no attempt to camouflage their action; it took place in full view of publicity and, from the outset, was announced and acclaimed as an ideological struggle, a crusade. As Alvarez del Vayo, the Spanish Republican Foreign Minister, said, an 'international civil war' had started.

This is not the place to examine the background and vicissitudes of the 'non-intervention' policy theoretically followed by Great Britain and France. It did not prevent numerous volunteers from both countries fighting on the republican side. Moreover, the USSR took up the cause from the faltering western democracies, giving the international anti-fascist movement the direction and external assistance it had hitherto lacked. It also demonstrated the difficulty of uniting the movement: communists, anarchists and Trotskyists were frequently at each other's throats.

Drawn from all quarters of the earth, the volunteers formed 'International Brigades' which eventually reached a total of 35,000 men; the majority were communists – 50 per cent of the Frenchmen and as high as 80 per cent for nationals of countries where the communist party was banned. Up to this time the communist party had been noted for the violence of its 'anti-militarism' – L'Humanité generally labelled professional NCOs as 'bull-merchants'. The International Brigades lacked experienced cadres; they were necessarily thrown up from the ranks and had to learn the trade of fighting and the art of command while on the job. The communist party thus acquired a whole body of specialists in popular warfare; the importance of this development is shown by the quality of some of the International Brigade volunteers – Longo from Italy, Tito from Yugoslavia, Ulbricht from Germany, Lecoeur, Billoux and Marty from France, Ferenc Munich from Hungary[1] and Szyr from Poland,[2] among others.

[1] President of the Republic for a time after the war.
[2] At present Vice-President of the Polish Council of Ministers.

3

Anti-fascists from some fifty countries, therefore, came to know each other and fought together in actual warfare. The resulting political fusion was no less important than the military co-operation; fighting beside the communists were to be found socialists like Willi Brandt from Germany or Nenni from Italy, Trotskyists, syndicalists, anarchists and also anti-fascists who belonged to no specific grouping, such as Malraux from France or Picciardi from Italy.

In Spain, therefore, anti-fascism graduated from the battle of the mind to that of the guns, from invective to rifles. There were highly symbolic engagements; on the plateau of Guadalajara, for instance, Blackshirts fought Italian anti-fascists and were routed. Nationally the opponents of dictatorship gained a new solidarity; for instance, the Italians united in a 'Popular Union of Emigrés'; it published a newspaper, *La Voce degli Italiani*, large enough to ensure a wide dissemination of its views.

Admittedly this great effort ended in defeat: Franco was victorious and 10,000 volunteers of the International Brigades died in Spain. Because failure, even more than exile, is a source of major quarrelling, international anti-fascism emerged from the Spanish war more divided than before. Nevertheless, the lesson was not lost. The volunteers of the International Brigades had served their apprenticeship in the Spanish Civil War and many of them became partisan leaders.

Governments-in-exile in London

As the Wehrmacht's conquests extended and fresh countries fell to the nazi axe, a growing flood of exiles left occupied Europe to find, on the territories of countries still at war with the Axis, either asylum or a springboard from which to pursue the struggle. Many went to the United States, where the largest colonies of Italian and German anti-fascists were already to be found. Frequently they were men of the highest qualities – politicians, authors, journalists, scientists or artists. After the defeat of France, for instance, refugees to the United States included men and women as eminent and as diverse as Pierre Cot, Alexis Léger (who was both Secretary-General in the Ministry of Foreign Affairs and, under the pseudonym Saint-John Perse, a poet of high repute), J. Romains, André Maurois, H. Bernstein, H. de Kerillis, Geneviève Tabouis, E. Bois, Eve Curie, H. Focillon, René Clair, J. Renoir, etc. They wrote in the press, they talked on the radio, they taught in universities, they gave lectures. They therefore helped to keep American public opinion informed before the entry of the United States into the war. But their political role was small and their rivalries as bitter as they were numerous. Whatever their personal prestige, they represented only themselves.[1]

The responsible politicians of the occupied countries were a different matter, for they remained in Europe to be nearer the oppressed peoples. Accordingly Beneš, the President of Czechoslovakia, Sikorski, President of the Polish Republic (with his government), M. Pierlot and the Belgian government, took refuge initially in France, whence they were hunted by the rapid advance of the German tanks. A second exodus then took place to London, where they joined King Haakon of Norway and Queen Wilhelmina of Holland; later arrivals were King Peter of Yugoslavia and King George of Greece. London became the headquarters of a sort of international movement of sovereigns and governments-in-exile, among them General de Gaulle's 'Free France', which seemed to have special characteristics.

Admittedly none of these visitors, whether royalty or minister, brought any great material contribution to the common struggle against the Axis. They did, however, control much of the Danish merchant marine, most of the Norwegian and Dutch fleets, the Belgian Congo, French Equatorial Africa, the Dutch East Indies until late 1941 and contingents of volunteers who had escaped from occupied Europe; all this constituted a significant reinforcement. Moreover the British government decided to accept and assist all of them; none could have existed without the generosity of the British Treasury, and the small forces which each had contrived to preserve could not have continued to fight without the equipment and supplies provided by the British.

The presence in London of authorities from the occupied countries, even if only symbolic, was of immense psychological value to the nationals of those countries; it was an encouragement against despair and complete submission to the exactions of the occupying power. The hope was kept alive that one day a sort of

---

[1] An exception was the field of nuclear research. There a remarkable conglomeration of foreign scientists, who had left their respective countries because of totalitarian persecution, played a major role in the Allied victory by giving the United States the monopoly of the atomic bomb.

immense 'fifth column' would appear to gnaw at the enemy's vitals. In the long term the British hoped that their support would bring them greater influence in a post-war Europe, grateful and conscious of the debt it had incurred.

In general, the British government had no major problems with the Norwegians, the Dutch or the Belgians, who were all too weak to be other than docile protégés. Over Poland, Yugoslavia and Greece, however, the British had to make a difficult choice between the government-in-exile and resistance groups. There were special problems with France: General de Gaulle was not content merely to direct the Free French movement which he had created, but claimed to speak in the name of France as a whole; he proved to be an alert and fractious defender of the rights, interests and prestige of his country.

Free France

Contrary to British expectations, when France was defeated no well-known French statesman, no senior military commander and no Governor-General of any of the colonies[1] made up his mind to fight on, despite the appeals of a certain acting Brigadier-General who had spent a few weeks as Secretary of State in Paul Reynaud's government, and had arrived in London by 17 June 1940. His name was Charles de Gaulle. Churchill allowed him time on the BBC and de Gaulle made a number of speeches, known as 'the call of 18 June', containing phrases which were to prove prophetic – 'France has lost a battle, but she has not lost the war, for this is a world war'. He did not attract many followers, however, because of Marshal Pétain's prestige in France and also because of the British action at Mers el-Kebir. Only a few thousand volunteers presented themselves, coming either from the French forces located in Britain or from groups of Frenchmen resident abroad. From these de Gaulle formed the movement which he called 'Free France' and the little army known as the 'Free French Forces'.

These volunteers were soon in action alongside British forces – in the Battle of Britain, in the Abyssinian and Libyan campaigns and in the Battle of the Atlantic. Some of the French colonial possessions (Oceania, India, French Equatorial Africa and the

[1] Except General Catroux somewhat later.

Cameroons) joined General de Gaulle, giving him more extensive territory, but they were poor, under-populated countries. Unfortunately, at Dakar in September 1940 the General failed to bring over French West Africa and in June 1941 he was able to assert himself in the Middle East only at the price of fratricidal operations when Frenchmen were pitted against Frenchmen.

Though he loyally supported de Gaulle, Churchill never gave up hope of a change in the attitude of the Vichy régime, which would have brought over far more valuable military forces, particularly the remnants of the French fleet which would have changed the balance of force in the Mediterranean. For this reason, although Pétain and Weygand regularly rejected the approaches made to them in the conviction that a German victory was inevitable, Churchill, supported by Roosevelt, refused to recognise the 'French National Committee' as the true legal government of France. He did no more than subsidise it; he even hesitated to send the few brigades which it had raised into action – so much so that de Gaulle considered sending them to fight in the USSR.

De Gaulle, on the other hand, maintained that his movement alone represented France because the Vichy régime, the legitimacy of which he denied, was not a free agent and, in addition, had embarked on a policy of collaboration with the occupying power. Consequently there were frequent clashes, sometimes bordering on severance of relations. The British supported some breakaway movements within Free France in the hope of finding more pliable men to lead it. The nadir was reached when de Gaulle took possession of the islands Saint-Pierre-et-Miquelon despite an American veto; though of no real importance, this incident soon developed into a bitter diplomatic quarrel. The British, moreover, had no hesitation in suborning and recruiting volunteers who had come over to join Free France. De Gaulle protested violently against such encroachments on his authority and threatened to withdraw to Brazzaville. The story is told that on one occasion Churchill, exasperated by the bitterness of the discussion, exploded with: 'The heaviest cross I have to bear is the Cross of Lorraine' – the symbol of Free France.

Nevertheless, the fact remains that the Free French Forces fought – and fought well. Small forces under Leclerc started from Chad and chased the Italians out of the oases of Kufra and Fezzan, General Koenig's brigade held up Rommel at Bir Hakeim.

contributing to the defence of Egypt. In Russia the *Normandie-Niemen* regiment fought well in the air.

At the same time information issuing from France showed a growing body of support for de Gaulle. This being so, the British government allowed him to exercise real authority over the French clandestine resistance movement. Alone among the governments-in-exile Free France was permitted its own special services, the 'Central Information and Action Bureau' [*Bureau central de renseignements et d'action* – BCRA]. Close ties were established between Free France and the Resistance, which recognised the authority of General de Gaulle from mid-1942. The title of the movement was then changed to 'Fighting France'.

PART II

Origins and Organisation of Clandestine Warfare

History is full of terrible conflicts in which peoples have defeated and enslaved their neighbours. History also shows that whole populations have been massacred or reduced to slavery, and yet have sometimes, by a desperate struggle, contrived to retain their identity and regain their independence. No situation, however – and this is the 'pitfall of history' – ever repeats itself exactly. Nevertheless, the defeated and oppressed of the second world war were inspired by legendary precedents. They knew instinctively that geography (islands or mountains) offered some refuge to the rebellious, and that to survive they must retain their national solidarity; memories of past glories sustained them; if only for convenience, they were prepared to insist on the preservation of their language, their customs, their beliefs and, if possible, their frontiers.

Yet among the occupied peoples the dominant feeling was one of impotence. Their armies had been defeated; their government had disappeared or become the enemy's tool; the enemy himself was moving from victory to victory. What could they do against him with their bare hands? For a long time they resigned themselves to the loss of their freedom and tried to make the best of it. Defeat had dulled the intellect and subdued the spirit; the few explosions of wrath were aimed primarily at the nation's own military or civil leaders.

For most of the period of occupation the attitude of the majority was one of lethargy. Material things were scarce, and people were fully occupied with attempting to obtain them. Léon Blum said of France: 'The country remained silent and inert. It was still suffering the effects of shock, using the word in its pathological sense, in other words from a sort of anaesthesia.' This did not apply solely to France.

If the occupying power showed his teeth at once, as in Poland, any opposition seemed that much more perilous; if, as in Paris, he was ostensibly 'correct', people inevitably began to wonder what his true intentions were; in any case why not profit from his goodwill, even if only for tactical reasons, and why change the situation by irritating him? The obscurity of the situation was further aggravated by the existence on national territory of more or less free and legitimate governments. Of course they were only there with the consent of the victor and they advised, even demanded, that nothing be done against him. But perhaps they had some ulterior motive. Were the people to refuse them their confidence because they were headed by a Hacha, a Pétain, a Horthy, an Antonescu or a Nedich?

In fact each individual was thrown back upon himself: he was the target of intensive propaganda; he was forced to exist by guile; he was overwhelmed by personal or family worries; he was convinced of his own impotence. So he had to find his own reasons for acting when all seemed hopeless, and persisting when success was denied him. The birth of resistance as a vocation remains shrouded in the mystery of the choice made by thousands of individual consciences. Although certain external or private impulses may have helped it grow, nowhere did the Resistance spring fully armed from the depths of the people's misery.

CHAPTER 4

First Moves

Considerable time passed before the occupied peoples made up their minds to take the first hesitant, faltering steps towards clandestine warfare; much wavering, many backslidings and numerous setbacks were the order of the day. For many, the simplest and most effective solution was to escape from the country and fight from outside.

Escapes[1]

Before the complete domination of Europe by nazi Germany it was comparatively easy to leave. On the very day when German troops moved into Bohemia, for instance, Colonel Frantisek Moravec, head of Czech Army Intelligence, fled with his entire staff; until Christmas 1939 other Czechs were still leaving via Hungary. After March 1938 certain Austrian exiles set up in Paris an 'Austrian socialist representation abroad' which moved to New York in June 1940. After the defeat of Poland the French and British missions in adjacent countries helped young Poles (soldiers, sailors, airmen, engineers) to escape first to France and then to Great Britain via Rumania, Hungary or the Baltic States. General de Gaulle left by air for London as soon as he heard that the new government of Marshal Pétain had requested an armistice. Such actions were typical of all countries.

From the time German troops lined the entire coast from the Baltic to the Bidassoa and were capable of reaching the Mediterranean, surveillance became stricter, escape both more difficult

---

[1] I would emphasise, once and for all, that I make no attempt to give a *complete* account of the action of the Resistance; it amounted, in fact, to millions of tiny operations. I have confined myself to recounting and comparing certain actions which seemed of significance to my subject.

and more dangerous. At this point the Resistance was primarily concerned with prisoners of war and its first moves were made on their account. Prisoners were too numerous all to be taken to Germany at once, and initially they were held in improvised, poorly-guarded 'front stalags'. Every subterfuge was employed to obtain for them cigarettes, food and later, if they wished, civilian clothing, sometimes with false papers provided by co-operative officials in mayors' or police offices. The first escape lines were organised for prisoners who no longer had a country – from Poland via Slovakia into Hungary or across the Vosges; on some days as many as thirty fugitives would pass through a certain forestry hut in the Vosges. When the wretched columns of emaciated and ragged prisoners marched through towns or villages en route for the 'oflags' or 'stalags' of Germany, expressions of sympathy were to be heard on all hands – a girl in Alsace shouted to the French: 'We would like to go with you.'

The Germans had carved up the occupied countries into zones of differing status which they surrounded with artificial but hermetically-sealed frontiers known as 'demarcation lines'. One of the first actions of the Resistance was to organise the crossing of these lines – at least they were thus breaking the enemy's rules and rendering themselves liable to punishment. Karski, the Pole, has given an account[1] of his journey from Warsaw to Lwow in Russian-occupied Poland – through woods and fields, bogs and streams; the route was complicated but perfectly safe and he was led by guides living near 'the line'. In France drivers and guards of trains authorised to cross from the occupied to the so-called free zone used every trick to help clandestine line-crossers: bunks were rigged up in the engines using the fibre-glass panels which insulated the machinery; children were given sleeping pills beforehand. Everywhere the demarcation line was riddled with holes; if a factory or yard lay astride it, workmen were continually coming and going – but they were not the same in each direction; fake furniture vans and hearses made the crossing. The Armistice Army's secret service despatched 'workmen', in reality young soldiers in disguise, to North Africa, where supervision by the Italian Armistice Commission was more lax.

The main destination for escapers, however, was Great Britain,

[1] In his book *Mon Témoignage devant le monde,* Paris 1948.

where they could continue to fight.[1] Karski, for instance, went by train to Zakopan, crossed the mountains on skis and reached Slovakia, whence he was passed on (by car) to Budapest; there, after a period of recuperation, he was simply handed a false passport and a railway ticket for Milan. As soon as they heard of the signature of the armistice, French Air Force pilots took off for the nearest British airfield: Great Britain, Gibraltar, Malta, Cyprus, Egypt, Palestine, Zanzibar – even Singapore. Success frequently demanded much ingenuity and perseverance; one young Breton concealed the parts of a light aeroplane in his family's country house, assembled it and, in November 1940, crossed the Channel.

Sailors were obviously the best placed to reach the British Isles. In June 1940 the entire able-bodied male population of the island of Sein – 130 in all ranging in age from 12 to 60 – left for England. On the same day a party of volunteers left the island of Batz, accompanied to the quay and cheered by the whole population – there was not room for everyone. Fishermen became experts in 'two-way journeys'; one completed no fewer than five crossings before being caught.

Switzerland too was a refuge, but did not offer permanent asylum. When the students of Guebwiller college were sent to the vicinity of Lake Constance, several of them swam across the lake and reached the Swiss shore. Numerous volunteers, more or less well disguised as peasants, crossed the Jura from Annemasse and threaded their way through the Italian Alps by mountain paths, crossing frozen rivers.

Such exploits demanded courage, initiative and also resources – money or undercover assistance – not available to everyone. Karski notes that the innkeeper who lodged him, asking no questions, raised his prices in his case. A 'guide' on one occasion took 120 people across the demarcation line free, but others would fleece their 'customers' and then callously abandon them in the really dangerous sector; other 'guides', when arrested by the Germans, entered their service and handed over to them the unfortunates who were relying on them. In Hungary the Germans

---

[1] Analogous to this type of operation was the removal from German reach *before occupation* of the Norwegian and French stocks of heavy water; on 16 March 1940 400 lbs arrived in Paris from Norway; in June 1940 the scientists Joliot-Curie, Halban and Kowarski despatched the stock stored in Riom prison to Bordeaux and thence to England. Joliot-Curie remained in France; the other two offered their services first to the British and then to the Americans.

discovered lines leading in from Poland; on these they established their own agents and the users found themselves in Germany. Treachery and heroism were permanent bed-fellows; no action, however minor, could be taken against the occupying power without major risk to the doer of it.

Non-acceptance of occupation

Those both able and willing to leave their country, not just for security abroad but to continue the fight, were never more than a minority and their numbers decreased as the enemy's information improved, his precautions became more widespread and his penalties more severe; the 'escapers' went primarily to swell the ranks of the little contingents supporting the governments-in-exile. The mass of the people was forced to remain and live under constraint; only through a general uprising could the Resistance become more than a band of knights, a gallant few. To act as yeast in the dough many of the exiles later returned as agents, instructors and channels for weapons, money or orders. In the meantime the infant opposition could proclaim itself only by modest gestures, the first being, quite simply, non-acceptance of the occupation, the determination to behave as though the occupation did not exist.

To begin with, everyone passed through a phase of self criticism. Léon Blum, for instance, reproached both himself and the socialist party for failing to convince the working classes that they could make their voices heard in a democratic régime and that, in defending it, they were defending themselves. Admission of past errors, however, could not be allowed to develop into masochism or it would be of assistance only to the enemy; each country could not be held responsible for the causes of its own defeat – be they the refusal of autonomy to the Sudeten Germans in Czechoslovakia, Polish nationalist policy in Posnania or the French rejection of Hitler's proposals in October 1939. In other words the real enemy was Hitler and nazi Germany.

This being so, an attitude of dignity was required of the occupied peoples. Weill-Curiel tells how, shortly after his arrival from London, he heard two girls in Paris put a German who had accosted them squarely in his place, much to his confusion; he had said that he was a native of Danzig, whereupon the girls replied: 'So you're a Pole then', and turned their backs on him.[1] In Strasbourg use of the French language was subject to a fine; on entering some government office a woman said *bonjour* and then paid the fine twice over remarking 'That's for next time'. When the schools in Colmar reopened the students of philosophy refused to give the Hitler salute; one day, when the only German student on the course was absent, they all rose shouting *Vive la France*.[2]

In Holland, if a German entered a café, everyone paid their bills, got up and went out.[3] In Warsaw and Prague the word was passed round one day not to buy a German newspaper; the few who disregarded the warning found a sticker on their backs saying: 'This swine supports the Germans.' In Warsaw new sign-boards appeared one night on walls, lamp-posts and street corners; they carried the names of Polish heroes or foreign states-men whom the Poles admired, such as Roosevelt and Churchill. This re-christening of the Polish streets left its mark even after all the signs had been removed; in trams the passengers would call out to the conductor: 'Put me down at Kozciusko Square.'

For the French Jean Texcier wrote his 'Advice to the occupied' in August 1940: 'Have no illusions: they are not tourists; they are conquerors. Behave correctly towards them, but do not try to curry favour by anticipating their wishes. They will not thank you for it in any case. . . . You do not know their language or alternatively you have forgotten it. If one of them speaks to you in German, signify ignorance and go quietly on your way. If he asks you a question in French, do not feel obliged to tell him the way. He is not going the same way as you are. . . . If he tries to enter into conversation in a café or restaurant, give him politely to understand that what he is about to say to you does not interest you. If your haberdasher has seen fit to put up a notice *Man spricht deutsch*, go next door whether the man really knows German or not. If you see a tart talking business with one of them, don't be enraged. The man will get what his money is worth – and that's nothing. . . . Study of our daily papers has never been advised as a method of learning to express oneself correctly in French. Still less so today – the Paris dailies do not even think in French.'

[1] *Eclipse en France,* Editions du Myrte, Paris 1946, p. 143.
[2] J. M. Bopp: *L'Alsace sous l'occupation allemande,* Mappus, Le Puy, 1945, p. 319.
[3] H. Bernard: *Histoire de la Résistance européenne,* Gerard & Co., Verviers, 1968, p. 215.

Another method of denying the presence of the occupying power was refusing to obey his orders. In Poland the Germans had instituted a privileged category of Polish citizens, analogous to the 'Racial Germans'. Despite German propaganda and certain advantages, particularly as regards rations, very few Poles enrolled themselves and those who did so were despised by the majority. In Chartres Jean Moulin, the prefect, sent instructions to all mayors not to post German notices on the walls of their offices. At Bar-le-Duc the Secretary-General of the department put the French flag at half-mast and refused to take it down. One mayor in Seine-et-Oise stopped the town hall clock to show that he did not recognise the 'new times'. When the Germans were trying to collect non-ferrous metals in the department of Eure, 'volunteers' brought them insultingly small quantities – a few pounds.

All these minor actions were of course no more than indications of a spirit of revolt; they were a source of consolation to the occupied rather than anxiety to the occupier, for whom they were mere irritating pinpricks. The game tickled the imagination of the vanquished, however, giving them some secret satisfaction and a sense of taking revenge; by making him look ridiculous they lowered the status of the conqueror in people's eyes. Humour played a special role in the game of restoring confidence to the conquered.

Malicious humour

In Alsace humorous alterations were made to German words: the notice in trains *Achtung, Verdunkelung* (Warning, black-out) turned into *Achtung, Verdun*; an 'h' was added to the word *Offen* (open), making it *Hoffen* (hope); *Raucher* (smoking compartment) became *Rache* (revenge). One journalist invariably made the same typing error: instead of Hitler's *Mein Kampf* he would write *Mein Krampf* (cramp).

In Poland the name of a senior ss officer stationed in Warsaw was Moder, but he was always referred to as *Mörder* (murderer); *Hitler* was altered to *Hycler* (dog-shooter). On walls the slogan *Deutschland siegt an allen Fronten* (Germany is victorious on all fronts) became *Deutschland liegt an allen Fronten* (Germany is prostrate on all fronts).

Once started in this vein inventiveness was limitless. In one town in Alsace the best joke was the fact that the *rue du Sauvage* had been renamed *rue Adolf Hitler*. Warsaw possessed 'Independence Avenue'; passengers on public transport would ask each other: 'Is this Independence?' the reply to which was: 'No, that's for next year.' In the departments of France occupied by the Italians the girls went about with sticks of macaroni in their buttonholes. When the Greeks were pushing the Italians back in Albania, a notice appeared at the Mentone border: 'Greeks, stop here; this is France.'

In December 1943 the corpulent 'Reich Marshal' Göring 'honoured' the city of Colmar with a visit. The people of Colmar gave out that he had done them a favour. 'How? Well, he showed them something they hadn't seen for a long time – fat and a full belly.'[1]

The Parisians were a match for the Alsatians. One story ran: 'Hitler, at his wits' end to know how to cross the Channel, found out that an old rabbi knew the secret, handed down from father to son, of the method used by the Hebrews to cross the Red Sea dryshod. He summoned the rabbi and promised to release several thousands of Jews if told the secret. Without further ado the rabbi indicated that the Hebrew leader had had a small magic wand which was able to part the waves. "This wand, I must have it at all costs," the Führer shouted. "Where is it?" The answer was: "In the British Museum." '

While standing in a Brussels train a German soldier trod on a Belgian's toes and at once the Belgian hit him. Another Belgian, following his example, pummelled the German with his fists. Both Belgians were arrested and interrogated. The first said: 'He trod on my toes,' the second: 'When I saw the German taking it, I thought it was permissible.'[2]

On occasions this mockery was humiliating to the victor's pride. In Poland a somewhat pornographic cartoon was circulated reminding German soldiers of the good time their wives were having during their absence. Another cartoon emphasised the numbers of foreign workers on German soil and implied that this might result in disastrous consequences for the purity of the race. So, for the occupied peoples, laughter was some consolation for their miseries. Humour is a sedative producing temporary oblivion; it revives hope because it is a relaxation and reduces

[1] Bopp, op. cit., pp. 191–2.
[2] Galtier-Boissière: *Mon journal sous l'occupation*, La Jeune Parque, Paris.

mental turmoil. But more concrete reasons for action were required and to establish these the occupied peoples were eager for information and for pledges of change – no matter whether they looked to heaven to provide them or picked them up by listening to the radio.

Mysticism

As with all the great plagues, the nazi virus produced a resurgence of mysticism. Despairing of the present, people were prone to believe in some miracle; old prophecies, forgotten in happier times, were revived and applied to the present; people looked to them for some hope of the future. 'In Alsace, for instance,' says J. M. Bopp, 'a most popular prophecy was that of Don Bosco. It consisted of three visions of the future of France. The first referred to a war in which France would be defeated; this was obviously the war of 1870–71. Then there would be a second war in which, after prolonged tribulation, France would be victorious, a clear reference to the war of 1914–18. Finally would come a third war in which Paris, the modern Babylon, would fall to the enemy on the 285th day. Four hundred days later, however, a warrior from the north would liberate the country. He would combine with the Papacy to re-establish peace and a new order. Obviously this prophecy came to light after the capture of Paris by the Germans in 1940; nevertheless, to give it greater force, those who spread it round swore that it was to be read in Volume IX of the words of Don Bosco.

'Another fashionable prophecy in October 1940 was that of a certain Italian, R. P. Pillot; he predicted that the war would be over by Christmas. This particular prophecy, however, was most discreet since it omitted to specify which Christmas.

'Finally, according to some Alsatians, Saint Theresa of Lisieux in person had given forth a prophecy, and in writing too. With the utmost seriousness the faithful maintained that a note in Saint Theresa's handwriting had been found on the altar of Lisieux cathedral; it said that the war would end on 6 August 1941. Many were disillusioned when the great day passed without the happy event taking place.'[1]

Nostradamus, Saint Odile and Saint Geneviève were all invoked

1 Bopp, op. cit., p. 187.

and some most peculiar prayers were intoned, such as the following in Paris in late 1940: 'The Virgin Mary has been evacuated,
Saint Joseph is in a concentration camp, the Three Kings are in
London, the ox in Berlin and the ass in Rome' and so 'there will
be no Christmas'.

In similar vein sensational reports spread like wildfire: German
forces attempting to invade Britain had been destroyed by walls
of flaming oil; Hitler had been assassinated; Mussolini was on the
verge of abdication. Allied forces had landed in Europe at least
twenty times before June 1944!

Clandestine radio

Fortunately there were other and more reliable sources of information, the news broadcast by neutral or allied radio stations; both
Sottens and Boston had a large following in France. But it was
above all the BBC which had the ear of the enslaved peoples,
despite the facts that listening to it was forbidden and its broadcasts were jammed. This was, after all, the voice of Great Britain,
the country which for months was fighting alone, the country
whose victory would put an end to the nightmare, the last stronghold of freedom where falsehood and oppression did not rule. In
Norway as in the Basque country, in Belgium as in Brno, every
evening the shutters would be closed early, the lights extinguished
and the inmates of the houses gather in silence round the radio
set, the family's altar of hope, straining their ears to catch the
muffled indistinct news.

Catholics also listened to the 'Voice of the Vatican' which 'in a
broadcast, half meditation half sermon, advised clear thinking
and composure, recalling the great principles of Christianity as an
antidote to spiritual abdication'.[1] So the occupied peoples began
to emerge from the night of oppression, a night made darker by
their ignorance of the world around them and the propaganda to
which they were subjected; thus they gained the courage to
initiate action, modest admittedly and still largely ineffective, but
invariably dangerous.

---

[1] Bedarida: '*Aux origines du temoignage chrétien*' in *Revue d'Histoire de la deuxième guerre
mondiale,* No. 61, January 1966.

Caches of arms

As they retreated, the troops defeated by the Wehrmacht frequently threw away their weapons. Obviously no one could hide a tank or a gun, but many people did collect and hide submachineguns and rifles; in northern France some were fished up from canals. A proportion was later recovered by the Germans, usually as a result of denunciation. In France, for instance, between June and December 1940 they uncovered small clandestine arsenals near Belfort, at Sèvres, at Fontenay-la-Vicomte, at Saclay, at Sainte-Geneviève-des-Bois. Yet some caches remained undiscovered. According to M. Pyromaglou, after the invasion and capitulation of Greece between 100,000 and 150,000 rifles were successfully hidden in the mountains of Epirus and in Thessaly.[1]

The 'occupied' were careful to keep such personal weapons as they had; a revolver, a sporting rifle or some trophy of the 1914–18 war was easy to conceal in a barn or granary. When the occupying power issued orders to hand them in, the acquiescent or fearful minority obeyed but many more refused to comply.

In unoccupied France the Armistice Army maintained a complete organisation to deal with the concealment of arms. They were hidden on private estates, in caves and in the depths of woods. Ex-servicemen were the first to help. Much valuable assistance was also provided by large-scale organisations with vast depots and storage sheds, such as the railways, 'Roads and Bridges' and the Post Office.

Preservation and concealment of arms was admittedly not as good as using them. But it could not be done solely by individual initiative; accomplices were required; several people became involved in keeping a secret.

Demonstrations

For those infuriated by the behaviour of the nazis it was difficult to conceal their revulsion for long. To salve their consciences they displayed their disapproval openly despite the dangers involved.

[1] Address at the Milan symposium in 1961 – see *European Resistance Movements*. Vol. 2, Pergamon Press, London 1964.

To taunt the occupier people hoisted forbidden flags: in France the Cross of Lorraine appeared on watch-chains, fastenings of handbags and as ornaments on dresses; tricolour dresses, badges and ribbons were also to be seen. At Gisors on 14 July 1941 a girl wore a tricolour scarf inscribed 'Vive la France'; a man wore a tricolour hat. On 23 June 1940, Prince Bernhard's birthday, thousands of Dutch wore a white carnation in their buttonholes, as the prince used to do; the Germans were not slow to grasp the significance and snatched many of the flowers away. Henri Bernard, however, records that 'many of the demonstrators had concealed a razor blade underneath the flower; the effect on the predatory hand was therefore easy to imagine.'

Malicious inscriptions were to be found everywhere. In Gaillon communists painted the words 'Down with Hitler, down with Darlan' on the roads and decked the inscription out with hammers and sickles. The easiest sign to produce, and the one most widely used, was the 'V' – V for Victory. This had been thought up in London by Laveleye, the Belgian ex-minister, and Churchill, when touring bombed areas, used to make the sign with two fingers. People daubed it on German notices with such regularity that the occupation authorities tried in vain to appropriate the sign themselves.

The darkness of the cinema was obviously conducive to whistling and hostile cries; in Paris the Germans replied by closing all cinemas for a week; then they decided that they should remain lighted while German newsreels were being shown. Gradually, however, the opposition gained confidence and the number of public demonstrations increased. National anthems were sung in public places; national flags were hoisted on town halls and clock towers, even on top of the Acropolis in Athens. Flowers were regularly laid on statues or monuments to the great men or deeds of the past – Joan of Arc, Clemenceau, Saint Wenceslas; and when allied airmen were shot down solemn crowds followed their remains to the cemetery.

Whether ordered by governments-in-exile or semi-spontaneous, mass demonstrations underlined the people's unanimity of view. On 30 September 1939, the anniversary of the Munich Agreement, the Prague population boycotted the trams, which ran empty; on 28 October they marched through streets decorated in Czech colours; German signs were torn down and thunderflashes went off beneath the windows of the 'Protector', von Neurath. In spring 1941 the Germans had decided on major celebrations for the feast of the Czech patron saint, Mathias, but the Czechs boycotted the theatres and the casts played to empty houses.

On 11 November 1940 the traditional parade at the tomb of the unknown soldier in Brussels was banned; the day before, however, the Belgians marched past the 'Column of Congress', the monument to national independence. On the first anniversary of invasion all demonstrations had been strictly forbidden but students boarded the trams, made them slow down as they passed the 'Column of Congress' and threw out bunches of flowers.[1]

On 11 November 1940 numbers of Paris students climbed the Arc de Triomphe, some of them waving two sticks and shouting 'We want *deux gaules*' (literally 'two poles' but pronounced 'de Gaulle'); they swept up the passers-by as they moved; there were scuffles and the German police intervened, injuring some and arresting many more.[2] On 28 March 1941, when the Belgrade *putsch* occurred and King Peter of Yugoslavia rejected Hitler's ultimatum, the people of Marseilles collected in front of the plaque commemorating the assassination of King Alexander. On the national holidays in France (1 May, 14 July) people assembled at war memorials or in the main streets of towns at some specified hour; alternatively, on orders passed by word of mouth, the same streets became deserted. In offices and factories work ceased for several minutes – primarily in memory of the hostages shot at Nantes and Bordeaux.

For the occupying power these demonstrations were tantamount to provocation. They enabled possible resisters to get to know one another, sometimes to their considerable mutual astonishment. Their effect on public opinion was immense. They gave rise to persistent stories, such as the death of some demonstrators in Paris on 11 November 1940. They constituted a public call to direct action.

First actions

These were, of course, only minor sabotage operations, aimed rather at public opinion than at doing the enemy any real damage.

---

[1] See Henri Bernard: *La Résistance 1940–1945*, Renaissance du livre, Brussels 1968.
[2] Josse: '*La naissance de la Résistance étudiante à Paris*' in *Revue d'Histoire de la Deuxième Guerre mondiale*, July 1962; G. Tillion: '*Première Résistance en zone occupée*', ibid., April 1958.

They were the work of individuals acting for their own reasons and against targets within their limited range. If repeated often enough, however, these little exploits irritated the occupier, gave him the not altogether erroneous impression that he was living in a hostile environment and ultimately drove him to reprisals which backfired psychologically. The extent of these minor activities is best judged by a purely factual account of operations undertaken in France alone during the second half of 1940.

The cutting of telephone lines was comparatively easy and could be done quickly and quietly; as early as June this had started in the departments of Côte-d'Or, Nord and Pas-de-Calais. In July the Germans reported cable cutting in six fresh departments and in August in a further six. In one village the population was forced to act as cable guards; one of the guards cut it again, was caught and condemned to death. In September cuts were even more numerous in the same areas and particularly in the neighbourhood of Paris. In October, November and December the habit became general and no part of France was immune. The same cable was sometimes cut in several places and on several days running; on other occasions yards of cable were removed. During the month of December 101 instances of cable-cutting were recorded in the Lille area.

The saboteurs also attacked the property of the occupying power. His notices particularly infuriated them. Defacement of a Wehrmacht poster meant a fine of 10,000 francs for the parish concerned; the culprits were frequently found to be small boys and their parents were then arrested. In many places special targets were posters picturing the attack on Mers el-Kebir and entitled 'Don't forget Oran'. Swastika flags and portraits of the Führer were also fair game.

On 8 December a man was sentenced to three months' imprisonment because, with his wife and family, he had torn down a poster caricaturing Churchill. In Lille schoolboys attacked a statue of Hitler with hammers – the headmaster, assistant master and ten boys were sent to prison. On 5 December Mourgues, a Bordeaux wine merchant, was shot for 'sabotage'; on the notices announcing his execution some unknown hand had written: 'Murderers, is that collaboration?'

German reports make frequent mention of brawls in cafés and other public places between Frenchmen and Germans. Drink or women were usually at the bottom of these quarrels. Incidents in which German soldiers were killed were, however, more disturbing to the occupation authorities. On 28 June, for instance, a sentry was killed in the Somme department. On 21 July rifle shots were fired at a German lieutenant in the department of Doubs. At Rennes two students were arrested near a German sentry post; they were carrying revolvers. Elsewhere a sentry was attacked in a railway station, two German soldiers were wounded, a French coloured soldier was shot after attacking some Germans with a knife, German soldiers were assaulted by 'civilians'. On 13 August three sentries were attacked in Paris while on guard outside the building occupied by the German Naval Commander; another sentry on guard outside the offices of the navy at Royan was attacked on 15 August.

The Germans took reprisals – fines on parishes, curfews, seizure of hostages. To intimidate possible recalcitrants threatening notices were posted on walls telling the population in general of the severe measures to which they might be subjected through the fault of a few eccentrics, though when the culprits were arrested their trial led nowhere. These early resisters belonged to no group, but were lone wolves who did not know each other. Resistance was born of a spontaneous reaction by certain Frenchmen who dared to do what many others dreamed of without yet having the strength of mind to act. But example was infectious.[1]

Thus it became clear that resistance would not develop its full potential strength until it became the expression of the will of the majority of the subject peoples. To convince them to act a vast propaganda campaign was instituted.

[1] All the incidents quoted are taken from German reports. See the author's *Vichy année 40*, Laffont, Paris 1966, pp. 422–4.

CHAPTER 5

Propaganda

When members of the French Resistance daubed 'V', 'RAF', hammers and sickles or the Cross of Lorraine on walls, they were in fact obeying the first rule of psychological warfare: show the enemy that a hostile and elusive force exists, and encourage one's unknown friends by proving to them that they are not alone. The nazis had presented the war as an ideological crusade and Goebbels had accordingly established a vast engine of deception. The Allies were forced to invent some counter-propaganda, explaining their own reasons for continuing to fight and refuting the enemy's arguments. They used two main weapons: radio broadcasts outside occupied Europe and the clandestine press inside. Both grew to an unprecedented size.

Rules of psychological warfare

According to Maurice Megret psychological warfare is 'a substitute for force which takes as its tactical objective the mind of the enemy and makes use of the intellect to compensate for inadequacy of resources.'[1] It is, therefore, the weapon *par excellence* of the weak – and the Resistance was inherently weak. Great Britain was in little better shape when left facing nazi Germany alone after the defeat of France; Russia was in the same situation from June 1941 to July 1943. Moreover, all links between the occupied peoples and the outside world, above all with the Allies, had been severed; contact was re-established through the radio and by leaflets. For the desired object to be achieved certain precautions had to be taken, as the British and then the Anglo-Americans of the 'Psychological Warfare Division' gradually discovered. Less is known of Soviet arrangements.

In the first place propaganda must be geared to the psychology of the peoples to whom it is addressed, as far as possible taking

[1] *La Guerre psychologique*, Presses Universitaires de France, Paris, 1956.

into account national and social peculiarities; before attemping to guide public opinion, care must be taken not to offend it by bringing propaganda into line with current ideas. In unoccupied France, for instance, it would have been most inept to vilify Marshal Pétain when his popularity was at its height; it was wise never to attack him directly but to aim at his 'entourage', or to make insidious references to the evil effects of old age and fence-sitting.

Secondly, information disseminated must be correct: any error which can be ascribed to bad faith destroys confidence. A precise picture of the military situation must be given – without concealing setbacks, as the enemy's propaganda will publicise them in any case; it is even wise to anticipate him by announcing them – proof of self-assurance and self-confidence.

Propaganda must, therefore, be closely co-ordinated with diplomatic and military activities. It cannot be a substitute for military action as if it were 'an independent arm . . . which can do miracles on its own'.[1] In other words if, by exaggerated propaganda, the Allies raised the hopes of the occupied peoples too high, they risked involving them in premature action, which would lead to failure and the loss of their co-operation at a later stage.

If it is to become 'a sort of infallible guide' (in the words of Dimitrov, the secretary of the Comintern) propaganda must have a good intelligence network. In this case the internal and external resistance was rather like a blind man and a paralytic: the one could not assist the other unless he provided information. In other words, the radio and clandestine press had to be mutually supporting. If this could be done the occupied peoples could be given a plethora of news and directives, creating the impression of a ubiquitous omniscient power, stirring euphoric reactions of hope, helping them to forget the anguish of their situation, leading them on gradually to take action within their capabilities, but also indicating courses of action on which they might not have embarked if left to themselves.

Action from outside – pamphlets and newspapers

Early in the war the British and French had believed that they could affect the morale of the German people and persuade them

[1] Richard Crossman, lecture at RUSI London, 1952; Bruce Lockhart, ibid., 1950.

to divorce themselves from their leaders by dumping tons of pamphlets over the Reich from the air. It failed, largely because the inactivity of the Allied armies was an admission of weakness and not a precursor of victory.

When left alone in the war, the British nevertheless continued this policy, initially somewhat ineptly. The pamphlets were suspended from balloons or dropped in containers and were frequently lost either by missing their mark or by being scattered. Those destined for Holland were written in extremely elementary Dutch. Later, miniature books and regular newspapers such as the RAF Post and the Voice of America were dropped. These were well-prepared, even expensive, news sheets which alleviated the feeling of isolation among the occupied peoples; in fact they were 'friends from the sky'. But although the news they gave was reassuring, they lacked the flexibility to adjust to varied and changing situations; sometimes they fell behind developments, thus losing credibility.

The British never entirely abandoned the despatch from London of newspapers destined for the occupied countries, primarily Belgium, Holland and Norway. They were of a higher standard as emigré nationals had participated in the drafting, but gave their readers the unfortunate impression, fanned further by German propaganda, that the governments-in-exile were mere puppets with the strings pulled by 'perfidious Albion'.

Films were hardly more successful and were only used in occupied Belgium. Some agents who were dropped carried reels of Allied news film, but these then had to be shown. For security reasons this could not be done to large audiences so the general public was not affected.

Radio broadcasts

The great advantage of radio broadcasts was that they knew no frontiers and could penetrate into every house possessing a radio set without the occupiers having any real means of stopping them. Moreover, they could be closely 'moulded' to events and could announce any development immediately: they established direct contact with the listener. All the major Allies stepped up their broadcasts but the BBC reached a peak of perfection in this respect.

Direction and control of British broadcasting was vested in the 'Political Warfare Executive' (PWE) which included representatives of all ministries concerned with war propaganda – Foreign Office, Ministry of Economic Warfare, Admiralty, War Office, Air Ministry, etc. Overall directives for each country were worked out at weekly meetings; all senior personnel were of British nationality.

Considerable use was made of emigrés, however, as executive personnel in the 'country sections'. In 1943, for instance, the 'German Department' of the BBC was employing more than a hundred people and it sometimes used lecturers of high repute such as Thomas Mann. A certain number of broadcasting hours were placed at the disposal of the Belgian government, when politicians or professional broadcasters whose voices could be recognised, spoke to occupied Belgium. Similarly, the Dutch had 'Radio Orange'. The Belgians, however, also had a broadcasting station of their own which was consequently not subject to censorship. A station supposedly transmitting from Warsaw was placed at the disposal of the Polish government, and as very few British knew Poland or the Polish language the government enjoyed considerable freedom of expression – a fact of which it made full use, far more than the British wished, during the Warsaw rising.

The case of Free France raised additional problems. The BBC included a French Section, which was under British orders although manned by French journalists such as Pierre Bourdan. General de Gaulle, however, insisted that Free France itself be allowed to broadcast regularly; its spokesman was Maurice Schumann. Efforts were specially concentrated on the French – for obvious strategic and political reasons.

Crémieux-Brilhac says: 'Almost all the French broadcasts were made simultaneously on one frequency in the long-wave band, one in the medium and three to six in the short. From autumn 1943 two additional frequencies in the medium-wave band (285 and 261m) were made available for the evening broadcasts.[1]

'The length of French broadcasts beamed on France gradually increased until it reached a total of $5\frac{1}{2}$ to $5\frac{3}{4}$ hours (including half an hour in morse) depending on the day of the week; this was more than double the time allotted to any other occupied country.

[1] Free France set up a high-powered transmitter of its own, first in Brazzaville and then in Algiers.

The following table shows the daily distribution of foreign language broadcasting time by the European Service of the BBC on 1 January 1943:

France	5 hrs 30 mins
Germany and Austria	5 hrs
Italy	4 hrs 15 mins
Holland	2 hrs 30 mins
Poland	2 hrs 10 mins
Norway	1 hr 45 mins
Czechoslovakia	1 hr 45 mins
Yugoslavia	1 hr 35 mins
Belgium	1 hr 30 mins (half in French half in Flemish)
Greece	1 hr 20 mins
Portugal	1 hr 45 mins
Sweden	1 hr 45 mins
Denmark	1 hr
Finland	1 hr
Bulgaria	45 mins
Albania	15 mins
Luxembourg	15 min (in dialect four times a week)[1]

The BBC also had something to say to its enemies. For example, a station supposedly located in occupied Belgium followed the line of the pre-war Flemish separatists, the object being to emphasise the betrayal of separatism constituted by the leaders' collaboration with the occupying power.

The BBC's principle was the exact opposite of that of Goebbels – 'not to tell lies'. It sought its effect through being 'completely candid'. In general it tried to appeal to reason, to the critical faculties of its listeners, not to their emotions; it made great use of sarcasm, songs and humour and seldom resorted to insults or tampering with the truth except in the case of certain Aunt Sallies such as Hitler, Himmler or Göring. It made many mistakes of course – for instance, it announced the liberation of Paris twenty-four hours too early, which could have been costly for over-enthusiastic Parisians – but taken overall its success was colossal, as witnessed by the thousands of letters from listeners arriving via

[1] Crémieux-Brilhac: 'Les émissions françaises à la BBC' in Revue d'Histoire de la Deuxième Guerre mondiale, No. 1, November 1950.

Portugal, and statements from people who had managed to escape from the occupied countries.

The Americans set up an 'Office of War Information' divided into two branches, one dealing with news for home consumption and the other with news for overseas. Its purpose was to publicise the attitude and aims of America at war. Many of its executive-level staff, however, lacked both experience and knowledge, and in addition American transmitters were too distant for the broadcasts to be easily audible in Europe, though the situation improved after the landings in North Africa and Italy. The us Army also formed 'psychological warfare sections' which were better placed to understand the special characteristics of the various occupied peoples.[1]

Under the authoritarian, ideologically-based Soviet régime propaganda was a function of the Central Committee of the communist party; its role was to produce complete centralisation and permanent mobilisation of public opinion for ends formulated by Party headquarters. The war merely accentuated this rigidity of control. So long as the Wehrmacht was in occupation of a large area of Soviet territory Stalin's main aim was to 'raise the morale' of the people and of the Red Army; directives were given to foreign communist parties over the radio but they were kept confidential and had no direct effect upon public opinion in the occupied countries as a whole. In 1942, however, when Stalin learnt of the exploits of Tito's partisans, he set up a powerful transmitting station at Tiflis, known as 'Free Yugoslavia'. Besides acclaiming Yugoslav action, it kept the partisans *au fait* with the Red Army's battles. The partisans sang Soviet songs and looked upon the ussr as the great sister of the new Yugoslavia which would be born from the partisan struggle.

Similarly, for Bulgaria two transmitters, *Christo Bolev* and *Naroden Glass*, theoretically located in the country, in fact broadcast on behalf of Dimitrov in Moscow. Another transmitter, *Za slovensku Svobodu* (For Slovak freedom), incited Slovaks who had joined the anti-bolshevik crusade to desert in the name of Slav brotherhood; it made frequent reference to the exploits of Janosik's 'mountain lads' in the eighteenth century, broadcasting

[1] In French North Africa, for instance, the 'psychological warfare section' was well aware of General de Gaulle's popularity and understood the reasons behind it; the White House and State Department, on the other hand, persisted in supporting General Giraud.

poems, songs and folk tales on the subject.[1] A similar policy was adopted towards Poland, broadcasts issuing first from Kuibishev and then from Moscow over a semi-clandestine station entitled *Kosciuszko*.

The clandestine press – its difficulties and techniques

It is not easy to estimate the effect of radio-disseminated propaganda. How is one to know the number of listeners, their readiness to receive, or the degree of their support? One of the first tangible results of the BBC broadcasts was to stimulate the production of a clandestine press in the occupied countries; in France its news bulletins were copied and distributed; in Holland regular newspapers appeared entitled simply BBC or BBC *Bulletin*, BBC *News*, *British News*, *London News*.

Nevertheless, the clandestine press was in most cases the result of spontaneous and continuous effort by the occupied peoples themselves. It started from nothing and was one of the first signs of the spirit of resistance. Everywhere it encountered enormous difficulties, in essence all the same. Every normal part of the newspaper process, from editing to printing and distribution, presented the clandestine amateur journalists with problems resulting from shortage of equipment and the security precautions which had to be observed.

Every paper started with handwritten or roneoed pamphlets; a roneo press was comparatively easy to obtain and conceal, and the number of copies did not necessitate large stocks of paper. Production of a proper newspaper was a different matter. A rotary press was difficult to obtain, expensive and bulky; in addition it required space, a special typewriter to produce the plates and large quantities of paper. The ideal was to recruit professional printers 'of good will' who would use their own equipment – stocks of paper, printing ink and type. Failing this, people did the best they could, buying expensively on the black market or 'cleaning out' offices, warehouses or even agencies working for the occupying power. For security reasons it was advisable, but not easy, to use several printers simultaneously; changes and moves were,

---

[1] The Russians were the only one of the Allies to make any real attempt to turn the Germans against Hitler through the 'Free Germany Committee' – see Chapter 11.

unfortunately, frequently necessary as a result of arrests by the enemy.

Editing was not easy either. How was the staff to get its news? Monitoring foreign and neutral radio services of course provided some; allies within the enemy-controlled administration formed a further source. Eventually, however, it became necessary to set up regular clandestine press agencies, as Jean Moulin did in France, which collected reliable information from all sources and distributed it through a periodical bulletin passed to the newspapers as regularly as possible. But readers not only wanted news. They were thirsting for appraisals of the military situation and for orders – anything to distract and feed the mind. A clandestine news sheet only turned into a 'major newspaper' when it became the mouthpiece of a large-scale resistance group – for which it became a good recruiting agent.

The most tricky part was distribution. The first method, simple but expensive, was to put the copies in the post, but there was no certainty that they would be delivered. Haphazard distribution on the street was spectacular but dangerous and in each case only a limited number of people were affected. It was essential, therefore, to use well-wishers as couriers, although their packages were liable to be opened during some spot check; but they delivered only to known allies and, gradually, distribution widened to include even the enemy – in the shape of the police and collaborator groups. No one could tell beforehand, however, how many readers would see each number; sometimes a complete issue would be confiscated while still at the printers. Here again things were easier if the newspaper was in regular touch with a large-scale resistance group.

The price paid by the clandestine press was high because of the number of people involved and the fact that it had to operate more or less openly; Lejeune estimates the losses in Belgium at 50 per cent of those concerned. Bruneau says: 'With the clandestine press every job, even the most humble, was made difficult by the lack of telephones and transportation, by the rationing of essentials, the overcrowding on trains and incessant checks – and, always, always one was beginning again. One had not time to breathe between one issue and the next.'[1]

The Poles had valuable experience in this kind of work. In 1901,

1 F. Bruneau: *Essai historique du mouvement né autour de journal Résistance,* Sedes, Paris 1951.

after all, Joseph Pilsudski had printed *Robotnik* (The Worker) in a shack in Lodz. As they had been under Czarist tyranny, little hand presses were operated under German occupation; they were located in the cellars of town houses or, if too noisy, in the woods. News from all over the world was collected by strings of radio receivers concealed in sound-proof cellars, forest huts or barns with false roofs. There were well organised 'press agencies' with regular correspondents abroad. Farmers' carts brought paper to the printers concealed under loads of vegetables. Distribution was done on the 'threesome' system: each distributor knew only the man who handed him the paper and the one for whom it was intended; news sheets were also distributed through shops, concealed in the goods, or even through the regular kiosks, the clandestine paper being handed to a known ally wrapped inside a German newspaper – which otherwise no one would have bought.[1]

Extent and diversity of the clandestine press

To the outward eye all clandestine newspapers were similar. They were small, in order to economise paper and facilitate the concealment of copies; printing was hurried and often defective; very few could afford the luxury of photographs.[2] Nevertheless, they diversified to cater for the varied needs of their clientele.

In Belgium the first two clandestine newspapers appeared as early as 15 June 1940 – *Chut* in Brussels and *Le Monde du Travail* in Liége. By July 1941 there were some forty of them and just before liberation 275, many in Flemish. On 1 July 1940 the first issue of *La Libre Belgique* appeared, carrying on the tradition of its famous predecessor of 1914–18. The Germans had appropriated the great daily paper *Le Soir* which the Belgians thereupon dubbed *Le Soir volé*; on 9 November 1943 cyclists delivered to all the Brussels kiosks thousands of copies of a fake *Soir*, a precise replica of the real one but carrying anti-German and anti-collaborator articles.[3]

---

[1] Karski: op. cit., pp. 251–7.
[2] In France the paper *Bir-Hakeim* was thought too expensive and so immediately became suspect; the editor had great difficulty in clearing himself, almost having to make excuses for the facilities he used which had enabled him to bring out so high class a paper.
[3] Similar tricks were also successfully played in Lyon and Turin.

In Holland a tapestry-maker from Harlem launched the first news sheet on 15 May 1940, called *Action of the Gueux*. By the end of 1941 two socialist papers, *Je maintiendrai* and *Watchword*, and *Free Holland* were each running at 50,000 copies. Then came a communist paper, *Truth*, followed by Catholic, Protestant and student newssheets. In 1941 there were 120 clandestine newspapers all told and by 1943 the total number of copies in circulation was estimated at 450,000.

In Denmark the clandestine press made its appearance in 1941. By March 1943 there were eighty news sheets and the number rose to 265 by March 1945; in all some 500 papers of varying longevity were counted issuing a total of 150,000 copies, some of which were on public sale. Great writers and artists participated in their production, including Pastor Kaj Munk, who was executed by the Germans. Information was assembled by a clandestine press agency which had a secret telephone line from its 'office' to Stockholm.

In Czechoslovakia the most popular newspaper was *Into Battle*, the mouthpiece of UVOD, the strongest resistance movement; others to appear were the *Czech Mail*, the *National Liberation Information Service* and the communist *Rude Pravo* (Red Law).

In Italy the anti-fascist press, initially printed abroad, returned home and flourished as soon as fascism showed signs of weakening. Each political party issued several papers, the most important being *L'Italia libera* for the Action Party, *L'Unita* for the communists, *Avanti* for the socialists and *Il Popolo* for the Christian democrats. In addition to the nation-wide weeklies provincial editions, magazines and books were published; the partisans of the 'Matteoti brigades', for instance, read *Il Partigiano*, which ran to 5,000 copies.

Clearly the importance of the clandestine press increased in proportion to the population's educational level and the necessity to convince people; it was of less value, for instance, in eastern Europe where the severity of the occupation régime was the best recruiting agent for the Resistance. Nevertheless, both in Russia and Yugoslavia clandestine news sheets were printed, the main aim in the latter country being to educate the people politically rather than to vilify the Germans. Even in Bulgaria, which was not occupied by the Wehrmacht, 140 clandestine newspapers were appearing by 1944.

The most successful efforts were made in Poland and in France. In Poland nearly 1,400 news sheets were issued, not counting those distributed openly during the Warsaw rising; 325 appeared throughout the occupation. The main ones were the mouthpieces of the Home Army or the Government Delegation in Warsaw. All the political parties, however, had their own papers and they were highly popular with their public; before the war Poland had been a dictatorship supported by strict censorship and so, paradoxically, under German occupation all shades of opinion felt free to express themselves. The newspapers published poems by ancient and modern Polish authors and their influence on public opinion was great; children learnt them by heart at school; they emphasised the permanence of Polish culture. The Ukrainian, Byelorussian and Jewish minorities also had their own news sheets.

In France the first clandestine newspapers were issued by movements with the significant titles *Combat, Libération, Franc-Tireur, Résistance, Défense de la France, Valmy,* etc. From the time of their approval of the Russo-German pact the communists issued *L'Humanité* secretly; following their example, the socialists issued *Le Populaire* and the radicals *L'Aurore.* The right-wing parties had no real clandestine paper of their own.

The French clandestine press was very varied. The policy of the National Front was to address itself individually to all social strata and even to individual professions, and as a result there were papers for women, farmers, railwaymen, students, traders, youth, doctors, universities, the *maquis,* etc.; in addition monthly literary publications appeared such as *Les Lettres françaises* and *Les Etoiles,* and numerous magazines such as *Cahiers politiques.*[1] In all there were over 1,200 different letter-heads and it is estimated that in 1944 the clandestine press was running at over a million copies.

In addition a clandestine 'publishing firm', *Editions de Minuit,* produced brochures written by the most eminent authors such as François Mauriac, Aragon, Elsa Triolet, Eluard, Aveline, Debu-Bridel, Jean Cassou and A. Chamson. A great writer, Vercors, made his name through his *Le Silence de la mer,* which achieved worldwide success.

---

[1] Published by the *Comité général d'études,* set up by Jean Moulin.

4

Subject-matter of the clandestine press

The clandestine press was necessarily geared to the special circumstances of each national struggle. Nevertheless, everywhere it had certain similar aims.

The first tasks were to shake public opinion out of its apathy and counteract the effects of the enemy's propaganda; the next step was to hammer into people's minds a certain number of overriding ideas which would gradually take root and provide the impulse first for their thoughts and eventually for their actions.

The first keynote of the clandestine press was the obnoxious nature of the occupation; every decision, every action by the occupying power was turned against him. Key phrases calculated to make a deep impact constantly recurred, such as 'plundering our food', which touched upon one of the reader's more pressing anxieties – fear that he might be unable to feed himself properly. There were many reasons for food shortages, but only one was highlighted – the occupation; the others were either passed over in silence or connected to the occupation.

The second keynote was to emphasise the inevitability of the enemy's defeat. German victories were minimised and, on the other side of the coin, his setbacks magnified. Certainty of the enemy's defeat had to be inculcated into the Resistance, but it was also important to suggest the same to the enemy himself, to awaken in him a desire to return home to a normal existence, constantly to remind him of the danger to his family from the systematic bombing of Germany cities. Other pamphlets, therefore, appeared addressed to the German soldiers in their own language or, even more frequently, to the foreign units incorporated in the Wehrmacht.

Hatred of the occupying power was roused by emphasising his crimes, such as arrests or execution of hostages; this, plus the conviction that he was not invincible, helped to inspire confidence in the men of the Resistance. But their activities could not be confined to longings and imprecations. The most effective method of encouraging direct action was to cite the example of other people, and the smallest acts of resistance were therefore publicised, sometimes analysed and invariably repeated.

The ideas of reward and punishment came as the final stage.

Chastisement awaited the villains; their misdeeds were listed with names attached and they were thus pilloried with severe punishment to come. To the heroes were held out all the joys of a world fashioned by them and conforming to their wishes. Certain words – 'liberation' for instance – thus acquired a sort of euphoric magic, opening up vistas of happiness; others, such as 'collaboration', were steeped in ignominy.

Effect and limitations of psychological action

It is difficult, if not impossible, to estimate the impact of radio propaganda. It was, of course, restricted by distance and by the small number of receivers, particularly in Poland. The Germans also took measures to hinder reception – rewards for denunciations, punishments for listening (in the case of certain Dutchmen this even meant consignment to a concentration camp), confiscation of sets. This last was never fully effective – out of one million sets in Holland it is estimated that at least 200,000 were never handed in.

Nevertheless M. Wittek's estimate of listeners to the BBC as one to three million is probably below the mark; these figures would probably be correct for France alone. What is certain is that Goebbels took the BBC broadcasts very seriously; on several occasions he replied to them personally in *Das Reich*. For many Frenchmen the 'British radio' showed that an embryo government and army existed in London; General de Gaulle's great popularity dates from this moment. Those Frenchmen who were opposed to the armistice and refused to resign themselves to defeat had thus found a standard to follow, often sinking their differences and past antagonisms. It is probable that these same methods consolidated the loyalty of the Norwegian, Dutch and Belgian peoples to their sovereigns and legitimate governments.

The impact of the clandestine press is equally difficult to gauge, though something can be deduced. The number of clandestine newspapers, their circulation and their longevity furnish some guide, as does the uniformity of class at which each aimed – communists in the case of *L'Humanité* or *Rude Pravo*, Catholics in that of *Témoignage chrétien* or *Il Popolo*. Nevertheless, these criteria do not provide a complete answer; those who spread the word never knew how many determined spirits they activated. It is a fact, however, that the Germans were alarmed enough by the influence of this clandestine literature to produce many fake pamphlets and documents, and to punish printers, editors and distributors most severely.

In short, taking the war as a whole, what was the importance of clandestine radio and press propaganda? In the occupied countries it was undoubtedly helpful in maintaining morale, in preparing for action and then organising and directing that action. Moreover, primarily in France, clandestine literature played a part in preparing for the post-war period: it studied and examined problems with a fresh eye, drafted concrete plans, drew up laws and regulations.[1]

The question remains whether an equal success was achieved as far as the Axis countries were concerned. In Italy dissension in the fascist camp was undoubtedly increased, but nazi Germany remains a question mark. The morale of the German soldiers hardly seems to have been affected since they fought valiantly to the end; the threats made against the nazi leaders led none of them to recant; as far as the German civilians were concerned, bombing certainly carried more weight than any speeches which they heard and probably only half understood.

For the countries liberated by the Red Army the problem was different. The Rumanians, Hungarians and Slovaks had not followed the Wehrmacht into Russia with any great enthusiasm.[2] Soviet historians record numerous desertions – 10,000 from the Rumanian army alone; 86,000 other Rumanians are said to have been sentenced by court martial for failing to comply with their call-up orders. But the disintegration of Germany's satellite states was probably due more to the Red Army's brilliant victories and the formidable threat posed by its advance than to any radio or newspaper propaganda. Conversely, while Great Britain was on the defensive, no armies rose to her aid on occupied territory.

In other words propaganda, whether by the written or spoken word, was capable of creating a climate of insecurity, raising doubts and awakening the conscience of the élite; but for a change in the attitude of the mass of the people only the

[1] See the author's *Courants de Pensée de la Résistance*, Presses Universitaires de France, Paris 1962.
[2] The situation was somewhat similar in the case of Alsatians recruited into the Wehrmacht.

great events counted, the developments which brought about sweeping changes in the situation. Wars are won by armies, and if it was to play its part in the final victory the underground, with its myriad little battles, had to become an army.

CHAPTER 6

Movements and Circuits

The occupied peoples were living in mental darkness. The old groupings – primarily the political parties – had either vanished of their own accord or been banned by the occupier and his puppet governments. The atmosphere was oppressive, full of mutual suspicion and potential denunciations. Everyone was inclined to caution and so was condemned to silence and reduced to isolation. Those who tried to face up to the enemy in spite of his strength and brutality were hampered by inexperience, lack of resources and, even more, the difficulty of telling who among their countrymen had taken the same resolve. In France, for instance, the collective trauma of defeat and the fall of the Republic had led to violent changes of beliefs and attitudes. Friends, meeting each other, never knew beforehand whether they would find themselves in agreement or not.

Gradually things clarified and a new dividing line ran through the temporarily enslaved peoples. On the one hand were those who resigned themselves to occupation – or who profited from it; on the other, growing steadily more numerous, were those who decided to do something to end the degrading situation. In the early months, however, public opinion resembled a shapeless lump of dough, rising for a time only to fall back into inertia when the course of the struggle favoured the Axis or the early acts of opposition were unsuccessful. In this depressing atmosphere many people thought it courageous and right to parade their feelings, to spread 'the good word' and display some assertion of their resolve – wearing a 'seditious' badge, for instance. They courted action by the oppressor and their punishment served as a warning to others.

The wiser heads acted only after cautious probing. The first underground 'cells' were formed with care, among relatives, friends and workmates. The circle of sympathisers widened as people listened to the radio together, passed clandestine pamphlets from hand to hand, took part in demonstrations or showed solidarity on behalf of the victims of occupation. Sometimes agents from abroad, better provided with resources and orders, acted as recruiting agents and formed new cells.

Movements and circuits thus gradually formed. They provided a new framework for public opinion; in them the volunteers of clandestine warfare could gather to train each other, to direct their type of action and increase its efficiency while reducing the risks. Movements were formed spontaneously from within; sometimes they were a cover for political parties or the answer to their bankruptcy – in all countries, for instance, the 'National Front' was a cover-name for the communist party acting clandestinely but non-politically. More often 'movements' and political parties existed side by side, each recruiting and controlling its own supporters. In countries such as Belgium, Holland, Poland and Italy where political parties quickly revived, either because they had not been discredited or because they had little difficulty in reconstituting themselves, movements were less successful in gaining the ear of the people. Nevertheless they inspired the political parties with their desire for battle. Through the Resistance the political parties were re-shaped, making fundamental and lasting changes in their cadres, methods and programmes. In some cases movements even aspired to total transformation of the political life of their country in and through the struggle for liberation; this was the case particularly with 'Justice and Liberty'[1] in Italy, the 'Kreisau Circle' in Germany and above all with many groupings in France.

Movements, a special manifestation of the Resistance, arose spontaneously in an unprecedented situation. They were seldom specialised in their activities: they were an amalgam, ill-defined in outline, uncertain in numbers, amorphous in structure, brittle and unstable; they split more easily than they coalesced; each aspired to be the nation's common denominator, which resulted in acute rivalries between them; they placed much store by propaganda; they ran great risks by perpetually improvising.

The 'circuit' was, equally, a novel organisation, but it was formed from outside and was of a fundamentally different nature. A 'circuit' was set up to carry out a specific type of operation; its objectives were carefully defined and it worked in a limited geographical area. The number of its members might vary, but was

[1] Later the 'Action Party'.

always strictly limited and the pyramid of authority rigidly laid down. In the movement it was difficult to divorce action and politics; the circuit was a military organisation, under strict discipline, its activity severely circumscribed, forbidden to trespass outside the field of action allotted to it. Admittedly on occasions movements and parties equipped themselves with circuits – this happened in France in the case of the 'United Resistance Movements [*Mouvements Unis de Résistance* – MUR] and the 'Civil and Military Organisation' [*Organisation Civile et Militaire* – OCM]; in some cases, but less frequently, a circuit sought to perpetuate itself. In general terms, however, movements and circuits remained distinct organisations in all countries, each functioning in its own way.

The movements

How did a movement originate and exist? There being no precedents, it was clearly entirely a matter of improvisation. Frequently it resulted from some individual initiative, its founder's personality playing a major role in its development. As a rule the original cells were formed by groups of friends, colleagues in the same workshop or office, members of some old association. Initially homogeneous, with some social, professional, religious or political background, they merged into an entity at once more extensive and more nebulous. Germaine Tillion has aptly compared this continuous process of fusion and expansion to 'crystallisation; each crystal, with its numerous facets, touches other similar crystals and, as they come into contact with the mass, still inert and fluid, that mass crystallises in its turn'.[1]

For example, in Paris ex-members of the 'Education League', having made sure they were in agreement, worked with leaders of the 'Middle Classes Organisation' and members of the 'Intellectual Workers' Federation'. Blocq-Mascart, the leading spirit of this latter group, also found recruits among his friends in the Ministry of Public Works and on the staff of the Chamber of Deputies; the first volunteers were civilians from the higher levels of the administration and of industry. At the same time Arthuys, another 'promoter', hit upon the idea of canvassing for sympathisers among the Regimental Associations and in particular the

---

[1] '*Première résistance en zone nord*' in *Revue d'Histoire de la Deuxième Guerre mondiale*, April 1958.

Old Comrades Association of the Cavalry School, Saumur. When Arthuys and Blocq-Mascart met, they were overjoyed to find that their views were identical and they realised that the teams which they had formed could complement each other. They decided at once to merge, thus giving birth to a stronger movement which they called simply 'Civil and Military Organisation'.

Another example, also from France but this time in the unoccupied zone, is of a number of professors from Montpellier University who were joined by colleagues from other universities and produced *Libertés*. At the same time, using his army connections and chance encounters, a regular officer named Frenay had formed *Verités* which was joined by other officers and issued a small roneoed news sheet entitled *Les Petites Ailes*. The two organisations combined to produce *Combat*, the most active movement in the southern zone.

The 'crystallisation' process was not peculiar to France. In Norway the first members of resistance groups came from youth associations, rifle or sporting clubs, ex-servicemen's associations or the trade unions – who were the first to form cells. In Poland political parties had been banned under the 'Colonels' Régime' and were not, therefore, strong factors. The first little groups were the result of individual initiative; their titles were telling – 'The Avengers', 'The Judgement of God', 'The Bloody Hand'. By the end of 1940 they had become one organisation, the 'Association for armed conflict', later, after considerable expansion, known as the 'Home Army' (AK).

The diverse backgrounds of recruits were due primarily to the distintegration of the old leadership, but also to the barriers dividing public opinion and, at least initially, to the small number of volunteers; any who offered themselves had to be accepted without excessive scrutiny. Sometimes the net was spread very wide – 'from the renegade communist to the reformed rexist', as Ugueux, one of the leaders of the Belgian movement, put it. In 'Combat' were to be found soldiers who had few republican leanings and might even still be Vichy supporters, socialists, Christian democrats and a few communists divorced from their party. The core of a movement, the solid kernel, asserted its authority through its homogeneity, the extent of its resources, its widespread connections or the impact of its newspaper. Recruitment was obviously easier if the leading spirit could draw upon a plentiful supply of well-disposed people, the Freemasons in

4*

'Patriam recuperare', the socialists in *Libération-Nord*, the syndicalists in *Libération-Sud* and students in *Défense de la France*. Sometimes a catalyst was available based on local connections, such as the Alsatian refugees in Lyon and Clermont-Ferrand.

Very few of the emergent movements gave themselves a 'registered trade-name'; they were forced to adopt some title when they published a newspaper or because external contacts made them define their character and size. Choice of a title was important, it must strike the imagination and mean something. Some titles were fortuitous, however – one Belgian group called itself B B because the cover-names of two of its agents started with the letter B.

To be effective a movement was forced continually to expand its contacts and to recruit more supporters; the more active it became, the greater its requirements and the larger the number of members needed. The object was to cover the country with a continuously expanding web. But expansion led to increased vulnerability – if a traitor could infiltrate, he could eat his way through the whole network like a canker. As a movement expanded, moreover, a close-knit organisation became more difficult; the moment might come when security reasons or sheer size prevented the original leader from seeing and knowing everything and he would no longer be recognised as leader by one of his subordinates. This could lead to quarrels, disorder and, worse still, splits and schisms.

Very few movements could put together an effective administrative structure. An exception was *Combat*. There Henri Frenay made a distinction between the various functions to be performed and set up services with expanding staffs for such things as recruitment, organisation, propaganda, safe houses and Secret Army. A similar organisation was adopted by the French resistance as a whole when it was united under Jean Moulin.

In their spirit of enthusiasm and self-sacrifice the movements were eager for action; they wanted to do everything at once. As soon as it was formed o c m was planning: to set up escape lines into the unoccupied zone, to form an intelligence service and to publish 'Letters to the French' to arouse public opinion. Differences in environment led to differences in ideas; in occupied France, for instance, where the Germans were on the spot, people were more 'activist'; in the unoccupied zone, where the Vichy régime acted as a sedative for public opinion, more effort was devoted to propaganda and people were more politically-minded, an attitude criticised by the Resistance in the north. In general terms, however, the movement was identified with the nation in revolt. In Belgium, for instance, the 'Belgian National Movement' (MNB) manufactured forged papers, collected information, planned to set up armed groups in the Ardennes, helped recalcitrants and Jews, censored correspondence, organised sabotage and surprise attacks – what more could it do?

With so many enterprises a movement could not remain a closed order, and this made infiltration easier. However well organised, the structure of a movement was fragile. It could not live on its own resources indefinitely; it needed money, weapons and all sorts of other things in increasing quantities and these it could only obtain from outside. At the same time, however, each 'chief' was convinced that the movement he had created was his own property. He demanded assistance; he considered that this assistance was his rightful due; he shouted 'Treason' if it was refused or restricted; he acknowledged no rules and no master; he expected to be given a certain autonomy in action and complete freedom of judgement; he regarded the Allies as sources of supply and the governments-in-exile as symbols; he insisted that he spoke in the name of his muzzled country. Since the same claims were made by all the leaders, rivalries and enmities were endemic. In fact, as far as the movements were concerned, the Resistance was in danger of degenerating into a series of private armies.

We shall show later why and how this was avoided. In fact the work of the movements was of prime importance, particularly in France. They dragged public opinion out of its apathy and resignation; they took up the running from the old leaders who were broken or incapable; they pointed the way and often discovered the methods to use. Only through unity, however, could they ensure strength, permanence and success.

The circuits

In occupied Europe a circuit was set up whenever the Allied command considered that it would be useful; a circuit was, in fact, a sort of commando, consisting of one or more agents sent in from outside who then recruited helpers on the spot. Circuits thus stemmed from a variety of sources, British, Soviet or American; moreover in any one country, Great Britain for instance, several separate organisations might be involved. In addition, Free France and the Polish government in London were allowed a certain autonomy, enabling them to set up their own circuits under more or less strict British control. In France's case the organisation in Algiers was further complicated by the rivalry between Generals de Gaulle and Giraud, which for a time meant that there were two French secret services despatching separate, if not rival, teams to France, until eventually the 'Directorate-General of Special Services' (DGSS) was formed. There could, of course, be no question of co-ordinating circuits except at the level of the Allied High Command, which used them for purely tactical purposes. In the field they were kept strictly separate; in areas of major strategic importance, such as Normandy, several circuits existed side by side, knowing nothing of each other.

Members of a circuit were soldiers, and their activities were similar to those of the traditional military secret services: they had to be technically trained; good communications with headquarters were essential; security precautions were extremely strict. Action by members of a circuit was obviously more secret and, when the story was revealed, seemed more spectacular than the humble thankless tasks carried out by the members of the movements. The circuits produced some sensational incidents in the 'spy war' and a whole series of bestsellers have recounted them. In fact, however, the great innovation of clandestine resistance was that it relied on patriotic volunteers rather than on professional agents or mercenaries; the volunteers made up for their lack of experience by knowledge of the problems with which they had to deal and of the human environment in which they worked. The few brilliant successes were counterbalanced by the tiny modest efforts of hundreds of men. The shadow war was a war of self-denial and self-sacrifice rather than one of spectacular exploits.

Escape lines

Circuits were differentiated by their fields of activity: there were action circuits, intelligence circuits and escape circuits. We shall be dealing with action circuits in connection with the armed phase of resistance. Escape circuits were formed earlier; they knit to-gether escape channels which had been arranged spontaneously to assist people in danger, such as escaped prisoners of war, Jews and political emigrés. They only became firmly established, how-ever, when intensive bombing of occupied Europe and in parti-cular of Germany began; Allied airmen were shot down and were such a valuable fighting asset that any price was worth paying to recover them.

Escape 'lines' were thus formed. They ran sometimes from Holland or Belgium right across France, later from northern Italy or Yugoslavia; they terminated either in some neutral country such as Spain, Switzerland or, (from Norway) Sweden or at some point held by the Allies such as Gibraltar or the liberated area of Italy. A uniform pattern of organisation was soon adopted. The first essential was to reconnoitre and collect the airmen who were wandering aimlessly or had been found and harboured by private citizens; for this purpose 'scouts' were employed to cover the whole country. Then they had to be housed, kitted out in civilian clothes, fed and even kept amused – all difficult matters in a time of acute shortages. The little company was provided with false papers and taken either to some frontier or to the coast; in the first case they were taken over by guides and conducted to neutral territory, in the second they were placed on board feluccas or submarines.

The work was delicate, and was often dramatic or humorous as well. The airmen frequently had no conception of the risks they were running and security gaffes were legion – their guides re-ferred to them as 'the children'. Until November 1942 the crossing of the Pyrenees was easy but after that it became extremely ardu-ous; many 'escapers' were recaptured. If this happened on the French side they were despatched to a concentration camp; if on the Spanish side they were interned in Miranda camp on the Ebro. In 1944 some 50 per cent of the crossings were successful. The Allies literally bartered wheat for internees with the Spanish government.

Escape lines probably existed in eastern Europe, particularly in occupied Russia, but we know little about them; the size of the country diminished the difficulties and dangers. Escape lines were specially active in France and Belgium – it is estimated that in France several thousands of people were involved. Belgian cir-cuits were helped by the fact that all Belgian diplomatic representatives were loyal to the Allied cause; at Montauban, for instance, the Belgian consul played an important part as the collecting centre for Spain. The exploits of the escape lines were innumerable; 'Pat O'Leary' could boast 700 successful escapes and at one time 'Shelburn' was organising nearly sixty a month; in 1943 departures for Spain were taking place practically every day; from Norway it is estimated that some 50,000 people succeeded in reaching Sweden without great difficulty.

Special preparations were made for political figures or resistance leaders summoned for consultation – for example Papandreou from Greece, Massigli and Vincent Auriol from France.

After November 1942 a new type of 'escaper' used the lines from France – volunteers who wanted to enrol in the new French army being formed in North Africa; they were either young men or regular officers who felt ill at ease in a clandestine atmosphere. Probably some 20,000 made the attempt; between April 1943 and August 1944 some 7,000 were counted passing through the eastern Pyrenees lines alone.

Intelligence circuits

The escape circuits were engaged in a sort of rehabilitation operation; like doctors putting the wounded back on their feet, they despatched to the Allied armies either combatants temporarily out of the battle or volunteers wanting to get into it. The task of the intelligence circuits, on the other hand, like that of the intelligence sections of conventional armies, was to keep the staffs informed. The situation was so complex, however, that the scraps of intelligence they collected could not be confined to locations, movements and equipment of enemy forces; account also had to be taken of the supply situation in occupied territory, arms manufacture, morale of the subject populations, transport, effects of Allied propaganda, activities of the satellite governments, and so on. In fact the entire life and attitudes of an occupied country had to be faithfully recorded – photographic aircraft were used for the same task but they could only capture the outlines. The job was immense and required the connivance of an innumerable number of people rather than the employment of a few highly-qualified agents. The occupying forces of course thought of members of intelligence circuits as spies in accordance with the laws of war.

The members themselves, on the other hand, who were operating in their own country, proudly claimed the title of patriotic combatants.

Whatever their origin, intelligence circuits were all organised for the same purposes, and they soon became similar in outline. At the 'sharp end' were the observers gathering information; everyone could pick up something from his window and the occupier was spied upon daily by millions of watchful hostile eyes – the railwayman who made a note of the passing of a train, the pilot who knew better than anybody when ships entered or left a port, the officer's landlady who overheard snatches of conversation. In principle nothing was too unimportant. The raw material was then collected in 'postboxes' and the initial sifting process took place. This was both difficult and important – if a valuable piece of information was overlooked, it was lost for ever; if comparison of the various reports led to a wrong conclusion, the user might be led to take a false step with incalculable consequences.

The next step was to transmit the information to its Allied destination as quickly as possible and by the most secure means. The initial procedure was to use carrier pigeons. Then parcels of documents were passed across the frontiers like the 'escapers' into neutral countries. The parcels sometimes fared better than the men as they could travel in the security of a diplomatic bag. Neutral Switzerland thus became an intelligence centre; all the embassies turned themselves into miniature espionage offices. Great progress was made with the microfilming of documents; weight and bulk were considerably reduced and secure hiding places were easier to find. By far the best solution, however, was to locate radio transmitters in occupied territory, with operators (known as 'pianists') sending information in an agreed code, on an agreed wavelength and at an agreed time of day; as a rule they encoded their messages without attempting to understand them. The organiser of a new circuit was dropped into his area armed with a radio transmitter (they became increasingly light and portable) and accompanied by an operator.

To ensure the rapid collection and despatch of material, and also for security reasons, an intelligence circuit could not expand its activity too far or employ too many people, and under the guidance of their Allied directors they became increasingly specialised. When Christian Pineau returned from London, for instance, he had been commissioned to form a group consisting of a few supply specialists. Gradually all intelligence circuits adopted a similar layout. The headquarters comprised the organiser, one assistant and one secretary; if possible an emergency headquarters was also provided. This formed the receiving point for mail, money and orders; it distributed questionnaires to its agents; it read, sifted, collated and encoded their replies; it organised mail despatch. The headquarters also had to provide itself with auxiliary services – inspection, liaison, communications, false papers, accommodation for radio operators, security and even counterespionage to keep track of enemy agents.

As an example the headquarters of the *Confrérie Notre Dame,* the circuit formed and controlled by Rémy, was located in a building in Paris where there was much coming and going; to all appearances it was some firm's office, but there were two exits. Documents were brought by courier; the telephone was never used and the post seldom. Papers left in the 'postbox' were in double envelopes, the first giving no indication and the second carrying a numeral and a key phrase identifying the agent. Reports were drafted to contain neither the name nor the code-name of the agent and gave no indication of objectives. Reports arrived in clear and were then encoded according to a complex system: they were assembled in no particular order, so that it was impossible to tell to which part of the whole each message referred. Such precautions inevitably led to errors either in the encoding or in the decoding at the receiving end.

To work satisfactorily a circuit needed the experience and technical expertise of a few people and the goodwill of the majority in the occupied country. Every circuit therefore included full-time professional agents (or men who became such), volunteer agents and 'casuals'. All sorts of people were recruited but some, such as railwaymen, post office workers or employees of German agencies, were better placed than others to observe. Every organiser was also compelled to make maximum use of his relatives, his friends and his professional contacts. Out of a thousand members of *Zéro-France,* for instance, some 200 were employed on the railways and almost as many were officials; the circuit also included workmen, policemen, traders, housewives, craftsmen, members of the liberal and teaching professions, farmers, nurses and concierges.

On occasions an intelligence circuit would bring off a sensational coup, such as the theft from an office of the 'plans for the Atlantic Wall'. Even then there could be no certainty that these were the authoritative plans, that they would not subsequently be changed or that the Allies would realise their importance and make good use of them. Most of the reports were in fact collections of bits and pieces with many gaps, wrong deductions and unintentional exaggerations. Everything depended on the use made of them, first by the specialists whose staffs were responsible for translating them into lucid conclusions, then by the responsible military authorities who took the final decisions in the light of numerous factors, of which intelligence was only one. It is therefore extremely difficult to be dogmatic about the part played by the intelligence circuits in the success or failure of military operations.

We do know that the Red Army was taken by surprise because Stalin refused to believe the unanimous intelligence reports of the imminence of the German attack. On the other hand inadequate intelligence – the fact that the presence of German armour was not known – led to the failure of the airborne operation at Arnhem. On the credit side, a Belgian circuit succeeded in photographing the German night fighters; a Norwegian officer landed by submarine and initiated the entire operation which ended in the sinking of the *Bismarck*; a French circuit was instrumental in the bombing of the *Scharnhorst* and *Gneisenau* in Brest – even though its reports that they would attempt to pass up the Channel were ignored; Polish circuits kept watch on all German economic activity in the Baltic, including the construction of electrically-driven submarines. The technical organisation of a circuit sometimes reached a remarkable degree of perfection. In Belgium, for instance, 'Mill' succeeded in arranging secret telephone lines which kept him in continuous touch with his observation posts, German orders for the movement of troop trains were intercepted through the teleprinters and orders were passed to his secret transmitters over a distance of more than thirty miles. To give an idea of the volume of traffic from the intelligence circuits – between 1940 and 1942 20,000 telegrams reached London from Czechoslovakia and in May 1944, on the eve of the Normandy landing, 3,700 were despatched from France.

The circuits paid a heavy price in blood and suffering. German direction-finding trucks often discovered the radio operators; some were killed on the keys of their set; others were captured and tortured, and some talked – a chain-reaction of arrests followed. Because the security of the German army was at stake the occupation forces made great efforts to break up the intelligence

circuits. Sometimes they were adroit enough to take control of
the organisation and personnel of a circuit without their knowledge and use them to deceive the Allies.

The V1 and V2 – a remarkable intelligence achievement

Hitler was determined to pay Britain back in her own coin for the
large-scale bombings to which Germany was subjected, and he
pinned his faith on the production first of 'flying bombs' and then
of rockets, known respectively as the V1 and V2. Warned from
various sources of what was being planned against them, the
Allies activated all the intelligence resources at their disposal. The
result was a remarkable example of teamwork between Belgian,
Danish, French and Polish circuits and one of the major intelligence
successes.

In the spring of 1943, through a German NCO who had lived
in Bromberg (Bydgoscz) before the war, the Polish 'Home
Army's' agencies on the Baltic learnt that a German establishment
of a very special nature existed at Peenemunde on the island of
Usedom at the mouth of the Oder; it was carrying out trials of a
new weapon. This information was studied by a Polish engineer
who had specialised in espionage on German aircraft; he came to
the conclusion that the Germans were trying out rockets. This
information was transmitted to London; it was confirmed by a
photograph taken by a Danish officer of a V1 which had been
launched from Peenemunde and had landed by mistake on the
Danish island of Bornholm. Polish deportees at Birkenau had
also warned the Home Army that 'commandos' were working on
some strange project in underground factories.

London accordingly decided to photograph the entire area of
Peenemunde from the air. Then, on 17 July 1943, 600 bombers
attacked the Peenemunde base – one of the most important
operations of the war.

The Germans then built an experimental launching ramp at the
village of Blizna near Rzeszow, out of range of Allied bombers;
the missiles came down in the area of Sarnaki, north of Siedlce.
The Polish Resistance discovered this ramp; they concluded that
the flying bombs had a range of over 200 miles and that the
Germans could, therefore, bombard London from the French
coast. The Home Army ordered its agents to collect fragments of

these bombs; they were not sufficient to reconstruct one – each bomb comprised 25,000 parts – but they did show the factory of origin which the Allies then bombed. The delicate choice of targets for the bombers was, therefore, decided by the Polish resistance.

The Home Army then worked out a plan to seize a complete weapon while it was being transported by train, but early in May 1944 a V1 fell into the River Bug without exploding and local peasants hid the wings, the only parts protruding above the mud, so the Germans were unable to find it. Polish engineers then arrived to take it out of the water, but the bomb broke in two and the warhead remained on the river bottom. Piece by piece the bomb was sent to Warsaw, where it was exhaustively studied by specialists who kept the Polish government in London closely informed of the progress of their examination.

Their researches led to the conclusion that the German rockets were guided onto target by radio signals transmitted on a specific wavelength. From this it was deduced that they could be diverted by similar signals. A Polish radio technician carried out experiments which proved the point – and the house in which he worked was occupied by a German airman.

But this was not enough for the British and Americans; they wanted to study the rocket in their own laboratories. It was decided to collect the parts by air from Poland, where two aircraft had already landed, though not without difficulty. A Dakota from Brindisi landed near Tarnow. It had to wait several days before leaving again because of wet ground. Eventually the operation was completed on the night of 25/26 July 1944. The rocket parts were loaded, but before the aircraft could take off it was necessary to dig out the wheels which were stuck in the mud; planks were placed under the wheels and the entire 'reception committee' pushed.

In the meantime the first V1s had fallen on London just at the moment when the troops of the Normandy landing were finding the going difficult. It was essential to locate and neutralise the camouflaged launching ramps along the North Sea and Channel coasts, and all the French and Belgian circuits set to work, each without knowledge of the other – which explains why they each claim sole credit for the discovery. In fact they all discovered something, in most cases by infiltrating members into the Todt Organisation;[1] one young engineer even contrived to copy the

[1] The German military construction agency.

plans of a launching ramp. Owing to their size the ramps could neither be moved nor reconstructed; one after another they were discovered and heavily bombed.

The 'rocket affair' was among the undoubted successes of the intelligence circuits, but at the same time it illustrates their limitations. Despite the accuracy of the information provided, the vast resources used and the undoubted achievements registered, neither the production nor the launching of these missiles was arrested: barely even impeded. The Allied armies had to cross the Rhine finally to bring the launchings to an end. The new weapons did indeed fail to achieve their object, but this was due to the fact that Hitler, obsessed with the idea of retribution, insisted on firing them on London instead of on the units and stocks of equipment massed in the British ports before the Channel crossing – an easy target of capital strategic importance.

Soviet circuits

The Soviet Union has published nothing, not even reminiscences by agents; we therefore know little about the Soviet circuits with the exception of those discovered by the Germans. They seem to have differed from western circuits on two main counts: in the first place they followed the traditional pattern of small groups of highly-trained spies – in the clandestine war outside the USSR communist volunteers were hardly ever used as collectors of information[1] – and secondly the aim of the circuits was conventional military espionage; their primary, if not their sole, purpose was to inform the Red Army about the dispositions of the Wehrmacht. It should be added that they never co-operated with the French, British or American circuits; they never passed on information, not even when the great alliance was at its peak after the Teheran Conference.

One group worked in Germany itself until November 1942; the Germans called it *Rote Kapelle* – Red Orchestra. One can only speculate on the precise sources available to it and the importance attached to its reports by the Soviet authorities.

[1] In France the FTP did possess a small circuit called 'Fana' which enabled them to remain in touch with the BCRA, from which they received certain resources; with this exception the communists knew nothing of the circuits and as a result were extremely suspicious of them.

Another group was active in Switzerland; its head was a cartographer named Rado who had worked for the Soviet Union in Paris as early as 1934. He was given active assistance by the Swiss communists – they advanced money, reported on the attitude of the Swiss police and even recruited helpers. Rado possessed three radio sets in Geneva and Lausanne over which thousands of messages were transmitted to Moscow. One of his main informers was a journalist, a German emigré who had joined Swiss Army Intelligence. Consequently, like Sorge in Japan,[1] Rado warned the Russians of the imminence of the German attack in June 1941. Probably the Soviet authorities thought this a plot – an 'exaggeration' – engineered by the Abwehr[2] to mislead them. The Germans were aware of the existence of Rado by August 1941, and by 1943 they seem to have known all about him. Nevertheless, it was the Swiss police who broke up the circuit, arresting the agents and confiscating documents and radio sets.

This brief picture produces more shade than light, and these are not the only obscure points. It is certain that throughout occupied Europe responsible communists on the whole remained loyal to Moscow, but we know nothing of the contacts they established, the orders they received, the information they provided or the exchanges of agents which may have taken place. It is probable that the USSR attached little importance to what was happening elsewhere unless it could alleviate in some measure the terrible pressure to which she was being subjected. Only when the Red Army had seized the initiative at Stalingrad and began to near other occupied countries, did the USSR take advantage of the underground. We shall return to this subject later.

[1] I do not propose to deal here with Sorge; much has been written about him.
[2] German Military Intelligence.

CHAPTER 7

External Contacts

Occupied Europe had become a vast prison, living according to German rules, a place of which the Allies knew nothing. If it was to increase its strength in order to attain its own objectives, the emergent underground must tunnel through the walls of its prison and establish as numerous and as regular links with the Allies as possible.

Airmen, volunteers, politicians and Jews in peril had been helped to leave, but in return something had to come in from outside. Isolated and left to itself the Resistance was impotent; it could not fight the enemy with its bare fists. It must receive from outside the weapons, equipment, training, money, orders and, later, the cadres for its ill-equipped and inexperienced troops Without this support it was condemned to wither and die.

For their part the Allies wished to make the best possible use of this convenient fifth column – a parachute force already on the spot, but they felt that they must first channel and direct the efforts of this impetuous, undisciplined force. The governments-in-exile, considering themselves legitimate rulers, wanted to assume command, fearing anarchy or the rise of rival leaders to be the likely alternatives. First the British, then the Americans and Russians, and finally the governments-in-exile despatched throughout occupied Europe a stream of agents to carry out diverse and dangerous tasks. Two-way traffic was thus established under the very noses of the Germans; a sort of blow-hole was drilled, through which a breath of fresh air might enliven the stifling atmosphere of Fortress Europe. Allied knowledge of occupied Europe gradually increased through reports from these agents and the Resistance itself.

Training of agents[1]

Agents were all volunteers; all had the same desire to serve, but not all had the necessary qualities. Colonel Passy records: 'By the end of 1942 the British had organised a remarkable system of tests, under a first-class psychiatrist, to categorise potential agents. As a result we managed to eliminate a certain number of volunteers held to be ill-fitted for clandestine warfare; the percentage of errors made in the selection of agents fell during the following months by more than 10 per cent and this naturally led to a considerable reduction in the number of mishaps in France. The conclusions of the most up-to-date psychological studies formed the basis of the tests. For the agents they were a formidable ordeal to which they only submitted with obvious displeasure. Very often they pretended to find them ridiculous and puerile but most of them were forced to admit that a series of conclusions resulting from purely mechanical tests conducted by experienced technicians and all pointing in the same direction, were probably accurate.'[2]

Once accepted, the agents-to-be were given intensive training in special schools. Physical training instructors made them run, swim and climb cliffs; doctors supervised their feeding and noted their reactions; engineers taught them how to sabotage bridges, railway engines or ships; experts explained the various types of explosives. Other 'instructors' taught them the art of picking a lock or the best methods of passing through a barrier with concealed documents or even weapons.

Regular courses of instruction then followed, giving the agents a grounding in German army organisation and the methods of the police forces in the occupied countries. They were given detailed information on the country in which they were to work, primarily on the changes in day-to-day life brought about by the occupation – ration cards, passes, traffic regulations, rules laid down by the occupying power, and so on.

Then they were trained as parachutists, learning to jump into the unknown and to fall without hurting themselves. This was followed by a number of 'exercises on the ground' – how to

---

[1] This entire section deals primarily with Great Britain who, in many respects, was the initiator of these methods.
Colonel Passy: *Mémoires*, Vol. 2, p. 179.

follow a trail, to find a stranger, to attack him or defend oneself against him. During all these various stages of training, of course, the men's characters emerged and their performance was meticulously noted and criticised. In fact they underwent a continuous examination which naturally some failed; these were then despatched to another camp, where they were held in cold storage until the knowledge they had acquired could no longer be of use to the enemy.

Radio operators were in addition given the necessary technical training. For their 'exercise on the ground' they were sent off to some nearby town where they had to find themselves a lodging, set themselves up and establish communication with another set. They were of course followed, and had to try to give their pursuers the slip by frequent changes of direction or by diving into shops with more than one entrance; when installed they had to watch for a possible enemy approach and be prepared to decamp quickly and unobtrusively. As the final test they were interrogated by a 'policeman' who had 'arrested' them – an alluring prospect!

At the last moment agents were given their instructions. They signed an 'ordre de mission' (operation order) summarising the action they were to take and, pending their return, this was held in the London or Moscow files. A 'working agreement' was drawn up containing the texts of messages to be exchanged, passwords, cover-names, safe addresses, etc. They were given money to enable them to exist pending absorption by one of the clandestine groups. A whole range of equipment was prepared for them: civilian clothes, chocolate containing a sleeping drug for the enemy and chocolate for themselves containing a stimulant, various tools, cyanide capsules to swallow in the event of capture. They were issued with false papers and assumed completely new identity. Armed with one or two safe addresses (or addresses thought to be safe) the agent, or to be more exact a small group of agents,[1] was dropped into enemy territory; in spite of their intensive training they encountered more unknowns than certainties, more enemies than friends and more mishaps than favourable turns of fortune. Each agent was simultaneously a scout, prospector, recruiter and instructor; some were trained for intelligence work, others for sabotage or escape lines; they were called

---

[1] Agents were generally dropped in pairs, an organiser and a radio operator, but there were also many threesomes and three was the regulation number for the 'Jedburghs' (see p. 316 below).

upon to act as teachers in radio transmission, handling of explosives, collection of information and use of weapons; they were the connecting link between the Allied Command and the clandestine Resistance, the true advance guard of the invading hosts.

Naturally they had to have an adequate knowledge of the country in which they were to work and, even more important, of its language. Some were 'escapers' from the country concerned, who agreed to go back quite soon after having left it; others were exiles who had been away from their country for longer and might not be altogether at home there. The need was such, however, that it was also necessary to use British, American or Russian agents who had spent some time in Europe but who would have more difficulty in concealing their origin and their accent. Casualties among these agents were very heavy: aircraft were shot down on the way, parachutes failed to open and sometimes the enemy was there when they landed. Many were captured during their mission – to face torture and consignment to a concentration camp. Of 250 agents who left London for Belgium, for instance, 145 returned to Great Britain but 105 were arrested; of the latter 25 were executed, 20 died from maltreatment and 40 were deported, of whom only 20 survived. The casualty rate was therefore a full 25 per cent.[1]

The Special Operations Executive (SOE)

The British were the first to establish communication with occupied Europe, and they remained the most active participants in this field throughout the war. They did not make their mark, however, with the same rapidity, ease or permanency in all countries. Nevertheless their contribution was immense and they scored some brilliant successes. The credit goes primarily to SOE.

Denmark. Initial approaches were made from Stockholm. The first agent was dropped in December 1941 but he was killed on landing; regular contact was not established until April 1942. The

---

[1] Jean Moulin's team, which was parachuted 'blind' into Provence during the night of 31 December 1941/1 January 1942, consisted of three men: of these one died under torture, one was shot and the third was arrested and deported – he returned from a concentration camp in the state one would expect.

main difficulty was the fact that very few Danes lived in Britain
and very few Englishmen spoke Danish; a total of fifty agents was
despatched during the war. Given Denmark's special position,
they played a role without parallel in the rest of Europe; all the
directives and all the weapons received by the Resistance came
from SOE. A major and spectacular success was the escape to the
United States in October 1943 of Bohr, the atomic scientist; he
became one of the leading members of the remarkable team to
whom the Americans owed their victory in the race to produce
the atomic bomb.

Norway. As early as 1939 the intelligence service had laid the
foundations by appointing undercover agents to the staffs of
British consulates; they were the genesis of SOE's Norwegian
section. Parachuting immediately proved too dangerous because
of the broken nature of the country; the regular and most secure
means of communication was by sea. Since the Norwegians were
totally inexperienced militarily and ill-suited by nature to clandestine work, SOE's agents were initially instructed not to work
with the local Resistance. This decision fluctuated and was the
cause of some dissension. It did not remain the rule.

Holland. The situation here was one of particular difficulty owing
to the country's geographical position, the fact that all surrounding areas were hostile and the German coast-watching precautions
– the islands were a forbidden zone; additional problems were the
persistence of fog at night and the high population density. Consequently there was no real contact until late 1941, and throughout
the war only 200 Dutch agents succeeded in returning to their
country; their casualties were high, moreover, since Holland was
on the Allied bombing route to the Ruhr and the German
concentration of radar and anti-aircraft was dense; parachuting
was therefore both difficult and dangerous.

France. Since the British wished to maintain good relations with
the Vichy government, SOE's French section frequently worked
separately from and without the knowledge of Free France. In the
occupied zone, therefore, its agents' contacts were not always the
best available; they were often forced to engage in improvised and
unwise commitments with helpers who did not always turn out to
be well-chosen or disinterested. The first radio operator was

dropped near Chateauroux on 5 May 1941; by 1942 the first groups had been formed and 53 agents despatched.[1] In all, 92 circuits were organised and 1,400 agents sent to the field, some British, some French and some French-speaking Canadians. The British had established the 'Patriotic School', a screening centre for 'escapers' from France; there they recruited volunteers, sometimes diverting them from the Free French forces.[2] Almost two-thirds of the operations were successful; the importance of the work done is proved by the figures – almost 10,000 tons of equipment and 400 million francs were delivered to France.

Italy. The first team was dropped in December 1942. Not until after the fall of Mussolini and the signature of the armistice by Badoglio, however, did SOE really address itself seriously to backing up the Italian Resistance in the north of the country, then occupied by the Germans. In September 1943 an SOE section set up a base, including training schools, at Bari. Its main area of operations was northern Italy but it also dealt with central Europe, the Balkans and Poland. An SOE agent was responsible for Benedetto Croce's escape from Sorrento. A total of 48 teams was sent in to northern Italy.

Greece. The country was most easily reached from Cairo. Between 1941 and 1944 a total of 1,072 agents was despatched in 82 operations; 435 of them were Greeks. The first team, consisting of twelve men, was dropped in October 1942; in all some 5,000 tons of supplies and 1,000 tons of arms and ammunition were delivered.

Yugoslavia. In accordance with Churchill's policy the country figured high on SOE's list. In the light of information received in London the main beneficiary was Tito's communist movement. The start was difficult owing to distance, ignorance and the difficult topography of the country. Out of eight operations despatched between summer 1941 and summer 1942 two never arrived, the members of the third were captured and the remainder had to be written off, contact with them having been lost. It was

---

[1] The figure for containers dropped rose from 9 in 1941 to 5,300 in 1943 and in 1944 to more than 48,000.

[2] General de Gaulle protested at what he called these attempts at enticement; he did not accept that Frenchmen should enter the service of a foreign power, even an Allied one; they would form a sort of Foreign Legion in their country, he thought.

December 1942 before a few agents managed to reach Mihailovich and April 1943 before similar contact was made with Tito. After the British and American landings in Italy, however, followed by the establishment of a base on the island of Vis for the exclusive use of the partisans, the rate of despatch of agents and stores rose sharply. The Yugoslav resistance movement was the only one to receive any significant quantity of machine-guns, mines and bombs; they were even sent guns and artillery ammunition. The entire country was 'chess-boarded' by liaison missions, so that touch was maintained with every important partisan unit.

Czechoslovakia. The British were only semi-successful in gaining or maintaining contact with the countries of central and eastern Europe. As far as Czechoslovakia was concerned, radio communication was established early and never ceased; despatch of agents, on the other hand, was a hazardous business. The country was entirely surrounded by the enemy; in the early days of the war only the western portion was within aircraft range; nothing could be done during the summer as the nights were too short and in winter any operation was dangerous because of bad weather. In addition Bohemia, the most densely populated area, was geographically unsuited to clandestine action. Until 1944 the ratio of successes to failures were one to seven. Not until spring 1944 could an operation be mounted into Moravia – from Italy; in June of that year a team was sent to Slovakia. Nevertheless Czechoslovakia was the scene of one of the most sensational clandestine operations carried out by agents from abroad – the assassination of the German 'Protector', Reinhard Heydrich.

Rumania. SOE sent in two missions, in the spring of 1943 and at Christmas that year. Their purpose was to assist the opposition to overthrow General Antonescu's régime. All the agents were arrested, but not before they had provided information which assisted in the bombing of the Ploesti refineries.

Bulgaria. Only one mission was despatched and both its members were killed.

Albania. Failure here was complete but in this case the fault was that of the communist leader, Enver Hodja.

During the war, therefore, SOE despatched a total of nearly 7,000 agents to occupied Europe, coming from nineteen different nations. In certain countries the British were gradually replaced by the Americans or Russians, who were both stronger and nearer; in others they were forced to allow considerable freedom of action to the governments-in-exile, the French and Poles in particular.

Land and sea communications

One of the great novelties of the war – successful parachute and air landings – were only possible when appropriate equipment became available; in the early days communications were restricted to more pedestrian methods – overland lines in the case of the occupied peoples and maritime operations in that of the British.

Overland communications functioned throughout the war; people were always crossing from France into Switzerland or from Poland into Hungary via Slovakia, but these routes were slow and insecure. The Belgians, for instance, organised a line from Brussels via Roubaix and Paris ending in Lyons; thence travellers were passed on to Portugal either by sea from Marseilles or overland across the Pyrenees and Spain. Only the final stage of the journey, from Lisbon to England, could be completed more rapidly by air. It was soon realised that, for security reasons, each stage must be independent so that in the event of a 'knock-out' the other stages would still remain, though the line would be cut; and there had to be a reserve line, likely to be equally slow and hazardous.

The Dutch were forced by geography to make do with this type of communication. Through the World Council of Churches and with the help of Dutch nationals living in Brussels and Paris a regular fortnightly 'mail' was instituted between Amsterdam and Geneva; since there was no air connection between Switzerland and Great Britain, however, a long detour was then necessary via Portugal or Sweden. Reports were microfilmed and hidden in scientific books.

The French circuits succeeded without great difficulty in persuading a number of Breton fishermen to carry clandestine passengers; at an agreed point at sea they would rendezvous with a

British ship which took their passengers and handed over others coming from England. On the Mediterranean coast operations were generally carried out in small boats launched from a larger ship sailing from Gibraltar and then run up onto a beach. All these methods were somewhat elementary; if a German patrol discovered the hide-out or if a storm blew up, the rendezvous at sea, on which everything depended, could not take place. Passengers were anything but comfortable in their restricted hiding places on board. Gradually, however, improvements were made which ensured the maximum chance of success – precise co-ordinates of the meeting point, agreed sentences broadcast over the BBC beforehand, information on the German coastal watch and sea patrols, exchange of meteorological data, accurate timing of the operation.

Between Norway and the Shetlands communication became so regular and secure that the Norwegian sailors who ran the line under British direction referred to it as the 'Shetland bus'; although boats were slow, by the end of 1944 400 tons of arms and 60 radio sets had been delivered to Norway by sea. From Greece, thanks to the large number of islands, movement to Turkey and later to the Middle East was continuous. Traffic from Denmark to Sweden presented little difficulty: in summer it took place via the ferry and in winter on foot across the ice; movement proved to be on such a large scale that a Danish resistance leader had to be permanently established in Sweden. Departures from Holland were equally numerous but more difficult. In Leyde the students were inspired to take advantage of a communal drinking match in which the Germans guarding a certain stretch of coast indulged at a certain time of day every week; under cover of the curfew a boat would put ashore an agent in evening dress, apparently drunk and brandishing a bottle; on occasions the sentry took pity on him and helped him keep his balance. Picturesque though they were, such methods were not very effective. Communications to Groningen improved when Swedish sailors agreed first to carry mail to the Dutch consul in Stockholm and later to take 'escapers', particularly students from Leyde. Unfortunately this line was cut in July 1943 as a result of treachery.

The noisy engines of patrol boats made them unsuitable vessels, but submarines, being comparatively silent, were an essential means of transport for the more numerous groups. The vessel lay on the bottom by day, surfaced at night and sent boats in-shore to discharge their human cargo and load up another one. The British frequently used this method, expensive though it was. The most brilliant feat by a submarine was undoubtedly that of the French *Casabianca* (Captain Lherminier); after refusing to scuttle herself at Toulon with the rest of the French fleet she was used to transport weapons from North Africa to the Resistance in Corsica and then to move an entire 'shock battalion' which fought alongside the *maquis* and drove the occupying forces out of the island.[1]

Parachute and air landing operations

The first parachuters who risked their lives were dropped 'blind'; as best he could the pilot found the point selected, frequently on the basis of sketchy information; the aperture opened and the man was swallowed up by the empty blackness. Navigational errors were numerous and accidents frequent. Even if the operation was successful, the agent was then alone in a country perhaps unfamiliar to him; at the outset he did not even know which door to knock at; some old friend, on whom he thought he could rely, might well be only too eager to denounce him.

Gradually an astounding system was developed. The early agents, if lucky enough to reach their destination, recruited 're-ception committees' for the more fortunate ones who followed. Dropping areas were carefully chosen; they had to be adequately flat and completely open, at a sufficient distance, therefore, from houses, forests, roads or high-tension lines; their minimum dimensions (400–500 square yards) and their co-ordinates were transmitted to London by radio. At the same time the agents signalled the types of weapons and explosives they required and the number of containers they could receive. Each dropping area was given a code-name and the day of the operation was announced by broadcasting over the radio a pre-arranged sentence, incomprehensible to all but the initiated.[2]

As soon as the sentence was heard the reception committee,

---

[1] Other French submarines, *Perle* and *Protée*, carried out similar operations; the first soe agent despatched to Yugoslavia was landed on the Montenegro coast from a submarine.

[2] Messages such as: 'The raven croaks'; 'The chiropodist is ticklish'; 'The verdigris is cold', etc.

some ten men, moved to the dropping zone; this they marked with four electric torches or four bonfires laid out on a pre-arranged pattern indicating the direction of the wind; torches and fires were lit as soon as the aircraft's engines were heard. The pilot circled above the markers for a moment to get into the best position and then dropped his cargo of men and/or containers. The former were quickly taken to the hideout prepared for them, while the reception committee, with some of its members on guard, set about burying the parachutes and concealing the containers (they weighed 225 lbs) in some safe place pending distribution of their contents.

The main risk in this system was that the lights might attract the attention of some German aircraft flying in the vicinity – and it would not hesitate to machine-gun any suspect area. This danger was eliminated by the 'S-phone', which provided direct communication between the aircraft and the ground at a range of several thousand yards. Once contact was established recognition signals were exchanged fearlessly. Other problems remained such as the transport, maintenance and employment of the equipment dropped, but all were solved in time.

The problem of clandestine landings or 'pick-ups' was more complex. The area had to be selected with great care if the aircraft was not to be damaged; there must be no furrows or mounds. The areas were too small for normal aircraft so the British recalled to service an obsolete light aircraft, the Lysander; it required little space in which to land and, though unarmed, was protected by its manoeuvrability and the fact that it flew very low, underneath the German radar coverage. The cockpit could not hold more than two men and a few packages in addition to the pilot, but landing was the only method of picking up agents and urgent but bulky mail. Once the personnel were well trained the whole process of landing, unloading, loading and take-off could be completed in a few minutes.[1]

All these methods postulated a combination of high-grade technique, accuracy, dedication and large-scale detailed organisation. From the point of 'those outside' they had to provide an adequate number of aircraft – and there were never enough – train

[1] Passy records that he suggested to the British that flying-boats might land on deserted stretches of water. This was turned down as it would have been impossible at night and without landing lights to estimate the actual height of the aircraft above the water – op. cit., Vol. 2, p. 176.

the pilots, design and manufacture the containers and make provision to hold stocks of a wide range of equipment – documents, revolvers, sub-machineguns, ammunition, grenades, time-pencils, truncheons and daggers, abrasive paste, radio sets, Bickford fuze, detonators, primers, to say nothing of operation orders, cigarettes and a few bars of chocolate for the reception committee.

From the resistance point of view a complete organisation had to be formed from nothing to recruit, train and assemble the men, house the passengers, store the containers and transport both the one and the other. This was just one aspect of clandestine organisation; when a group had successfully received an air operation it became both more determined and better equipped to try for more; the equipment received helped to arm other groups who could then receive in their turn and so on. In France a full-scale organisation to deal with air operations was formed on Jean Moulin's initiative. It had various titles; an 'office' dealt with mail, internal communications, radio, security, false papers and welfare; a second section dealt with dropping zones, external communications and finance; though the reception committees were made up of part-time volunteers, instructors and heads of section worked full-time. France was divided into six regions, the heads of which were given radio sets, cars, a personal bodyguard, accommodation, etc. Similar systems operated in other countries.

But however good the organisation, success depended on the weather. Operations were possible only at full-moon periods, so during the winter months the number of attempts which could be made was restricted; wind and rain added to the failures – in December 1943 only two out of more than a hundred operations were successful. The experience of Poland is a good illustration of the difficulties.

Polish territory could only be reached from Great Britain by aircraft with a range of 2,000 miles. An initial operation, planned for December 1940 had to be cancelled for lack of a suitable aircraft. Then a modified Whitley was used but it had to turn back after covering 850 miles; it dropped its three agents over 60 miles from the boundary between the area annexed to Germany and the Government General. Fortunately they met some Polish sympathisers but their weapons were lost. After this setback the Air Ministry was unwilling to loan aircraft and very few operations were carried out in 1941. The Poles tried hard to obtain some aircraft of their own but did not succeed. In July 1942 three Halifax were allocated but it was up to the RAF to decide. In January 1943 six operations took place. The Home Army thereupon reported that it would be forced to reduce activity unless it received the necessary equipment.

A large-scale plan was then worked out for the period September 1943–May 1944; there were to be 300 sorties delivering 300 tons of equipment, but on the first operation four out of eleven aircraft were lost. Sights had to be lowered and in September only twenty-two operations (sixteen successful) were undertaken instead of thirty-six. From January 1944 operations took place from Italy but in the first three months there were many failures owing to bad weather. In April there were 65 successful deliveries out of 132; in April and May 104 agents and 170 tons of equipment were despatched (double the figures achieved during the whole of the preceding three years); no operations were possible in June; in July 1944 of 63 sorties half were successful. In all, as far as Poland was concerned, 1,300 operations were requested, 858 were attempted and of these 483 succeeded in dropping 345 agents, 600 tons of equipment and 40 million zloty. Eastern Poland was always out of range. This scale of assistance could support limited action but was inadequate for the preparation of a national rising.

Sometimes the forces of occupation put spokes in the wheel of this complicated machine. In Holland of 600 drops attempted 400 failed and more than half the 35,000 weapons despatched fell into German hands. How and why will be explained later.

Radio communications

Whatever the operation, whether transmission of information or exchange of agents, good radio communications were an essential condition of success. They had to be two-way, however; in other words the Resistance had to have not only high-quality receivers, which was comparatively easy, but also transmitters for passing on their requests – and these had to be provided. The first sets sent to France were very bulky; they weighed at least 65 lbs, were ill-concealed in heavy suitcases and were certainly not very handy. As a result, although by December 1942 ten radio operators had arrived, only four were in a position to transmit – from

Bordeaux, Arles and Paris. The others had either lost their sets or their code on landing or had encountered serious personal difficulties.

From September 1943 smaller sets were mass-produced. They were better camouflaged, either in a portable gramophone or a small double-bottomed suitcase. By December 1943 thirty-two radio operators were working in France. It was a highly dangerous trade. The average life of a 'pianist' was six months, particularly when the number of messages and time on the air increased, as this raised the German's chances of detecting the set.

A message consisted of: first a key sentence including the names of the originator and addressee – or rather their code-names – then the message itself. For instance: 'Husky Tortoise to Navicert: What are you doing?' meant that the BCRA (Husky Tortoise) was worried about what was happening to one of its agents whose cover-name was Navicert. The latter had to reassure the office at once by telegraphing his news, in the agreed code of course. Too prolonged a silence or an error in transmission cast doubts on the agent's freedom of action and a further pre-arranged message would then be sent. Failure to reply correctly was proof that the set was being worked by the enemy.

It is easy to see why, under these conditions, the Germans attached such importance to the capture of codes. For this reason they used every method, ranging from torture to corruption, to make captured radio operators talk. In some cases they managed to continue working a set to London and the men and equipment from subsequent operations fell straight into their hands.

To detect the secret transmitters the Germans used direction-finding trucks. Messages were first intercepted by a static station; a truck was then despatched which gradually pinpointed the position of the transmitter by registering the maximum and minimum strength of the signals through a rotary aerial. As soon as intercepted, each transmitter was listed showing its normal time on the air, frequency used and assumed location; in this way it was gradually pinpointed. Once the truck had indicated a building, experts carrying miniature receivers determined the floor and then the apartment from which the 'pianist' was working.

To baffle the pursuers time on the air was reduced, the coding system was frequently changed and, more important still, the operator moved house periodically – but as a result he knew too many people to remain unknown for long. These precautions did not prevent the 'pianists' paying a heavy price; some, taken by surprise while actually working, were killed at their set.

Once communications with the outside world were established, however, the Resistance was no longer isolated nor weaponless. Henceforth it could act on its own, as it wished, but it could also co-operate with the Allies to the advantage of all.

PART III

The Component Forces of Resistance

Fascism's creed was one of total revolution; it was therefore opposed on principle to everything other than itself. It did not, however, succeed in destroying either the economic or social structures in the countries which it controlled or which its armies had conquered – this is as true of Germany as of Italy or Spain but its instinctive violence was backed by insidious propaganda, adept at sowing discord among its enemies. Initially, therefore, seizure of power or occupation of territory by totalitarian forces merely increased and exacerbated the long-standing divisions among the peoples, widening the gulfs separating opposing blocs. In practice all social political, professional and religious groupings, and even families, were divided, and opposed each other on the attitude to adopt, thereby greatly assisting the victory and establishment of totalitarianism.

The protraction of the conflict, however, worked against fascism. It destroyed the prestige gained by its *blitz* victories and it forced it into savage exploitation of the conquered peoples, thus increasing both the discontent and the number of its enemies. As time went on hardly a section of any occupied people was to be found which could not voice some grievance or did not harbour some fear. In face of this common danger there gradually formed an extraordinary alliance of all, whatever their background, who were victims of the occupation or feared that they might become so one day. In Italy, for instance, communists recognised the authority of King Victor Emmanuel; in France priests and freemasons sometimes fought side by side.[1]

The Resistance, therefore, drew its recruits from all classes and levels of society; it was the prerogative of no one – no man, no class, no party. But it did not impinge everywhere at the same

[1] A similar process of coalescence was to be seen in the forces outside occupied Europe. Free France, for instance, was a remarkable conglomeration of people – see the author's *Histoire de la France Libre*, Presses Universitaires de France, Paris 1967.

tempo or to the same depth; the national climate and differing mentalities or circumstances meant that in one place a certain section of the community might appear as a collaborator of fascism and in another as its enemy. To differentiate between the various components, therefore, and to be fair to everybody, it seems necessary to survey the attitude and activities throughout occupied Europe of the whole range of forces involved – social (by class and profession), intellectual (political parties, Churches, Trade Unions); we shall also attempt to define the nature of the opposition displayed by 'captive societies' – prisoners of war, inmates of concentration camps and populations of annexed territories. A special case were the Jews, who were nationals of all countries and members of all human groupings. The same applies to the communists who played a great role and displayed intense activity.

CHAPTER 8

Classes and Groups of Society

I propose to deal in turn with the attitudes of the upper or ruling classes (obviously excluding the USSR), the working classes, the agricultural population, the intelligentsia and finally regular officers.

The ruling classes

In general terms, before the war began, the *aristocracy* had ceased to play any role of political importance in Europe, except in Poland, Slovakia, Hungary and Rumania where great landed proprietors were still to be found. Elsewhere, in Belgium or Holland for instance, they had some post at court; or as in Germany, Italy or France, they had found scope for the exercise of their talent for service to the state in the army; they also occupied important posts in the diplomatic service and the higher levels of the administration. They were inherently opposed to the liberal democracies since they were actuated and governed by the bourgeoisie; they were even more opposed to the socialist and communist ideologies which, being both atheist and materialist, seemed to them the negation of Christian civilisation. The aristocracy, therefore, showed some sympathy for the fascist parties which were destroying democracy and fighting socialism and communism. On the other hand the aristocrats mistrusted and despised certain basic manifestations of fascism, which they considered plebeian, coarse and vulgar – the nazi Storm Troops and the fascist Black Shirts.

The aristocracy thought it could see its way clear when men of its own stamp (or who claimed to be) came to power – Horthy in Hungary, Antonescu in Rumania and above all Pétain in France. The Vichy régime in fact signalled the end of the Republic of the old school tie and the professors. Though Marshal Pétain himself

was neither titled nor a royalist, the wording of his decisions –
'We, Philippe Pétain, Marshal of France, Head of the French
State . . .' – had a smell of the fleur de lis about it. Many country
gentlemen returned to active service in the ranks of the Vichy
régime, its youth movements or its fighting 'Legion' [*Légion des
combattants*].

But these 'halfway house' régimes were hardly permanencies,
as they were threatened by fascist groups more submissive to the
Germans, such as the Arrow Cross, the Iron Guard or the French
collaborationist parties. The choice had to be made. Some aristocrats opted for the anti-communist crusade – a Bassompierre was
a Militia leader in France and Prince Borghesa one of Mussolini's
most faithful disciples.

In contrast certain aristocrats joined the clandestine opposition
where they rubbed shoulders with the most astonishing allies. In
Germany the 'Kreisau circle', whose leading spirit was von
Moltke, included aristocrats, jesuits and social democrats; many
a castle in Piedmont harboured communist partisans; among the
leaders of the new French army were many names which included
the 'de'. Some titled gentry even reverted to tradition and turned
into defenders of their own estates, becoming leaders of volunteer
units raised to expel the invader – there was a 'red Marquis' in the
Nievre.[1]

The *upper middle class* – industrial, commercial or financial – had
many links with the aristocracy and shared many of their views
but at the same time they were concerned to act in accordance with
certain principles and, as their calling dictated, to defend as best
they might the vast interests which they controlled. In their eyes
no smell was attached to money. In Germany, Italy and Spain
they had subsidised and in some cases openly supported the fascist
parties on their road to power – even at the price of civil war. A
fascist victory was in many respects their victory for it carried
with it the priceless advantage of an end to social agitation, to
workers' demands, to strikes and to trade union disputes; it
strengthened their authority. Arms contracts, with the resulting
economic boom, increased their profits. From this point of view
Hitler's war against the USSR represented the ultimate stage of
a social house-cleaning since it would eliminate once and for

---

[1] This in some degree explains the ease with which General de Gaulle, with his
nationalist background, reached agreement with the communists. 'I wanted them
to serve,' he explained in his war memoirs.

all the hotbed of world revolution constituted by the Soviet régime.

In the occupied countries bourgeois capitalists inevitably viewed with alarm the consequences of defeat and the presence of the enemy – temporary stoppage of production, necessity to adjust to a difficult situation resulting from the enemy's extortions and the suspension of foreign trade and the advent of a new-style 'continental system'. In order to get their machines running again, reopen the bank counters or refurbish their stocks many businessmen not only showed no aversion to economic collaboration with the enemy but even wished and looked for it. In particular a whole swarm of racketeers placed themselves at his disposal to collect the products he required; some scandalous fortunes were made in this way.

Nevertheless, although the Germans did not actually expropriate the great financial, commercial or real estate barons, some of the measures imposed reduced their profits and even threatened their existence. The hand-over to 'Ostland' settlers of abandoned or requisitioned farms in the Ardennes and Lorraine and the acquisition of an interest, either by purchase of shares or forced mergers, in major business concerns such as Rumanian oil, the French chemical industry, the Lorraine ironworks, Czech banks, etc., were such instances. As soon as it was clear that the Germans were losing the war, the businessmen deserted the German camp. Whereas the sympathies of the aristocracy were with Great Britain and her monarchy, the business community nailed their colours to the mast of United States capitalism, the champion of their social and economic order. Some even went so far as to subsidise resistance groups, some of which were under communist direction; but they were the exceptions.

The *middle classes,* who had in general failed to adjust themselves to the growth of an industrial society, had largely assisted to swell the ranks of fascism which they regarded as their defender against a creeping proletarianisation. To many of this class – producers, craftsmen and traders – occupation and the resulting general poverty brought unexpected riches and social advancement – they no longer had to solicit and convince their customers; the customer came to them begging for their products and asking no questions about price. Nevertheless, the lower middle class was the stronghold of patriotism and particularly in France it provided some of the first members of resistance groups – though admittedly they

5*

were primarily officials and members of the liberal professions.

Three conclusions emerge from this examination of the attitude of the ruling classes: none formed a solid bloc; on the contrary all were divided; the majority found that its wishes and its interests were best represented by the 'halfway house' régimes which were both fascist-inclined and ostensibly 'national'; two minorities diverged; one inclining to collaboration and the other to resistance, the latter growing as German fortunes declined.

The working-class and the agricultural population

Among the occupied peoples *the workers* suffered worst from the deterioration in the standard of living. In all countries the occupying power left the indigenous administration in being for his own purposes, and forced it to decree a wages and prices freeze and institute a strict rationing system. In fact this was only partially successful in checking the rise in the cost of living; the majority of goods essential to existence could only be obtained in adequate quantities on the black market at prices bearing no relation to wages. Unemployment was always in the background and as a result working-class families had little time to think of anything other than what they were to live on – which they only obtained with great difficulty.

The apathy caused by this disastrous material situation was increased by uncertainty of mind. All the fascist or fascist-inclined régimes proclaimed their determination to promote the working class once they had rid it of its 'evil shepherds'; in some cases, for instance in Germany, Italy and even in occupied Poland, the rules and regulations did produce certain advantages – greater security of tenure, increase of wages, social benefits. But the workers were even more dependent on their employers than before. They were left helpless by the suppression of the professional or ideological organisations such as the trade unions or the socialist and communist parties, in which many of them had fought to improve their lot. Persistent propaganda convinced many of them that the capitalist democracies were their enemies as much as the fascist dictatorships. When the Russo-German pact was signed and approved by the majority of national communist parties, slogans proclaimed that in this 'imperialist war' with Germany and Italy on one side and France and Great Britain on the other, the interest of the working class of the world was to remain neutral.

For all these reasons comparatively few workers were to be found in the early resistance groups.[1] Even after the German invasion of Russia many were attracted by the higher wages and agreed to work for the occupying power either in their own country or in his. In no country did the working class really begin to contribute to resistance until their old organisations, the trade unions or political parties, had secretly reconstituted themselves and until the occupier exerted a blanket threat by trying to force them all to work for him; in most cases this entailed a move to the Reich with its accompanying dangers. The end of the working class attitude of indifference was marked by the refusal to obey the forced labour call-up.

Even then, however, the working class did not take part in all forms of clandestine action; it played hardly any role in propaganda, escape lines or intelligence. It did, on the other hand, provide technicians for sabotage groups, and evaders of the compulsory labour service joined the *maquis* or the partisans, well away from industrial cities. In fact the working class showed its hostility primarily by use of its own specific weapon, the strike; it finally returned to its traditional nineteenth-century role during the risings in the great cities – Paris, Warsaw and Prague.

Nowhere, except in the USSR, did the *agricultural population* form a distinct social class. The world of the countryside was a complex one with many divergent interests; it included large landowners, small landowners, yeoman farmers, tenant farmers and farm workers linked to the crafts and rural trades. Only in rare cases did this mixed society really coalesce in defence of its interests. The peasant parties in Poland and Hungary, like the Chambers of Agriculture in France, were no more than devices to protect both the large- and medium-sized landed proprietors; the socialist and communist parties had few adherents in the agricultural labour force.

In general, conditions in the countryside did not deteriorate as a result of the war, except in the areas annexed to the Reich, where expropriation and deportation of populations was the rule.

---

[1] Certain professions became involved earlier than others – railwaymen for instance; in addition, particularly in France, the first battle groups were formed from 'immigrant labour', which frequently consisted of stateless persons or anti-fascist emigrés.

In the occupied and impoverished countries there was even a relative improvement; far from producers having difficulty in disposing of their wares, purchasers descended on the farms begging them to sell and they were able to obtain the essential manufactured goods by a system of barter or through the black market; instead of selling their best-quality produce, they ate it themselves. In addition rural areas were not subjected to bombing from the air – unless, of course, the land was being devastated by military operations anyway. The occupation forces were not so strong that they could be physically present everywhere.

In many areas, such as Flanders, Brittany, Slovakia, Poland and Southern Italy, the agricultural population was politically less well educated than the city workers; they were amenable people, under the influence of their local dignitaries. Occupation increased their isolation by making transport slower and more spasmodic. The local newspaper still appeared but its message was one of conformism and compliance and as radio receivers were less numerous than in the towns news from the outside world barely penetrated to enliven and alert the mind. Finally, from time immemorial armies had drawn their rank and file from the agricultural population and so on many farms in Poland, France, Yugoslavia and Russia the breadwinner was a prisoner of war.

The countryside was brought into touch with the resistance with the development of the *maquis* and of guerrilla warfare, but not always in a manner to its liking. At least in Norway, Belgium, France and Italy the agricultural population was less affected by the compulsory labour service and so it provided the partisans with food, information and lodging rather than volunteers. In eastern Europe, however – Russia, Poland, Slovakia and above all Yugoslavia – clandestine military action took the form of full-scale peasant risings. We shall be explaining the reasons later.[1]

---

[1] These social distinctions even extended to the underworld, of which every country could provide representatives. The occupying forces recruited from it some of their most sinister minions – informers and torturers. Equally, however, the resistance recruited some for more worthy causes, the reason for the arrival of these unexpected volunteers generally being: 'Those guys – the occupation forces – I can't take them.' At a certain trial in France after the war the presiding magistrate was highly incensed when a senior police officer gave evidence in favour of a gangster – whom he had known and grown to respect in prison under the Vichy régime, the régime to which the magistrate had sworn an oath of allegiance.

The intelligentsia

In every country the people who created the greatest difficulties for fascism or the forces of occupation were the intellectuals – writers, artists, members of the liberal professions, teachers, students. This section of the population was clearly the best qualified to expose the fabrications of fascist ideology and the crudity of its propaganda, the most prone to suffer from its intolerance, its dictatorial methods and its disdain of the individual, the best placed to denounce the iniquity of its plans for the future and the mendacity of its slogans.

Goebbels was not stupid, however. He knew only too well how to play upon the writers' and artists' somewhat infantile yearning for adulation, their exhibitionist tendencies and their need to express themselves. He offered them newspapers and magazines in which to write, theatres in which to produce their plays, exhibitions in which their works could be displayed and luxurious trips to Germany when they savoured the sweet smell of admiration. Many succumbed to the temptation and made both a fortune and a reputation, frequently without perceiving the trap which had been set for them. A world-famous French pianist, for instance, never understood why he was ostracised after the war because he had gone to Berlin to play to a uniformed German audience. Abetz, Ribbentrop's Ambassador to France, showed himself particularly persuasive and generous.

In general, however, the writers' world proved difficult to penetrate – more so than that of the artists. Many emigrated to the Anglo-Saxon democracies to recapture some freedom of expression. Others who remained at home decided to preserve an heroic silence, although in some cases the existence of the 'halfway house' régimes, Vichy in particular, led to statements and commitments which their authors – François Mauriac and Paul Claudel, for instance – were later destined to regret bitterly. In still other cases, and not those of minor figures only, their pen became their weapon and they joined in editing clandestine newspapers and magazines; sometimes they were even at odds with their political friends. In February 1941, for instance, Rosenberg arrived in Paris to give a lecture; Politzer, the communist pundit, flayed him, writing in *La Pensée Libre*: 'Under the National-Socialist revolution's régime human relationships have reverted to the barbaric level associated with the darkest period of the

Middle Ages. . . . What is the cultural level of nations deprived of their freedom? . . . According to the racist creed the most frenzied reaction is known as revolution and a policy tending to turn an occupied country into a vassal state is called national'. At the time when this was written the Russo-German honeymoon was at its height and Moscow was frowning on even the slightest attack on Berlin.

Though by nature disinclined to action, some writers joined the underground and there lost their lives – to name Frenchmen only, Marc Bloch, Jacques Decour, Vildé, Cavailles, Benjamin Crémieux and J. Prévost, this last being killed in the Vercors *maquis*.

Moreover, even when committed to guerrilla warfare, the resistance volunteers needed to be told why they were fighting, to be encouraged to persevere, to be given a song as a morale-raiser. In the latter connection the success of the 'Song of the Partisans' was little short of miraculous; it was written in London by J. Kessel and Maurice Druon and set to the music of A. Marty; none of these three had any personal experience of guerrilla warfare yet their song exactly caught its agonising but exhilarating atmosphere.

The liberal professions also produced their resistance. In Norway the German High Commissioner failed to keep his promise to respect the independence of the courts; after an initial protest, therefore, the Supreme Court of Justice refused to carry out its functions and its action was approved by the Bar Council. In Holland, when Seyss-Inquart attempted to impose the nazi system and force all lawyers into corporations, the majority refused, in some cases openly.

Doctors provided evaders of the compulsory labour service with false medical certificates; in the *maquis* they looked after the wounded and in some cases organised rough and ready hospitals and medical services. Doctors in Holland went on strike rather than join the nazi professional organisation.

Teachers carried an even greater responsibility, for they were instructing the young whom fascism was doing its best to woo. Opposition was perhaps more widespread and more violent here than in any other profession. In Norway the teachers, as a body, refused to join the single compulsory corporation set up by Quisling; thirty professors and 1,200 students were arrested in November 1943. Others were banished to the outer islands where conditions were so severe that several of them died. The rector of Oslo University was deported and the student association closed; university life was virtually at an end from September 1941. Brussels University was threatened with closure in August 1940 and was in fact closed in 1941; according to Henri Bernard Louvain University 'refused to be supervised by German universities or to exchange chairs with them'. In Holland both professors and students went on strike in protest against the exclusion of their Jewish counterparts. In April 1944 sixty-six well-known Rumanian intellectuals, mostly university professors, drafted a memorandum demanding that Antonescu democratise education – and put an end to the war against Russia.

In France education was a field in which the Vichy régime failed to play its role of chloroform pad between the occupier and the people, since it opposed a secular university. The Sorbonne professors protested against the establishment of a chair of Jewish anthropology but it was set up against their advice. Students were the first to demonstrate in Paris on 11 November 1940; they caused regular disturbances at nazi propaganda functions such as film shows, lectures, concerts or exhibitions; they formed their own 'movement' and issued a newspaper entitled '*Défense de la France*'; at Montpellier J. Renouvin recruited the first saboteurs in the unoccupied zone from among the student population.

Universities became the guardians of the great human and national values. At Ghent, the stronghold of the Flemish movement, both professors and students refused to compromise their cause by collaborating. Strasbourg University, which had refugeed to Clermont Ferrand, remained a centre of resistance to the German annexation of Alsace until eventually the teaching staff and several students were sent to Auschwitz.

The most striking case was Poland. There the Germans proposed to deprive the nation of any élite. Accordingly they closed Cracow and Warsaw Universities,[1] deporting the teaching staff, and abolished all higher education – Poles were to be given primary education only, as this was thought to be adequate for the German slaves which they were intended to be. The first essential, if the nation was to survive, was to preserve the Polish language and culture. Clandestine universities were set up – that of Warsaw was run by a certain Professor Manteuffel, a Baltic baron by origin.

[1] Poles were expelled from Poznan University which was open to Germans only; the Poles met once more in the clandestine universities.

The university worked in hundreds of different localities; examinations were organised and diplomas issued, drawn up in code and signed by the professors using code-names. Despite the difficulties of access to libraries or laboratories 150 scientific books dealing with all subjects taught were written, printed and distributed; literary, medical, legal and scientific doctoral theses were written – and all this starting in November 1940! In addition valuable articles such as manuscripts, instruments and research dossiers were saved. A new feature of great social significance was that entry to the clandestine universities was free. In Warsaw the law faculty comprised no fewer than 600 students; in fact everything was studied – except German.

Regular officers

The intellectuals played a vital role during the counter-propaganda phase by instilling a sense of obligation to resist; from the time when the Resistance was ready to resort to armed action the military men played no less essential a part, but their participation was productive of much misunderstanding, difficulty and frustration.

The training of an officer, which was very similar in all countries, in no way prepared him for clandestine warfare. He had been brought up in the tradition of the 'respectable' battle, against an enemy basically comparable to himself. He tried to apply traditional methods to revolutionary situations whose true import escaped him and whose apparent disorder annoyed him. He had little understanding of the intrigues and problems stemming from the political context in which he was disinterested – he was making war not on nazi Germany but on the Wehrmacht. If needs must, regular officers would agree to become intelligence agents,[1] but they had no liking for guerrilla warfare – no uniforms, no 'rules of war', a real squaring of accounts in fact, in which one got one's hands dirty. When they were persuaded to participate, they tried to form their men into regular units, thus arousing the suspicion of their subordinates. Alternatively they failed to grasp the rules; being accustomed to think in terms of victory won by a concentration of force superior to that of the enemy, they found it difficult to accept the dispersion essential to the *maquis*, which

[1] One French naval officer agreed to work as an intelligence agent in the occupied zone but not in the unoccupied.

produced the mobility without which guerrilla warfare would have died out. Finally it was unthinkable that these regular officers could ever have turned into rebels or conspirators.

This mentality was not confined to the regular officers of any particular country; it was the same in the British and American armies as in the German and Italian; even the Red Army, although prepared for political struggles, was not immune to a certain mistrust of partisans – one never knew precisely who, where or how many they were, what they were 'cooking' or thinking. This attitude of mind explains the Wehrmacht's submission to Hitler despite frequent conflicts and considerable mutual distrust; the German military were so blindly obedient that they even accepted the independent status of the Waffen-ss – they could not punish an ss man without reference to Himmler. In January 1944 they hardly raised a protest against the appointment of genuine nazi political commissars to every headquarters down to battalion level. Only the catastrophic defeats of summer 1944 led a handful of officers to conspire against the Führer's life.

The position of the Italian Army vis-à-vis fascism was more independent since theoretically its Commander-in-Chief was the King, not the Duce. Despite numerous defeats, however, it remained loyal to the régime until its fall. After this it split; certain generals fought against their former allies and some units joined the Anglo-Americans, but others rallied to the fascist Salo Republic; very few decided to join the partisans.

In the occupied countries the patriotism of officers was admittedly never in question; cases of genuine collaboration were very few indeed. But resumption of the struggle was another matter. Many Dutch officers refused to help the first agents arriving from London, holding that they were committed to observe a sort of neutrality towards the Germans because they had been set free a few weeks after the May 1940 capitulation. Obedience to orders was so deeply ingrained in regular officers that, as prisoners of war, they reacted automatically to German orders; P. Gascar says: 'They disciplined their men and insisted that orders received be carried out without taking account of the fact that they were thereby turning themselves into enemy auxiliaries.'[1]

Nevertheless, in many occupied countries, the soldiers were

[1] *Histoire de la captivité des Français en Allemagne,* Gallimard, Paris 1967. The novel and film, *The Bridge over the River Kwai,* are illustrative of a comparable mentality in a Japanese prisoner of war camp.

among the first resisters. In Czechoslovakia nearly every high-ranking officer joined the 'National Defence' (*Obrada Naroda – on*), the largest clandestine organisation of the war, too large in fact for the security of its members. In Holland certain military groups formed automatically – the *'Orde Dienst'* (Law and Order Service) and the 'Front-line soldiers' Legion'. In Norway resistance was organised and commanded on military lines from the outset; *Milorg* was 20,000–25,000 men strong and commanded by General Ruge, Commander-in-Chief of the regular army. In Belgium regular officers formed the 'Belgian Legion' in 1940; in 1943 this became the 'Army of Belgium' and was recognised as such both by the Belgian government in London and by the British. In Yugoslavia Mihailovich, a regular army colonel, collected certain scattered units and refused to lay down arms. In Greece an organisation of senior officers known as the 'Six Colonels' maintained touch both with the King and the British.

Numerous though these military resisters were, the question remains: What did they do? In Poland their commitment was instantaneous and total, an affirmation of the nation's determination not to die. Elsewhere the officers formed secret armies, their headquarters neatly divided into the traditional four sections were the spit image of regular armies; their purpose, it was said, was to assist the Allies to liberate the country when the time came. Meanwhile they stood by with folded arms. In most countries the occupation police got wind of the movement; they arrested the leaders who were not very adept at adopting the disguises inseparable from a clandestine existence; they broke up the organisation and seized the stocks of weapons – this happened to the Danes, for instance, in August 1943. The military resistance sat on the fence but it paid a high price nevertheless. Sometimes the regular soldiers set themselves the goal of 'maintaining social order' at the same time as liberating the country. For them a mass of men, practically unarmed, without uniforms, without any real discipline and under leaders of their own choosing was tantamount to revolution.[1] The dramatic story of the Armistice Army in France illustrates vividly the inherent unsuitability of professional soldiers for the task with which defeat faced them, to which indeed it called them.

[1] The younger officers were quite capable of adapting themselves to guerrilla warfare but very few did so. See Captain Poitau: *'Guerilla en montagne'* in *Revue d'Histoire de la Deuxième Guerre mondiale,* January 1963.

The Armistice Army

After the armistice the majority of regular French servicemen suffered a particularly agonising crisis of conscience. All their life had been lived in the conviction that Germany was France's 'hereditary enemy'. They had only laid down their arms in face of the Wehrmacht's crushing superiority and they looked forward to a more favourable moment when they might resume the struggle.

The majority, however, succumbed to a perverted sense of discipline which, they had always been taught, formed the backbone of an army. Those who joined Free France did so in most cases before the Vichy régime was firmly established; after this recruitment for de Gaulle's breakaway movement died to a trickle, since it was held to be contrary to the traditional military virtues of respect for authority and senior officers. Inevitably the French regular officer regarded Marshal Pétain and General Weygand, the two most illustrious officers still alive, as his undisputed leaders. Inevitably he would tolerate no criticism of the behaviour of these two great soldiers nor doubt their perspicacity for a moment and this attitude was strengthened by the oath of allegiance sworn to the Marshal. It had always been his duty to obey; now failure to keep his word would be a breach of honour.

The military, moreover, had long been an object of mistrust to the civil power which all too easily conjured up the bogey of 18 Brumaire. Eventually they had come to occupy a position on the fringe of the nation, taking no part in the political battles – they had no vote – and were contemptuous of the parliamentary merry-go-round. In a sense the Vichy régime rehabilitated them and lifted them out of obscurity. It was headed by two great military leaders whose choice the nation had approved through its elected representatives, thereby absolving the army of all responsibility for a defeat which had not been due to any lack of courage or self-sacrifice on its part but which had been made inevitable through the inefficiency of republican governments incapable of preparing for war.

Accordingly, although the officers of the Armistice Army remained anti-German both in heart and mind, the only fighting they did between 1940 and 1943 was against France's allies, the British and Americans, or against their comrades of the 'Free French Forces' – at Dakar, in Syria, in Madagascar, at Casablanca,

Oran and Algiers. The most irretrievably committed were the sailors, among whom the Mers el-Kebir operation had revived a hatred of the British as bitter as in royalist days.

When, therefore, the emergent resistance attempted to equip itself with a secret army, very few regular officers volunteered although its leader, General Delestraint, was one of them. To them the underground conjured up visions of indiscipline and disorder; they found it hard to believe that it would carry any weight in the liberation of France.

Things changed when a properly constituted government was set up on French territory in Algiers under a well-known soldier, General Giraud. Before leaving France he had gathered around him most of the unit commanders of the Armistice Army. When this was disbanded on the entry of the Germans into the southern zone, many of its officers did their best to reach North Africa via Spain in order to join the new French Army which was forming with modern American equipment. In this way they could resume the fight in the manner which suited them, openly and according to the known rules of warfare.

At the same time officers remaining in France formed a clandestine organisation, the 'Army Resistance Organisation' (*Organisation de Resistance de l'Armée* – ORA), which produced one or two *maquis* leaders. In general terms, however, whatever the avenue used for a return to active service, the regular officer's attitude to the rough and ready resistance forces, the 'French Forces of the Interior', remained one of contemptuous distrust.

A certain general says: 'Psychologically the majority of army officers were not at home in clandestine work where it is not clear who is in command and there is no established channel for orders. In their view it was paradoxical that in the vanguard of resistance were to be found those who had previously had little liking for the army and whom the latter accused of being responsible for the disaster of 1940. They observed and deplored the fact that, instead of possessing a proper chain of command, resistance became an affair of committees, in which all sorts of subjects were debated in addition to the national problem of the struggle against the invader.'

On the lower executive level an ORA departmental head noted with sorrow that 'his training as an officer had not prepared him for a war which the enemy was waging in a repulsive manner. This is no battle in the open; this is not war with all that that word implies in the way of honour and nobility. If only we could be sustained in this struggle by certainty that our ideals would be achieved.'

The majority found the methods used in subversive warfare repellent – sabotage of railways, destruction of depots, murder of individual enemy soldiers. Such action, they thought, did not paralyse the German war machine, instead it assisted the Germans by hurting the French, causing inconvenience to the population, rendering it liable to reprisals and rousing public opinion against 'terrorism'.

Nevertheless very many officers did play a part in French Resistance. The number involved before the landings of June 1944 is estimated at 4,000 – out of 32,000 on the active list in 1939 of whom 12,000 became prisoners of war; 1,500 escaped to North Africa; 600 officers and 850 NCOs were deported.

Despite these casualties and their undeniable spirit of patriotism and self-sacrifice, the military were not prepared for clandestine warfare and found it difficult to adapt themselves to its rules, which for them were both novel and unorthodox. Resistance did not, therefore, receive all the help which it might have expected from their knowledge of the profession of arms. In fact the Resistance had to work out its own rules, using its own resources and without the assistance of the technicians of war.

CHAPTER 9

Political Parties, Trade Unions, Churches

The basis of fascism was the single party; other parties were banned and their members imprisoned. Fascism was basically opposed to all associations not under its control, sensing in them potential enemies. Nazism proclaimed a return to a mythical germanic paganism to counter the evil influence of Christianity and judaism. It would have been surprising, therefore, if fascism had not made many political and religious enemies. Many people, however, thought it either opportune or wise to avoid a head-on collision and to temporise. The general confrontation only developed with the passage of time; here again division was initially the rule.

The extreme Right

One of the more surprising phenomena was the apparent transfer of their allegiance on the part of many nationalists to the fascist cause – admittedly this occurred after its initial victories in most cases. One would nevertheless have expected these super-patriots to fight desperately against an avowed enemy of their country's independence. This did, in fact, happen in Poland; there supporters of the old 'colonels' régime' together with genuine fascist groups formed clandestine organisations, published newspapers and set up *maquis* – while all the while protesting their opposition to the Polish government-in-exile and its representatives in the country and without abandoning their basic anti-semitism.

In Poland, however, the Germans had no wish to come to terms with anyone and so they united everyone against them. Elsewhere the occupying power showed itself more accommodating and more adroit. As a result, faced with a complex and explosive situation, no group succeeded in maintaining complete unity, the price of which would have been abdication of their position and agreement on a policy acceptable to all.

In Belgium Van Severen had been the champion of Flemish independence and the union of Flanders with Holland; in 1928 he had said: 'Belgium! To hell with it!' Though his following had definite totalitarian leanings, he began to cut his ties with nazism as soon as the voracity of its appetite became clear – a great 'country of Thiel', yes, but a frontier province of the Reich, no. Van Severen was interned in May 1940 and later executed at Abbeville. His followers turned to resistance, incorporating their 'National Legion' into the Belgian 'Secret Army'.

In France Colonel de La Rocque's 'French Social Party' developed somewhat similarly. De La Rocque had been one of the leaders of the abortive *putsch* of 6 February 1934 and initially he rallied to the Vichy régime, at the same time accusing it of appropriating his own doctrine; he did much to swell the ranks of Vichy's 'Fighting Legion'. A sense of patriotism then drove many of his adherents towards the resistance; Charles Vallin, one of his assistants, made a spectacular departure for London in the company of the socialist, P. Brossolette; de La Rocque himself was deported to Germany. The ex-members of the *Croix de Feu* undoubtedly felt a sense of obligation towards Pétain; this and the mere existence of the Vichy régime led them to accept the equivocal policy of the Marshal, though frequently they did so with no great enthusiasm. Otherwise, being ex-servicemen and basically anti-German, they would undoubtedly have resumed the struggle earlier and in greater numbers.

Turning now to other extreme right-wing groups in France, movements as solidly organised as *Action française* or the *Cagoule* (the secret anti-communist society which had organised assassinations and planned a military *putsch*), were unable to remain united in the face of severe defeat. Some joined the nazis for ideological reasons; others, more numerous, followed Maurras in regarding Pétain as the country's saviour, an uncrowned king who, with his policy of retrenchment and 'reformation' summarised in the slogan 'France alone', would cure the nation of all the ills from which it had suffered since the revolution of 1789. Some of them, however, became pioneers of the resistance; ex-members of the *Camelots du roi*, for instance, were among the founding fathers of *Combat*; *Alliance*, one of the most important intelligence circuits, was formed by ex-cagoulards.

The moderates

Though conservatives were to be found in the Resistance, they came as individuals; there were no real conservative groups. In many countries they had been supporters of fascism before the war – in Germany and Italy, for instance; alternatively they had adhered, with greater or lesser enthusiasm, to the 'halfway house' régimes, parts of whose programme apparently tallied with their own. A particular instance of this was the attitude of Rumanian politicians such as Bratianu and Maniu towards Antonescu; it was held up against them for years. In Italy the traditionalist Right attempted to rally behind the King and Badoglio and was never more than on the fringe of Resistance.

As far as the western democracies were concerned, the Right was represented in the Norwegian, Belgian and Dutch governments-in-exile in London; it also played some part in the 'movements' formed in the occupied countries. The position in France was exceptional; the right-wing parties had never been more than electoral labels or at best headquarters with no genuine organisation in the country. Moreover many moderates opted for the Vichy régime owing to its paternalism, its support from the Church, its doctrine of social harmony and its reliance on the banking and industrial oligarchies. Only a few individuals had the courage to break away from the majority of their group, an example being Louis Marin of the 'Fedération républicaine'. When Vichy degenerated into collaboration, the moderates made some attempt to divorce themselves from it and rally around General Giraud in Algiers. After two-and-a-half years of fence-sitting, therefore, the French Right eventually joined the struggle against Hitler, but only in the forces outside France where a State and an army were being reconstituted. It played hardly any part in the underground, for which it was not fitted and which it continued to fear, not without some reason, as the standard-bearer of social revolution.[1]

As the situation developed, the radicals too tended to be obliterated. They had long been in power and so were under heavy attack as responsible for the country's defeat; certain of their leaders, such as Daladier, were imprisoned, but many more

[1] There were hardly any moderates in the 'National Resistance Council'; two of them were there to show the flag, but they had no backing; there was no representative of the Federation of Employers.

rallied to Vichy; Herriot and Jeanneney, for instance, testified in writing to their confidence in Pétain. Later several, such as Queuille and Mendés-France, departed for London and Paul Bastid represented the party on the 'National Resistance Council'. But all this did not amount to much. The Radicals were little involved in active resistance and, like the Right, emerged from the war much reduced. The resulting vacuum in French politics was the cause of much instability.

In contrast there was one segment of the political spectrum, of only minor importance at the time, which played a considerable role both in France and Italy: the Christian Democrats.[1] Their motives were admittedly political but they were religious as well. To situate and understand their attitude that of the Catholic Church must be analysed first.

The socialists

Before the war socialists had formed an International and it had undoubtedly been a force of some substance; in all countries the socialists had been represented both in the parties and the trade unions and sometimes they had been in power, in Denmark and France for instance. But solidarity was not their strong point. In the first place under the fascist-inclined régimes – Poland, Rumania, Hungary, Yugoslavia – the party was banned and its leaders were either in exile, in prison or at best in cold storage. In the western democracies socialists were divided over the attitude to be adopted towards the fascist dictatorships; they were, of course, unanimously opposed to them but they were torn between their ideology which prescribed firm active opposition, and their inherent pacifism which moved them never to turn down an agreement. The result of this dichotomy of views was the existence of 'tendencies', divergent wings of the party in fact. During the Spanish Civil War this lack of unity had led the French Popular Front government to adopt the so-called 'non-intervention' policy which had had much to do with the republican defeat.

The German, Italian, Austrian and Spanish socialists were in exile, first in France and later in Great Britain and the United States. They could, of course, count on the support of the British

[1] They were also in evidence in Belgium, in the German opposition to Hitler and in Poland, where they adopted the label 'Labour Party'.

Labour Party and certain of the great American Trades Unions, but their following and their impact in their own countries was small. Moreover they were divided; some favoured agreement with the communists; others feared that an Allied victory would benefit only capitalism and bolshevism.

In the occupied countries the attitude of the socialists differed according to the local situation. Socialists were represented in the Czech, Polish, Belgian, Dutch, Norwegian and Free French governments-in-exile in London. In Denmark, where they were in power, convinced that they could do nothing, they counselled passivity tantamount to resigned inactivity. In Poland, on the other hand, where they were well schooled in clandestine action, they profited from the general revolt on the part of the population; they published over seventy newspapers; they announced a programme of nationalisation of production resources, a planned economy, distribution of land to the peasants and establishment of a parliamentary democracy – all ideas which had never been so well publicised before. The Russo-German pact, however, followed by Stalin's hostility to Poland, ruled out any agreement with the communists. Once more the socialists were divided – between WRN (Liberty, equality, independence) and PS (Polish socialists); there was also a Jewish socialist party, the 'Bund'.

The most complicated situation, as usual, was that in France. In Vichy the majority of socialist members of parliament had admittedly opposed the grant of plenary powers to Pétain. Some, of them, however, including Paul Faure, the Secretary-General, subsequently supported the new régime. In the occupied zone others, though admittedly not very many, were such convinced pacifists that paradoxically, with their republican and secular background, they were more opposed to the Vichy régime than to their foreign fascist conqueror, and prepared to accept occupation.

The party was therefore much diminished; it was a target for attack by Vichy. It was accused of responsibility for the defeat and was prosecuted as such at the Riom trial. This was the organisation which Léon Blum, from his prison, tried to reconstitute clandestinely, initially under the deliberately discreet title of 'Socialist Action Committee'; the party itself did not re-form under its proper title until 1943, aping, and at the same time betraying their fear of, the communists. Nevertheless, some leading socialists such as A. Philip, F. Gouin and P. Brossolette joined General de Gaulle in London; others formed resistance movements, mainly in the north, and still others organised intelligence circuits such as 'Brutus' and 'Cohors Asturies'; they were, in fact, the backbone of many of the non-communist resistance groups and later were represented both in the Algiers government and on the 'National Resistance Council'.

In all the occupied countries, therefore, the socialists were a major factor in resistance, but they were the theorists rather than the leaders; with an eye to the post-war period, they attempted to channel it towards a certain programme – their own. Yet although, throughout Europe, they emerged from the struggle strengthened by the part they had played, the socialists never solved the dilemma which had faced them ever since the bolshevik revolution: whether, by combined action, to renew their accord with the communists or whether to place the emphasis on the democratic and liberal aspects of the major reforms which they advocated, thus perpetuating the political division of the working class.

The trade unions

Nowhere in Europe, except in the USSR, had the trades unions achieved solidarity. Though anarchist tendencies had disappeared nearly everywhere except in Spain, the trades unions of western Europe were divided between three main blocks, the communist, the socialist and the Christian. Only a minority of workers, however, belonged to a trades union at all. In central and eastern Europe, where the economy was mainly agricultural, trades unions were weak and banned to boot. In Germany and Italy they had been replaced by State organisations, whose leaders were nominated by 'The Party' and who dutifully played their part in the totalitarian orchestra.

In occupied Europe the victor or his minions attempted to impose unity on the trades unions. In Belgium, for instance, a 'Union of manual and intellectual workers' was formed. In Vichy France under the 'Work Charter' the same arbitrary treatment was meted out both to the trades unions and employers' organisations; they were simply dissolved, leaving only officially inspired unions in each firm or works. The question was whether to accept these travesties of a trade union in order to preserve some small possibility of defending the workers' interests or whether to refuse them. Some trade union leaders opted for the first alternative; one of them, R. Belin of the post office workers, even became a Minister in the Vichy government.

The first sign of trades union resistance was their rejection of the strait-jacket of official trade unionism despite the attractive offers sometimes coupled with it. The occupier clearly had two purposes in mind – to make claims by the workers impossible and integrate the mass of the labour force into his war effort. Being opposed on principle in this way, many of the more militant trade union leaders issued pamphlets explaining their position and then formed groups to resist this state of affairs. The trades unions were therefore the originators of movements in France such as *Libération-Nord* and *Libération-Sud*. In Poland the 'Association of Polish trade-unionists' published some ten newspapers. An organisation entitled *Raclawice* spoke for urban workers originating from the country.

Later, assisted by the revival of the political parties, the trades union leadership re-established itself underground. Faced with a common enemy, old quarrels were set aside and agreements were concluded between socialists and Catholics on the one hand and socialists and communists on the other; in France, for instance, the CGT [*Confedération générale du Travail* – General Confederation of Labour] was reconstituted. The situation also forced the trade union leaders to abandon their policy of confining action strictly to the defence of the workers' interests; they realised that national liberation must precede any claims for social betterment. In Belgium, Norway, Denmark and Holland, therefore, they participated in attempts to create a clandestine state; in France both the CGT and the CFTC [*Confedération française de Travailleurs chrétiens* – French Confederation of Christian workers] were later represented on the National Resistance Council, the Departmental Liberation Committees and the Consultative Assembly.

Trade union resistance activity, therefore, became part of the action of the underground as a whole. Under communist influence for the most part, it assumed certain specific forms in places of work such as factories, offices or goods-yards. By 'infiltrating' the official unions or through the clandestine unions it became closely associated with demands for an improvement in living conditions and with the sabotage of production for the benefit of the occupying power. It formed the bridge between professional grievances and patriotic motives. Through the trade unions, even more than through the 'left-wing' political parties resistance came to be angled in two directions, that of popular mass action and demand for a new social order. In this both the Christian trade unionists and Christian democrats were naturally much influenced by the attitude of the Catholic Church in general and the Pope in particular.

Position of the Catholic Church

The least that can be said is that Pius xii did not lay down any clear line of conduct for the priesthood, or for Catholics in general. Admittedly the Pope refused to associate himself with the anti-bolshevist crusade. He made numerous démarches to improve the lot of Catholics in Poland and the Vatican became an asylum for victims of occupation; most explicit papal bulls were issued condemning the nazi neo-paganism and these were broadcast in paraphrase by the 'Voice of the Vatican'.

On the other hand the Papacy was linked by concordats to the German State and, reaching even further back in history, to the Italian. These, particularly the latter, accorded it a privileged position, the counterpart of which was implicit acceptance of the totalitarian régimes; the Pope could therefore hardly condemn them root and branch.[1] Lastly the stubborn silence of the Vatican, well-informed though it was, in face of the terrible fate meted out by the nazis to the Jews was a source of sorrow to some and scandal to others; in any case it was at the time a sign of indecision hardly calculated to clarify the conscience. Under these conditions the national church leaders turned their attention to their churches rather than their countries. They rendered unto Caesar most of what was due to him – and left the faithful to their own devices.

In Germany, moreover, certain bishops resolutely professed faith in nazism; Mgr Groeber was nicknamed the 'brown-shirted Archbishop of Freiburg im Breisgau'; Bishop Hudal even tried to prove the important contribution made by catholicism to the nazi ideology. Other bishops, however, Cardinal Faulhaber and Bishop von Galen for instance, condemned the nazi racist neo-paganism from the pulpit – 'the adulation of a mortal man, the contempt for the sanctity of life, the violation of basic rights';

On 31 December 1939 Pius xii awarded a 'golden spur' to Count Ciano 'as a a reward for his services in the cause of peace'.

they proscribed the nazi bible, Rosenberg's 'Myth of the Twentieth Century'. Many priests denounced anti-semitic measures or euthanasia for 'unproductive citizens'. Several hundreds of them met in Dachau concentration camp. Nevertheless, condemnation was confined strictly to the religious level. Having given forth their criticisms, the bishops, the aristocrats of the Wilhelmian era, would pray for 'the German people and its Führer'; they ended their letters to Göring with the 'German greeting'; they remained silent about the Russo-German pact; at no time did they urge disobedience.[1] German Catholics who refused to serve the régime had to make the decision in the secrecy of their own consciences; far from supporting them, the episcopal hierarchy disowned them by its silence; one prison chaplain even refused the sacrament to a conscientious objector because he regarded refusal to bear arms as tantamount to a dereliction of a Christian's civic duty.

In Italy the priesthood, taking its cue from the Pope who, after all, was an Italian citizen, made no distinction between the cause of Italy and that of fascism; in Northern Italy there were some, such as Cardinal Schuster in Milan, who acknowledged the legitimacy of Mussolini's authority and the Republic of Salo to the very end. Nevertheless, 'in a spirit of evangelism' many priests tried to mediate between the warring Italian factions in order to save the population from excessive hardship. The attitude of the lower-level clergy, who were in closer touch with the people, differed from that of the bishops; in Northern Italy it became increasingly favourable to the partisans; there were chaplains in the *maquis*, even in the communist 'Garibaldi' units. This was the origin of the 'Peppone – Don Camillo' legend.

In Croatia, now independent, Pavelic decided to 'convert' the orthodox Serb minority to catholicism. He sent peremptory letters to the bishops. The methods used ranged from intimidation to massacre. Yet Archbishop Stepinac rejoiced over this 'progress of Christianity'; the Archbishop of Sarajevo wrote a poem in honour of Pavelic; Franciscan friars participated in killings and ran concentration camps. The Roman curia, with the exception of Cardinal Tisserant, showed itself favourably inclined to the 'Ustashi State'. The Pope received Pavelic with the honours due to a Head of State.

The Catholic Church in Croatia, therefore, reverted to the

[1] In Poland the German bishops were zealous agents of the germanisation and nazification of the annexed territories.

methods of the Albigensian crusade; nowhere else was the priesthood so extreme in its acceptance and approval of the established régime. Neither did the Church resist the less outrageous temptations offered it by régimes claiming to be defenders of 'Christian civilisation' – Vichy for instance. In France the Catholic Church, long the supporter of the monarchy, had rallied to the Republic slowly and without great enthusiasm. The long-standing quarrel over schools, with the Church demanding complete jurisdiction over those under its control and the Ministry of Education trying to ensure a monopoly for secular schools, had aroused passions never really pacified.

As a result of these quarrels the senior clergy saw the Third Republic disappear with no great regrets. Not only did they recognise the successor régime as a matter of course, but very soon they were giving it their full support. The persecution of the freemasons, subsidies to private schools, plans for religious instruction in schools, the importance attributed to family life and morals in the social ideas of the new State, the respect shown for religion by the Head of State – all this created an atmosphere of 'moral good order' which the bishops found highly satisfactory. One of them even went so far as to render unto Caesar more than his due, proclaiming that 'Pétain is France and France is Pétain'.[1] Although they did not actually collaborate, the dignitaries of the Church became one of the pillars of the Vichy régime – the Fighting Legion [*Legion des Combattants*] which volunteered for the anti-bolshevist crusade, took a bishop with them as their chaplain. Gradually, however, the Church's hostility to nazi paganism became more marked. Several bishops protested against the treatment meted out to the Jews by the Germans and by the Vichy régime also. The fact remains, that, when General de Gaulle entered Paris in triumph, the Paris resistance ruled out a welcome on the steps of the cathedral by the reigning archbishop because of the latter's previous attitude. Cardinal Suhard was not the only bishop to be regarded with well-merited distrust.

In fact the 'condemnations' of the occupying power voiced by bishops were contained in veiled muted messages characterised by extreme caution. Not until 15 March 1943 did Cardinal Liénart

---

[1] Conversely in the overseas territories which joined General de Gaulle, Saint-Pierre-et-Miquelon or Gabon for instance, the bishop was opposed to Free France. Things only changed with the establishment of the French Committee of National Liberation in Algiers.

openly proclaim that obedience to the compulsory labour service call-up was not part of a Christian's duty – 'it may be evaded without sin'. At the same time, however, in the Church's name the bishop advised young Christians to 'share in the common trial'. So what were they to do – stay or go?

Nevertheless, in France too, the country priests were in closer touch with the average Frenchman than their superiors. In the Eure department M. Baudot counted a number of parish priests who were resolutely hostile to the Germans and 'all parishes received a letter, carrying the bishop's forged signature, ordering the reading from the pulpit of the cardinals' message condemning the compulsory labour service'. In Savoy some priests joined the *maquis*.

In Belgium, says M. Lejeune, 'the Church officially ignored the Germans. On the other hand if any of its rights were infringed, it protested with the utmost vehemence'. Unofficially it warned Catholics against the doctrines and parties of the 'New Order'. It waged a resolute struggle against Rexism and the VNV [*Vlaams national Verbond* – Flemish nationalists] Cardinal Van Roey made no secret of his disapproval of the *Pays réel*[1] policy. At Bouchout on Whit Sunday 1941 a priest named Wouters refused communion to a group of young Flemish nationalists who arrived at the altar in uniform. Two years later Degrelle the Rexist leader took violent action against the Dean of Bouillon who refused him communion because he attended dressed as a German officer. At a sign from Degrelle his bodyguard seized the priest and threw him out of the church. After this scandal Degrelle was excommunicated by Cardinal Van Roey himself, who announced the fact at a meeting attended by all Brussels clergy.

When the regulations for the compulsory labour service were published the Cardinal reiterated his protest and demanded the withdrawal of the measure. 'These measures requisitioning human beings,' he proclaimed from the pulpit, 'are totally unjustifiable; they are a violation of natural law, international and Christian morality. They take account of nothing, neither of the basic dignity and freedom of the human being . . . nor of the welfare and self-respect of families . . . nor of the overriding interests of Society.'

This attitude was clear and courageous, but the Cardinal's strictures were directed less at the Germans than at their minions.

[1] A publication produced by Degrelle.

Catholics in the Resistance

The shepherds, therefore, gave no clear indication to their flock of the path they should take. Yet in all countries many Catholics committed themselves to the Resistance. Not in Germany, however. Admittedly some Catholics preferred exile or arranged to serve in the Wehrmacht's auxiliary services. After prolonged research, however, G. Zahn could only discover seven Catholic conscientious objectors and six of these were Austrians. Seeing that Catholics in Germany numbered over thirty million, of whom fifteen million were of military age, the effect on the nazi Reich of a refusal to follow the Führer into an unjust war would have been considerable. The 'Kreisau Circle', however, which admittedly did no more than plan, and the small students group known as 'White Rose' did distribute anti-nazi pamphlets with a Catholic background.

In Italy, although the Christian democrats did not go all the way with the communists and socialists, many of them came out against fascism. They must, therefore, be counted among the parties which controlled resistance and they had their place in its co-ordinating organisations. But they would have no part nor lot in the revolution preached by their fellow-resisters; they remained loyal to the monarchy. They did agree, however, that the dispute between the Vatican and the Italian State should be settled once and for all; they no longer questioned democracy and liberalism; they adopted them. Even so they could not quite bring themselves to accept a secular state; even when liberated from fascism Italy was to remain to a large extent permeated by Catholicism. As a result of this attitude of moderation the Christian democrats fought somewhat halfheartedly and, primarily in the Mezzogiorno, the party became the refuge for much of the Italian Right with fascist leanings.

In France between the wars a democratic and social trend had developed among Catholics; though still a minority view, it was on the increase; it carried the torch of *Sillon*.[1] Though condemned by the Pope, it was 'swimming with the tide of history'. Even though certain orders such as the Dominicans and the Franciscans, tended to favour it, the movement's leaders were secular and at loggerheads with their priesthood. A representative of 'Young Republic' became a Popular Front Minister; among this section

[1] Mari Sangnier's publication which marked the birth of social Catholicism.

of opinion the right-wing revolt had been immediately condemned. Through the resistance this trend grew and was consolidated. Following the dictates of their conscience as Christians, for instance, the founders of 'Christian Witness' decided to 'draw up their battle lines against Hitler. Spiritually it is our duty to resist and to organise resistance to nazism'. They argued that national-socialism was animated by an anti-Christian mystique in face of which no Christian could remain neutral. They protested against anti-semitic action, whether inspired by Berlin or Vichy, and against the annexation of Alsace, a subject on which the French government preserved a discreet silence.

Consequently French Catholics fought in *Libération*, in *Combat* and in the CFTC; they were responsible for the more important Jewish rescue operations; they were represented on the National Resistance Council; some, such as Georges Bidault, joined hands with communists in the 'National Front'. In no other country, apparently, did Catholics play so great a part in the Resistance. As a result, on liberation, the small democrat-popular group in parliament turned into the great political party, the MRP [*Mouvement républicain populaire* – Popular Republican Movement] the true force of which was somewhat obscured by moderate elements which streamed into it regarding it as the lesser of two evils.

The other Persuasions

In Germany and Holland Catholics and protestants frequently co-operated because the Evangelical Church's episcopate was fairly closely linked to that of the Catholic Church. The protestants, however, seem to have been more outspoken in their criticism. Bishop Wurm, for instance, had the courage to proclaim that 'the Allied air raids were Heaven's punishment for the crimes committed against our Jewish brethren'.[1] In Norway Bergrav, the primate, was a determined opponent of Quisling's nazi party, the Nasjonal Samling; all seven Norwegian bishops protested against the excesses of the Hird, the collaborationist Storm Troops, and for the guidance of the faithful they reiterated their condemnation in a pastoral letter; they even urged their flock not to attend services conducted by the few priests who had joined the Nasjonal Samling.

[1] Henri Bernard, op. cit., p. 61.

The protestant opposition was greatly encouraged by the pronouncements of Karl Barth, the celebrated theologian of Basle University; after the defeat of France he stated that 'under no circumstances could the Church conclude peace or an armistice with Hitler'. In Belgium the Federation of Protestant Churches registered a protest against the compulsory labour service with General von Falkenhausen, the German military commander. In France protestants were less eager than Catholics to support the Vichy régime; their past history of persecution had ingrained the habit of non-conformism more deeply in them than in the Catholics; they were extremely active in circles where they were numerous, such as the teaching and liberal professions.

Thanks to the policy of national union inaugurated by Stalin in the USSR the orthodox church achieved a sort of international renaissance. Russian patriarchs from Moscow harangued the Bulgars, Serbs and Greeks, the first being the most receptive. In Greece the orthodox church attempted to mediate between the rival royalist and communist factions, for whom ruthless internecine struggles were taking precedence over resistance to the forces of occupation. Damaskinos, the patriarch, who had been instrumental in many escapes, was therefore accepted as regent by the majority of public opinion pending decision on the question of the King.[1]

The attitude of Moslems in the Middle East was governed by their desire to see the disappearance of the Jewish national home in Palestine in accordance with their repeated demands to the British. The defeat of France aroused major hopes among Arab nationalists, not only in North Africa but even in Egypt and Iraq. Their protagonists, led by the Mufti of Jerusalem, looked upon Great Britain, France and Italy as the main colonial powers and therefore backed a nazi victory – little realising that, had it happened, the Arabs would have been subjected to the servitude reserved for inferior peoples by the 'Aryans'. In pursuit of this astonishing misconception Moslem legions were raised in Bosnia and from Russian prisoners originating from Azerbaijan and Turkestan; 'volunteers' were even accepted into Himmler's Waffen-ss, the guardian of 'racial purity'; this was not the only ideological deviation, however, to which the nazi leaders were reduced as they saw defeat approaching. Concentrated though this propaganda was, it did not prevent many Moslems from

[1] The rabbinate will be dealt with in the section devoted to the Jews.

French North Africa enlisting in the new French army; they did not, however, play any part in the Resistance despite the fact that certain Moslems were sent to concentration camps.

Freemasonry

The freemasons formed another international community; as a result the same accusation of corrupting society was hurled at them by the nazis as at the Jews, the marxists or the 'plutocrat democracies'. In France freemasonry was accused, particularly by *Action française* of being the real power behind the throne and exerting an evil influence for certain dark purposes in furtherance of cliques, personal ambitions and business interests. In fact, although a whole body of highly-coloured literature emphasising the symbolism of the masonic ritual, had drawn a picture of a mysterious and disquieting force for the general public, the freemasons were divided between differing and rival allegiances; varying shades of political opinion were represented among them and they were far from possessing either the solidarity or resources ascribed to them in current legend.

Little is known of their wartime doings in France, and even less elsewhere. One thing is certain – there were many shortcomings; a Grand Master wrote an abject letter of submission to Pétain; an ex-'brother' became a Vichy minister; others followed dark paths of collaboration. Singling out one department of France only, Baudot has listed a number of these surprising 'about-turns' – 'the Jewish mayor of a small town in the department, very well thought of in liberal circles pretended to disown his past and so escaped the concentration camp and the gas chamber; a dignitary of the "Grand Orient" lodge came to terms with the supporters of the New Order so as to evade government measures against active members of secret societies; the Chairman of a Chamber of Commerce, known for his freemason affiliations, obtained a vote of confidence in the Marshal from his Chamber as early as 19 November 1940'.[1]

Throughout occupied Europe or wherever collaborators were in control, however, there was no further place for freemasonry; the lodges were disbanded, their possessions confiscated and their records seized. Freemasons were banned from public office and

[1] Baudot: *L'Opinion publique sous l'occupation.*

became the target for a systematic campaign of vilification expos-
ing them to public disapproval. They thus became one of the
victims of the 'New European Order'. In general they recovered
quickly and launched themselves into active opposition; in this
they were assisted by their habit of secrecy and their numerous
links with all circles of society. Freemasons were therefore to be
found in all resistance groups of all types in France and it may be
assumed that the same applied throughout western Europe. In
some instances, having discovered 'brothers' among the civil or
military personnel of the occupation forces, the freemasons made
good use of them – to extract information or demoralise the enemy.
Moreover the lodges continued to function underground, with a
simplified form of induction; in some places new lodges were
apparently set up. The number of freemasons interned, tortured,
shot or deported was high.

Resistance, therefore, drew its recruits from every ideological
grouping; their religious and political convictions were diverse
in the extreme. In their common distress they forgot what divided
them and became increasingly aware of what united them. Fruit-
ful links were thereby forged. Meanwhile what were the captives
in the oflags, stalags, concentration camps and ghettos doing –
what could they do?

CHAPTER 10

The Captive Societies

In Hitler's Europe the victims of nazism were numbered in millions. They included prisoners of war, wretchedly treated and ground into the Reich's war economy; conscripts of the compulsory labour service who, though admittedly better protected, were forced to work far from their homes; inmates of concentration camps, huddled together under the most ghastly conditions and destined to die of malnutrition; Jews, herded into ghettos pending extermination in chain-belt slaughter-houses or scientifically designed gas chambers; populations annexed to Germany without their consent, humiliated and ground down as inferiors, if not slaves. These millions of human beings, both men and women, certainly had no love for the nazis. What could they do against them? What did they actually do?

Prisoners of war

The Wehrmacht had captured between seven and eight million enemy soldiers, mostly Russians, French, Poles, Yugoslavs, Belgians and, from September 1943, Italians. All these prisoners were men in their prime, ex-servicemen, enemies of the Germans. All were longing to return home and their common tribulations ought, one would have thought, to have instilled into them a hatred of their gaolers and led to continued well-nigh irresistible resistance.

It was not quite as simple as that. In the first place, once their battle was over, although still in uniform these men mentally reverted to civilians with differing points of view; their appearance of solidarity was superficial only. More important still, they felt themselves beaten, disarmed and disorientated. In many cases their resilience was gone. As J. M. D'Hoop writes: 'They took more than a few days to recover from the shock they had suffered. In the course of a few weeks the majority had been hurled from barrack life into battle and thence through retreat into captivity; they were short of food and sleep; they were incapable of initiative or sustained effort. Moreover, faced with the Germans, whose might had just submerged them, many were paralysed by a sort of mixture of fear and admiration.'[1]

The prisoners of war were on a slippery slope: impotence bred an attitude of resignation which led all too easily to neutrality, if not of semi-collaboration extremely well analysed by P. Gascar: 'Was defence of the prisoners' short-term interests invariably compatible with a policy of systematic opposition to the Germans? The word "systematic" is important: under all circumstances nazi Germany remained the enemy. The German object, however, was to disarm opposition by certain concessions in matters of food, comfort, working conditions, freedom of movement, freedom of worship and entertainment. In their struggle for security and well-being, were the prisoners not in danger of drifting into actual collaboration? In many camps they formed a police force – in Stalag IA, for instance, there were ninety amateur French policemen. Undoubtedly these kept order more fairly than the Germans would have done, but they relieved the Germans of this duty, thus making them available for other military assignments and so, to a degree, became auxiliaries of the Wehrmacht. The rank-and-file prisoner never received an order from a German soldier. Orders were given him by Frenchmen without reference to the camp authorities. This was a dangerous game. It is useless to pretend to be free and independent when one is in fact in slavery. In an attempt to safeguard his dignity, the Frenchman runs the risk of turning into the model prisoner. One of the tragedies of captivity is that it forces Frenchmen and Germans to live cheek by jowl. If forced to live together people are inclined to look for a compromise, a modus vivendi. Of their own volition the prisoners in the Oflags and Stalags maintain and create no serious difficulties for the Germans. This is a counsel of impotence.'[2]

The unhappy prisoners were not only cut off from their country and their families and starved of news, but were also subjected to incessant propaganda. How should they refuse to work for the Germans when their country's government, under an illustrious

[1] J. M. D'Hoop: 'Les Evasions' in Revue d'Histoire de la Deuxième Guerre mondiale, January 1957.
[2] P. Gascar: Histoire de la captivité des Français en Allemagne, Gallimard, Paris 1967.

soldier, told them that it was their national duty to do so in the name of 'collaboration'? Moreover, obedience and 'good conduct' were rewarded by early release. From the fortress of Koenigstein, where he was incarcerated with nearly 200 other French generals, General Giraud commented regretfully: 'The majority were resigned; most of them were dumbfounded by a defeat which they had never even contemplated before 1940. All had brilliant first world war careers. The blitz and brutality of modern war based on tanks and aircraft had disorientated them. Now captivity was weighing hard on them, but they were far more inclined to try and obtain a release for health reasons than to face the risks of attempting to escape.'[1]

Finally, for many of the prisoners of war was the German really the enemy? The Flemings, the coloured troops from the French and British empires and certain nationalities of the USSR had been dragged into a conflict which, after all, was not theirs. When the Wehrmacht invaded the USSR or the Germans took measures against the Jews, how could the anti-communists and anti-semites in the Oflags and Stalags fail to be pleased? German propaganda was adept at sowing the seeds of division; after all General Vlassov raised a veritable army to fight the bolshevist régime and his men came from the Soviet prisoners of war, even from the actual Russians among them.

In short opinion in the prisoner of war camps differed little from that in the occupied countries; the vast majority was inert, passive and acquiescent; a minority opted for collaboration but there was also a minority of 'irreconcilables'; for their benefit the punishment camps of Lübeck, Colditz or Rava-Russka were opened. What forms did their opposition take?

The first method consisted of demonstrating, even parading, a basic attitude of hostility; when a German officer visited a camp, for instance, everyone vanished in order to avoid saluting him; other morale-raisers were facetious gestures such as a sardonic salute to a German with a broom-handle or an umbrella; noisy demonstrations took place when news of a German defeat arrived; symbolic parades were organised for national festivals – on 14 July 1942 thousands of men in Rava-Russka marched past a French flag hoisted on some improvised flagstaff singing 'You shall not have Alsace-Lorraine'.

Such actions may seem somewhat puerile and ineffective but at

[1] General Giraud: *Mes Evasions,* Julliard, Paris 1946.

least they raised the morale of those involved in them and also of those who knew about them; moreover they were severely punished. Other actions in contravention of camp rules, though apparently equally ineffective, had a much more definite purpose. When, for instance, the arrival of a parcel containing forbidden articles was announced, a whole team would co-operate to exchange it for another innocuous parcel; in Colditz parts for four radio receivers were smuggled in in this way and all officers involved gave their word of honour never to disclose their existence, even should they be released.

A genuine clandestine existence requiring a minimum of regrouping was built up inside the camps: news was listened to and then spread by word of mouth, pamphlet or even clandestine newspapers; false papers were prepared; an intelligence service, and even a counter-espionage service, was set up to discover friends and eliminate enemies; contact was established with the outside world. The clearest evidence of this attitude and of the newly-formed 'hard core' lay in its solidarity; French cadets, who were confined in a special camp unanimously refused to allow special treatment to be meted out to the Jews among them; in Rava-Russka prisoners employed in the German offices tore up the papers of the few Jewish prisoners and substituted those of men dead or escaped.

This passive resistance culminated in a refusal to work for the Germans; this was proof of rejection of all propaganda and 'brainwashing'. Under the Geneva Convention officers and NCO's were not compelled to work, but the resulting material advantages proved to be a bait which some were unable to resist; moreover the collaborator governments, Vichy in particular, urged them to turn themselves into 'free workers', which in fact meant only partially free.

The rank and file could not evade work but they used every ruse to do as little as possible. Russian prisoners were particularly good at moving with robot-like deliberation as if on a slow-motion film. This go-slow was sometimes accompanied by more spectacular acts of sabotage. These were, of course, as Gascar says, often impossible – 'when prisoners were employed on the vital parts of some machine such as the engine or steering of a vehicle, the electrical fittings of an aircraft, the safety system in a ship or submarine, etc., their work was always carefully checked by the Germans, using mechanical controls. In other

6*

cases, even if sabotage were successful on one occasion, it could not be repeated since the Germans immediately took measures to stop it. Major acts of sabotage were therefore rare – in all the five years of war only some 3 to 4 per cent of the offences committed by French prisoners were brought before German tribunals.

'Some sabotage demanded considerable courage. In a certain foundry the French used to throw lumps of lead into a mass of boiling metal. They discovered that, if these lumps were first dipped in freezing water, a violent reaction took place when they struck the boiling mass. Frequently the force of this sort of explosion was sufficient to crack the oven. Whenever they were unattended the prisoners arranged that this should happen. Several of them were burnt by splashes of boiling metal. In a certain aircraft factory prisoners threw quantities of explosive rivets down the drains.'[1]

The attempt to escape, however, constituted the prisoner's real method of resistance and for this purpose miracles of ingenuity were performed. Underground tunnels were dug, identities were exchanged on departure of a detachment, barbed wire fences were cut, prisoners admitted to hospital with non-existent ailments, disguises of all sorts used, double-bottomed trucks employed as hiding places, holes bored in railway wagons during a journey; prisoners concealed themselves in refuse carts, let themselves down from windows by ropes of knotted sheets, escaped through the sewers, in beer barrels, etc.

Sometimes escapes were opposed by the camp's 'prisoner authorities'; one French colonel, for instance, drew up a note stating that 'escape was an egoistic act'. Those left behind did in fact have to endure reprisals, but in most cases escapes were occasions for demonstrations of solidarity and for deception of the camp guards, all of which amounted to acts of genuine resistance. Moreover, they necessitated the formation of teams for the manufacture of false papers, photographs, assembly of stocks of clothing and theft of essential tools. Sometimes they were organised by genuine little offices; in one Oflag, for instance, the Belgians set up a finance office, a tool shop, a section producing compasses and keys, a team for concealing articles in parcels, a system of camouflaging the absence of escapers at roll-calls, 'specialists' in false papers and genuine rubber stamps, an observation service, map-makers and craftsmen in all professions.

[1] Gascar, op. cit., pp. 192–3.

The number of attempts at escape rose continually – in the case of the French from 16,000 in 1941 to 33,000 in 1943, in other words from 1 to 2.9 per cent of all prisoners. What happened to the escapers? Many reached some neutral country – Sweden, Switzerland and, until 1944, Hungary; the majority placidly awaited the end of the war. Others, however, were determined to fight once more; Captain Billotte, for instance, led a party of French escapers from a camp in Poland into the USSR; there they were interned at first but eventually managed to rejoin Free France in London. Another party, hunted out of occupied Hungary, took part in the fighting in Slovakia. General Okecki counted 240 French prisoners fighting with the Polish Resistance. Slovak, Rumanian and Hungarian prisoners of war were the Red Army's source of recruitment for the agents it despatched to these countries as cadres for the partisans.

Nevertheless, although acts of resistance on the part of prisoners of war were innumerable, they were the result of individual initiative rather than of any genuine organisation. Only on rare occasions were links established with the clandestine resistance in any country, although *Défense de la France* had a line into an Oflag where the prisoners clubbed together to help distribution of the clandestine newspaper in France. The Allies did not perhaps make the most of this immense Trojan Horse made up of the millions of men held prisoner in Hitler's Reich.

Conscripts of the compulsory labour service

Only a small proportion of the workers from all over occupied Europe arriving in Germany were volunteers; some were deceived by the nazi propaganda and by operations of the 'relief of prisoners of war' type thought up by Laval, under which two healthy young men were sent to work in Germany in exchange for one aged or sick French prisoner of war; others were lured to Germany by the high wages. The majority, however, had been forced to leave their countries when Sauckel was commissioned to plug the holes left in German factories by the mobilisation of their workmen; complete villages of Ukrainians, Russians or Poles were 'displaced'; many only arrived after having failed to evade and they were, of course, potential recalcitrants.

Millions of foreigners, both male and female – the French alone numbered 600,000 in 1944 – were therefore living in Germany; the majority were young and of working class origin. Admittedly they were not always to be pitied; they drew wages, they were decently housed, they could send money home, they enjoyed a certain freedom of movement and they were allowed 'leave'. Nevertheless, cut off from home, many felt angry and resentful; Allied air raids with their resulting casualties made the anticipated advantages seem illusory and the Germans did not have many friends among the compulsory labour service conscripts.

But apart from their common fate, the conscripts had no unifying bond; in fact they were a real Tower of Babel. Those from eastern Europe had to rely upon themselves, since there was no longer any national authority in their countries; the Italians were similarly cut off after September 1943. The French, on the other hand, were regimented by the Vichy régime which urged them to maintain order and discipline and to work. In any case all these people were civilians, unarmed and disorientated by their ignorance of the German language and of Germany; they became lost souls, carried along on the eddies of the German defeat.

Nevertheless, it seems that they frequently showed hostility to their employers, to judge from the number of them consigned to concentration camps – several thousands of Frenchmen alone were treated in this way. The reasons were sabotage of production and, even more often, relations with German women. No balance sheet has been drawn up for this mass of small-time actions; they represented a trend rather than resistance; many will never be known. All that we know comes from the beneficiaries – certain gestures of sympathy and solidarity towards prisoners of war and inmates of concentration camps. It does not amount to much.

Yet these 'worker conscripts'[1] were to be found everywhere, for they were free to travel anywhere in the Reich; they could have sabotaged the entire German war production – agriculture, mines, workshops; and what a mass of information they could have collected! But they were never organised, directed or utilised. Only the communists, apparently, had the idea of infiltrating a few of their own people into the departing contingents;[2] German communists distributed pamphlets to the French which

---

[1] As is only right, the word *déporté* will be applied only to inmates of concentration camps.

[2] Pajetta: *Douce France,* Editori Riuniti, Rome 1956.

were mere calls to bolshevisation. In general the resistance movements did their best to dissuade the conscripts from leaving; this done, they devoted their efforts to assisting the evaders. As far as the Allies are concerned, even including the British and Russians, everything goes to show that they never realised the immense potential force at their disposal. Perhaps they were taken by surprise; perhaps it seemed too great or too dangerous an undertaking in view of the anarchy which it might have spread throughout the Reich, or perhaps they did not have the time. The compulsory labour service did not become a major factor until 1943.

Whatever the reason, no more use was made of the opportunity than in the case of the prisoners of war.

Resistance in the concentration camps

To what extent can one refer to resistance in the concentration camps and what did it consist of? The majority of concentration camp inmates were determined opponents of the nazi régime; the camps had been opened for Germans who had tried to oppose its rise to power, primarily communists and socialists; later Resistance prisoners were sent to them. By their very nature, therefore, the concentration camps were permanent centres of hostility to nazi Germany.

The inmates had generally first been imprisoned or interned in their own countries, making their solidarity greater; they had learnt to hold their tongues, to be on their guard and to help each other; many had already tried to escape. So clandestine organisations edited news bulletins; conversations and lectures helped to maintain morale; links with the outside world still existed. Sometimes revolts broke out, such as that at Eysses which was brutally suppressed by the Militia. The concentration camp inmates were proven fighters; sometimes they had been deported as a group, but in any case there was never any lack of recognition between them.

Nevertheless, their task was not eased by the nazis' planning, location and organisation of these camps. In the first place the resisters were intermingled with the other inmates who were not their former comrades but hostages, victims of manhunts or people deported by mistake; in Dachau one day the French resisters were astounded to hear French voices singing 'Marshal, here we are'; they were products of an outsize manhunt and were merely hoping to prove the purity of their intentions and absence of any animosity towards the Germans. Fellow-prisoners such as these were not only a deadweight but could easily turn into enemies or stool-pigeons. Even worse was the calculating way in which the nazis had introduced common criminals into the camps – thieves, anti-socials, sexual maniacs, even murderers; they were given junior posts of authority and allowed to impose their own jungle law, so that the ss might be left in peace and quiet.

The ss were adept at exacerbating divisions among the inmates which were already deep for other reasons – differences of language (twenty-two nations were represented), social and professional background, political or religious beliefs; the obstacles to mutual understanding, to co-ordination or co-operation were numerous and formidable. Such time as the prisoners were allowed and such energy and fighting spirit as remained to them were fully taken up with the difficulties of their ghastly daily existence; for them everything constituted a problem. The hunger which gnawed at them, the blows which rained down on them and the hard labour to which they were subjected led to incessant rivalries and internecine struggles.

What, then, could concentration camp prisoners do? The camps in which they were huddled were far from any habitation and the prisoners lived in a vacuum. They could never really be alone; they ate, slept, washed and did their daily duty together, under each other's eyes; no hiding place was secure; hostile ears might be listening to any conversation. They were weaker, more emaciated and more helpless than the prisoners of war; they received neither letters nor parcels. They were a natural prey to despair and accordingly the number of what concentration camp jargon called 'moslems' increased – living skeletons who had ceased to strive, dead in spirit though not in fact.

Under these conditions it is little short of miraculous that any organisation existed and any anti-nazi action took place in the camps; in any case it could not be of great importance or really effective. Nevertheless certain groups did emerge from the chaos; their genesis is described by Poliakov as follows: 'When one shares one's morsel of bread with a friend – and the normal man can barely imagine how difficult this is when one is hungry oneself – the foundations are laid for resistance to the determination of the ss to produce a situation described by a camp commander as follows: in Auschwitz a prisoner who does not "organise himself" cannot live more than three to four months. The seeds of resistance are old friendships, identity of beliefs and national affinities. The first task of these little groups is to ensure the survival of their members, in so far as this is possible in Auschwitz.'[1]

The inmates of the camps manifested their resistance by refusal to acquiesce to the divisions systematically fostered by the ss. The meagre morsels were shared; the skills of some were employed to serve others, manufacture of little articles, for instance, or repairs to clothing; the sick were cared for; by substituting names on the lists the weak were directed to working parties where the work was less strenuous.

But, if they were to help each other in these ways the prisoners had to infiltrate themselves into the machinery of camp administration. As a result a silent struggle developed, particularly in Buchenwald, between the 'politicals' (the reds) and the common law criminals (the greens). The communists, who had the longest experience of these camps and who had representatives of all nationalities, were the first to organise themselves and they became the natural leaders of the 'reds'. The most urgent problem was to place reliable anti-fascists in most of the jobs open to prisoners – hospital, secretariat, cookhouses, etc. In this way a number of lives might be saved.

It was indeed difficult to do more. Links with the outside world were to all intents and purposes impossible in Germany; there the population was extremely hostile to concentration camp prisoners since they had been proclaimed as the Reich's worst enemies. In Poland things were easier; the Auschwitz prisoners, for instance, managed to contact the local resistance groups and smuggle out photographs of the camp which were then sent to London. As a result the BBC was able to relay stories of the abominable crimes perpetrated in the camps, accompanied by threats to the torturers. Cyrankiewicz, the socialist who headed the Auschwitz 'organisation', was appointed to his post in proper form by decree from the Polish government in London; it arrived concealed in a pencil.

Nevertheless, in the nature of things genuine acts of resistance which did actual harm to the Germans and assisted the Allies, were very few. Escapes could be counted on the fingers of both

[1] L. Poliakov: *Auschwitz*, Julliard, Paris 1964, p. 220.

hands.[1] When prisoners were employed on working parties in the mines or factories, they were able to sabotage production, but at enormous risk and taking the strictest precautions.

Kogon says:[2] 'Direct sabotage, such as damage to machinery or weapons, was possible only in isolated instances. Generally speaking, sabotage had to assume forms that were hard to recognise. The primary possibility was manpower utilisation. Naturally the prisoners preferred to assign skilled workers only to plants that were not directly concerned with arms production. The latter were sent mainly unskilled help. The German civilian foremen and engineers in charge of production were poor in technique and organisation, since they were almost without exception regular nazis. They often had to depend on their prisoner experts. As a result it was possible to conduct a comprehensive programme of sabotage by means of faulty planning and building, delays in procuring machinery, tools and materials, fostering internal jurisdictional disputes, applying official regulations and test standards to the letter and similar methods.'

Under these circumstances the fact that concentration camp prisoners could contemplate armed action and prepare themselves for it in such conditions constituted real resistance. Yet in Dachau, Auschwitz, Buchenwald and Mauthausen 'international committees' were set up under communist leadership; they included all nationalities and all shades of anti-fascist opinion. The fittest men were armed with the few revolvers, rifles or grenades stolen or concealed from the ss and were formed into small combat groups. In the first place they were to fight if the guards decided to exterminate the prisoners; then they were to contact any Allied troops or parachute detachments which might reach the area; finally they were to disarm and neutralise the ss in order to accelerate the camp's liberation. These plans were never implemented owing to the disintegration of nazi Germany and the flight of the ss; they did, however, enable the prisoners to administer their camps themselves on liberation.

---

[1] In Mauthausen several hundred Soviet officers attacked the ss, broke through the electrified barbed wire and disappeared into the countryside with casualties not exceeding double figures; almost all were recaptured. See De Bouard: 'Mauthausen' in *Revue d'Histoire de la Deuxième Guerre mondiale*, July–September 1947.
[2] Eugen Kogen: *The Theory and Practice of Hell*, Secker & Warburg, London 1950, pp. 243–4.

Jewish resistance

Jews accounted for a high proportion of the concentration camp population; the death camps had been opened specially for them; their situation was much like that of other concentration camp prisoners. Since they were the nazis' selected victims, the nazi scape-goat, how could they fail to be enemies of nazism or to behave as such? But for a number of reasons, mostly rooted in the past, the Jews were not predisposed to fight. Non-religious persecution had been endemic and had taught them the value of turning the other cheek, of ostensible submission, of the waiting game. The nazis had been adepts at arousing hatred of Jews, fanning jealousies and instigating denunciations; more than any other people, Jewish resisters felt themselves cruelly alone in their struggle. Finally they too had their own authorities in their communities whose duty it was to speak for them; this was the 'Judenrath' or Jewish Council which was supposed to represent the Jews vis-à-vis the occupying power; naturally it did its best to alleviate the misfortunes of its co-religionists but by its very functions it set an example of co-operation with the enemy.

More than all the other victims or enemies of nazism, therefore, the Jews had good reason to sit on the fence, to put themselves in the hands of their God and to place their hopes in the hereafter without attaching too much importance to the length of their existence in this hell on earth, this valley of tears. In fact hundreds of thousands of Jews allowed themselves to be torn unprotestingly from their work and their homes, stripped of their possessions and taken they knew not where; finally they climbed docilely and apparently without fear into the trucks which took them to the door of the simulated 'bath-houses'; when, to their horror, they discovered the fearful truth that they were in a gas chamber, it was too late either to escape or to sell their lives dear.

In the concentration camps it was practically impossible for a Jew to occupy any of the main administrative posts open to prisoners, such as camp leader, block leader or 'kapo' [prisoner in charge of a working party]; they were accepted only as lowly employees in offices or workshops or as maids-of-all-work in the latrines or huts. It was to the advantage of the other prisoners, who were better off, to leave to the Jews the monopoly of the

toughest assignments. Despite their relative homogeneity, therefore, it was more difficult for the Jews than for any other group
to organise themselves.

In addition Jews were moved into certain areas, even into
certain defined quarters of a city. This made their enemies' task
much easier whether it was to keep track of them, to number
them, to exploit them or to exterminate them. In eastern Europe
the nazis began by compelling Jews who had left the ghettos to
return to them; they invariably gave out that this would have no
serious consequences; despite crowding, lack of hygiene and the
difficulty of finding a decent living, the Jews, they said, would be
returning to their own environment; this would give them a false
sense of protection and security – like a return to their mother's
womb.

Nevertheless, in all countries many Jews were to be found in the
Resistance. In France, for instance, they were to be seen at every
demonstration, in every region and at every moment when resistance showed itself. There were Jews in General de Gaulle's
entourage in London, among the non-Gaullist French emigrés in
Britain and the United States, in intelligence, escape and sabotage
circuits, in resistance movements both in the occupied and unoccupied zones, in the first cells of the communist party's 'special
organisation' and among the supporters of the socialist party, in
all stages of production of the clandestine press, in the *maquis* –
the Vercors particularly – in the French Forces of the Interior and
in the Liberation Committees.

Frenchmen of Jewish faith or nationality were to be found as
leading spirits in the resistance, organisers of parachute drops or
maritime operations, heads of circuits, Free French agents in
occupied France or commanders of *maquis*. The much-publicised
and effective *putsch* in Algiers on 8 November 1942 was conducted
by a few hundred volunteers, the majority of whom were Algerian
Jews. It is difficult, if not impossible, to support one's conclusions
by figures or percentages, but one would seem to be near the
truth or at least in the area of probability in stating that, if the
component elements of Resistance be considered from the religious or ethnic angles, the Jews made the greatest contribution of
anybody in proportion to their numbers among the population
as a whole.

Nevertheless, the question remains whether this *action by Jews
within the Resistance* can properly be called *Jewish resistance*. It

would seem that in western Europe there was no such thing; except for those who had recently fled as refugees from Germany the majority of Jews were completely assimilated and had no desire to be any different from their fellow-countrymen; many were no longer practising Jews. In the Resistance, therefore, the behaviour of the Jews in no way differed from that of other Frenchmen, Belgians or Dutchmen. Probably, however, the anti-Jewish measures stirred their sense of nationhood – many Israelis had never been zionists. Apart from certain demonstrations of solidarity there was no specifically Jewish organisation, but the destiny in which all shared lay at the root of the rebirth of a Jewish national entity.

In eastern Europe this entity already existed; there the Jewish population was both numerically and proportionately greater and they had retained a basic individuality in language, dress and customs. Here resistance was specifically Jewish, particularly where whole communities revolted. Such revolts were numerous; they took place in at least eight camps and in most of the ghettos – Cracow, Bialystock, Czestochowa, Tarnow and Lodz. The most important of all, of course, was that of Warsaw; there in April 1943, after several months of fighting, the Germans had to bring tanks and armoured cars into action and blow up whole blocks of houses to drive the Jews from their bunkers; on 15 May the ss General Stroop finally registered his satisfaction, saying that 'The Jewish quarter has ceased to exist'; earlier he had congratulated his men on their 'indefatigable enthusiasm'.

Naturally such damage as the Jews could do to their enemy bore no relation to the immensity of the suffering he inflicted on them – a few thousand Jewish resisters on the one hand and victims in millions on the other. To be precise, Jewish resistance was the outcome of despair; it was doomed to failure from the outset since it lacked all the conditions necessary to an enduring resistance which could grow and on occasions be victorious. In all countries the clandestine resistance was only one aspect of national resistance; the other, into which it had to dovetail, was the resistance outside the country concerned. During the war, however, there was no Jewish state or Jewish army to help those who fought in the ghettos; moreover, even at the height of the nazi era, the Jewish settlers in Palestine continued to regard the British as their enemies because of the obstacles they had placed in the way of expansion of the 'National Home' to avoid displeasing the Arabs. As far as the Allies were concerned, they refused to aid the Jews as such; they would give assistance to Poles or Frenchmen, but not to some mythical Jewish nation; they missed many opportunities of saving groups of Jews from genocide. The ghetto revolts had no alternative but to die in the flames of the fires lit by their adversaries.

Moreover, one of the rules of guerrilla warfare is that, if it is to be effective and to have some prospect of continuance, it must have space. A ghetto was certainly a fortress, a 'strong point', but it was also a prison; no relieving column would try to break through from outside; the garrison's inexorable fate was extermination; from the outset they were paralysed by what might be termed an 'Alesia complex'.

One solution was to escape from the ghetto and answer the 'call of the forest'; in Lithuania, Poland and the Ukraine many did this and formed groups of Jewish partisans. But as a result their relatives remaining in the ghetto were the target for severe reprisals; moreover, it meant exchanging collective segregation for individual isolation. The Jewish partisans could not count upon any assistance from professional soldiers, agents from outside or a political or professional organisation; worse still, as eastern Europe was basically anti-semitic, they were without informers, guides, medical care, hide-outs and food; sometimes they were victims of denunciation which the Germans expected and rewarded – on occasions denunciation even came from other resistance groups which had remained anti-semitic.

It is, therefore, right to refer to Jewish resistance, even though it remained on the fringe of the overall conflict and had no links with the remainder of European resistance or with the Allies. With great skill the nazis had driven the Jewish people into a position of weakness in which it could do no other than tear itself to pieces in the first place and then go under. Jewish resistance wrote one more magnificent page of history to prove the fighting qualities of the Jewish race and its will to live.

CHAPTER 11

The Communists

Of all the forces in the Resistance the communist party is at once the most distinctive and the most difficult to study. No other party executed such changes of attitude in conformity with the course of the war; it swung from neutrality towards nazi Germany to the most savage struggle against her. The historian is confronted with three obstacles, if not three riddles. In the first place he does not know what directives the communists received from Moscow; yet it is certain that the party remained faithful to the USSR throughout. Secondly he does not know what discussions went on inside the directing agencies, what cabals were formed or what scores paid off; the veil is only partially lifted on these, *a posteriori*, by expulsions, demotions and promotions. Viewed from the outside, the party invariably presents itself as a monolithic bloc. Finally the communists regard history as a library of arguments in favour of their policy; they emphasise the version of events which they consider most favourable to their purposes of the moment. Consequently they are frequently inclined to assert rather than prove and sometimes, come hell or high water, to uphold indefensible theses, quoting supporting 'documents' in evidence, even though they may have to make an about-turn later. In particular the part the communists played in the Resistance has enabled them to establish themselves in undisputed power in the people's democracies; they accordingly magnify their own resistance role while minimising or disregarding that of their erstwhile partners.

The Russo-German pact

The Russo-German pact posed a dramatic problem to the communists of Europe. It was concluded by Stalin and Molotov without consulting the international party leaders or even the

Russian communists. Surprise was such that certain French communists treated the news as a propaganda manoeuvre by Goebbels. Ever since 1935 the USSR, with the entire international party machine behind her, had been the most resolute opponent of nazism; she had been the main source of arms and volunteers for the republican side in Spain; she had formally condemned the 'shameful' Munich agreement which had handed Czechoslovakia over to the Hitlerite ogre and yet had not preserved the peace. Now, all of a sudden, the communists were expected to denounce a war between the democratic states of France and Great Britain on the one hand and nazi Germany on the other as a clash of rival imperialist forces, something of no concern to the peoples since the Soviet Union had no desire to become involved in it.

The Russo-German pact probably had no serious repercussions in Hungary, Rumania, Bulgaria or even Yugoslavia where the communists were weak at the time. In Italy it did not reduce their hostility to fascism but it did impede co-operation with other anti-fascists. In Poland and Czechoslovakia, however, the pact divorced the communists from the rest of the nation for a time; in Poland the USSR became an enemy equal to Germany in the eyes of the emergent resistance. The German communists were reduced to silence.

The drama was at its most acute in France. There the communists were torn between their duty to their country and loyalty to their ideology; the rigidity of Stalinist monolithic theory left them no room for manoeuvre. Having first voted the war estimates, the party leaders reluctantly conformed, but certain of the leading lights such as Gabriel Peri were not convinced; the rank and file were nonplussed and evaded the issue; many militants broke with the party with a flourish; many more left it on tiptoe. Through its press, now clandestine, the party machine issued calls to defeatism and disobedience; their effect is difficult to estimate but it was probably small; the causes of the French disaster lie elsewhere. The fact remains that, at one of the gravest moments in its history, the French people was divided; the edge of the anti-nazi sword was blunted.

With the collapse of the French army another period opened; the steps taken by the Danish, Dutch, Belgian and French parties were so similar that one cannot avoid concluding that they were acting on directives from Moscow. They demanded a sort of legalisation of the party by the occupying power, release of their militants who had been imprisoned and the right to publish their newspapers; in Belgium local newspapers censored by the Germans did in fact appear in Antwerp and Brussels over a period of two months and a communist publishing firm was functioning in Brussels until June 1941. In France permission to publish was given for a time and then withdrawn; militants were arrested by the French police.[1]

The tentative steps towards collaboration were therefore halted. The party press did continue to preach 'fraternisation' with German soldiers, referring to them as 'workers in uniform'; it reminded people that only the communists had opposed the war; it launched continuous attacks on 'The City of London' and the 'henchmen of plutocracy', coupling Benès with de Gaulle.[2] At the same time, however, as anti-communist action intensified, they reacted against the 'halfway house' régimes whom they held responsible – Hacha in Czechoslovakia and the Vichy régime in France – labelling them 'bandits' and 'minions of the foreigner'. To defend the distributors of its press the French communist party formed security teams, the 'special organisation'.

The party machine clung to the official line in blind docile obedience to Moscow, but it was neither approved nor followed by many of the militants who probably neither knew nor understood it very well. In France individual communists joined the early resistance groups despite the fact that *L'Humanité* had characterised the first acts of sabotage as 'provocations'.

The communists of the USSR

Their precise role is difficult to estimate, since communist propaganda is all-powerful and governs their interpretation of history; it credits the party with every virtue and deliberately passes over the setbacks which are laid at the door of 'deviationism'; there were always enough men beaten in the struggle for power, such as Beria, to serve as scapegoats. Nevertheless, it is clear that the role of the party was of fundamental importance; it is equally

[1] According to certain renegades from the party such as Auguste Lecoeur, the leaders had deliberately ordered the party to work in broad daylight – 'on the café pavements' – to demonstrate that it was the only political force in existence in France at the time.

[2] In Czechoslovakia the party press denounced Benès as 'mud in the aristocrat morass'.

clear that it was closely bound up with personal action by Stalin.

In any case a distinction must be made between those areas of the USSR untouched by invasion and those occupied by the Wehrmacht. In the former the Soviet state was still in existence and the communist party was its backbone; party members, with their affiliated organisations such as the Komsomols and Kolkhozes, regimented the entire population in the interests of the war effort and the battle itself; they spurred the people on, they called for increased arms production, they reviled the enemy and they denounced the halfheartedness of some and the weaknesses of others. To defeat the invader a broad base was needed for national unity; officers imprisoned during the 'purges' were released, even though their background was 'Czarist'; condemnation of past 'obscurantism' became muted, and national heroes were placed on a pedestal – Alexander Nevsky, Ivan the Terrible, the celebrated Einstein, Peter the Great, Kutusov, Suvorov. This was no longer the bolshevik régime fighting to preserve the power it had conquered, as in the civil war; this was eternal Russia, embodied by the Soviets, fighting to safeguard her independence, to preserve her unity and reconquer her temporarily lost provinces.

In short Stalin formed a 'national front' in the USSR. The invader with his armed forces and his ideology was the common enemy. All must combine to defend the country, the national heritage, and safeguard the future – communists in the lead, but also workers, peasants, the intelligentsia, even the Orthodox Church and yesterday's criminals such as the former kulaks. The party, of course, kept its hand firmly on the levers of power but greater latitude was allowed to the Red Army, the administration, public opinion and the scientists, provided that all contributed to the common effort.

In time such a concentration of energy was bound to have its effect in the occupied areas, but not immediately. In the early days, whether as a result of the military debacle or the nazi policy of liquidating political commissars and bolshevik leaders, the party was disorganised, if not destroyed; all of a sudden the people had lost their familiar leaders, rigid though they were; without them they were at a loss. Groups were apparently formed spontaneously on the initiative of 'non-party' men, whom subsequent propaganda adroitly acclaimed as citizens who had felt the call to become courageous party members. But in the vast occupied areas, apart from 'Radio Moscow', all links with the legal authorities were severed. Stalin's directives hardly penetrated and in any case they lacked precision, except for the 'scorched earth' orders which the inhabitants could hardly bring themselves to implement.

The best recruiting agents for the Resistance were the savagery of the ss, the ineptitude of the occupying régime and the severity of the economic exploitation. For the party the problem was to reorganise itself and infiltrate back into the occupied areas, then to re-establish control over the underground and the 'wildcat forces', groups of soldiers who had evaded capture and retained a proportion of their weapons. As early as 1942 agents were parachuted in; several thousands landed in the Ukraine. The managers of collectivised undertakings, which the Germans had left intact for their own purposes, became the natural leaders for clandestine action; veterans of the civil war assumed leadership in the clandestine war.

As the Red Army's resistance stiffened and turned into victory after Stalingrad, the party became stronger, more sure of itself and more influential. In late 1942 Stalin summoned to Moscow a number of the new leaders who had asserted their personality during the struggle and whom he wished to bring under control once more. From 1943 the party was in a position to return to its normal methods of local meetings at which propaganda and political instruction went hand in hand with weapon training and the handling of explosives. A second phase began later when the Red Army took control of guerrilla activities and integrated them into its own strategic operations.

In the ussr, therefore, Stalin and the communist party demonstrated how to subordinate all objectives and activities to the patriotic struggle. They showed how it was possible to move from neutrality vis-à-vis the Germans to all-out warfare against them. Their teaching was that communists, without in any way abandoning their revolutionary calling, could and should become leaders in the battle for the liberation of the country by allying themselves with all whose aim was similar. Throughout occupied Europe, throughout the entire world in fact, the communists heard the call and understood the example given; they answered the call and were inspired by the example.

The communists and the USSR

In the main communists of all countries faithfully obeyed the orders from Moscow transmitted by their leaders who had taken refuge there.[1] The only exceptions were those who had left the party after the Russo-German pact, the more forceful of whom became such violent anti-communists that they even collaborated with the occupying powers.

When Stalin decreed the abolition of the Comintern, several of the older militants could not suppress some note of regret or bitterness but they all conformed. Togliatti alone, faithful to the teachings of Gramsci and apparently far ahead of the others in his thinking, seized the opportunity to forcast a polycentrism which Stalin was in no mood to consider. In fact throughout the war communists patiently accepted orders given them by Moscow and carried them out to the letter, with only a few exceptions. Throughout occupied Europe, therefore, a communist clandestine warfare strategy came into being, the prototype of which the USSR had produced on her own territory.

In the communist press the USSR was no longer held up as the country of peace; it now showed the way to war and the road to liberation. It was, of course, still praised to the skies as the only true democracy – 'all power belongs to the workers' – the 'home of socialism and science', the land of prosperity thanks to collec- tivisation and a planned economy, the people's paradise 'where unemployment does not exist and misery has disappeared'. Stalin, its 'leader genius', also led 'the workers of all countries'; in addition he became the unparalleled strategist, the implacable enemy of nazism, the rock on which the Wehrmacht would founder. In all countries the columns of the party's clandestine press were full of his orders of the day, his proclamations, accounts of his services and catalogues of his accomplishments.

The war forced on the USSR was now no longer an imperialist struggle. 'It is a holy war for the freedom and dignity of man . . . the peoples of the USSR are fired by the same passion as the de-

---

[1] Pieck and Ulbricht from Germany, Togliatti from Italy, Vlakhovich from Monte- negro, Dolores Ibarrubi (*La Passionaria*) from Spain, Thorez and Marty from France, Friedrich from Austria, Bierut from Poland, Rakosi from Hungary, Kuusinen from Finland, Gottwald from Czechoslovokia, Anna Pauker from Rumania, Dimitrov from Bulgaria, etc.

fenders of Valmy, by Saint Justs' vision of bliss.' The USSR was strong because 'the Red Army is closely linked to the people, the factories, the schools and the collective farms'. Moreover, the war would not arrest social progress – 'though the home of socialism knows how to defend itself, it continues to pursue its ideal, always greater well-being for the people'.[1]

The Red Army, naturally, was extolled to high heaven – 'its morale is perfect, its contempt for death complete . . . discipline is strict but freely accepted, promotion is based solely on merit . . . for months it has carried the weight of the war alone'. Every action by the USSR was approved. So as not to alarm anyone it was said that, although in a socialist economy trusts had been abolished, 'private property, the reward of work, was not only allowed and secured but was flourishing'. It was impossible to deny that marxism was atheist, 'but the constitution of the USSR guarantees religious freedom'. As a matter of course 'the USSR has no territorial claims vis-à-vis other nations, great or small . . . the Soviet government has proved yet once more its respect for the right of nations to run their own affairs'. When the mass graves of Polish officers were discovered at Katyn, the communists had not a moment's doubt that the nazis were to blame and they denounced 'the campaign of anti-Soviet calumny'.

British and American communists were among the first to reaffirm their 'unconditional loyalty' to the USSR; after June 1941 they vied with each other in calls to national unity and attempts to raise the warlike ardour of their fellow-countrymen. British communists were loud in their condemnation of the Indian nationalist leaders who refused to grasp the fact that this was no time for the struggle against British imperialism. They demanded to be accepted into the trade unions and it was the labour leaders themselves who found this sudden conversion unconvincing and refused to have them. American communist workers became champions of increased arms production and opposed all strikes which might affect it; Thomas, the socialist leader who showed his approval of them, was branded as an agent of Hitler. Communists had played their part in the 'America first' neutrality campaign and in this connection had been the prime movers of the 'American peace mobilisation' movement; keeping the same

[1] These quotations come from the French communist party's clandestine press – see the author's *Courants de pensée de la Résistance*, Presses Universitaires de France, Paris 1963, pp. 589–98.

initials, they now turned this into 'American People's Mobilisation' – total mobilisation for war.

Communists in all countries were clearly happy not to have to choose between their material home and their spiritual home. All were now actuated by the same motives and under the same leadership; in all the occupied countries, therefore, they followed the same clandestine warfare strategy, aiming towards broad-based unity, continuous bellicosity in the short term and 'mass action' to further simultaneously the material interests of the workers and the liberation of the country. The most far-reaching steps in this direction were taken by the USSR and the German communists when they formed the Free Germany Committee.

The Free Germany Committee

In various agencies the British and Americans made some use of anti-nazi refugees; whenever, on the other hand, there were indications of some secret approach by them to nazi emissaries, Stalin cried treason. This did not prevent him attempting a bold experiment with German national communism; for this he assembled a number of heterogeneous and apparently irreconcilable ingredients – long-standing German communists who had been away from their country for ten years and a number of Wehrmacht officers, some of whom had previously been heavily implicated in nazism.

This development originated in the ineffectiveness of German communists in their own country which the Russians could not deny. It was, therefore, necessary to turn to other quarters which might make more impact. The Stalingrad prisoners were subjected to concentrated propaganda pointing out that the Führer had incautiously committed them and then abandoned them to their fate; then, in July 1943, the 'National Free Germany Committee' was formed. Its president was Weinert, the author, and it included communists, kept discreetly in the background, and a number of officers including a descendant of Bismarck. The Committee called upon the German people and the Wehrmacht to overthrow the Hitler dictatorship and sap their own country's war potential by acts of sabotage and assassinations. It produced its own newspaper, *Freies Deutschland*, which was distributed in the German prisoner-of-war camps; it spoke to the German people through Radio Moscow and despatched representatives to the Red Army to be near the front. It is difficult to estimate what actual effect all this had; desertions from the Wehrmacht owing to war weariness were already numerous and the Gestapo retaliated with multiple arrests. No revolt of any sort occurred.

Then in September 1943 a sort of replica of the Germans' 'Vlassov's Army' appeared; this was the 'Officers League' formed by six generals who had served under Paulus; it was eventually joined by the Field Marshal himself, obviously a recruit of some importance. The Committee continued to address itself to the mass of the German people; the League, on the other hand, called upon the senior officers of the Wehrmacht to overthrow Hitler, pointing out that his madness was leading Germany to ruin. Its success was meagre; efforts to canvass for recruits in the German prisoner-of-war camps were generally met with hostility and contempt; propaganda behind the German lines had little effect, even on units which were surrounded. The attempted assassination of Hitler on 20 July 1944, however, seemed to show that this astounding initiative was justified. Some fifty generals joined the League at once and Paulus exhorted the Wehrmacht to make a further attempt to rid itself of Hitler.

The extent of the reprisals against the families of the 20 July conspirators and those of the members of the League doused the latter's enthusiasm. The Russians weighed up the pros and cons of this setback and concluded that nazi Germany was not going to produce a General Yorck or sign a new Treaty of Tilsit. From this they drew their lesson; as they approached Germany they withdrew the German generals from the front, leaving only proven communists to contact the German people in liaison with the Red Army. A split thereupon developed in the League; nevertheless two generals agreed to take marxist courses of instruction and so the cadres which later were to become the German Democratic Republic were formed.

The ultimate outcome of this experiment was failure. Had Stalin made an error of psychology in trying to mix oil and water? Clearly the German generals' main fear was that, after defeat, Germany might relapse into permanent disorder; we know little of the promises by which the Russians sought to convince them, in particular what were the proposed frontiers of Germany after defeat – a question certainly of major importance to the generals. Stalin and the communists obviously had other plans; in their eyes the German generals were no more than a means to an end, a sort of lever which they would throw away as soon as it ceased to be useful or became embarrassing.

Looked at overall, therefore, the resistance strategy perfected by the USSR and the communist parties produced the expected advantages. It reintegrated the communists into the nation, it enabled them to infiltrate into the directing agencies of the Resistance, it produced a notable increase in the prestige of the party and the number of its supporters. In the USSR the bolshevik party became the accepted heir of the line of great Russian statesmen-builders.

In three countries, however, Stalin was unable to do what he wanted or was forced to employ other methods at greater risk and with less success. These were Yugoslavia, Greece and Poland. We shall be reverting to them later.

This study of 'component forces' has shown what a heterogeneous assortment went to make up the Resistance. In fact many resisters, perhaps the majority, certainly most of the younger ones, belonged to no group or had broken with their group when they first took clandestine action. The ranks of the 'Shadow Army' were swelled by individual recruits rather than commitment by specific groupings. The Resistance rank-and-file consisted of 'all comers', of the 'average man' who considered that for his own private reasons, probably different in each case, he ought, for the sake of his country and his own sake, resume the fight against the occupier. What was still to be decided – and the problem was of capital importance – was the form the battle would take. At the outset no one could have told.

Note

The *Comité d'Histoire de la Deuxième Guerre mondiale* [Historical Committee on the second world war] is working on figures of Frenchmen deported to nazi concentration camps. From the Paris area 21,517 have been traced and there is reason to think that this is well below the truth owing to the high proportion of Jews which it includes. Of this total 6,290, or three-tenths, were women.

Naturally all these deportees were not resisters; the exact number of resisters is still unclear since many did not divulge their real activity

when arrested; similarly in the case of 7,315 person, their profession
at the time of arrest is unknown.

It is nevertheless of interest to have an order of magnitude of the
social and professional categories represented in the concentration
camps. Of the 14,280 whose type of activity has been discovered, nearly
6,000 were craftsmen or traders (a figure to be explained by the high
proportion of Jews), 615 belonged to the liberal professions, some
thousand were executives, 2,160 employees and 3,160 workers. One is
given to think that the 7,315 of 'no established activity' were women
or young people – nearly 2,000 were less than twenty years of age.

The list obviously includes no farmers, miners, foresters or fishermen since they did not exist in the Paris area; they are to be found in
the figures for other departments. Although the study is not yet complete, it is clear that *all categories of Frenchmen, both by class and profession,
were represented in the Resistance,* the highest percentages being those of
the 'executive' and 'intelligentsia' classes.

Women in the Resistance

So far no precise statistical study has been made for any country of the part played in the Resistance by the various social classes and professions and it is doubtful whether this could be done; in any case it would not take account of the role played by women since the majority of those who worked in the underground were young girls or housewives without a definite profession. The men had gone – as prisoners of war, compulsory labour service conscripts, in the *maquis* or with the partisans – and so the woman was often running the home; the difficulties of day to day existence increased her problems. Perhaps these new responsibilities brought a deeper understanding of the nature of the occupation. In any case the fact remains that women played an important role in the underground.

Although few women actually controlled movements or circuits, they were to be found at all levels and in all positions in the resistance. Many were arrested, some were tortured, many were sent to concentration camps – in Birkenau a special section was reserved for women and a complete women's camp was opened in Ravensbrück.

In eastern Europe, where women were tougher, they actually took part in fighting with the partisans, and not merely as auxiliaries; primarily in Yugoslavia, they were to be seen in the firing line. In western Europe they played a more normally feminine role. They assisted in the printing and distribution of the clandestine press, housed resisters and acted as secretaries for circuits. A girl was the moving spirit behind the Belgian escape line *Comète*; 'escapers' were convoyed to the Pyrenees primarily by women – they were adept at smiling their way past some suspicious guard. The British parachuted fifty-three women into France and fourteen of them were killed; female militants, communist, socialist and trade unionist, gave their lives for their beliefs. The nurses in the Vercors caves were mown down by machine-guns like the wounded they were tending; in *Défense de la France* female students were as courageous as their male counterparts; some women were even to be found in the 'sharpshooter groups'.

Women were particularly suitable, however, for carrying messages, transmitting orders and warning those threatened; they were efficient liaison officers. Karski, the Pole, describes the role they played and the risks they ran as follows:

'Nobody, not even my own liaison officer, was allowed to know my surname nor the details of the false papers which I carried in my pocket. This being so, it was practically impossible for members of the resistance to communicate with each other. The problem was solved by the women who manned the liaison service. If I wished to contact a political leader whose cover-name and address I did not know, I got in touch with his liaison officer.

'The women who acted as liaison officers, however, were very much in the open. A liaison officer's apartment was frequently placed at the disposal of the resistance. She must never be lost sight of; she had to live somewhere where she could easily be found and she could change neither her name nor her address without permission. So long as she was acting as a liaison officer, she could not look for somewhere else to go or she would have severed the contacts between the members and the various branches of the resistance. The female liaison officer and her apartment were always kept under careful watch by a special "observation" service.

'She was, therefore, in permanent danger. Many people inevitably knew every detail of her life – and in clandestine work that was bad. She almost invariably had compromising papers on her. Her comings and goings were calculated to arouse suspicion and she had to be present in many dangerous places. The average "life" of a female liaison officer was no more than a few months. They were inevitably caught by the Gestapo and in most cases treated with bestial cruelty in the nazi prisons. Among all the resisters their task was the most demanding, their sacrifices the greatest and their work the least recognised. They were overloaded with work and doomed from the start.'[1]

For tactical reasons the communists allotted another role to women; they became the instigators of demonstrations. They were expected to demand increases in the ration, to protest against the compulsory labour service and to press for the return of

---

[1] Karski, op. cit., p. 266.

7

prisoners of war. By these means they could assist in sabotaging production and encourage their men to initiate actual fighting; naturally they ran great risks in the process. The part women played in the resistance was undoubtedly an important factor in their post-war social advance and emancipation.

PART IV

Hundredfold Battle

Armed clandestine warfare only took shape with the entry into the resistance of the communists, who possessed very precise ideas on the subject and well-tried methods. Before that the resisters were divided over the type of operation they should carry out in each case. Even well-constructed plans had to await the necessary resources and seize a favourable moment. The people paid a high price for the clandestine action which was trying to liberate them; before initiating anything it was necessary to weigh the pros and cons with care and be sure that the price was not too high in relation to the anticipated results. In the case of the resisters themselves an incautious step, a miscalculation, lack of self-control and technique might lead to arrest, the torture chamber and the firing squad.

The resistance struggle was waged in diverse and overlapping forms. I do not propose to attempt to deal with them in strict chronological order; in most cases all the methods were in use at the same time. In general terms, each member of the resistance graduated from one form to the other as circumstances dictated. The simplest and easiest way of opposing the occupier was to behave as if he did not exist, to pretend not to understand his orders, to think out ways of carrying them out badly, to serve the occupier as little as possible and in the way most costly to him, but without allowing him to perceive that the object was to do him damage; in this way the resister could not be accused of more than incompetence, ill-will or negligence.

A stage was reached when actual acts of sabotage were committed against the German war machine and a further stage when enemy soldiers or their friends were assassinated. This spectacular action was taken as deliberate provocation, and brought severe punishment with it – fines, penalties, seizure of hostages, imprisonments, shootings. As a body the Resistance arrived at this solution only after much discussion and argument.

Another method, one that was very much of a gamble, was to attempt to reverse the situation to the advantage of resistance by seizing power, the *putsch* or conspiracy. The most important example of this was the attempt to assassinate Hitler in July 1944.

Whatever tactics he used or whatever enemy he confronted, the resister was condemned to live disguised, alone, hunted, often misunderstood. He faced enemy police forces who were both brutal and clever. The fate which awaited him was as certain as it was frightful. His days were numbered. He was on the road to his Calvary.

CHAPTER 12

Passive and Administrative Resistance

The occupying powers were faced with the dilemma of assertion of their authority and assuring of their peace and quiet. They should have placed no confidence in the occupied peoples and left them no powers, but they did not possess a sufficient number of qualified officials to administer the whole of Europe. Moreover, as Hitler explained to Mussolini in Munich on 17 June 1940 in regard to France, orders and instructions issued to the vanquished direct by the victors would appear more vexatious and be carried out with less good grace than those received through the channel of their own fellow-countrymen. The occupier was, therefore, compelled to let the occupied peoples carry out their own administration with the proviso that he would keep it under close surveillance, punish any shortcomings, change those in positions of responsibility from time to time and be prepared to intervene if necessary.

Examples of administrative resistance

The occupied could always take advantage of the low density of occupation – there could not be a soldier behind every inhabitant; they could also profit from the occupier's ignorance of their language, local customs and technical problems to delay completion of orders, conceal required articles and exaggerate the difficulties of carrying out an order. Doctors could reduce the enemy's labour force by declaring large numbers of men unfit for work. In workshops a few minutes deliberately wasted by numbers of men added up to millions of working hours lost. Machine maintenance could be neglected and damage repaired either badly or very slowly on the pretext that the problem was highly complicated. In a large concern it was possible to bring co-operation between the various complementary workshops and offices to an end simply by leaving the initiative to someone else; delays in delivery of a certain part could stop the entire production. A skilled technician could say that the work demanded of him was beyond his competence and so on. The list of possibilities is endless.

When the compulsory labour service was instituted the Belgian Courts and Bar Council protested, pointing out that the enemy's measures were in contravention of Article 52 of the Hague Convention. On 20 March 1943 the Supreme Court sent von Falkenhausen a letter which soon became public knowledge and was reproduced in millions of copies; among other things it said: '. . . As the highest authority of the judicial hierarchy the Belgian Supreme Court has the duty, both to itself and to the nation, solemnly to denounce the injustice done to Belgians and to point out that the measures taken contravene not only the provisions of the Hague Convention, signed both by Germany and by Belgium, but also the overriding dictates of conscience.'

Subsequently the Belgian Supreme Court protested on several occasions against the extortions of the Germans' auxiliary police; it even sent personal letters to some of these mercenaries reminding them of the responsibility they were incurring. Similar protests were frequently made against the crimes committed by the ss – and it took some courage to do so; when the population of Oradour-sur-Glane was massacred, the Prefect of Haute Vienne condemned the murderers in a letter to the German authorities and the bishop did likewise from the pulpit. After another massacre at Charleroi the Secretary-General of the Belgian judiciary wrote at once to say that the 'occupation authorities had disgraced themselves'.

In fact, any official could play his part in this silent orchestra of hostile non-co-operation without running any great risk. In France 'Roads and Bridges' and local Engineers and Surveyors employed theoretically demobilised officers in camouflage jobs. Rationing offices provided cards and meal tickets for people on the run. Valuable articles and documents were placed out of German reach well in advance; when the Germans arrived in Grenoble, Gosse, the Dean of the University, contrived to secure all the archives, catalogues and delicate instruments belonging to the research group of which he was in charge. A small number of officials of the national museums in France played the German agencies which were 'recovering works of art of germanic origin' against each other; they concealed masterpieces which the Germans wanted, refused all 'disinterested' exchanges and relinquished pictures of little value in order to save their priceless treasures.

By the nature of their functions some organisations were under greater pressure than others and their men were, therefore, in positions of considerable delicacy; the most obvious examples were the police and the gendarmerie. For them it was practically impossible to evade their duties all the time and they were forced to assist the Germans in some of their more revolting operations, particularly in the man-hunts for Jews. On the other hand, the French police were very lenient in dealing with demonstrations; after the marches organised on 1 May 1942 a report reached London saying that 'the police had been very half-hearted' and that quite clearly 'many of them secretly approved'; though they arrested a few people, they let others go. Gendarmes were the bearers of clandestine notes, they would warn people before arriving at their homes to interrogate them, they looked at peoples' papers with a vacant stare and pretended not to see things which leapt to the eye; it was the police who enabled the main escape line across the Pyrenees via the Llivia enclave to function with such regularity. The Germans were forced to recruit more reliable auxiliary police from the collaborator groups or from the dregs of the population. On many occasions they judged it wise to disarm the police and gendarmerie.[1]

The communists had grasped the fact that millions of apparently inoffensive gestures could add up to mass opposition. One of their pamphlets merely advised farmers 'to delay delivery of corn to merchants as long as possible, only to deliver cattle incapable of breeding, to refuse to pay fines, to receive inspectors with a pitchfork, to refuse to give details of their stock in order to save their herd, to withdraw their money from the savings banks and not to subscribe to Vichy's loans'; they should realise, they were told, that 'they had the numbers and the power'.

Every inhabitant of an occupied country could, therefore, do something, however apparently minor; their strength lay in their repetition and multiplicity. Railwaymen and postal workers were particularly well placed to operate effectively.

---

[1] In Greece General Manoussakis, commanding the gendarmerie, was a member of the Edes resistance movement.

Railwaymen and postal workers

Another communist pamphlet told French railwaymen that their 'role was to disorganise and paralyse transport; not a single loco- motive should emerge from the depots and those which must do so should break down after a few miles'; this was followed by technical instructions on ways of putting engines and carriages out of action – 'remember that if a suburban train carrying 1,500 workmen arrives 30 minutes late, that means 750 hours lost to the Boches . . . repeated small hitches disrupt the system and are good business'.

The French railwaymen became so punctilious in applying the rules that delays piled up. The more important pieces of paper, such as the bill of lading of a wagon, were accidentally lost; some small irregularity, whether deliberately caused or not, was blown up into an incident necessitating trans-shipment from one train to another; some mistake on a docket, some error in shunting or some exchange of labels – and the truck went off to some wrong destination where it had to be discovered and returned to its proper one . . . unless some other mistake occurred, etc., etc.

As for the postal workers, those responsible for construction and maintenance of telephone lines would destroy during the night what they had repaired during the day; for anyone other than a technician it was impossible to disentangle the jumble of wires in the junction boxes. In the telephone and telegraph exchanges it was tempting to take a copy of messages or make notes of a conversation. The Germans, of course, hastened to install their own circuits but they could not work these without some help from people of the occupied countries and, once installed, they were in an even better position to operate.

In normal times diverting mail is something dishonourable, something forbidden both by the professional's conscience and by the law, but the rescue of people in danger was an even more overriding duty. When letters addressed to German agencies arrived in the sorting offices, they were likely to contain something which it was entirely permissible to know; in this way denuncia- tions, information of use to the enemy or proposals for collabora- tion might end in the wastepaper basket; if the writer had registered his letter, the 'R' was ungummed and fixed haphazard to some other letter; to their great astonishment, therefore, people would receive registered letters containing nothing but family news. The Belgian postal workers hit upon the idea of diverting the thousands of letters addressed to compulsory labour service volunteers or the Waffen-ss militia fighting on the eastern front – lack of news from home was a good method of lowering their morale. Their letters home, on the other hand, were a good source of information which the Allies could use.

A certain source known as 'K' showed the lengths to which, in exceptional cases, this subversive work could go if carried out by a professional. For months R. Keller and his team studied the long-distance telephone and telegraph communications between Paris and Metz; then, on the pretext of repairs to an underground cable, they cut the circuits which they knew to be the most important and diverted them to a neighbouring house which they had rented and equipped as a listening post. A whole mass of information was thus obtained and recorded; it concerned the Luftwaffe, the German navy, strengths and locations of units, movements of squadrons and ships, operations carried out or planned – a miraculous haul. But at this degree of perfection, one is no longer in the realm of purely administrative resistance; this was the start of a true intelligence circuit.

Rescue of Jews

In several countries the Jews, who were the most threatened and the most savagely treated by the Germans without any provocation whatsoever, were the recipients of spontaneous assistance from societies, the administrative services or individuals horrified at the ghastly treatment meted out to them. When it was learnt that whole families had been rounded up and herded into trains at Lyons, various officials combined with the clergy and the laity of the 'Christian Friendship' society to save at least the children; they took them in, fed them and found them some safe hiding place. In Italy the churches, the convents and even the Vatican returned to their traditional mediaeval role of offering asylum, and hid Jews on the run.

In Belgium both Queen Elizabeth and King Leopold intervened with the German authorities on behalf of the Jews. Cardinal Van Roey ordered all religious institutions to take these unfortunates in whenever they could; he forbade any religious proselytisation;

7*

this was purely an operation of charity and of rescue, he said. Convents, parish priests, hospitals, church schools and child welfare institutions accordingly hid both parents and children, often the latter alone. Of 66,500 Belgian Jews, 32,000 were deported, but 34,000 escaped and of these 25,000 remained hidden in Belgium.

In Holland 20,000 were rescued against 120,000 deported. A writer and a sculptor set up a complete false papers office for them; a full-scale volunteer organisation, set up by a society lady through her contacts, destroyed dossiers in Amsterdam and stole identity cards from town halls with the tacit connivance of the officials. In Denmark success was complete since the entire population from the King downwards participated. In 1943 7,200 Jews were evacuated to Sweden by sea. Only 570 of the less fortunate ended in Theresienstadt; they had initially been hidden in a large hospital, but the fishermen, when asked to assist and provide boats, proved to be unco-operative; they made much of the risks involved and the majority demanded payment, and at a high rate. A nation-wide collection was thereupon organised which brought in a million kroner; each passenger cost 500.

In Bulgaria, where the Germans were present but not in occupation, numerous approaches were made to the government to cancel planned anti-semitic measures; forty-three members spoke against them in parliament. On 23 and 24 May 1943 'mass demonstrations' took place in the streets of the main towns; at Kustendil people rushed out of their houses during the night to rescue Jews who were being arrested. Success was complete; not a single Bulgarian Jew was deported.

Unarguable though these successes were, they illustrated the limitations of such action; they did not and could not prevent the murder of millions of Jews; rescue on that scale was beyond the resources of any resistance organisation, however strong and well organised. One of its more important results, however, was that through it men of goodwill were found, organised, guided and utilised; propaganda on a small scale was necessary to make these rescue operations effective – to reduce the anti-semitism of the Poles, for instance. The Jews thus rescued could only survive if they were determined to defend themselves and were not left alone to do so. Solidarity developed in this way grew naturally into association and action.

Limits of administrative resistance

Passive resistance is the least obvious of all forms of clandestine action; it is certainly not the most effective. It may annoy the occupier, always provided that he notices it; it can only weaken him in the long term; it hardly demoralises him; it does not bring him to his knees. Moreover, he himself is neither inactive nor impotent. Theoretically he may be at a loss when the majority of an occupied population is against him, but he can always impose exemplary punishments calculated to discourage some and scare others; he has no lack of reliable candidates for posts of authority. If he feels really threatened he can arrest or charge the various office-holders. The Germans, for instance, insisted on the recall of General Weygand from North Africa and removed Horthy, the Hungarian Regent, from power in order to instal Szalassy.[1]

If they were to retain some freedom of action and the minimum of forces, the governments of the occupied countries had to show that they were worthy of the confidence placed in them by the victor. Acts committed against the occupier were balanced by others favourable to him. Some officials might destroy dossiers or address communications wrongly in order to sabotage the compulsory labour service; the majority, however, did their work correctly out of discipline, conviction, ignorance or fear. Many swung first one way and then the other, day by day and as occasion served in order not to 'come out into the open' too much. In most cases, if his duty was not clear to him or if he had not the courage to do it, the official was guided solely by his own interests; he 'covered himself' both ways, so as to be in good shape whatever the outcome of the war. The investigators into crimes of collaboration after the liberation of France were not a little surprised to find that some of the most heavily compromised had been careful to run with the hare and hunt with the hounds – the current phrase at the time was 'everyone had his own Jew'.

There is, moreover, a point beyond which administrative resistance cannot go. It cannot become general without directives, without control, without a minimum of centralisation and direction. If it becomes too widespread, the occupying power will

[1] In France the Germans arrested many of the departmental prefects; in their zone the Italians arrested the majority of the pre-war mayors.

inevitably soon come to know of it. If, furthermore, it is not linked to other forms of action, administrative resistance remains purely negative and entirely defensive. The most it can do is inconvenience the enemy and make him feel insecure.

Worse still, administrative resistance may become an actual disadvantage since it must work in the dark. Carried to its logical conclusion it would end in 'scorched earth' tactics or at least in a sort of economic harassment analogous to a blockade. By depriving German production of raw materials, agricultural or manufactured products, means of transport or hours of work, people could, of course, hope to obstruct development, perhaps even bring about gradual strangulation. But if people who lived solely off their work had to destroy the fruits of their labours, was this not tantamount to condemning them to slow hara-kiri, to demanding that they deprive themselves of their own means of livelihood? In short resistance could be self-destructive – this was one of the agonising problems it faced in relation to sabotage. It was essential to be able to choose between the various targets for attack and to deal only with those which could do real damage to the enemy without unnecessarily sacrificing the occupied peoples.

Penetration of public offices

If resistance was not to do great harm to the people and forfeit their co-operation, it could be no more than an advanced guard, at least until the time came for a national rising. Meanwhile, acts of resistance must not be undertaken merely by well-intentioned and more or less well-informed men inspired by the right ideas. When, for instance, railwaymen succeeded, despite the watchful eye of the German supervisor, in changing the labels and numerals on a train carrying important goods and despatching to Quimper trucks expected in Hamburg, a whole series of manoeuvres was needed. They had perhaps shunted other trains in between themselves and the Germans on guard. The whole action had been minutely planned and carried out with the assistance or connivance of signalmen, foremen and shunters; unco-ordinated action would not have produced the result. In fact a complete organisation, a 'circuit', had to be formed, on a small scale perhaps but consisting of experienced and reliable men. When Keller installed his clandestine listening post, he had to have a whole range of delicate and expensive equipment, in particular switches for circuit selection and amplifiers; while he was at work the French testers at the nearest repeater stations argued with the German supervisors to distract their attention; trained technicians were required to hear, transcribe, translate and understand the intercepted information. In short, here again numerous accomplices were essential but to ensure success only a small number could be 'in the game' and they must be fully aware of the risks they ran, resolved to take them and bound together by mutual confidence – once again, a circuit in fact.

Without a definite structure, administrative opposition could not become resistance in the true sense of the word. It could, however, give considerable assistance to organised resistance, if the latter pressed it into service when necessary; telephone operators could pass the word down the line to the *maquis* that German columns were approaching; factory watchmen could indicate when sabotage was possible or necessary and then be found tied hand and foot by the saboteurs; tax collectors or inspectors could become more or less willing treasurers of resistance groups; equipment intended for the 'Chantiers de la Jeunesse'[1] could find its way into the hands of the French *maquis* and so on.

One of the first tasks of French Resistance movements, *Combat* in particular, was to separate the wheat from the chaff in the French administration left in being by the Germans.[2] Lists of people in all the services were prepared showing who might be needed, because of the position he occupied or his qualifications, whether he was a sympathiser and whether he was helpful – a complete census, in fact, of men of goodwill or ill-will.

The latter were denounced, as they deserved; open references to them in the clandestine press left them in no doubt about the threat of eventual punishment hanging over them. Public servants thus came to be classified by a new criterion of merit; the resisters knew whom they could trust and, even more important, whom to avoid. As time went on, this classification roused supporters to further enthusiasm and caused opponents to reflect and proceed with caution.

There was a moral aspect to this 'penetration'. It showed the

[1] A Vichy paramilitary organisation eventually disbanded by the Germans.
[2] This search for conveniently placed accomplices undoubtedly took place in all countries; as far as one knows, however, it was most systematically organised in France.

determination of the Resistance to judge men, whoever they might be, by their patriotism and courage in troublous times rather than by their professional qualifications; personal problems of salaries and promotions had no bearing on the matter.

At the same time, however, this 'penetration' was analogous to the 'fifth column' method which had proved itself during the Spanish Civil War. A web was woven within the enemy organisation, each reliable contact being a thread. In this way police action against the Resistance could be anticipated and thwarted, decisions could be known before they had been implemented, plans could be betrayed when they had barely been formulated. The NAP[1] became a vast intelligence service; the occupying power was its target but it worked through the Vichy régime and, through the Resistance movements, its information became available to Free France and the Allies. Conversely the slogans and orders of the Resistance were distributed in circles assumed *a priori* to be hostile; cells were formed and multiplied, manned not merely by activist sympathisers but by men who had a certain authority; their growth indicated the increasing power of the Resistance, and the gradual loss of authority by the French state.

Seizure of power, one of the distant aims of the Resistance, could be prepared gradually from within; in some cases it had in effect occurred even before the Germans had been actually defeated. The Vichy administration was paralysed from within, either because orders were not carried out or because heads of department were persuaded not to issue them.

Thus 'penetrated' the various administrative and governmental services could go into action as a body when the moment arrived; the Paris rising of August 1944 was triggered off by a general strike of the transport and public services; the first to use weapons, the few weapons which the Germans had thought it wise to leave them, were the gendarmes, the police and the inspectors from police headquarters. Before this, however, the Resistance had had to form its own volunteer fighting groups – 'movements', circuits, saboteurs, independent units, partisans and the *maquis*.

[1] *Noyautage des administrations publiques* – penetration of the public services.

CHAPTER 13

Sabotage, Assassinations and Strikes

The Resistance was divided on the advisability of attacking the occupier immediately. In France controversy raged between the 'Gaullist' resistance movements supported by the Free French leader and the communists, culminating in a 'truce' at the height of the Paris rising in August 1944. The story is typical of resistance all over Europe.

'Wait and see' or 'immediate action'

Through their press the French resistance advised people to await the favourable moment before initiating direct action. A headline in *Défense de la France* read: 'Frenchmen, you are not the stronger side. Have the wisdom to await the moment.' The Allies were also advised to wait and not to launch ill-prepared landing operations which would merely create pitfalls for the resisters; they would be forced to expose themselves and so become an easy prey. *Franc-Tireur* proclaimed: 'We should say to the British – take your time and leave nothing to chance.' Delay did not imply lack of interest in the battle but preparation for it – 'we must first be mentally prepared for battle and organise ourselves'. In April 1942 Rémy considered that immediate preparations should be made for a rising 'which must occur immediately *after* the landing'; meanwhile so secret an army should be raised 'that even its members would not realise that they belonged to it'.

This concept of a cautious clandestine struggle was in line with that of the Allies who feared that action might be premature. It also coincided with that of the Belgian, Dutch and Norwegian emigré governments. Two cogent arguments were advanced in favour of these tactics. If the Resistance plunged too soon into operations for which it was neither morally nor materially prepared, it would be decimated without damaging the German war

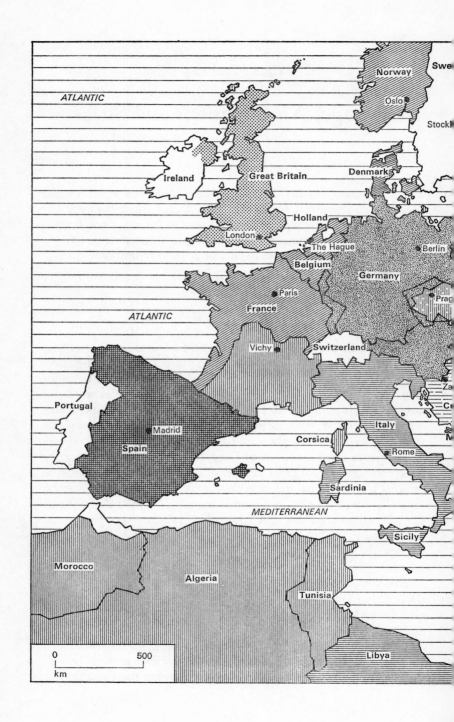

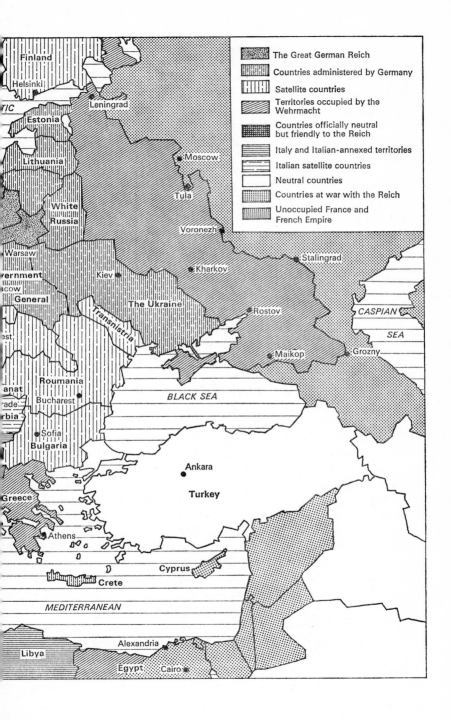

The Great German Reich
Countries administered by Germany
Satellite countries
Territories occupied by the Wehrmacht
Countries officially neutral but friendly to the Reich
Italy and Italian-annexed territories
Italian satellite countries
Neutral countries
Countries at war with the Reich
Unoccupied France and French Empire

Finland
Helsinki
TIC
Leningrad
Estonia
Moscow
Lithuania
Tula
White
Russia
Voronezh
Warsaw
Stalingrad
ernment
Kharkov
cow
Kiev
General
Rostov
The Ukraine
CASPIAN
Transnistria
SEA
est
Maikop
Grozny
Roumania
anat
Bucharest
BLACK SEA
ade
rbia
Sofia
Bulgaria
Ankara
Greece
Turkey
Athens
Cyprus
Crete
MEDITERRANEAN
Alexandria
Libya
Egypt Cairo

machine; then, when the moment came, it would not be there to answer the call. Secondly, direct attack aroused both the fear and hatred of the occupying power and savage reprisals were the result; the death of ten Frenchmen was a high price to pay for the elimination of one German soldier. Moreover by acting in this way the Resistance might risk losing the support of public opinion, stopping its own recruitment and providing grist to the collaborationist mill.

The view of the communists was quite different, and they did not mince their words. Their decision to reject the 'wait-and-see' policy was a political rather than a military one. In July 1941 they responded as best they could to Stalin's call for help addressed to all supporters of the communist International; they were determined that the USSR should not suffer from a repetition of the tragic error of autumn 1939 when Poland was crushed in the east while the French army remained motionless behind the Maginot Line. The principle was laid down by *L'Humanité*: 'Our duty is to help the USSR by every means' and the paper elaborated as follows: 'By sabotage at all times, by unceasing action to prevent Germany drawing supplies from our country, we shall weaken Hitler and so advance the hour of his defeat. What do we require in order to accelerate the hour of victory of the USSR, its allies and the oppressed peoples? Action, again action, always action.'

Once the decision had been made, the party would hear of no argument against it. To the objection that action was premature Grenier's reply, aimed at a London journalist, was: 'What are the RAF raids on our railways supposed to do then? Are our patriots to be forbidden to do what is permissible for your airmen?' If security reasons were cited together with the fear that the best clandestine fighters might be lost prematurely, the party replied: 'The losses will not be among the brave. In fact thousands of militants have been arrested owing to carelessness and an idiotic legalistic outlook.' Bold action would itself produce security since it might, for instance, rally a crowd which would act as cover for brave spirits. Risks were minimal for those who reacted as revolutionary fighters should. 'It is not true that action inevitably leads to repression. It is non-observance of the rules of security which leads to repression.' In any case what was the good of doing nothing? The enemy would certainly not remain inactive. 'If we leave the Boche alone, he will put us all slowly to death, some by starvation, others by imprisonment and still others as hostages. It is better to fight, it is better to risk everything rather than submit to such a fate.'

Moreover by participating in the common struggle resistance would establish 'an imperishable claim to the gratitude of the Allies and every people on earth'. It would thus 'not only assist the formation of the second front by weakening the Reich but also inspire the Allies to act sooner than they intend. . . . It would issue an appeal to allied strategy, the echoes of which could not fail to be heard'.

One wonders whether the party really expected success from this plunge into action for which it was not really prepared. We do not know. Experience, it maintained, would prove that its decision was right – 'the national rising can only take place if leaders have been trained in action'. Finally a negative argument – 'formations which do not fight cannot learn how to do so; moreover they divide, grow weaker and distintegrate'.

The communists were not alone in adopting immediate action tactics; they had been used by Mihailovich in Serbia for a time and with even greater determination and persistence by the Polish resistance which took its orders from the London government. But in western Europe, as in the satellites of the centre and east, it was the communists who laid down the policy and set the example; the rest eventually followed them with greater or lesser enthusiasm. Before blossoming out into guerrilla units which led to the apotheosis of the national rising, the resistance struggle initially took the form of sabotage, assassinations and strikes.

Sabotage

In the communist view the notion of sabotage should be interpreted as broadly as possible. According to them every member of an occupied people – official, housewife, worker, farmer, intellectual – was capable of damaging some part, however small, of the German war machine. Young people, for instance, 'even though unarmed, could do harm to the enemy by tearing down his direction signs, setting fire to his labour exchanges, smashing his windows and punishing traitors'. Housewives could 'raid food stocks destined for the Boches and so recover some of the goods they had stolen'. Such widespread sabotage, it was admitted, could lead to great difficulties – 'the question of daily bread was a terrible one' – but it was essential in order to implant fear, confusion and a sense of impotence in the heart of the enemy; 'repeated acts of sabotage force the enemy to guard vulnerable points and so immobilise thousands of soldiers'.

The Allied military leaders counted primarily upon bombing to destroy the enemy's war potential and exaggerated its effects. SOE, however, was convinced that sabotage was less expensive and could be more effective. In France, for instance, a raid on the Peugeot factory, which was making tanks for the Germans, destroyed numerous warehouses and workshops but failed to stop production. Some SOE agents then contacted the Peugeot family; they proved to be pro-Allied and agreed that some small explosive charges should be placed at certain well-chosen points in the factory, to disrupt production without destroying the factory; as a result both human life and useless destruction was saved. This procedure was not generally used – bombing was more spectacular and after the Anfa conference the British relied primarily upon this method of winning the war cheaply.

The governments-in-exile were not over-enthusiastic at the prospect of large-scale destruction of their countries' resources by repeated sabotage – Benès and the Dutch government were particularly vocal, but members of the Resistance who were on the spot were even more afraid of blind bombing which frequently missed its target and turned their cities into ruins and slaughter-houses. In November 1943 the Norwegians protested at the bombing by 158 Flying Fortresses of the factories at Rjukan and Vemork which produced heavy water; the material damage and loss of life, they said, was out of all proportion to the results achieved. The French Resistance movements advocated sabotage 'which was equally an operation of war but saved human lives'; naturally the necessary equipment must first be received and targets be carefully chosen. According to Henri Bernard, G. Burgers, head of a group in Belgium, considered that 'destruction of a factory should be neither total nor permanent since this would entail deportation of the labour force to the Reich whilst partial but effective destruction kept the workers in the factory; the time required for repairs added to the stoppage of production implied a serious loss to the enemy'.[1]

[1] Henri Bernard: *La Résistance belge* (op. cit.), pp. 82–8.

SOE set up special workshops manufacturing sabotage equipment of increasing perfection and ingenuity – 'sausages' to be placed on German aircraft and adjusted to explode at the right moment, magnetised boxes to be attached to a tank or armoured car, explosive 'horse-droppings' and pebbles to burst the tyres of a vehicle, plastic explosive of all shapes and sizes – a particular favourite of the resisters which has given a new word to the French language, 'plastiquage'. The art of sabotage was taught in the training schools for agents. For their part the resisters obtained such explosives as they could from quarries or mine depots; the most fortunate, or most intrepid, were the Belgians who 'recovered' thousands of pounds of dynamite, thousands of yards of Bickford fuze and detonating cord, thousands of detonators and several hundred rifles from the national arms factory in Herstal. Using their own resources they also manufactured incendiary bombs and darts filled with phosphorous, steel-pointed devices known as 'crabs' to burst the tyres of vehicles, white lozenges known as 'aspirin' which adulterated petrol, etc.

The resisters gradually discovered that sabotage meant learning difficult techniques demanding psychological, professional and economic knowledge. If it inconvenienced the population too much, it became counter-productive – a power cut might be more effective than a costly explosion. Inventiveness and ingenuity were their stock in trade. To be fully effective sabotage had to be supported by propaganda; it accordingly had a part to play in psychological warfare and for this reason the clandestine press reported, magnified and sometimes even invented it. It was important that operations should be numerous and continuous to keep the enemy on guard, play on his nerves and compel him to disperse his forces. Care had to be taken to avoid ill-considered destruction which might even be harmful; if a lift was to be blown up in a coal mine, for instance, it was essential to choose a moment when it was untenanted since, if a miner were killed, the psychological effect might be the opposite of that intended. In general terms, if the main object was to lower or even stop production, too many workers must not be thrown out of work for too long or they would be taken to work in Germany. All this was frequently difficult to appreciate. In fact resisters attacked everything within their capabilities – factories, stocks, warehouses and businesses of all sorts; transport and communication facilities such as bridges, canals, telephone lines and railways were favourite targets; owing to their length they were poorly guarded and therefore easy to attack with only minor risk.

During the period 1940–44 in Poland 1,300 German trains were derailed, 7,000 locomotives, 20,000 railway wagons and 4,000 vehicles were damaged; 800 'communal administrative offices' were destroyed in order to obstruct delivery of agricultral products. As early as April 1940 Frank, the Governor-General, was noting in his diary that many ammunition depots had been blown up – and he attributed this to the 'thousands of armed resisters'. From 1943 trains only ran on many lines at restricted times of day or under escort or not at all; in 1944 cases of railway sabotage averaged ten a day. The German general Haenicke confirmed that 'roads and railways could no longer be considered secure for the movement of reinforcements to the East'. This sabotage was obviously of major assistance to the Red Army.

By November 1941 production at the Ploesti oil wells in Rumania had fallen by 20 per cent; an anti-tank mine depot had been blown up; many shortcomings in arms manufacture had been discovered. On 12 June 1942 the military arsenal at Tirgoviste was set on fire; during the winter of 1943 the arms depots at Mirsa suffered the same fate. In Bulgaria thirty acts of sabotage had been recorded in Sofia by July 1941; a petrol depot was set on fire at Varna; the number of sabotage operations rose from 12 in January 1943 to 280 in November of that year. During the occupation of Greece saboteurs derailed 117 trains, destroyed 209 locomotives and 1,540 railway wagons and damaged nearly 20 miles of line, 5 tunnels, 67 railway bridges, 136 road bridges, 800 vehicles, 17 ammunition depots, 16 tanks and 5 aircraft on the ground.

In Belgium 'Group G' specialised in the sabotage of high voltage lines; the method had been worked out by a genuine 'planning office' manned by professors of science and technicians from the electrical industry; Henri Bernard says that this resulted in the 'loss to the occupier of 20–25 million working hours, more than ten million in the night 15/16 January 1944 alone'. In Norway power stations on the west coast provided current for the manufacture of aluminium; since they were on the outskirts of towns great precautions had to be taken; groups were specially trained in Scotland to sabotage them; similarly German boats were sunk in the port of Oslo, foundries and chemical factories were dynamited.

These figures and this catalogue of sabotage are only examples drawn from the complete list which is far too long to quote here; they show, however, that the German war machine was put to a severe test and that nowhere was it secure from action by the Resistance. In addition to this ceaseless underground activity, resistance was also involved in operations of genuine strategic importance which could not have succeeded by other means. In Greece, for instance, the SOE mission for once succeeded in uniting the Elas and Edes partisans and in November 1942 blew up the Gorgopotamos viaduct on the Athens–Salonika line, thus hampering the movement of reinforcements to the Afrika Korps, which was then under attack by the British Eighth Army at El Alamein. In the summer of 1943, before the landing in Sicily a whole series of sabotage operations against railways and road bridges caused the Germans to fear a landing in Greece; as a result they held a complete Panzer division in the Peloponnese, far from the actual theatre of operations.

In 1943 General Alexander asked that the vast railway viaduct at Stampetov in Yugoslavia be destroyed, as this was on the Trieste–Ljubljana line it would hold up despatch of enemy reinforcements to Italy. The viaduct was heavily guarded and so the Yugoslav partisans had to attack the guards, hold them at gun-point for several hours, drive them from the viaduct and prevent them returning until after the explosion; the demolition was successful thanks to powerful explosive charges despatched from Great Britain. In 1945 the main railway line running through Norway from north to south and its extension into Denmark was cut several hundred times to prevent the despatch of German occupation units to Germany as the British and Americans advanced.

The most celebrated instance of sabotage and the most telling from the point of view of co-operation required and results achieved was the destruction of the installations manufacturing heavy water in Norway; for the Allies this was tantamount to victory in the race to produce the atomic bomb, on which the outcome of the war might depend. SOE initially dropped parachutists in October 1942, but the aircraft and gliders were shot down and the survivors executed. It was necessary to turn to the Norwegian resistance; on 28 February 1943 nine of them gave a sort of model demonstration of clean, complete and economical sabotage, destroying the installations of the Vemork factory, which was located in the depths of a mountain valley, without loss. The Germans repaired the damage and the Allies decided to bomb the entire installation; they did destroy the hydro-electric power-station but not the operative circuit which was protected by several layers of reinforced concrete. The Resistance was called in once more and in January 1944 they sank the ferry used for moving the stock of heavy water to Germany.

Other forms of sabotage demanded pertinacity as well as expertise. Three employees on Aalborg aerodrome, for instance, were only permitted to take in one package each day and were not allowed to take it out again; it was their lunch. They substituted plastic explosive for their sandwiches and did without their lunch for a fortnight. Then, one day in the autumn of 1944, they placed their charges on everything they could see – aircraft, fuel depots, workshops, canteens, offices. It all went up that night without the loss of a single life.[1]

These few examples show the results which can be achieved by sabotage; in fact they were exceptional. During the darker periods of the war, when Germany was advancing on all fronts, sabotage was inevitably working in the dark; its sole purpose was to envelope the occupier in a climate of insecurity, to cause him gradually to lose his arrogance and confidence and to begin to feel that he was the hunted. When the Allies were on the offensive, however, sabotage could be co-ordinated with the operations of the Anglo-American armies in the west and the Red Army in the east; in the rear of the combat zone it could cause anxiety to the enemy, hamper his movements, subject him to a permanent threat and force him to divert part of his forces away from the real front. Nearer the front the object of sabotage was to assist the advance of Allied forces, but if it took place haphazardly it might hinder them; sabotage, therefore, had to take its place in the wider plans and thus it became an integral feature of the national rising and seizure of power. At this stage it also had to be linked to security operations and counter-sabotage to prevent the enemy holding up the Allied advance. However this may be, one cannot but agree with a telegram to London from the 'delegation of the MUR' in Geneva: 'If you provide the explosives and indicate the targets, our groups are ready to undertake any form of demolition and to extend this action; this would avoid costly and inaccurate bombing which damages the morale of the popu-

[1] See Henri Bernard: *Histoire de la Résistance européenne*, p. 233.

lation'. The Allies undoubtedly committed a major error in disregarding such appeals and in persisting to bomb Europe – including their friends of the Resistance.[1]

Assassinations

The Resistance, therefore, gradually reached agreement that the best and least expensive method of striking at the enemy which was within its capabilities, was repeated sabotage; it did not, however, altogether succeed in convincing the Allies of this. Resisters remained in disagreement, however, on the usefulness and advisability of assassinations, particularly in the case of enemy soldiers. In fact in western Europe – the situation was different in Poland – only the communists continuously advocated widespread assassination and minimised its unhappy consequences. Although their call to 'strike down in turn the traitors of the Militia and the others who have sold themselves to the Boches' left the Germans comparatively unmoved, it was a very different matter when their own soldiers were attacked. The communists then found themselves facing a vast wave of public emotion aroused by seizures of hostages and shootings. Their first reaction was to reply by increased terrorism – 'we must avenge the murdered patriots. For every Frenchman ten Germans or creatures of the Germans calling themselves Frenchmen will be executed without hesitation'.

In fact the opposite occurred: the Germans executed numbers of people vastly in excess of those they lost through 'terrorism'. The communists then set about whipping up popular emotion and sympathy, sometimes by sentimental accounts of the martyrs' deaths, sometimes by organising a commemorative ritual – 'in the workshops, in the cloakrooms, on the machines lay flowers on photographs or nameplates of our late lamented comrades . . . institute stoppages of work . . . observe a minute's silence'.

The party refused to recognise the inexorable cause-and-effect relationship between assassination and repression. Grenier wrote to London: 'It is untrue that an increase of activity on the part of the *Francs-Tireurs Partisans* led the enemy to execute hostages – untrue both politically and historically. The first hostages were

[1] For the effects of bombing see the author's *Seconde Guerre mondiale*, Presses Universitaires de France, Paris 1969, Vol. II, pp. 160 *et seq.*

shot in Paris in July 1941, whereas the first *Francs-Tireurs* detachments were formed two months later.' Grenier knew perfectly well that the French had been horror-struck by the executions of hostages; horror had turned to anger paralysed by fear.

In fact the cause-and-effect relationship did exist and it became more obvious as time went on; there was a limit to the number of assassinations which the resisters could carry out; there was no limit to the reprisals which descended on the heads of the occupied peoples. The communist party seems to have realised and accepted the risk from the outset: 'The blood which stains our paving-stones is the seed of future harvests.' . . . 'The glorious death of our heroes has called forth others in thousands.'[1] This was the background to the call by Charles Tillon, head of the FTP, 'Let each man get his Boche,' and it led the party to conclude 'The battle and political sagacity are one and the same thing.'

Non-communist resisters, on the other hand, and most of the governments-in-exile were more afraid of the unhappy consequences of assassinations and belittled their effectiveness; General de Gaulle formally disapproved of them.

The case against premature action

'We advise everybody to refrain from useless demonstrations which do not contribute to the good of the country. . . . We formally dissociate ourselves from the assassination of an officer of the army of occupation which recently took place at the Barbes metro station.' This reproof was based on moral as much as practical considerations – 'We have no taste for political assassination and any fanatic who instigates such attacks seems to us a criminal worthy of condemnation. No one has ever brought about a lasting victory for the cause which he serves through eliminating his political enemies by violence.'[2]

In any case, owing to German reprisals, assassinations resulted in many more deaths. Admittedly 'these Frenchmen fell in battle' but 'ten to one is too high a price to pay'; therefore 'all elimination of individual Germans is premature'. But it was necessary to

---

[1] *La Vie ouvrière*, No. 50 of 16 August 1941 and No. 109 of 17 October 1942; see also the statements made to Rémy by a communist leader in *The Silent Company*, p. 328 – for each man lost fifty new recruits were enrolled.

[2] *La France continue*, No. 5, September 1941.

differentiate between the victims: 'An attack on a collaborator is an execution, not an assassination; courts martial not being available, rough justice is meted out to traitors; this is not civil war, it is simply war.' In fact in the southern zone the *Combat* activist groups formed by Jacques Renouvin organised the assassination of several collaborators which led to a favourable swing in public opinion.[1]

In spite of these distinctions, however, it was argued that assassination tactics failed to serve the purpose in view – 'Killing a German soldier on a street corner one evening can in no way influence the outcome of the war. It cannot be compared to the essential sabotage of equipment, transport or, even more important, war production.' *Libération-Nord* accordingly advised its readers 'not to be lured into useless individual actions'. In its issue No. 89 of 14 August 1941 the same newspaper reiterated that 'since the majority of German soldiers in Paris are headquarters clerks, their corpses are of less value for the cause which we serve than the dishonourable remains of one French Hitlerite'.

Punishment of traitors

All resisters were agreed that traitors – collaborators – should be punished; the communists initially included in this category comrades who had left the party after the Russo-German pact. In France the example was set by Paul Colette, a lone operator who wounded Pierre Laval and Marcel Déat with revolver shots. Hungarian partisans placed bombs in the Budapest municipal theatre where 2,000 members of the 'Arrow Cross' were meeting. Many a Gestapo informer was kidnapped and executed as he left work; stickers were placed on doors – 'A traitor lives here'; lists of collaborators for whom exemplary punishment was promised were published in the clandestine press and read over the London and Moscow radios. Sometimes tragic errors were made; a magistrate of Aix-en-Provence was executed and it was later discovered that, far from being harsh on resisters, he had been trying to save them. On other occasions personal accounts were squared under cover of patriotic motives. No error was made, however, when resistance struck at the leaders, thus impressing

---

[1] They also blew up kiosks selling German newspapers after having first warned the proprietors. Renouvin refers to these operations as *kermesses* (fêtes).

upon the public that no one was secure from their attacks; the young Bonnier de la Chapelle struck down Admiral Darlan in his office in Algiers; a group of the MUR [United Resistance Movement] forced its way boldly into the hotel room occupied by Philippe Henriot, the Vichy Secretary of State for Information; in Bulgaria an ex-Minister of War and an ex-Chief of Police were liquidated and in Holland an ex-Chief of Staff of the Army.

Raiding parties

The Resistance directed its attacks more frequently against installations than individuals. In the Ministry of Labour in Paris, for instance, a small group from *Ceux de la Résistance* led by Leo Hamon destroyed an entire card index – over 200,000 cards – compiled to assist in the enforcement of the compulsory labour service. Everywhere partisans used armed raiding parties to obtain stocks of tobacco, ration cards, official papers and money; an attack on the postal giro office in Brussels brought in 14 million francs and in the Dordogne the French Forces of the Interior laid hands on over a milliard francs belonging to the Bank of France.

The most remarkable raid of this type was undoubtedly one organised in Poland. Periodically a quantity of banknotes were transported, with a German police escort, from the issue bank in Warsaw to Cracow. The Home Army decided to intercept one of these convoys. Through informers in the bank it obtained essential information on the sums transferred, the days when this took place, the strength of the escort, etc. The route, however, was fixed at the last moment by the convoy commander. Learning that a transfer would take place on 12 August 1943, the Home Army blocked with simulated roadworks one of the possible routes leading from the bank. The convoy was, therefore, obliged to use the other street. A lorry carrying armed partisans hidden under a tarpaulin drew up alongside the bank courtyard railings. As the vehicle carrying the money was about to emerge a van full of large blocks of wood spilt its load as if by accident bringing the bank vehicle to a halt. The resisters opened fire on the German police. Two of them leapt into the truck and laid hands on the money-bags – 100 million zloty! The Germans issued notices promising a reward of five million zloty to anyone giving information leading to the recovery of the money and identification of the culprits. To these notices the resisters added stickers promising ten million zloty to anyone providing information which would enable them to repeat so profitable an operation. The raid had taken place in front of the statue of King Sigismond III; the Germans received a letter signed by the King, saying: 'I saw it all, but I have no need of money, so I shall not say anything.' Success was complete.

Localities used by Germans became targets for increasingly frequent attack; sometimes the object was to rescue fellow-resisters under arrest, sometimes to retaliate for executions. During the war 250 armed attacks took place in Warsaw and in the course of two years 165 in the Radom district alone.

'On 26 March 1943 members of the clandestine organisation "Szare Szeregi" rescued one of their number Janek Bytnar ("Rudy") and twenty-four other prisoners from the Avenue Szucha while they were being moved to Pawiak prison. On 24 October 1942, in retaliation for the hanging on the 16th of fifty members of the Polish Workers Party, a detachment of the Peoples Guard under Roman Bogucki hurled grenades into a dance-hall known as the Café-Club which was reserved for German soldiers. On 11 July 1943 a detachment of the Peoples Guard under Miroslav Krayevsky ("Pietreci") attacked the same café in retaliation for the shooting of two hundred political detainees in Pawiak prison. On 23 October 1943 another group of the Peoples Guard attacked a night club and as a result twenty-two ss and Gestapo men were killed.'[1]

Only the Czechs seem to have used these terrorist methods in Germany itself. The Czech resistance movement UVOD claims to have placed a bomb in a Munich beer-cellar where Hitler was due to speak and to have caused an explosion which partially destroyed the Anhalter station in Berlin.

Some spectacular assassinations

In most countries Germans occupying senior positions were

---

[1] The Polish War Crimes Study Group has published a brochure specifying the localities in which acts of resistance took place; practically every street in Warsaw is mentioned. See *Lieux de lutte et de martyre*, published by Council for Preservation of monuments to battle and martyrdom, Warsaw 1965, p. 362.

struck down by a few determined men – and not by communists alone. Colonel Hotz, military commander in Nantes was killed on 20 October 1941; Ritter, aide to Sauckel the head of the compulsory labour service, was struck down by Manouchian's group near the Trocadero on 28 September 1943; Rauter, the Commissar-General in Holland, was murdered on 7 March 1945. Attempts were not invariably successful; the FTP machine-gunned the car of General Schaumburg, the military commander in France, but by chance it was empty. Nevertheless the public heard of these exploits and admired the courage of those involved; people gradually became convinced that no German was unassailable and concluded that the Reich was not winning the war.

Two assassinations made a particular impact – that of General Franz Kutschera, the ss commander in Warsaw, and in Prague that of an even more eminent personality, Reinhard Heydrich, the 'Protector' of Bohemia and Himmler's immediate deputy.

Kutschera went from his house to his office every day by car, although the distance was only 150 yards. The rule in the Home Army was that only heads of the German agencies of repression should be attacked but that this should be done in the most spectacular manner possible in order to impress the Poles as well as the Germans. The Army condemned Kutschera to death but the operation had to be organised with the utmost precision because of the short time available. For several days three girls stationed along the route studied exactly what Kutschera's chauffeur did. At 9.0 a.m. on 1 February 1944 they took up their positions and, by agreed signals, gave warning of the passage of the car to the resisters who were to strike down its occupants, Kutschera, his ADC and his chauffeur. At a cross-roads a car, apparently very badly driven, cut across that of Kutschera, forcing it to brake and almost stop. As the car drove quickly away several men, who were apparently waiting for a bus at a near-by stop, drew sub-machine-guns from beneath their long winter overcoats and opened fire. At the same time several others threw hand grenades at a neighbouring German police post in order to neutralise it. The whole operation lasted barely a minute; only nine men took part and their leader was only twenty years old. Kutschera and four other Germans were killed and four of the attackers wounded; two of these died of their wounds and another, who escaped from hospital, was killed during the Warsaw rising.

Heydrich had been assassinated nearly two years earlier, on 27 May 1942; the murder squad consisted of several dozen Czechs, who had left for France in March 1939 and then made their way to Britain whence they were parachuted into Bohemia. They had much difficulty in recruiting assistants but eventually found them in the Czech Red Cross and the Sokol organisation. Two of them posted themselves on the route regularly followed by Heydrich's car at a point in a Prague suburb where the road bent sharply at the bottom of a hill and there was a tram stop; here the car must inevitably slow down. Heydrich was only wounded but died of his wounds. Treachery enabled the Germans to discover the attackers who, with other resisters, had taken refuge in the crypt of a church, an old dank cellar. There they were besieged; they defended themselves desperately until eventually the Germans flooded the cellar. Three were killed and four others committed suicide. Their bodies were laid out on the pavement to impress passers-by.

The attack on Kutschera formed part of a prolonged sequence of violence on the part of the Polish resistance; that on Heydrich was quite a different matter. In fact the operation was decided upon in London, by the Benès government alone and not by SOE; orders for it had been sent to Czechoslovakia a month before it took place. This attitude is all the more surprising in that the London Czechs and their supporters in Bohemia were in principle opposed to 'immediate action', considering it too expensive for the results to be expected from it.[1]

It must be admitted that the price exacted for such resounding feats was extremely high. The result of the assassination of the military commander in Nantes was the shooting of fifty hostages on express orders from Hitler; they included those from Chateaubriant and further hostages who had been arrested. When a German officer was assassinated in Holland 688 people were deported to Neuengamme. In Prague 540 people were arrested at once; there followed mass deportations of officials, writers, priests and communists; 252 of these were shot in Mauthausen as accessories to the operation; in addition the village of Lidice was burnt to the ground and its population massacred as a reprisal.

It seems questionable whether acts of resistance liable to be

[1] During a conference in Oxford M. Keary propounded the theory that the Czech government had learnt of severe anti-resistance measures shortly to be taken by Heydrich.

punished by such violent reprisals are necessary or even useful. Their effect is purely moral and the enemy's strength remains intact; retaliation is aimed at the most determined and most prominent of the resisters.[1] The organisation of resistance requires resources, time and energy and these could be devoted, at less cost and with greater efficiency, to a large number of more remunerative operations.[2] It may also be thought that a population which needs to be shaken out of its apathy by such methods, has no great predilection for clandestine work. It must not be forgotten, however, that the Czechs and Poles were fighting for their very existence and that, particularly in the case of the latter, they were engaged in a remorseless struggle for which the nazis were responsible; they had wanted it that way. However this may be, assassinations are only one of the tactics employed by the underground. Strikes also have their role to play.

Strikes

Here the communists were undoubtedly the experts both in theory and practice. In their view, although individual action is certainly not to be disregarded, only 'action by the masses' can be really effective. Taking conscription for the compulsory labour service as an example, they felt that if not a single conscript appeared for mustering or medical examination; if their mothers, wives and sisters were the first to advise them against doing so; if removal of a man from a factory led to a stoppage of work or the entry of the police to a violent reaction; if officials provided evaders with false papers and farmers gave them food and shelter and if, finally, arms were dropped to them by parachute so that they could defend themselves, then the question of the compulsory labour service would end in the total defeat of the occupier.

Such a combination of effort is exceptional; nevertheless it is

[1] The Czechoslovak historians, who have long been extremely hostile to Beneš, have frequently condemned the assassination of Heydrich as a 'provocation' – a peculiar attitude on the part of communists, and explicable solely by the political situation.

[2] Resistance cannot always have the last laugh as it did in Warsaw. There a fine of a million zloty, imposed as the result of an assassination, had no sooner been deposited in a bank than it was spirited away by a Home Army raiding party.

not mere fantasy provided meticulous preparations have been made. For this reason 'communists must always be able to sense what the masses are thinking, to understand their needs and interest themselves in their claims . . . avoiding, according to the teaching of Stalin, anything which might lead to lack of understanding between the masses and the party'.[1] Now what do the masses constantly think about? The difficulties of daily life. What weapon can they use to alleviate them? The power they derive from their participation in production and the threat of withdrawing this participation by going on strike.

Any claim for better conditions was, therefore, worthy of support since it might lead to action against the occupation; in the circumstances it inevitably assumed a political and nationalist character – 'we shall not, all of a sudden, persuade the 150,000 miners of the Nord department to take armed action, but they will strike heroically to obtain soap and a Sunday's rest'. Continuous claims, for whatever purpose, created an atmosphere of unease and increased hostility towards the occupying power – 'the battle to defend one's daily bread is a battle against Hitler who is starving us'. This type of exhortation led to demonstrations when men marched shoulder to shoulder and the irresolute were carried along by the fervour of the crowd.

This mass action should be both spontaneous and the result of agitation; in any case it must be channelled and directed by the party. Its ultimate aim was the strike which was in fact the perfect act of sabotage, '*the* weapon *par excellence* to use against the enemy'. But the general strike could not be improvised nor should its success be compromised by risky experiments; it should be the culmination of a series of partial strikes which it would co-ordinate and 'raise to a higher level'.

Once initiated, the general strike was the true workers' battle into which the party threw all its forces. It prepared its troops with care, like a general sending out his patrols to gain contact with the enemy before a major clash. The party instructed its members how to initiate a strike under these exceptional conditions and what lessons to draw from its development, its success or its failure. 'As soon as work in a factory ceases, we must remember our experience of 1936: organise occupation of the workshops, block their exits, prepare their defence; warn neighbouring firms at once and invite them to join the movement;

[1] *La Vie du parti,* August and September 1942.
8

alert the population in areas adjacent to the factory so that they may support the strike from outside; finally defence of the strike inside the factory requires the formation of special fighting groups to disarm the enemy and turn his own weapons against him'. A strike might, therefore, spread like an oil slick, mobilising the working population. Stoppage of work might even lead to armed action since it was itself a battle.

Once a strike was over, an exhaustive post mortem took place. Many valuable lessons could be drawn from a successful strike, but if it had been only partially successful there was even more to be learnt. At Firminy 'the workers should have organised the strike inside the factory. Once they had left the factory the workers were dispersed and the places in which they might have assembled were guarded. Isolated in their homes, the workers were without information or directives and this reduced their capacity to continue their struggle. Had they occupied the factory, the strikers would have brought the whole population into action, since they would have gone to the factory to feed the strikers'.

A vast mechanism of warfare was thus organised and gradually perfected. In this field 'activism' was also a paying proposition. 'After a strike it is certain that groups of *Francs-Tireurs Partisans* will form'; at Anzin 'the tendency to sabotage is greater; production is already falling'. From Algiers, Lucien Midol drew the conclusion: 'Strike action gives the workers confidence in their collective strength; it is good preparation for the people of France for those supreme acts of courage which the final battle will require. Moreover, these strikes have brought to the fore claims which affect the entire population. They have assumed a national character. At this moment the CGT is France's most powerful army.'

All over occupied Europe, therefore, strikes took place on the most diverse pretexts – supply difficulties, the arduous nature of the work expected, inadequacy of air raid shelters (tantamount to holding the national or occupation authorities responsible for the loss of life resulting from Allied bombings), solidarity with other strikers, protests against arrests, low wages, demonstrations against shooting of hostages, demands for higher rations, distribution of clothing coupons, hostility to managers accused of collaboration, obsolescence of installations, increase in the cost of living, insistence on the observance of collective agreements, allocation of milk to children, observance of holidays, etc.

They were in fact dress rehearsals for the general strike. Durand has listed the signs pointing to the general strike of the French railways – stoppages of work at the Oullins workshops (engines and carriages) on 29 June, 25 and 26 July 1944, at the Venissieux depot on 29 June and 15 July, at the Conflans yard on 30 June, 14 and 15 July, at the Arles-Machine shops on 8 July, at the Lyon-Mouche depot on 16 July and at the Paray-le-Monial and Marseille depots on 18 and 21 July, finally at the 'minor maintenance' workshops of Villeneuve on 24 July.[1]

Elsewhere full-scale dress rehearsals took place, sometimes for reasons of patriotism, sometimes for some political purpose – the two were barely distinguishable. In the Jiu coalfield in Rumania a miners' strike at the end of 1941 lasted nearly a month; in Luxemburg, when military service in the Wehrmacht was introduced, the workers struck on 31 August 1942 and were supported by the students; several hundred people were deported. In Holland, when it was announced on 23 April 1943 that prisoners of war released in 1940 were to return to captivity – the Germans had decided on this as a security measure – workers in the Twente district struck and the strike spread to the rest of the country; farmers refused to relinquish their quota of agricultural products; the German reaction was savage – 150 Dutchmen were shot and all radio receivers confiscated. In Denmark, when the Germans ordered a curfew for Saint John's night on 26 June 1944, a general strike took place in Copenhagen; all public transport ceased; water, gas, electricity and telephones were cut off; shops and stores were closed, those belonging to 'collaborators' were looted and their owners manhandled; barricades appeared as if by magic. Faced with the threat of brutal German repression, the resistance organisations ordered a return to work on 3 July.

Italy was probably the country where the most significant stoppages of work took place. In March 1943 strikes occurred in Turin and Milan; there had been sporadic stoppages a few months earlier. This time, however, the movement was more or less general; work stopped for a few minutes in one place and for some hours in others. The reasons were perfectly normal – wage claims and demands for increased rations. Nevertheless, the impact was considerable; for the first time in twenty years an important section of the Italian people had dared to rebel against the fascist system, and in the middle of a war. In August 1943, after the fall

[1] P. Durand: *La SNCF pendant la guerre* (op. cit.), p. 515.

of Mussolini, the trend continued; internal factory committees were elected with communists and socialists as candidates; meetings were held, first at places of work and then in market squares. In March 1944 a genuine general strike was called; in some places it lasted a week and it continued to smoulder until September, when 80 per cent of the trains stopped. That autumn no more than half the men in the metallurgical industry were working; production fell and prices rose. The Salo fascist republic thereupon proposed to nationalise the firms concerned; of 32,000 men who voted in the Fiat factory only 400 supported the measure. The labour movement had come out fairly and squarely against fascism. It had become political, but had it become revolutionary?[1]

How was anyone to know? As the moment of the national rising and seizure of power drew nearer, the Resistance was compelled to ask itself what was its ultimate object. While still held together by the battle against occupation the resisters tried not to look too closely at the gulfs which were opening between them. But what then? The question was, of course, present throughout the struggle: what were they fighting for, what future did they want for their country? Through the strikes the answers began to take shape; some were assailed by anxiety, others proved disloyal. Patriotism was admittedly the cause of the majority of work stoppages, but unrest was there too. Was the proletariat to find its way via the Resistance to that promised land from which, according to Marx and Engels, capitalism had excluded it and which Jaurés had proclaimed would come via democracy? Or would the Resistance prove to be a spring-board for the social revolution? The communists did their utmost not to disturb the unity achieved in battle, but that did not mean that they no longer attacked management, capitalism and trusts. Nevertheless, it was possible to detect a certain divergence between their programme and their doctrine. The first question was: had the patriotic war changed the communist party and, if so, in what direction? Second question: would it attempt to seize power? Noncommunist resisters asked themselves these questions not without anxiety; mistrust began to grow and they were uncertain how far they wanted to go along the road of reform. But the answer would not be given by their country's communist party; it would be given by Stalin and it would vary according to the war aims of the USSR. This was why the national rising and liberation, the

[1] Germany was the only country where there were no strikes, only sabotage.

apotheosis of resistance, assumed such totally differing forms in different countries – and the deciding factor was whether they were preceded or accompanied by the entry of Anglo-American armies in the west or the Red Army in the east.

CHAPTER 14

Conspiracies

The object of resistance was to undermine the strength of the occupying power and one day, drive him from each occupied country and restore to it its freedom. The enemy, however, had created or taken into his service certain potent forces from the political, economic and administrative worlds, the military and the police. It was possible to 'penetrate' these groups from within, to search out the well-disposed and, with their help, neutralise those who proved hostile. But it was naturally far better to swing them all over at once into the anti-Hitler camp; in many cases all that was required was the seizure of power by men not over-compromised with nazism. This was what Great Britain vainly tried to do with the Vichy government. Churchill first attempted to divorce from it the Empire and colonial army which had accepted signature of the armistice with ill grace; he made use of Free France and General de Gaulle as levers to this end. Then, having failed to persuade Marshal Pétain to move to North Africa, he placed his hopes in a revival of anti-German patriotism on the part of General Weygand. Only after the failure of all these approaches and manœuvres did the Americans take up the running from the British and reach agreement with General Giraud, third in line as the leader of disaffection. Similar attempts were made in Rumania to persuade the more reputable politicians to oppose General Antonescu or even overthrow him, but with no greater success. The appearance of a dictator as totally committed to an anti-German line as Metaxas in Greece was a happy surprise; he was determined to fight the Germans as long as the interests of his country required. The Allies wanted to see this engineered elsewhere. After all they would merely be paying the nazis back in their own coin; they had placed in power puppets whom they manipulated to their advantage – Nedich, Hacha or Laval. Why not try to substitute pro-Allied leaders for them?

In the corridors of power clandestine activity was sometimes parallelled by a silent struggle for the exercise or direction of authority. Conspiracies accordingly ensued which according to chance sometimes succeeded and sometimes failed. Naturally the operation was easier when the Germans were not present; this was so in Belgrade in March 1941 when a pre-resistance coup d'état was successful and a government hostile to the Axis formed. A similar coup in French North Africa before the American landing was less successful. In Hungary, on the other hand, Admiral Horthy had little luck when, on two occasions, he tried to change sides. The whole course of events would obviously have been different if the Italian or German dictators had been overthrown or replaced; in Mussolini's case this did occur, but it came very late and the Italian resistance played no major role in his downfall. A small number of conspirators from the German resistance, however, did engineer an attempt to assassinate Hitler on 20 July 1944, backed by an abortive coup d'état; they only narrowly missed succeeding. It was one of the most extraordinary and most dramatic occurrences of the war.

Complete success – the Belgrade coup d'état

The Yugoslav leaders in the shape of Prince Paul, the Regent, and his government had acceded to the blandishments of Hitler and joined the Tripartite Pact. Their decision had not been without hesitation, but in view of Mussolini's unconcealed ambitions they could see no other solution than a position of subservience to nazi Germany. Nevertheless, not all of those in authority were convinced of the soundness of this policy. Early in 1941 the Italians were still marking time in Greece, which they had attacked in October 1940, and the British had a footing there. The British government and secret service had quite successfully brought strong pressure to bear on the Yugoslav leaders to give assistance to Greece.

As a demonstration of disagreement with the signature of the pact with Germany, three ministers had resigned and Cvetkovich, the Prime Minister, had had difficulty in replacing them. General Simovich, the Army Chief of Staff, had openly warned the Minister of War that 'the younger officers were discontented', meaning that he was no less so himself.

When Cvetkovich and the Minister for Foreign Affairs left for

Vienna where they were to sign the pact, 'spontaneous' demonstrations broke out which British agents, apparently, did their best to extend. Students shouted: 'Rather war than the pact'; ex-servicemen of the 1914–18 war met to declare their opposition and the orthodox clergy showed themselves to be equally hostile.

The co-ordinator behind all this was General Mirkovich of the Air Force. He decided to take action at 2.0 a.m. on 27 March using units of the Belgrade garrison. Without difficulty troops occupied police headquarters, the radio station, the War Ministry and the telephone and telegraph exchanges;[1] the Prime Minister was arrested. In an hour all was over with only one man killed. At 5.0 a.m. General Simovich formed a new government of national union in which all the recognised Serb parties agreed to participate. Prince Paul, who was on holiday in Croatia, bowed to the inevitable and resigned. The young King Peter was declared of age and a statement from the Prince read over the radio. The coup d'état was ratified by great demonstrations of popular enthusiasm.

The Belgrade *putsch* was basically little more than a pronunciamento, but it was carried out with the maximum legality thanks to the young King's agreement. It met with no opposition and its success was complete, undoubtedly because its instigators were expressing the feelings of the vast majority of the public, at least in Serbia. The Croats, however, were faced with a *fait accompli*; Matchek, their leader, initially advised the Regent not to give way but eventually himself bowed in face of the coup's success. The desired result was certainly achieved. Although General Simovich declared that he would pursue the same policy as his predecessor, he was in fact hostile to the Axis and everybody knew it. Yugoslavia had in effect changed sides, as Hitler realised only too well, and he immediately modified his plans to include an attack on the country. The British proved incapable of defending it and the army's rapid defeat accentuated the divisions in the country. Though apparently successful the coup had been undertaken somewhat light-heartedly and all its possible consequences had not been properly appreciated.

---

[1] According to an eye-witness the doors were opened by conspirators who had allowed themselves to be shut in overnight – see Simonin: *La France Libre dans les Balkans,* Editions du Scorpion, Paris 1950.

Partial success – the Algiers 'Putsch'

The policy of neutrality tinged with collaboration adopted by Marshal Pétain with Admiral Darlan and Pierre Laval as its champions had few supporters either in unoccupied France or the French empire, particularly after the United States entered the war. In French North Africa, on the other hand, the Vichy régime was fully accepted. The military, although basically anti-German, regarded Marshal Pétain as their revered leader; the 'colonials' appreciated the 'reforms' introduced by the 'national revolution' – authoritarianism, suppression of political parties, anti-semitic legislation; the mass of the native population was indifferent and, unexpectedly, the emergent nationalist groups had ostensibly ceased all activity after the fall of France in June 1940. Only the Jews – who had lost their French citizenship with the repeal of the 'Crémieux decree' – and some small factions in the administration and the University came out in favour of the Allies and against Vichy. Small 'Gaullist' groups had formed in Tunisia, Algeria and Morocco but they confined themselves to the collection of information and occasional sabotage of Italian ships; they made no real impact on public opinion. At the other end of the scale ardent supporters of 'collaboration' were to be found in the Navy, whose traditional anglophobia had been increased by the action at Mers el-Kebir, and in the *Légion des Combattants*, particularly its 'law and order service', which contained many admirers of fascism.

In this somewhat unfavourable atmosphere American agents masquerading as consuls patiently attempted to gather up the threads of a conspiracy against the time when the Allies might decide to land and turn North Africa into a new theatre of war. They made contact with a small group – 'The Five' – led by Lemaigre-Dubreuil, the industrialist, and including General Mast, Rigault the journalist (an extreme right-winger), Henri d'Astier de la Vigerie (his two brothers were gaullist but he himself was royalist), Tarbe de Saint-Hardouin the diplomat and Van Hecke, head of the 'Chantiers de la Jeunesse'. These men saw in the Americans the probable victors in the war, a bulwark against communism and a method of removing General de Gaulle who was suspect because of his 'republican' entourage and alliance with the communists.[1]

[1] In addition many officers were extremely hostile to the Free French Forces, having fought them in Syria.

8*

When the British and Americans decided to land in French North Africa (Operation 'Torch'), they wanted to ensure that the French forces would not stand in their way or fire on them. The policy in vogue in North Africa was that put forward by General Weygand as 'defence of the Empire against all comers'. Discreet contacts were made with French leaders, General Noguès, the Resident-General in Morocco, General Juin and even Admiral Darlan who, though no longer a member of the government, was still the Marshal's heir apparent and commander-in-chief of the armed forces; they proved disappointing despite one or two ambiguous remarks from the Admiral. American diplomats in Vichy thereupon made indirect contact with General Giraud, famous for his escape from Koenigstein; his hostility to the Germans was common knowledge since he took every opportunity of proclaiming it. Giraud agreed to work with the Americans and the 'Group of Five' recognised him as their leader.

An embryo organisation was now formed. The plan was that the American landing should be backed and assisted by a French conspiracy. In the first stage the conspirators would neutralise the Vichy authorities in Morocco and Algeria – the Americans felt it impossible to extend their action to Tunisia; General Giraud would then arrive from France at the opportune moment to assume command of the armed forces and legalise the operation. Under these conditions it was hoped that the American landing would take place without opposition and that finally French North Africa and with it possibly the whole French empire in Africa would re-enter the war against the Germans and Italians. This was what the British had been hoping for ever since June 1940 but had so far failed to bring about.

In fact the conspirators recruited quite a number of accomplices. Some of the military leaders, having been cautiously 'contacted', agreed to join – General Béthouart in Morocco, General de Montsabert, Colonel Jousse in Algiers and even a naval officer, Captain Barjot; they were joined by nearly a thousand 'civilians' led by Doctor Aboulker, including a few 'gaullists' from Algiers such as Professor Capitant, but no communists – they had taken the hint and made themselves scarce. Preparations for the operation were made at Cherchell between General Mark Clark, General Eisenhower's deputy who was to be in command of the landing, and General Mast.

From the outset the operation laboured under grave handicaps but it was the best that could be expected given the situation in North Africa. In the first place it was not aimed solely against the Vichy régime and the collaborators; no confidence was placed in General de Gaulle and Free France who, together with their French resisters at home, were kept at arm's length. Instead of paving the way for the unity of all Frenchmen opposed to the Germans, it accentuated their divisions. Secondly the disparity of forces was glaring; some thousand unarmed conspirators might well find themselves facing tens of thousands of soldiers – there were 11,000 in Algiers alone – and it was certain that the native recruits would obediently follow their officers; in addition there were the *Légion*'s paramilitary formations which were also armed. Finally and most important of all, a serious difference of outlook existed from the start which Americans took care to conceal. They were interested solely in the success of the landing and they had no wish to become involved in the problems of French internal politics or even to try to understand them, the more so since they hoped to avoid provoking too hostile a reaction from Marshal Pétain and the Vichy government. Consequently not only did they refuse to divulge their actual plans – a perfectly legitimate security precaution – but they made promises which they knew perfectly well that they could not keep; they left General Giraud under the illusion, for instance, that a landing would also take place on the Languedoc coast and that he was designated as Allied Commander-in-Chief.

Under these conditions it was little short of miraculous that the *putsch* scored even a partial success. In Rabat, General Béthouart surrounded the 'Residency' and demanded that General Noguès order the troops not to fire on the Americans. Noguès succeeded in raising the alarm outside, however, and it was then General Béthouart's turn to be surrounded and taken prisoner with the threat of being shot. The French Navy fired on the Americans as they landed at Casablanca and several hundred men were killed in the fighting.

In Algiers there was initially almost complete success despite the facts that the Americans had not provided the arms promised and that certain of the conspirators withdrew at the last moment, one of them giving the game away. According to plan groups of young people, mostly Jews (very few Arabs were involved), occupied the main installations such as the prefecture, the main post office, the radio station and the governor's summer palace; they set up their headquarters in the central Commissariat where, quite simply, they summoned those whom they considered their most dangerous enemies and locked them up. Small detachments armed with a few revolvers held General Juin, Admiral Mendigal and General Koeltz prisoner in their houses, and Admiral Darlan who was unexpectedly in Algiers. The general idea was that, with their most senior leaders absent or muzzled, the troops would obey General Mast, on whom authority would legally devolve; he would address them in the name of General Giraud, whose five stars would carry weight.

Various unforeseen developments, however, altered the whole basis of the problem. In the first place the presence of Admiral Darlan completely upset the local chain of command, since he headed not only the troops in North Africa but those in France as well; if he could be persuaded to join the plot this would be of the utmost value to the Americans, particularly if he would order the fleet to sail from Toulon for Algiers, but given his role and position at Vichy it seemed unlikely that he could so decide without out Marshal Pétain's agreement. Secondly General Giraud missed his appointment with history; when everyone was expecting him in Algiers, he was palavering with Eisenhower in Gibraltar. When he eventually arrived in Algiers he was confronted by an imbroglio which he took no steps to disentangle, particularly because his fellow-officers, far from welcoming him with open arms, cold-shouldered him, and Admiral Darlan, his superior officer, was on the spot. Most important of all, the Americans did not fulfil their promises; they did not land at the points or at the times agreed; worse still, they were late. When they did appear, the putschists, who were too weak to fight unsupported for long, had been routed out, disarmed and arrested, and so the tables were turned. The Vichy authorities, whom it had been hoped to remove, returned to their posts with a powerful reinforcement in the shape of Admiral Darlan. The French fired on the troops as they landed.

Under these conditions the Americans felt that they must cut the gordian knot and they, therefore, dealt with the most senior authority confronting them, Admiral Darlan. Adroitly interpreted telegrams from Vichy enabled the latter to state that, acting in the name of Marshal Pétain who was 'indisposed' (Darlan was the heir apparent), he had decided to order a 'cease-fire', sign an agreement with General Clark and bring North Africa back into the war under his leadership, both civil and military, giving him the title of French High Commissioner.

The Algiers *putsch* was, therefore, both a success and a failure. On the technical level it was successful – the putschists had gained all their objectives in the time allotted to them; from the overall political point of view it was also successful, since the entire French empire took up arms once more. But the conditions under which these successes were achieved nullified any favourable results. In fact North Africa was handed over to the Americans after considerable fighting, not by their friends of the Resistance, but by men who had refused to treat with them, and at the head of these was Admiral Darlan, a notorious collaborator, the man who had negotiated and signed the 'Protocols of Paris' of May 1941. This was the negation of morality and commonsense; Admiral Darlan hastened to arrest those responsible for the *putsch*, branding them as rebels; worse still, the resulting delays enabled Axis troops to gain a footing in Tunisia and months of heavy fighting were necessary to dislodge them. Moreover this success, instead of uniting the French, divided them even further. Though Roosevelt referred to Darlan as a 'temporary expedient', the Americans had apparently shown that they were quite prepared to negotiate with the Quislings of Europe if they thought it advantageous. Paradoxically, therefore, General de Gaulle and the French resistance at home were led to condemn a series of events which, viewed as a whole, were leading in the direction which they themselves had been the first to take.

The authors of the conspiracy could not be held responsible for these unhappy consequences; they acted in defiance of numbers, public opinion, legal authority and strength; in their favour they had nothing but their youth and their faith; they could rely only on the effect of surprise. But, just as the British had encouraged the Yugoslavs of Belgrade to court Hitler's rage when they had not the resources to protect them, so the Americans in North Africa had made use of the Resistance without attempting to understand it and were quite prepared to abandon it if their short-term interests seemed so to dictate. The lesson to be drawn both from Belgrade and Algiers was that a yawning gulf was in danger of growing between the resisters and their great allies of the outside world.

The tergiversations of Admiral Horthy

The Hungarians were no germanophiles but they had been drawn towards Germany by the Trianon treaties which had unjustly saddled them with equal responsibility for the Great War with the Germans. All Hungarian policy was aimed at the recovery of their lost territories; under the 'Munich agreements' part of the Slovak plain was returned to Hungary; in March 1939 she obtained Sub-Carpathian Ruthenia; on 30 August 1940 the Italo-German award gave her back much of Transylvania; during the carve-up of Yugoslavia in April 1941 Hungarian troops reoccupied the Banat. The Hungarian leaders would, therefore, have had every reason to be satisfied with the course of the war had not the advantages they drew from it been counterbalanced by a heavy-handed German tutelage. They joined the Tripartite Pact; they sent their troops on the 'anti-bolshevik crusade'; their entire economy was tied to that of Germany and the latter did not keep to the barter agreements, to the considerable disadvantage of her partner. A proud people wedded to their independence, the Hungarians looked askance at the Wehrmacht units stationed in their country 'in transit' to the eastern front; they were opposed to the totalitarian measures adopted under nazi pressure.

When Hitler demanded the arrest of Hungarian Jews, Horthy was hesitant to issue the order; he was susceptible to the wave of international protest raised against the nazi racist policies, but after some prevarication he gave way.[1] In July 1944, however, when the Allied landing in Normandy had succeeded and German pressure on central Europe seemed to be lessening, Horthy thought that the moment had come to rid himself of Sztojay's collaborationist government and replace it by a military cabinet which would be more politically neutral, though still retaining the confidence of the Germans. The fear inspired by the Germans was still so great that Horthy did not dare to act on his own but asked for prior agreement from Hitler. The latter, well knowing how much reliance he could place on his allies' loyalty since the about-turns by Darlan and the King of Italy, quickly grasped the purpose behind the move and his refusal was categoric – 'Any

[1] In July 1943 Hitler insisted on the dismissal of Kallay, the Prime Minister, who had made contact with the British and Americans.

deviation from the present line would have serious consequences.'
Horthy gave way once more.

After the Wehrmacht's defeat in Rumania in August 1944 the
Regent felt himself in a stronger position; he dismissed Sztojay
and commissioned the new government to ask for an armistice.
But he then found himself inextricably entangled. The greatest
fear of the landed proprietors who were his kith and kin, was
social revolution, which the Red Army would undoubtedly bring
with it; Horthy, therefore, turned to the British and Americans,
asking them for their terms. Their reply was also categoric:
Hungary was in the Soviet operational zone and he must reach
agreement with the USSR. Horthy resigned himself disconsolately
and decided to contact the few Hungarian resisters, weak though
they were; he would have nothing to do with the communists.
When he eventually steeled himself to approach Moscow, he
failed to carry his policy to its logical conclusion; Hungarian
troops continued to fight the Russians; they did not even disarm
the few thousand German soldiers stationed in Hungary; in this
way six weeks were lost. The Germans then pushed forward
Szalassy and his 'Arrow Cross', on whom they could rely, and
Admiral Horthy had not the courage to initiate a trial of strength.
He gave way, accepted Szalassy as head of government and
resigned. He was arrested and interned in Germany.

In this tight-rope walking exercise Horthy undoubtedly had
authority on his side, but he was not really supported by public
opinion; the forces behind him were weak and divided. Most
important of all, his initiative ran counter to the decisions of the
British and Americans with whom he wished to deal.

The fall of Mussolini

Despite the Duce's prestige and twenty years of monolithic
tyranny his fall on 24 July 1943 came rapidly and with surprising
ease. Both the man and the régime he had founded were equally
sick; the King, the military leaders and even the fascist dignitaries
were convinced of the necessity for fundamental change as a
result of the dictator's visible physical deterioration, the defeats
suffered by the Italian armies, the loss of the empire, the invasion
of the homeland and the serious economic and social crisis
besetting the country. Mussolini eventually lost his position and

his freedom as the result of two parallel conspiracies, one devised by his faithful disciples of the early days and the other hatched by the King, who the very day before had assured Mussolini of his staunch friendship.

Italian resistance played no direct role in all this; it was still too weak and disregarded by the Allies. Even more than in North Africa they restricted their dealings to the most exalted legal authorities, the King and Marshal Badoglio, his new Prime Minister. As in Algiers the American military were concerned solely with the success of their military operations and had no wish to become involved in internal Italian politics. To simplify matters they placed the liberated areas under an Allied military administration (AMGOT). Nevertheless, it was clear that the agitation instigated by the Resistance, particularly in the North, and its emergence into the open in Rome after the fall of the Duce presaged its re-entry into Italian political life. At second hand it had achieved the result it desired above all else, which had been its *raison d'être* from the outset – the fall of fascism.

The examples of Yugoslavia, North Africa, Hungary and Italy show that the success of a conspiracy and seizure of power by the Resistance depended on the fulfilment of a certain number of conditions, seldom all present at once. In the first place the conspirators had to have a minimum of authority and backing from public opinion, neither of which was the case in North Africa. A measure of Allied assistance was essential and this Admiral Horthy entirely lacked. Most important of all, the Resistance had to be sufficiently strong and united both to assert itself vis-à-vis the Allies and resist the enemy; this condition was not fulfilled either in Belgrade, Budapest, Algiers or Rome. As far as the brave German conspirators in the attack on Hitler were concerned, they had to rely on their resolution, determination and luck.

A dramatic failure – the attempted assassination of Hitler

Apart from communists and socialists, whose leaders were regarded as sworn enemies of nazi Germany, the nazi party did not withhold its favours from the 'rank and file', provided they took their place loyally in the new nazi order. Many had done so – no social, religious or ideological group in Germany could remain totally unimpressed by Hitler's victories, the glitter of the Reich, the return of prosperity and Germany's grandiose prospects.

Nevertheless small groups of wary dissidents remained. They came from the most diverse backgrounds – workers whose hostility took the form of sabotage which was hushed up by the press or denounced as the work of Germany's enemies, the survivors of the old political leaders, intellectuals in revolt against the denial of liberty, idealistic pacifists and Christians who disapproved of racial measures. But there were no links between them, they were practically powerless and were divided over the methods to be used.

In most cases an obsessional notion of their patriotic duty prevented them doing more than making proposals and criticisms of little practical significance. The remaining few were divided between supporters of the 'revolution from below', who wished to win over the mass of the population by agitation and propaganda, and believers in 'revolution from above', in other words a *putsch* designed to change the leadership of nazi Germany at a stroke.

To achieve their ends, they needed the active support of the only force in Germany which had kept itself in some degree aloof from the Party – the Army. The generals knew from experience that Hitler, and still more Himmler, had no liking for them and saw them as the last representatives of the aristocracy and the great landed proprietors of the Bismarck era; a silent struggle frequently raged between the army and the ss, the pioneers of the future Germany. But the German military had too deep-rooted a sense of discipline and their debt to Hitler was too great for them to rebel against him. The Führer, after all, had given the Wehrmacht back its strength and its prestige; he had expunged both the shame and the effects of the Versailles *diktat* and then had fulfilled the dreams of the pan-Germans.

Nevertheless, a few generals had been bold enough to protest against the inhuman treatment of the Poles; others had advocated a policy of *rapprochement* in the USSR either towards the local nationalists or the Russian people. The German defeats in Africa and Italy, the fall of Mussolini, the sacrifice of the Sixth Army at Stalingrad, the severe bombing suffered by Germany, the Führer's blind obstinacy in Russia and the success of the Allied landings in Normandy made clear, even to the most obtuse, that Hitler was leading Germany to defeat, and that he must be stopped while there was still time. In July 1944 Germany was still sufficiently strong to be able to discuss an honourable conclusion to the war with her enemies, whereas in September 1943 fascist Italy had been so weak that she had been forced to accept all the Allied terms.

So the conspiracy was formed under the direction of General Beck and Field Marshal von Witzleben, both long-standing anti-nazis and both on the retired list. They were supported by Generals Hammerstein, Hoepner and Olbricht, the latter a senior officer of the Abwehr [Military Intelligence]. They contacted certain civilians such as Goerdeler, the ex-Burgomaster of Leipzig. Cautiously they approached generals on the active list and recruited von Tresckow on the eastern front and von Stulpnagel in Paris; more senior officers, however, such as von Kluge and Rommel, merely hinted their approval. But these officers remained a closed circle; they did try to approach the socialists through Leber but, when he was arrested, did not persist. They, therefore, had no link with the masses; their following was restricted to a few small military circles; there was no guarantee even that the majority of the army would follow them. From the outset the basis of the conspiracy seemed extremely narrow.

But how to seize power? Some recoiled before the prospect of eliminating Hitler, wondering whether he could not be persuaded to retire or even whether he should be seized by force, but the Führer seldom left his headquarters and that was too well guarded for such an attempt. The decision was eventually taken by Colonel von Stauffenberg: Hitler must first be killed and then, taking advantage of the confusion among the leaders, the surprise of the people and the unquestioning discipline of the troops, the conspirators would seize power. This was Plan 'Valkyrie'.

What would the conspirators do after their victory? Despite the Allied decision to impose unconditional surrender on Germany, the majority hoped that the British and Americans would agree to negotiate with them; after all, they thought, their agreement with Soviet Russia which was not only difficult but unnatural, could not be everlasting. Others, including von Stauffenberg, thought that contact must also be made with the USSR, perhaps via the Free Germany Committee – they were, after all, patriots whose sole error had been to place themselves ostensibly at the service of an enemy power. The 20 July conspirators were good Germans, if not even nationalist; they wished to see Germany emerge from the war with minimum losses, if possible unoccupied and with her September 1939 frontiers intact. All the attempted, highly discreet, approaches made to the Allies, however, met with no response.

On 20 July 1944, during a briefing conference with Hitler in the chair von Stauffenberg placed a delayed-action bomb in the conference room of the Rastenburg headquarters. He left the room on some pretext, leaving his briefcase containing the bomb beneath a corner of the table; he heard the explosion and then succeeded in taking off in his aircraft and landing in Berlin. Here he learnt of the first hitch – because of a signals error Plan 'Valkyrie' was not yet in force and precious time had been lost. Then came the second piece of bad news – the Führer had been wounded but was not dead; someone at the conference had moved the briefcase and the heavy wooden table had saved Hitler. The gods were certainly not on the side of the conspirators.

When they did decide to go into action it was already very late. General Fromm, commanding the Home Army, who would have joined the conspiracy had it succeeded, took avoiding action as soon as he foresaw failure and rallied Hitler's supporters. Beck was cornered and committed suicide. In an unsuccessful attempt to make up for a moment of weakness, Fromm had the other conspirators, including Stauffenberg, executed after a travesty of a trial.

A savage wave of repression descended upon all those who had either directly or indirectly been connected with the conspirators. A parody of justice by a so-called 'Peoples Tribunal' was accompanied by torture, insult and degradation. Field Marshal von Witzleben, twelve generals and thirty-four colonels were hanged; hundreds of officers were sent to Oranienburg concentration camp, including Admiral Canaris, head of the Abwehr; they were massacred by the ss on the eve of the camp's liberation. In all some 5,000 persons were killed including priests, diplomats, pastors, socialists, scientists and even long-standing nazis.

The conspirators of 20 July 1944 were undoubtedly heroes inspired by the highest motives. Von Stauffenberg in particular seems to have been a man of exceptional stamp; he had been much impressed by Soviet Resistance and reached the conclusion that only a form of osmosis between the traditional Christian virtues and the promises of socialism could rejuvenate Germany.

The task was an exacting one and the conspirators had to steer a middle course between conflicting requirements: to preserve secrecy their numbers had to be kept as small as possible; to be effective they needed wide-spread support. In addition luck was not with them.

Nevertheless, it is clear that they did not use all the trumps in their hand and that they behaved somewhat like a suicide squad. Their leaders were too old, too tired and too long forgotten to have much chance of asserting themselves over the generals on the active list; they had not managed to enlist the support of any of the great Army Commanders who wielded real power. They had also under-estimated the fanaticism of the thousands of young officers who were blind disciples of the Führer.

Even if Hitler had been killed and the military leaders had joined the plot, there still remained the Party and the ss; would they have given way without a struggle? Might Germany not have embarked on civil war? It is also highly doubtful whether any of the Allies, all of whom were committed not to reply to separate peace proposals, would have agreed to negotiate individually with the insurgents and they could not know the true character or intentions of the new German leaders – soldiers, after all, if not ex-nazis. Alternatively it would have been necessary to capitulate completely in the west and open the doors of Germany wide, which would have been considered treachery by many people.

The seizure of power is hardly possible without a strong and coherent organisation – and there was no such thing either in the Wehrmacht or the German resistance. Such organisation can only be lasting if it has wide-spread popular support and on 20 July the German people did not move, did not even understand what was happening. Finally, unless the Allies were 'in the game' and had given their prior approval, no one could be sure of their support in the later stages. After all, they had brought the whole house of cards down in Algiers and there they *had* given prior approval. Clearly the Resistance had to use, to invent, methods other than conspiracy.

CHAPTER 15

The Resister's Calvary

Coming, as they did, from all quarters of the globe, the resisters were activated by the most varied motives, but as soon as they were committed they all faced the same risks. Whether they were members of a movement, a circuit or a party, printers or distributors of the clandestine press, agents dropped by parachute, guides for escapers, radio operators, providers of 'safe houses', liaison officers, saboteurs, office workers for the underground, members of a *maquis*, leaders of groups, members of a shadow government – all were subject to the same terrible dictates. They had to abandon their old identity and become someone else, to hold their tongues, to hide, to be vagrants, to live in a perpetual crisis, to accustom themselves to loneliness and destitution, to hate the enemy and trust no one. If they were captured, usually through treachery, the same fearful fate awaited them all – a noisome prison, torture, insult and generally shooting or deportation. Such was the resister's calvary.

Motives

Like all human undertakings Resistance had its adventurers,[1] attracted by the excitement of the life. Many joined without really knowing why – as a result of family ties, chance or opportunism. For the vast majority, however, the overriding reasons were patriotism and anti-fascism; these two soon merged.

Patriotism initially took the form of a prickly xenophobia, the instinctive aversion to the presence of the foreigner, particularly in a position of superiority. In face of the increasing misery and the growing difficulties of day-to-day existence German propaganda was doomed to failure; people with empty stomachs simply would not listen. There were many reasons for their misfortunes,

[1] And even its killers.

but as they thought them through, their residual reaction was one of anger and they held the occupying power responsible for all their sufferings. A wave of hatred swept over enslaved Europe.

This reaction was naturally more prompt and violent among traditionally anti-German peoples such as the Poles and the French; certain sections of the population, such as the ex-servicemen and inhabitants of areas which had already suffered occupation during the 1914–18 war, felt particularly acutely. For the Dutch, Danes and Norwegians it was a new experience.

Potent factors were refusal to accept defeat, fear of partition of the nation's territory, and memories of past territorial losses, such as the French loss of Alsace. Both inside and outside France, the clandestine press was full of attacks on Germany and the Germans – 'It is a lying, deceitful race, greedy for plunder; the German uses his intelligence solely to do greater damage; he has no delicacy, no true moral strength, no dignity; he will renounce anything. . . . He is bovine, ruled by the herd instinct and incredibly deceitful. The great men of Germany have no faith in their country; many have disowned her. . . . No one can unravel the mystery of the German soul since it is a tissue of negatives. Unable to be great individually, the German attempts to be so by force of numbers and therefore produces a substitute for greatness in the shape of military force.' The conclusion was obvious: 'Never forget to hate; every time we encounter a German soldier our desire for retribution increases. . . .' Soon after June 1940 General Cochet wrote: 'Only one enemy, the Boche.'

In the early days of the war the anti-fascist motive was a factor only in the case of a minority of intellectuals, trade unionists and political militants;[1] it was, however, obviously the sole motive of those Germans and Italians who opposed the dictators. In most occupied countries it gradually grew as the true nature of the occupation was revealed; the loss of liberty, lack of freedom of speech and movement were bitterly resented; the fascist leader-worship evoked sarcasm and irritation. It was primarily the fate of the Jews which opened and aroused general indignation; people still did not know the horrible fate which awaited them but what they saw was enough – whole families arrested, deprived of their

[1] The Russians realised that this motive was confined to a minority; their propaganda stressed the day-to-day inconveniences rather than the ideological aspect of the occupation; it invariably coupled the words 'invader' and 'fascist'.

possessions and branded with distinguishing marks like animals, the degrading spectacle of manhunts with the victims herded into trains or public places; they were apparently perfectly ordinary men, women and children who had done no evil. This horror evoked pity, protest and rage. Under no circumstances, people thought, would they participate in such crimes; later they would descend upon their authors and punish them.

Self-respect was the strongest impulse which turned a man into a resister. Acceptance of defeat whilst still capable of fighting was to lose one's self-respect; self-respect dictated that one should not yield to the blandishments of collaboration; it even demanded self-sacrifice in order to restore one's country, but, above all, it demanded belief in oneself and one's ideas. Resistance accordingly produced men – very few – who could fight German soldiers without hating them – 'My death must not provide sustenance for hatred of Germany,' Boris Vildé wrote before he was shot. In a splendid passage Alban Vistel has emphasised that 'resistance was a moral rather than a political phenomenon', springing from a deliberate determination to defend certain ethical values to the end through all tribulation and sacrifice. 'It sprang from will-power, not the passage of time; it offered only duty without hope of rest; it confirmed the virtue of pertinacity; for every man of the Resistance commitment implied a break with the mediocrity of the past and rejection of conformism, injustice and degradation; it was a development of a spiritual nature.'[1]

A hard and dangerous life

The propensity of the subject populations for clandestine warfare varied according to their past history and manner of life. An SOE agent, for instance, observed that the Norwegians, particularly those of the islands, were great individualists, that they liked to say what they thought even at the risk of unfortunate consequences for themselves. The Polish leader of an intelligence circuit told his French friends that he was one-hundred-and-fifty years ahead of them; the French, accustomed to speak freely, prone to criticise and indisciplined by nature, did not possess that caution which came naturally to the Czechs and which twenty years of dictatorship had taught the Italians. For all of them,

[1] Alban Vistel; *L'Héritage spirituel de la Résistance*, Editions Lug, Lyons, 1955.

however, work in the underground implied an arduous apprenticeship and condemned them to a life of harassment and danger.

Apart from the collaborationist minority which profited from
the miseries of the majority, occupation created enormous
difficulties for the inhabitants. An extensive and strict rationing
system was instituted everywhere. As a result a sort of paper
currency in the form of cards and coupons grew up, proliferating
in inverse ratio to its true value. By the winter of 1940 conditions
in France, a rich country before the war, had become those of an
under-developed area. Everything became short all of a sudden –
bread, meat, sugar, vegetables, pastries, shoes, underwear, clothing, coal, electricity, tools, etc. The smallest essential day-to-day
activity, formerly an easy matter, produced insoluble problems –
keeping warm, travelling, finding milk for the children, buying a
new toothbrush, getting one's shoes mended, obtaining some
darning thread, buying nails to mend a chair, providing school-
children with paper and ink, etc. The resisters, who were the
recalcitrants among the population, were always hungry, emaciated and in rags, with unnaturally shining eyes, for they had
decided, not merely to survive, but to fight. To do so the problems
they had to solve were legion.

It might seem simple to learn to hold one's tongue, to stop seeing
old friends who had chosen the other side and to give up all
thoughts of a career; it was more difficult to abandon one's profession. Moreover, as a man's commitments became more definite,
the dangers and difficulties increased. Action in the Resistance
was like a quicksand, engulfing more and more deeply those who
had allowed themselves to become embroiled in it. A man would
begin by distributing pamphlets, passing on orders, taking part
in demonstrations and providing lodgings for strangers. By this
time he was committed and a sense of solidarity led him into
action – some papers or equipment needed storage, some mission
had to be fulfilled; finally he would take part in an operation –
and there he was with a gun in his hand. As the older hands
became casualties, responsibility weighed more heavily on the
shoulders of the survivors.[1]

The time came when the resister had finally broken with his
previous existence. He had changed his name and cut himself off

[1] This 'changing of the guard' is magnificently expressed in the 'Partisans' Song':
'When you fall, my friend, another friend will emerge from the shadows to take
your place.'

from his family as a precaution; he became homeless and frequently penniless. He became accustomed to interminable journeys in overcrowded trains, to hotels which he left at daybreak before the police came; he tried not to show fear when Germans examined his false papers; he no longer entered a house without looking for the emergency exits. Gradually he learnt the thousand and one details of clandestine action – meetings in city squares and railway stations, changes of route to baffle the sleuths, the compromising suitcase left in a railway compartment other than his own, destruction of the smallest scrap of secret paper, etc.

Everyone had gradually to assume another identity, to change his outward appearance and even his character, to become someone else. Few could continue in their profession; as excuse for their continuous travelling, therefore, they had to invent some fictitious employment, a 'cover story'. Jean Moulin, who was an art enthusiast, decided to open a picture gallery which he stocked with his private collection, telling his manageress not to sell anything. Above all it was essential to be unrecognisable – wear a different hat and hair-style, put on thick spectacles, grow a moustache or shave it off. All this was relatively simple; it was less easy to change behaviour, voice, gestures or mannerisms. The resister might frequently meet old friends who quickly penetrated his disguise.

Agents dropped by parachute from outside were forced to change their identity at a stroke rather than gradually as could the people of the occupied countries. Before departure they carried out a final inspection of their gear, turning things inside out in case some label had been forgotten, emptying their pockets in case some London or Moscow bus ticket should still be there. Even so occasions arose when, on meeting at some railway station after the operation and before dispersing once more, they realised with horror that their type of hat or mackintosh, compared with those of the people around them, would inevitably attract attention. Moreover how could they rid themselves of a British or French-Canadian accent? To guard against such dangers they were forced to invent a complete past history – relations living in Australia, long stays in South Africa or Montreal, etc.

Day-to-day life in the underground was very expensive; frequent journeys, meals in cafés and restaurants, lodging in hotels were the daily bread of the profession, but they cost a great deal and were also dangerous. One exhausting method of remaining inconspicuous was to travel by bicycle, as did many people in the occupied countries who had been deprived of their cars.

A good description of the daily existence of a resister is given by Guillain de Benouville: 'I sleep one night in the house of a clergyman and the next in a hotel requisitioned by an armistice commission, where the proprietor is a friend of mine. I explain their precise job to those whom I recruit and put them in touch with the leader who must be nominated in each town. I weave them all into the spider's web. I go over with the "responsible person" in each city the opportunities he has and those that I can make for him by giving him a contact with other supporters; he will, of course, know neither their names nor addresses; they will all appear under cover-names and, to keep in touch, will use all the well-known methods – the "post-box" in a friend's house, for instance; there an unaddressed message can be left and, if the police arrive, the owner can pretend that he does not understand it at all since it will say: "Swallow will expect Apricot tomorrow at 5.0 p.m. at the same place as last week." Regular meetings take place in busy streets, the date and time being decided from one meeting to the next; it will be agreed, for instance, that if one misses a meeting on Thursday the 8th at 3.0 p.m. outside No. 20, the next will be on Friday the 9th at 2.0 p.m. outside No. 43, on the opposite pavement. When we meet, security considerations compel me to check my friends' notebooks to ensure that they have followed the instructions contained in a note on security issued under reference number 64 LB. Suppose a man is due to meet me at 3.0 p.m. on the 8th at an agreed point; my cover-name is Renault; if he really must write, he should note down "Fiat", "Citroen" or "Talbot" and "5.0 p.m. 10th", in other words change my cover-name and use a personal number which he adds to or subtracts from the true figures.'[1]

When two resisters were to meet, they took elaborate recognition and concealment precautions. Rémy gives an illustration as follows: 'When someone came into the bar with the German magazine *Adler* folded under his left arm and ordered a bottle of Vichy, the agent would ask him for a light. The man would reply: "I have a lighter but it's out of petrol." The agent would pay for his drink and leave. The liaison officer would wait for two or three minutes before joining him in the entrance hall of the railway station. At a propitious moment a report on construction at

[1] Guillain de Benouville: *Le Sacrifice du matin*, Laffont, Paris, p. 209.

the airfield would be passed to him and slipped between the pages of the magazine, where there were already reports of the same type. The agent would then take a train to z . . . where the most frequented library was situated opposite the municipal theatre. He would thumb through several books before asking for an agreed title. The librarian would reply: "It's out of print, but if you like to come back in a few days, I will try and get you a copy." "No thank you, I'm only passing through," the agent would reply and, touching his hat, depart leaving his magazine near the books he had just been looking through. The librarian of z . . . who collected in his "post-box" reports from the entire area, would remove the reports from the magazine, add them to the others which had come to him by various means and finally hand them all to another liaison officer arriving from Paris.'[1]

Naturally all this could not be organised straight away; time was required to perfect the system; there were mistakes and set-backs. The need of a secure, well-chosen hiding place from which to work was one of the resister's permanent anxieties. Rémy again is illuminating: 'Lodging us entailed much self-sacrifice for the men and women who did so; in emergency we could always move, but they were tied by their jobs and their family responsibilities. For this reason elementary honesty compelled us always to take account of the immediate or indirect risks they ran. We preferred to choose a quarter where traffic was heavy and varied since the enemy could not then post his spies at street corners to pick out unfamiliar faces. The best was a house in the centre of town, if possible without a concierge but with a fair number of tenants. I do not recommend suburban villas since the inmates are naturally inquisitive about each other. Apart from providing hospitality people who agree to house resisters should undertake no illegal activity. If they are reputed to favour the occupier, so much the better. Their address should be known only to a very small number of people.'[2]

Outside occupied territory the staffs of SOE or the BCRA could always draft large-scale, meticulously worked-out plans, covering every possible contingency; on the spot, however, any clandestine arrangement was built on shifting sands. The head of a circuit explained it to Passy thus: 'If you want to find a "safe house", your mind first turns to reliable friends and you send them a

[1] Col. Rémy: *Réseaux d'ombre*, p. 17.
[2] Rémy, op. cit., pp. 222–3.

liaison officer to tell them what it is all about. If the friend in question is resourceful, has the time and is in luck, the agent may return to see him in a week's time and be told that everything is all right. When the liaison officer eventually returns, some ten days after leaving, the leader will know whether or not he can count upon the "safe house" he wanted. More often than not some scruple on the part of the friend or the owner of the "safe house", omission of some detail or some unfortunate proviso will entail a second journey. Three weeks are essential to arrange a "safe house" properly. To arrange a "reception committee" you require six weeks if you are to be sure that it will function perfectly at the time required. You have to be quite certain since the leader will not be there to deal with any last-minute problems. Setting up a liaison headquarters with its "post-boxes" and internal communications to the organisations it serves is a considerable task which inevitably takes time. Remember that every link in the chain must have certain qualities and be free of certain defects. Every member must then be instructed independently and given his role; the time-scale must be such as to remove all doubt about the way in which he will play his part.'[1]

Moreover, if the ideal organisation proved impracticable or when the threads so patiently woven were severed by the enemy, the resisters had to work in the open – not very comfortable in winter. They would meet in public places, on benches in parks, in a busy street, a large store or a station entrance hall, where they could talk unobtrusively. Punctuality was very important – in certain places the police posted their informers and they were quick to spot some stranger apparently waiting about. It was better not to meet twice at the same place, though this was temptingly easy. In addition to passwords certain warning signals were agreed on for use as necessary – an opened-necked shirt, hat in the hand, waistcoat unbuttoned, etc. In principle it was better to write nothing down but this was difficult to avoid. In any case it was essential to destroy papers with great care – Jean Moulin used to roll them into a ball and chew them. As resistance became more general, however, it acquired a real administrative machine which secreted directives, reports and messages; double walls and double floors were used, double-bottomed drawers, the plumbing and lumber rooms. The best hiding-places, however, were the most obvious; Michel Debré simply used the offices of

1 Colonel Passy: *Mémoires* (op. cit.), p. 187.

the *Conseil d'Etat* [Council of State] – there were a lot of papers there!

The underground mentality

Only very few resisters, such as the 'secret service' men or communist party 'professionals', had had any training for this life. The majority found it a severe test of their nerves and physical endurance. There were, of course, happy moments, even open rejoicing – on regaining contact with a friend, on the success of a difficult operation, after playing a good trick on the enemy, on snatching a few minutes of relaxation, etc.[1]

But at every instant the resister had to be on guard. Before clearing a 'post-box' he must check that it was not under observation. His heart inevitably beat a little faster as he climbed the stairs to a friend's flat, looking out for danger signs. Would the friend be at home? If not, who would be there? If a colleague failed to appear at a rendezvous, waiting for him was torture – had he been arrested? Shall I be arrested next? He had to learn to listen at doors before going in and have an excuse ready if something appeared suspicious. Almost anything could be a danger signal – someone gazing at him in a restaurant, seeing the same person several times in a day, a wrong number on the telephone, police vehicles near his home, an unexpected visit, an unexplained noise.

Through living in an atmosphere of constant danger the resister became hyper-sensitive and alert, but fatigue and attrition inevitably led to a certain laxity, to the fatal moment of inattention, to the mistake which might give him away. The uplift, the sense of doing something great was quickly dissipated. The days were filled with endless small matters which were invariably tiring and frequently disappointing. Collecting some piece of intelligence was all very well, but then it had to be encoded and transmitted and one never knew whether it would be received, understood and utilised. Receiving containers at night was rewarding but the price was an interminable vigil for the agreed radio message and nights spent watching for the aircraft in cold, weariness and fear. Even after a success he could not show his pleasure to his neighbours. The pleasures and the pains, the secrets and

[1] Jean Moulin used to go to a cinema in Trévoux which was usually full of German soldiers.

the orders, even the reassuring news all had to be kept to oneself.

To add to this continuous tension the resister frequently suffered genuine crises of conscience. The most fortunate were the unmarried since they were endangering only themselves. But those who exposed their wives or children to the threat of reprisals were inevitably torn by anxiety. The Germans were quite prepared to make use of innocent hostages and many a resister gave himself up so that they might be freed, though this was often a vain attempt. In almost everything he did the resister was endangering other people; the agent who notified the location of an ammunition dump might cause the adjoining village to be bombed; a *maquis* camp near a farm might lead to it being set on fire; a bomb placed in a factory might result in the workers being deported. Others too had to wrestle with their consciences; the railwayman had always been taught that it was his professional duty, which he observed with almost religious piety, to ensure that wagons and goods reached their destination; he was now asked to divert the former and destroy the latter. What of the postman who diverted mail? What of the concierge lending the apartment of one of her tenants who was away? What of the engineer who gave wrong orders or the specialist who did bad work without always being sure that the enemy would be the recipient of his deliberately defective products?

Even if the moment arrived when he had had enough, it was difficult to stop. For a few of the leaders it was possible to leave the country for the haven of London, Algiers or Moscow. Not all did so, feeling that their mere disappearance would be enough to destroy all that they had built up. A few days before his arrest Jean Moulin simply cabled: 'I shall hold on as long as I can'; by then he knew that the Gestapo had his name and description, all his cover-names and hide-outs and had already swept up some of his relatives. At these moments of dejection there was a continuous temptation to give way to the 'psychosis of the underground', to a crazy desire to abandon everything, to make the fatal false step deliberately, almost hand oneself over to the enemy like the shipwrecked who, weary of struggling, deliberately let themselves drown.

False papers

To mislead their many pursuers who, though well equipped were not well informed, the resisters hit upon the idea of giving themselves cover-names both for correspondence and in conversation. It soon became the rule for every resister to have several false names which he used either in turn or simultaneously; he changed them according to his functions, his contacts or his misfortunes, using one name for the outside world and another for his circuit; Henri Frenay, for instance, was known under some ten different names.[1] A surname common to several resisters was concealed under differing cover-names and, to make matters more complicated, the same cover-name was chosen by different people. The results were duplication in estimating the numbers of resisters, confusion among their enemies and great complication in identifying anyone.

For purposes of day-to-day existence every resister had to be in possession of a whole range of false papers, the number and variety of which continually increased owing to police regulations and the extension of the rationing system. He might need any or all of: a demobilisation certificate, an identity card, ration card and coupons, work or residence permit, civil status certificate, movement permit, pass for restricted areas, etc. In addition some might need a registration paper for the compulsory labour service, medical certificate, exemption certificate for students, release certificate for prisoners of war, etc. All these were subject to continuous change; access to some area previously unrestricted would suddenly be banned or some new article would be rationed; the form and wording of papers would be changed.

The preparation of false identity cards required many precautions; in the case of France Ippécourt describes them as follows: 'It is best to keep the real christian name since the user is then less likely to make a blunder. One or two other christian names should be added since the single christian name is a rarity in France. For the surname one takes the initial letter of the real name and, starting from this, chooses some French-sounding

---

[1] London knew him as 'Charvet' or 'Nef', his friends of *Combat* or the MUR as 'Gervais', 'Tavernier', 'Xantrailles', 'Francen' or 'Henri'. In passing it may be noted that this procedure has turned resistance documentation into a real jigsaw puzzle and does not make life easier for the historian.

name in sufficiently common use not to attract attention but not one so overworked as "Durand" or "Dupont" which are too frequently used as cover. One should avoid using a name which might indicate Jewish origin and so one cuts out names like David or Simon. One must also take account of current usage in mayors' offices; the name is written larger than other entries on the card but not in block capitals. For date of birth it is advisable to keep to the real date. Place of birth must never be Paris or a major city since immediate verification would be too easy; it is better to choose a village or locality where the records have been destroyed during the invasion or by bombing. For residence one chooses a street which actually exists, consulting the street guide or telephone directory. As far as description is concerned, this must obviously be accurate and care must be taken to use only the terms currently employed in mayors' or police offices; colour of hair, for instance, must be either black, auburn, average or dark and for these colours clearly defined abbreviations must be used; eyes can be chestnut or green or blue or grey-green or blue-grey; black eyes do not exist under civil service rules. A whole range of descriptions is available for shape and width of nose, facial characteristics and complexion. The attestation of signature is productive of the most serious risk run by the forger. In the smaller places attestations are always carried out by the mayor; if a specimen is available, therefore, one forges his signature and if not uses an illegible signature with 'p.p.' added. The date is one of the most important entries. Under all circumstances it must be later than May 1940 since this was the time at which an identity card was made compulsory. Care must be taken not to use a date which was a Sunday or holiday since no mayor deals with papers on those days. Even after all this there is still much work to be done. The stamp, for instance, must be a 13-franc stamp but these are very difficult to come by since they were withdrawn from circulation to stop the production of false papers; in April 1943 they were replaced by 15-franc stamps. The 13-franc stamp can still be found in solicitors' offices.'[1]

The remaining problem was to obtain or reproduce the blank forms for the various certificates and the numerous stamps which they had to carry – in France a demobilisation certificate required some twenty different stamps. A convenient method was to use town hall employees who could produce completely authentic

[1] Ippécourt: *Chemins en Espagne,* Gaucher, Paris, pp. 187–8.

documents. The procedure was to find names of people who had left the parish several years before; for each name, which would be correct with correct legal status, some fifteen identity cards could be prepared; it would have been surprising if two of them had been presented at the same check point on the same day. But this type of game could not be repeated *ad lib*; it was possible only in small places and its scope was therefore limited.

Workshops for the manufacture of false papers appeared in all countries. The various forms were ordered from clandestine printers; stamps were procured by stealing specimens and manufacturing copies. A whole range of material had to be patiently assembled – indiarubber, zinc plates, special ingredients and machines such as electro-presses; experts such as draughtsmen or technicians had to be recruited. The student movement *Défense de la France* undertook to manufacture stamps for other groups – up to 500 at a time. It obtained specimens through a whole series of accomplices in various official positions – prefectures, mayors' offices, police stations, youth movements, hospitals, German agencies, the rationing system, universities, gendarmeries, etc. Its apparatus became so manifold and diverse that, to find one's way round, it was necessary to draft a 'perfect forger's manual'.

Betrayals and arrests

All these precautions, all this ingenuity and all this devotion did not prevent numerous arrests. In fact, in spite of the efficiency of his many forms of police force, the occupier would frequently have been at a loss to uncover and break down the circuits; he was, after all, working in a foreign country and he never knew the language, the localities or the customs perfectly. But he knew how to recruit mercenaries and traitors to do his dirty work; he also had fearsome methods of loosening tongues and taking advantage of a moment of weakness.

The resisters were hunted by two rival German police forces. One, the Abwehr with its counter-espionage service and the Secret Field Security Police, was subordinate to the military authorities. The other, the State Police, was an offshoot of the ss; since 1939 Himmler had been in charge of all state security agencies, of the service of investigation and enquiry both at home

and abroad and of the criminal and political record offices; together these all formed the *Reichssicherheitshauptamt* [Central
Security Department – RSHA]. In general terms the executive
agency was the Secret State Police, the *Gestapo*; it was in sole
charge of all 'political' questions – communism, marxist parties,
resistance groups, Jews, Churches, Freemasons and, in the
broadest sense 'enemies of nazi Germany'. Though initially introduced semi-clandestinely in the rear of the fighting troops, the
Gestapo gradually replaced the Abwehr and became *the* organ of
repression *par excellence*.

In all occupied countries the Gestapo made use of the national
police force, though placing little trust in it and had access to its
files and saw its reports; they recruited from it volunteers who
were completely at their service. The collaborator governments
played their part in pursuing the resisters; the Vichy government,
for instance, formed special 'anti-terrorist brigades' and a 'police
force for Jewish questions'; to speed up legal proceedings it set up
'special sections' in the courts against whose judgements there
was no appeal. The 'more zealous' members of the collaborator
groups also offered their services and they had the advantage of
knowing their fellow-countrymen well. They were joined by a
whole swarm of informers, thugs, old lags and sharks.[1]

On occasions resisters fell into the hands of the enemy merely
by chance, as the result of an identity check, for instance, or during a manhunt when an entire area would be cordoned off and
anyone on the move interrogated and searched. But the more
sinister German successes were the result of treachery. Frequently,
all too frequently, people who had some connection with the
Resistance attempted to profit from it; alternatively, when
arrested, they agreed to enter the enemy's service. In the
French *Mouvements unis de Résistance*, for instance, a man named
Multon, known as Lunel, was responsible for several hundred
arrests; it was through him that the Germans reached Jean
Moulin.

Severe trials awaited the resister when arrested. His false papers

---

[1] In Croatia the Ustashi set up thirty-four special tribunals, of which eleven were
on circuit; executions took place three hours after the sentence; one man was
condemned to death merely for distributing pamphlets; twenty-four concentration camps were opened for opponents of the régime. Even the German generals
were disgusted by these massacres, the victims of which were numbered in
hundreds of thousands. The nazis recruited policemen and informers even inside
the ghettos.

did not stand up for long; his address was soon discovered and his house searched; any unfortunates who arrived and knocked on the door found a trap awaiting them. All compromising documents were rarely destroyed and, by following up the clues such as a name or address in a notebook, the investigators could often work their way right through a circuit. As soon as it was known that a resister had been arrested (but it had to be known in time), all those in touch with him went to ground, changed their cover-names and appearance, hid their papers if possible, dismantled their 'offices' and abandoned their 'post-boxes'.

The Gestapo used a whole series of methods to make prisoners talk, ranging from intimidation or bribery to the most brutal barbarism. For the resister the really difficult problem was to know how far he could go in admitting facts in view of the knowledge already possessed by his torturers; moreover, either without his knowledge or through some dramatic confrontation, the Gestapo made use of other resisters under arrest to conduct a sort of bidding match.[1] 'Moral torture' was a favourite method; if the resister would not 'talk', his nearest and dearest were cruelly threatened – with arrest, consignment to a concentration camp or, in the case of girls, to a 'soldiers' house'. It seems likely that a threat of this nature hanging over his fiancée led to the collapse of the man who, although a brave and long-standing resister, was in all probability responsible for the arrest of Jean Moulin.

Sometimes, to his great astonishment, the prisoner was released – nothing had been discovered against him, he was told. In high spirits he would hasten to rejoin his friends, never suspecting that he was being followed and was leading the hunters to their quarry. As a result released resisters soon came to be regarded with the deepest and frequently quite unjustified suspicion; this applied even to those who had been clever enough to deceive their gaolers or brave enough to escape from their clutches.

But when the prisoner consistently refused to say anything the Gestapo thugs gave free rein to their brutality; even worse were their mercenaries who wished to curry favour with their masters at the expense of their fellow-countrymen. Blows rained down with the back of the hand or a club; limbs were twisted and broken, teeth smashed; the soles of the feet were burnt with a red hot

---

[1] As a result, when liberation came, the public was astounded to hear well-known resisters hurling accusations of treachery at each other's heads, whereas in fact both sides had simply been tricked by the Gestapo.

iron, an electrified wire passed around the genitals; nails and eye-brows were torn off. The torturers competed in 'ingenuity'. Masuy, a Belgian in the service of the Gestapo in France, was the inventor of the 'bath torture', described as follows by one of the unfortunate victims: 'Taking short steps, bent double, I eventu-ally reached the bath-room, or rather the torture-room. One of the men picked me up and thrust me into the water. The bath was full up to the brim with icy water. The torture of the night before was about to begin again. But this time was not to be just one session but three consecutive sessions that I was to undergo. They were all there standing over the bath and when my head came out of the water, I saw their eyes shining, glaring at me. And all the time I could hear Bernard and Masuy shouting: "Come on, now talk." At one moment, owing to my being pulled in and out of the water, one pair of handcuffs came off. Bernard put them on again and tickled the soles of my feet. Whenever my head appeared, he threw icy water in my face, preventing my breathing and hurting me dreadfully. Constantly pushed back under water, unable to breathe, my strength gradually left me – there was a continual ringing in my head. They pulled me up and pushed me down again and again. "Give us the address," they shouted.'[1]

Few could stand up to such suffering for long. Agents dropped by parachute had a means of avoiding it by swallowing a cyanide capsule immediately they were arrested. Others committed suicide, like Pierre Brossolette who managed to elude his gaolers for a moment and threw himself from the fourth floor of a building in the Avenue Foch. Some died under torture, like Jean Moulin – 'every vessel in his body burst'. Those who emerged from 'interrogation' alive, whether they had talked or not, were returned to their cells – whence they sometimes succeeded in escaping with the help of their fellow-prisoners.[2] Usually they only left them to face the firing squad in the pale dawn of their last day on earth or to arrive, huddled in a goods wagon, in some concentration camp, where slow but certain death awaited them.

Sometimes the Gestapo did its work too well and, by its bruta-lity, killed the goose which laid the golden egg. The Abwehr was cleverer; its favourite method was to infiltrate double agents

---

[1] P. Rémy: *Portrait of a Spy,* Arthur Barker, London 1955, pp. 122–3.
[2] Escapes were easier if the prisoners succeeded in getting themselves admitted to hospital; sometimes they were helped by the warders who also took to their heels.

into the circuits in order to break them up from within and make use of them, in effect taking them into service – without their knowledge of course. In this way some German spies contrived to reach Britain accompanying genuine 'escaped' resisters. The most remarkable success scored by this procedure took place in Holland; it was known as the 'Englandspiel'.[1]

SOE has been guilty of some indiscretions in Holland. Without adequate precautions one of its agents had contacted some Dutch officers, one of whom betrayed him. The first result of this was that the Germans broke the British code. In February 1942 they arrested a radio operator; he half-confessed and continued to transmit but making mistakes in order to alert the London end; being cautious, SIS broke contact but the less experienced SOE continued. Two other operators were then caught in the Abwehr's spider's web and one of them agreed to send messages. The British charged unsuspectingly into the trap set for them. Parachute drops were organised at various points, delivering all types of equipment; in London people were jubilant thinking that all was going well; in Holland the men and containers were swept up by the Abwehr as they arrived. Every operation added some threads to the web since each agent carried lists of names and addresses of which the Germans made good use. Finally, thirty-five experts were dropped intended for the training of a secret army; they were arrested at once. To deceive its British opposite numbers the Abwehr even pretended to organise some minor acts of sabotage – to the great joy of the Dutch.

The Dutch government in London was the first to have its suspicions when it found that all its most reliable political friends were falling into enemy hands one after another. But SOE still refused to be worried. In January 1944, when two agents succeeded in escaping to Switzerland, their story seemed so incredible that London was unwilling to believe them. By this time 4,000 telegrams had been exchanged with 'North Pole' and 400 agents arrested. The Dutch resistance had been totally destroyed.[2]

Many may think that the resisters were defenceless in the face of such resources and experience and frequently they were. They

[1] It was also called *Nordpolspiel* [North Pole game] because, when a Dutch nazi arrived with the news that British agents were reaching Holland, the head of the Abwehr replied: 'You can go to the North Pole with tales like that.'
[2] See De Jong: 'Britain and Holland' in *Proceedings of a Conference on Britain and European Resistance*, Oxford 1962.

paid dearly for their 'amateurism'; it is difficult to say how many died on the job; including shootings and deportations it was certainly in tens of thousands in France alone. But, as the Resistance became identified with the fate of the subject populations and the embodiment of their hopes, it was able to draw indefinitely on a vast reservoir. The intelligence and escape circuits, the reception committees, the agents dropped by parachute, the groups which printed and distributed the clandestine newspapers, the workers who initiated the go-slow, the members of the activist squads who sabotaged enemy equipment or liquidated his friends were the knights of the Resistance. They showed the way; their martyrdom and their sacrifices were the signposts.

Thanks to them the great battle could start, the *maquis* campaigns, the battalions raised in the villages and the provinces, the 'national risings'. Working with, often ahead of, the Allied armies, the Resistance became the great 'shadow army' drawn from every class and section of the nation. In the apotheosis of liberation this was the victorious army which marched through Wenceslas Square in Prague and down the Champs Elysées in Paris.

PART V

The Shadow Army

By means of sabotage, assassinations and partial strikes the Resistance served its apprenticeship. The communists were in no doubt about the ultimate object: as soon as possible resistance should take the form of direct armed action, bringing into it the largest possible number of available volunteers, not in a disorderly old-style *levée en masse* but through co-ordinated action by small groups, each working in its designated area and with the resources available to it. In areas of the USSR gradually liberated by the Red Army and in other countries numerous partisan units sprang up in the mountains and forests, and also in the cities. These the Red Army did its best to arm, train, staff and direct.

The British and Americans together with the governments-in-exile and the resistance groups dependent on them were somewhat opposed to the instigation of large-scale risings which they thought might lead to anarchy and be the forerunners of revolutionary movements. They preferred small groups formed as far as possible on regular army lines[1] and commanded by radio. To show the Germans, therefore, that victory did not mean security and to convince the populations that they had not been abandoned and as a rehearsal for larger-scale operations, the British launched harassing actions into Europe, raids in which the local resistance was involved to a greater or lesser extent; they ranged from the spectacular bombing of a building occupied by the Gestapo (in Oslo) or an air raid on a prison in order to free the inmates (at Amiens) to the temporary capture of a port (Saint-Nazaire and Dieppe) or the destruction of German installations (Bruneval). The most successful was undoubtedly the operation against the Lofoten Islands in Norway in March 1941; ships totalling 19,000 tons were sunk, eighteen cod liver oil factories were set on fire,

---

[1] In Holland SOE visualised formation of a secret army of some thousand men, preferably consisting of ex-officers.

213 German soldiers and 12 collaborators captured and 300 volunteers taken back to Great Britain.

In western Europe the communists were working on other lines and many other resisters also crossed swords with the occupying power. Certain of the governments-in-exile, especially the Polish, wished to prove to the world that the entire population of their country was behind them and the best method of demonstrating this was to put it into action *en masse*. In addition, as the Germans enforced the compulsory labour service regulations, the number of evaders increased and they moved from recalcitrance to open hostility. Steadily, under the pressure of events, occupied Europe became a vast furnace in which revolt was smouldering.

The spark was provided by armed groups known in some places as 'partisans' and in others as *maquis*; they operated in areas which armoured vehicles could not reach and they vanished when attacked by superior forces; sometimes, however, they stood firm and inflicted defeats on the Germans or even took the initiative, raiding deep into enemy territory, spreading an atmosphere of insecurity and imposing their summary justice in areas under their control. In certain cases guerrilla warfare became widespread and the occupying power was unable to stop it.

These men who fought increasingly in the open were not very numerous, but they were protected and assisted by a whole network of accomplices and well-wishers. They swept up the earlier resistance groups, the 'movements' and the 'circuits'. To coordinate and supply such variegated forms of action, the Resistance acquired a military and administrative structure. It regrouped and set up an efficient organisation and little by little, the machinery of a *clandestine State* appeared with, in some cases, a genuine government at its head.

Then came the moment for the long awaited and carefully prepared *national rising*. The entire machine began to move at the approach of the Allied armies. All underground forces were committed; sabotage increased on a planned basis, partisan attacks became bolder, strikes became general and whole cities or areas rose, frequently with success as in Bucharest or Paris, sometimes in dramatic failure as in Warsaw, Slovakia or the Vercors.

From this point resistance everywhere played a major role in the country's liberation. It had grown since the difficult early days but, as it reached its goal, all the internal fissures and rivalries which had undermined it came out into the open. In France and Yugoslavia it came to power, in the first case through national union, in the second at the price of civil war. In Central Europe it was the springboard that enabled communist minorities to seize power. In Poland and Greece it ended in dismal failure. Whatever the outcome, however, it was in the underground that post-war Europe took shape.

CHAPTER 16

Guerrilla Warfare – Maquis and Partisans

When civilians make war, fighting themselves, without uniform and without military status, they become partisans, irregulars, francs-tireurs, guerrillas, *maquis*, resisters – there are plenty of words describing them. The history of Europe is full of warfare of this nature – and the regular armies treat them, not as enemies but as outlaws. In general such warfare has been revolutionary and has occurred when minorities believe that they must resort to arms to defend their rights or their faith. Such was the case with the protestant Camisards in the Cevennes, the Vendéans against the Convention and the Spaniards and Prussians against Napoleon's armies.

The first essential in the struggle is to gain the approval and then the complicity of the population; this gradually strengthens as an administrative, economic, military and even judicial machine becomes established. Since, in most cases, revolts have been occasioned by despair, warfare is characterised by fury, violence and fanaticism, by massacres and exploitation. Before resuming the struggle against Napoleon after Jena, Stein laid down that 'The Landsturm will carry off all inhabitants with their animals and possessions; flour and grain will be removed or destroyed, barrels emptied, mills and boats burnt, wells filled in, bridges blown up and houses set on fire. The struggle to which the nation is called justifies all methods, the more terrible the better.' In Spain and then in Russia Napoleon's armies were met by a 'tactical desert', by 'scorched earth'. Guerrilla warfare has always led to enormous losses of life and property.

The marxists and subversive warfare

Communist theorists had devoted much study to these risings in which a few companies of determined men had succeeded in carrying an entire population with them and withstanding an apparently far more powerful army. Marx observed that the Spanish guerrillas had been everywhere and nowhere, 'they took their operational bases with them'. He had criticised the Piedmontese, who had been beaten at Novara, for having engaged the Austrians in battle when they were inferior both in numbers and arms; he concluded that 'mass risings, revolutionary methods and guerrillas everywhere are the means of re-establishing numerical and material equality'. This method of warfare, he said, was as normal and as 'noble' as any other. In 1870 Engels poured scorn on 'the civilised nations whom a certain sense of honour forbids to continue the war after the destruction of their army and official capitulation' and Marx had criticised the 'essentially Prussian idea that a nation which continues to fight after the destruction of its army is committing a crime'. Both were thus pleading the cause of the French francs-tireurs, shot by the Prussians on capture.

Lenin went further and emphasised the advantageous role which war could play in a revolution – 'it tears down false façades, lays bare the weakness of governments and uncovers internal putrefaction'. From this point of view a State's defeat might accelerate the revolutionary process; far from being feared, it should be assisted. For the communist theorists guerrilla warfare was subversive since its object was to enable a minority to assert itself; its aim was to overthrow an established political, economic and social order; it was essentially politico-military.

These quotations from the great marxist thinkers had become the bolshevik bible. The Congress of the 'Communist International' in 1928 had defined the political significance of partisan warfare, the transformation of 'imperialist warfare' into civil war in which each country's proletariat would rise against its real enemy, the class oppressors of its own country.

Mao Tse-tung turned these principles into concrete tactical teaching: 'The whole art of war is based on deception. If we are ready to attack, we must appear incapable of doing so; if we are close to the enemy we must make him think that we are far away and if we are far away that we are close. Put out baits to draw the enemy. Simulate disorder and crush him. . . . When the enemy advances, we retreat; if he withdraws, we harass him; when he retreats, we pursue him; when he is weary, we attack him. . . . If you have ten times the forces of the enemy, encircle him; if you have five times, attack him; if not, avoid battle. Wear the enemy down; draw him into our territory and attack from strength against weakness . . . live off the enemy . . . one to ten in strategy, ten to one in tactics. . . .'

But all these methods had been worked out on the assumption that the proletariat was seizing power from capitalism. The advent of the Soviets to power in Czarist Russia changed the basis of the problem. From then on the object in the event of attack was to fight to prevent the homeland of socialism going under; through the bolshevik revolution the workers of the USSR had found a country; at least initially, therefore, their war was not a political offensive but defence of the nation. The same applied throughout occupied Europe; Moscow's directive to the communists was the liberation of national territory; 'revolution would be achieved through liberation'. In any case, though the aims of guerrilla warfare might thus change, its rules remained the same.

Rules and conditions of guerrilla warfare

Lawrence had deduced from his battles with the Arabs against the Turks the principle that 'clandestine warfare partakes of the nature of an influence, an idea, something intangible, invulnerable, without front, without rear, spreading like a gas'. He thus emphasised that guerrilla warfare was effective only if the guerrillas believed that it could be; it was, in the first instance, the child of faith and propaganda. In Europe this feeling was kindled by an exalted sense of patriotism born of the occupation of the nation's soil by the enemy.

In addition certain conditions had to be fulfilled. Realisation of the enemy's crushing superiority must not lead to impotence. The resisters made a point of systematically belittling the enemy potential. 'An isolated Boche is a prisoner . . . weapons do not compensate for lack of numbers when an entire people is on the ground and can pursue the struggle in concert. . . . The nazi terror is operative only for those who accept it.'[1] History was combed for convincing illustrations of victory of the weak over the strong.[2] The fact remained, however, that in major strategic areas such as the Channel coasts, the Germans concentrated too

[1] *France d'abord*, June 1944.
[2] Charles Tillon, for instance, cites Du Guesclin, Marty and Joan of Arc.

many troops and took too many precautions for the underground to do more than collect information, at great risk.

But it was not the same everywhere. In fact Hitler's voracious ambitions had so extended the occupied territories that the German army and police could not supervise the whole area. This was one of the reasons for the institution of a régime of terror, which was in fact a confession of weakness. Moreover the war differed totally from that of 1914–18 in that there was no permanent static front; the combatants were intermingled and wide areas were left uncovered. Napoleon thought that 'the secret of warfare consisted in remaining master of one's communications'. As it moved across Russia, lengthening its supply lines by thousands of miles, the insatiable appetite of a mechanised army grew in geometrical ratio to the distance covered. The Wehrmacht was laid open to sabotage which it was barely able to check, still less to prevent. The fuel which gave the armour its irresistible strength, in a sense became its Achilles heel; if it did not arrive the Wehrmacht ground to a halt, a prisoner of its own requirements.

Because of the suffering and destruction it causes guerrilla warfare is less suited to peoples of a high level of civilisation than to those lower down the scale – where communications are sparser. Mountainous areas are particularly favourable; they offer a refuge; the occupation forces are hampered by the rough ground and by lack of information; they work in semi-darkness; co-ordination of movement is difficult as the troops must disperse and therefore adopt the same tactics as the partisans. Heavy weapons such as tanks, artillery and aircraft are less effective or cannot be used at all; regular forces advance less surely, sometimes even timorously. The partisans, on the other hand, are defending their own hideout; they know the country; observation is easy for them and they can detect the enemy's approach at once. Their weapons are their lungs and their muscles; they can use foot-paths and ridges to escape encirclement and vanish into the countryside. To a lesser degree large forests, even in flat country, play the same role.

A major urban area, however, with its labyrinth of streets and innumerable hiding places in buildings, can also harbour a *maquis*; for the saboteur a faceless crowd offers as secure a hiding place as a forest. More important still, cities contain numerous targets, whose destruction will greatly affect the occupying power – factories, railway stations, machine depots, stocks of weapons and supplies, road junctions, barracks; the presence of administrative offices facilitates the collection of intelligence and the density of the population assists propaganda. But supply is more difficult as the partisan is continuously underground, and above all the occupier can easily take savage reprisals which may turn the people against the resisters.

Without the support of the population guerrilla warfare is like a bale of wet hay into which a match has been thrown; it will smoke but will not burst into flame. Although, therefore, the partisans kept away from inhabited areas as far as possible, the supporting population formed the reserve on which they could draw. It was their source of supply, of medical aid if necessary and of information on the enemy's preparations. Mao Tse-tung summarised this essential osmosis in the famous phrase 'to be among the people like a fish in water'. In France a circular from the 'National Front' ordered *maquis* to 'set up in each village an aid committee to deal with reception of evaders, assembly of food stocks and collection of funds'.[1] Partisans who were not natives of the country encountered some difficulty and time was required before they became accepted by the populace; agents dropped by parachute had even greater difficulty.

If the population did not support guerrilla warfare it died away, for it could only continue through a constant influx of volunteers. High morale and an aggressive temperament were the hallmarks of the volunteer; since he had chosen his road himself, the man of the *maquis* was by nature more resourceful and more inclined to act on his own than the soldier who follows his officer blindly. However, this made it difficult for those in command to assert their authority and maintain discipline. At any time the volunteer might consider that he had a right to argue or refuse to obey an order, even to demobilise himself. Common convictions or customs – membership of a party or regimental association for instance – might mitigate these basic weaknesses, but a *maquis* remained a fragile institution. Splits, break-ups and reconstitution elsewhere were the order of the day. This basic inconsistency made it difficult to bring about agreement between different groups (particularly of differing ideologies) and to adopt and apply any common strategy.

Whatever happens the partisan must never become bored or discouraged. In the *maquis* a 'waiting game' is extremely dangerous; mere vigilance sends the partisan to sleep, ossifies his reflexes

[1] 'Push your tentacles forward; the inhabitants will be your eyes and ears.'

and gives him a feeling of uselessness; he begins to long for the peace of his home. The men of the *maquis* were defending their hearth and home and the further they went from it the weaker they became; major expeditions were difficult for them in any case since they had to move on foot. Moreover, they could not remain on the defensive without risking disintegration. 'The defensive,' Marx had said, 'is death to popular warfare; it is destruction even before commencement of the struggle.' Groups which fought were invariably stronger than those which remained inactive. The enemy captured most of his prisoners from the latter; conversely danger increased the solidarity and aggressiveness of a group. In addition, where the enemy would not fight 'the inhabitants gained the impression that the sufferings, destruction and casualties were a pointless burden and a total loss'.[1] For the guerrilla, therefore, attack was the best defence; moreover it kept the enemy at full stretch, wearing him down and demoralising him. Charles Tillon wrote: 'The tactical principle of the FTP was to strike at the enemy at once despite his strength, but each time to strike in such a way as to weaken the enemy and strengthen the forces of patriotism.'[2]

By its very nature guerrilla warfare had no power to annihilate the enemy, the aim of all war according to Clausewitz. It was no more than a series of endlessly repeated tiny operations, of assassinations, acts of sabotage and ambushes. Its margin of action was small – the difference, according to Captain Poitau, 'between the enemy's appreciation on which he bases his action, and our true capabilities; the first essential is to upset his calculations, to bluff him, never to do what he expects and to think up something different'.[3] Such flexibility precluded the employment of large units; only small teams could make a surprise attack and then withdraw with the necessary mobility and rapidity. In their *maquis* schools the FTP stressed 'the importance of movement over fire'. Lenin had advocated groups of two or three; the 'National Front' laid down the ideal number as eight to twelve.

Whatever happened, still following Lenin's teaching, one must 'seize any opportunity of doing real work ... never let slip an opportunity that offers'. If the enemy forces were too strong, the

---

[1] Circular from the 'National Front' in France.
[2] *Les FTP*, op. cit., p. 168.
[3] *'Guerrilla en montagne'* in *Revue d'Histoire de la Deuxième Guerre Mondiale*, January 1963.

partisans would withdraw without attempting anything – audacity was not to be equated with foolhardiness. Similarly they would refuse battle when the enemy was seeking it and force it upon him when he was not expecting it. Objectives were communication facilities, small detachments in transit, guard posts, depots and storage sheds, stocks of arms, equipment and ammunition – which also held out the advantage of replenishing the *maquis'* meagre arsenal. Liberation of an area, however, was not an objective in itself; defence of a piece of ground at all costs was tantamount to suicide; the guerrilla, after all, has no bases to maintain, no rear areas to protect. This too Lawrence had observed: 'The art of the guerrilla is always to evade the enemy; when regular troops are trying to maintain contact, the guerrilla refuses it; the regulars are trying to destroy their enemy, the guerrillas to destroy his equipment. Guerrilla warfare never consists of keeping and increasing some advantage, but always of moving and striking elsewhere.'

Whatever a country's history, traditions and mythology, however favourable its geography, however determined its inhabitants, nowhere and from no one section of any people did a flexible and widespread guerrilla movement spring fully armed from the presence of the enemy; a long apprenticeship was necessary. Eastern Europe proved more suitable than the west; mountain peoples adapted themselves more easily than city dwellers; the communist had the advantage of a half-forgotten doctrine, of a closer knit organisation, but the city workers were in no way ready for it. Most disconcerted of all were the regular officers; as Bugeaud had said to his officers involved in the struggle against Abd el-Kader, they had to 'forget much of what they had learnt'.[1] This was good advice for the Allied armies too.

Life in the maquis

The size of a *maquis* or group of 'partisans' varied considerably. Ideally the actual attacks were made by small groups of highly trained and resolute men, but day-to-day existence demanded genuine services – outposts, supply, communications, etc. Although the majority consisted of less than one hundred men,

[1] Quoted by Henri Bernard.

others, particularly in Russia and Yugoslavia but also in the Vercors and at Mont Mouchet, numbered some thousands of volunteers. Obviously everything depended on the role they were expected to fulfil. Whatever their numbers, the partisans came from the most diverse backgrounds. People were unsettled as a result of war and occupation, refugee movements and compulsory transfers of population; as we have seen, resistance fighters came from all quarters of the globe; finally the *maquis* provided a refuge for those persecuted by the enemy and they came from all walks of life. Research into the make-up of a small French *maquis* showed that most of its members were young; they included evaders of the compulsory labour service from all parts of France, Alsatian and Slovene deserters from the German army, gendarmes absent without leave, school-teachers, workers from the neighbouring towns, small shopkeepers, a few farmers, French and foreign Jews.[1] Numerous studies carried out in eastern Europe have reached similar conclusions in regard to the Polish, Russian and Slovak partisans; local resisters were joined by escaped prisoners of war or workers evading the compulsory labour service belonging to all nationalities.

This diversity rendered the maintenance of discipline difficult. In communist *maquis* the party kept control by means of the 'triangular system' expedient, three 'commissars' being appointed, one for personnel, one for operations and one for miscellaneous services. In a *maquis* recruited from regular army sources the leader was 'the most senior officer of the highest rank'. Most *maquis*, however, were basically 'wild', and consisted of people who had been on the run; in most cases they had chosen their leaders themselves, men who could assert themselves through force of personality, sometimes only for a very short time. The *maquis* tended to turn into gangs; one MUR leader described his men as 'rebels, ungovernable and ready for anything which would satisfy their thirst for action and revenge'. The French resistance leaders understood the seriousness of the problem and opened 'staff schools'. *Maquis* instructors dropped by parachute could often assert themselves as a result of their technical knowledge and the weapons and money they could provide. Punishments such as the forefeiture of tobacco, food or a weapon were difficult to enforce. The best method of ensuring discipline was to sink

[1] See Perotin: '*La Composition d'un maquis*' in *Revue d'Histoire de la Deuxième Guerre mondiale*, January 1963.

all differences in the cauldron of battle – if the leader was courage-ous, he could prove it in action and emerge with greater authority. Nevertheless there were numbers of 'two-timers' in the *maquis* who held people to ransom, kidnapped and executed them even after liberation; they were all the more difficult to identify since, in moments of danger, the 'genuines' were frequently compelled to resort to the same dubious methods.

The time of year, the possibility of enemy attack, and current operations all caused the *maquis* to move frequently. The moun-tains and forests provided fesh water, game and sunshine in the summer, but in winter it was necessary to come down and find some warmer hide-out, sometimes even in the valleys where it was obviously easier for the enemy to keep them under observa-tion; alternatively the *maquis* put itself in cold storage and vanished into the population, or they could dig in.[1] The area selected for a camp had to be one seldom visited, hard to get to but easy to guard; it must have several exits so that it could be quickly abandoned – a mountain amphitheatre, for instance, might mean a fight with backs to the wall. Captain Poitau says: 'As soon as a camp was discovered, even by a friendly lumberjack or poacher, it was moved at least two hours march away. Some camps, on a steep hillside and reached by the bed of a stream, were so well hidden, away from any path, that many a new arrival spent the night wandering around.' This was obviously easier for the smaller units. Once a place had been chosen tents and wooden huts were put up and tumbledown buildings repaired. There were many fatigues – for wood, water, food and cooking, etc.

Supply was the big problem; it forced the *maquis* to maintain a full-scale organisation in the valleys and even in the towns. Representatives toured the farms, appealing to the farmers' generosity, but they paid as well, sometimes in money, more often in '*maquis* vouchers'. The guerrillas, therefore, had a finan-cial problem – a minimum of pay had to be issued, particularly to heads of families. Fines were levied on 'collaborators'; sometimes a parachute drop provided a small quantity of fresh money. The easiest method was to rifle food stocks, steal ration cards and coupons from town halls, help themselves in shops or carry out an armed raid on public funds – in post or tax offices, for instance,

---

[1] An MUR pamphlet reminded people that the soldiers of the First World War were not cold in the trenches if they had an underground shelter since it was warmed by the body heat of the inmates.

but this led to charges of highway robbery being levelled against the *maquis* by its opponents. The most 'correct' solution, however, was to print stamps or vouchers acknowledging gifts and promising payment later; *maquis* leaders were provided with 'letters of entitlement' by the emigré governments or clandestine authorities authorising them to use this paper money; notices posted in the villages invited people to accept it. After all it was no worse than that issued in such profusion by the occupying powers.

Care of the wounded constituted a difficult problem. Sometimes the *maquis* applied to the doctor of a neighbouring village; on occasions a medical student was discovered among the evaders of the compulsory labour service. The larger *maquis*, such as Glières or the Vercors, were allotted volunteer doctors; a well-known New Zealand surgeon was parachuted to Tito. Makeshift operating theatres were installed with nurses who were usually amateurs. Collapsible stretchers were constructed, but frequently the wounded had to be taken to near-by hospitals in the hope that the staff would keep the secret.

The greater part of the time was taken up in training – handling of weapons, reconnaissance, drill for disengagement, plans of attack. Live firing exercises were held in the mountains, and the resulting accuracy minimised accidents. After this an initial operation, not too difficult or dangerous, was carried out to give each man his baptism by fire.

To obtain the necessary offensive and defensive intelligence a double network was set up. Around the camp, in the valleys or in the towns. friends kept watch on the enemy; liaison officers were chosen from reliable people whose profession allowed them to move around; any new face was suspect on principle. Further out other friends patiently observed possible objectives to discover the right moment when the *maquis* could descend.

Weapons, unfortunately, were scarce. Lenin had, of course, said that 'the fighting detachments must arm themselves with anything which comes to hand' and the FTP announced that 'any fitter could manufacture a hand grenade, tyre-bursters and many other useful things'; the fact remained, however, that the disparity of force was almost insurmountable. One solution was to organise raids to obtain weapons – more than one gendarmerie post lost its stock of carbines with its own connivance. The less formidable enemies such as the Italians were also a source of weapons; the principle was that 'each weapon should bring in at least one other weapon each week'. Finally stocks of ammunition had to be assembled, not an easy task with so mixed a collection. Toll was levied on the armies of the 'halfway house' régimes and deserters from them were always welcome in the *maquis*. The Italian capitulation in September 1943 proved to be a windfall for the partisans in the French Alps, Albania, Greece and Yugoslavia; a full-scale arsenal and much equipment was captured and some complete units even changed sides. A great gap remained, however, between the numbers of volunteers and the weapons at their disposal – the leader of a *maquis* in the Montagne Noire had only two sub-machineguns and some sixty rifles for several hundred men.

This continual lack of resources restricted partisan recruitment and reduced enthusiasm. The solution could only come from the Allies; they had to be convinced that their deliveries were put to good use which was not always the case; moreover the guerrillas could not operate too far away from the regular armies. It soon became apparent that the Red Army was the best prepared and the best placed for large-scale co-operation with the partisans.

Guerrilla warfare in Russia

On several occasions co-operation with partisans had been one of the themes of Red Army manoeuvres, but the speed of the German advance left the army little time to take advantage of this training.

Starting in 1942 two-way communication was established through a few radio sets and parachute drops became possible. A 'Partisan Headquarters' under General Ponomarenko was set up in Moscow as directing agency. In fact initiative came primarily from those on the spot. Local groups, sometimes commanded by officers, took advantage of equipment abandoned by the Soviet armies as they retreated. They enjoyed a large measure of autonomy since only they could discover the enemy's weak points and carry out operations with some prospects of success. 'Courses of instruction' were broadcast by radio and partisan schools opened in Moscow, Leningrad and Stalingrad.[1]

Partisans appeared everywhere. They were not very numerous

[1] The first landing by a Soviet aircraft on an airfield under partisan control took place on 10 November 1942; the news caused a considerable stir.

in the north, however, because of the severity of the climate and the fact that it was a secondary theatre of operations. Similarly, despite the stories of Stenka Razine and Pougachev, the steppes of the Ukraine offered few natural advantages. Plentiful hide-outs were to be found, on the other hand, in Byelorussia, with its forests and marshes, and in the mountains of the Crimea and Caucasus.

The role of the partisans varied with their location. Away from the front or in the towns activity consisted primarily of the distribution of propaganda leaflets, assassination of 'collaborators', sabotage of installations serving the enemy and the formation of sympathiser groups to provide hide-outs and supplies. A feature of Soviet guerrilla warfare was the organisation of long-distance raids by major units. The forest of Briansk, for instance, became a sort of fortress from which 'sorties' were made in all directions; one of these, made by several thousand men and directed southwards, crossed the rivers Snov, Desna, Dnieper and Pripet massacring any enemy unit it encountered and sweeping through villages where the 'law of the partisans' was in force for a time; another raid, starting in the Ukraine, ended in the heart of the Carpathians. In such cases the role of the partisans was to spread insecurity behind the enemy lines, demoralise the occupying power by surprise attacks and keep a grip on the population through a close-knit network of sympathisers; in certain cases towns were even liberated ahead of time, as happened at Pavlograd in February 1943.

In areas near the front, however, the partisans turned themselves into a genuine advanced guard of the Red Army – the most original characteristic of their activity. In principle they were subordinate to the army, both clandestine warfare and conventional war being directed on an equal footing by the 'Committee for Defence of the State'. Sometimes the Red Army's objective coincided with areas held by the partisans and then they were provided with the necessary heavy weapons such as machineguns and mortars. In June 1944 the Bobruisk-Vitebsk sector provided an example of successful co-ordination but the best illustration was the battle of Kursk in the autumn of 1943 which decided the liberation of the Ukraine. The Red Army's advance was preceded by the partisans who committed an average of twenty-five acts of railway sabotage per day; they built bridges over rivers and fought regular battles. The result was to produce a sort of corridor clear of the enemy from the Dnieper to the western Bug, into which the regular forces advanced and attacked the enemy in flank.

As soon as an area was liberated partisan units were disbanded; their members were registered and taken over by the army, some being drafted into security or mopping-up units for the rear areas, others simply being used as regimental replacements; officers were sent to refresher schools. An estimate can therefore be made of the true value of guerrilla warfare in the USSR. It certainly did not lack activity; for White Russia alone it can boast: 3,000 cases of railway sabotage, a similar number of trucks destroyed, 16 German battalions each of 2,000 men immobilised. The Germans were the first to confirm its importance. One of their reports of April 1943 estimated partisans in Byelorussia at 80,000 and admitted that they were the cause of 'considerable difficulties in railway traffic and agriculture'. According to Colonel Teske 175,000 German soldiers were killed by partisans in the Ukraine alone. Clearly the vast distances and the fact that the great majority of German units were at the front made it comparatively easy for large guerrilla groups to infiltrate. Since, moreover, after a period of uncertainty the 'Committee for Defence of the State' gave the partisans maximum support, guerrilla warfare reached proportions unknown elsewhere except in Yugoslavia; in the Ukraine alone 220,000 volunteers were 'counted'. Caught up in a battle of colossal numbers, the Soviets ignored Lenin's teaching that only small irregular units should be used. Nevertheless when the German general Dittmar, writing in July 1943 – at the height of the Kursk battle – said that 'partisans were doing more damage to the Wehrmacht than any other form of activity', he was exaggerating. The Soviet official history sets matters in their true proportion when it says that in the 'great patriotic war' the Red Army played the leading role, the partisans never being more than its advanced guard or auxiliaries.

Guerrilla warfare in Yugoslavia

With its mountainous broken country, extensive forests and hardy frugal inhabitants, Yugoslavia was particularly suited to guerrilla warfare and the savagery of the Ustashi turned it into an implacable struggle. Even before the Wehrmacht had invaded

Russia it was known in London that a colonel named Mihailovich had collected some scattered remnants of the Yugoslav army, routed before completion of mobilisation, and was continuing to fight in old Serbia. He was universally popular; he and his *chetniks*[1] became the symbol of European resistance; until 1943 the French communists had nothing but praise for him.

In fact Mihailovich was obsessed with the 'pan-serbism' of the Yugoslav leaders and he despised Croats, Slovenes and Bosnians; he seldom left his hide-outs to attack the enemy. He soon allied himself to other Serbs, also calling themselves *chetniks*, who were in fact servants of General Nedich's collaborator government in Belgrade. He was savagely opposed to other partisans, whom he attacked – those raised by the communist party and commanded by Tito, then completely unknown to the Allies who thought his name to be a cover or acronym. Chetniks and partisans were soon at daggers drawn and, despite counsels of moderation from Moscow and the directives of the government-in-exile in London, a furious battle developed. To their astonishment the British learnt from the reports of missions despatched to both sides that Mihailovich was flirting with the Italians, and was remaining strictly inactive, preserving his forces to square accounts with the communists on liberation. Only Tito and his men were really fighting and they were giving the Italians, Hungarians, Bulgarians, Germans, Ustashi and other *chetniks* a bad time. Churchill decided to transfer support to Tito.

Such was the beginning of the extraordinary story of a tiny group of Yugoslav communists – a few thousand only, though some were veterans of the Spanish Civil War – destined to rise from prison to power and give their country new political institutions and a new social structure. When the Germans invaded Russia they were scattered all over the country and, knowing the line to take with the inhabitants of the mosaic of provinces which still formed Yugoslavia, they preached agitation and then revolt. At first fighting was done only by small groups of ten or twenty men but, the flame of revolt gradually spread. As early as July 1941 the Italians in Montenegro were taken by surprise and given a bitter taste of partisan belligerence.

---

[1] *Chetnik* means member of a *ceta*, one of the companies of irregulars which fought against the Turks in the nineteenth century, in the Balkan wars at the beginning of the twentieth century and even during the Allied offensive at Salonica. The word was pregnant with historical significance.

The first Serbian units were formed principally of students and workers from Belgrade; they comprised some twenty detachments of one hundred men each. In September 1941 they 'liberated' the town of Uzice. There they found a small munitions factory in which, over a period of two months, they manufactured 16,000 rifles and thousands of grenades. The reserves of the 'National Bank of Yugoslavia' had also been evacuated to the town, and they laid hands on millions of dinars. A printing works was available, and they reproduced hundreds of thousands of leaflets with which they inundated the entire country.

This opened Tito's eyes to the possibilities. Henceforth the partisans' orders were 'to make good any loss of territory by capture of fresh territory, greater in size and importance', where social revolution and education of the masses was to go hand in hand with the struggle against the occupying power. On the subject of command Tito was quite inflexible; he paid little attention to the background of his volunteers but he insisted that command of all units down to company level be in the hands of communists only; a Party cell was immediately set up in any new group. The Yugoslav partisan movement thereby acquired a homogeneity and unity of direction seldom seen in other national resistance movements.

Between April and June 1942 Tito's troops were forced back into Montenegro and Herzegovina where they could not live off the country. Tito chose this moment to form them into four 'proletarian brigades'. He proposed to abandon static harassing tactics for a war of movement and form a mobile offensive force which could strike wherever necessary. The partisans pushed their way into western Bosnia and set up their headquarters at Bihac. An assembly was convened with delegates from all over Yugoslavia; it assumed the title of 'Consultative Assembly of the anti-fascist Council for National Liberation'. It decided on a policy of political education and instruction for the 'masses'; women dropped the veil and learnt to read. The 'brigades' then turned themselves into the 'Revolutionary Army of National Liberation'.

Early in 1943 this 'army' was attacked in Bosnia and Croatia by a force of 80,000 men; fighting went on along the Neretva for a month; ravaged by typhus, the partisans flowed back into Montenegro. In May 1943 a fresh enemy offensive drove them out of even this stronghold; for a month 19,000 partisans were surrounded, losing over 4,000 men; Tito himself was wounded and narrowly escaped death or capture.

This fluctuating fighting was exhausting for both sides, but even more so for the population which was subjected to the demands of both sides in turn. Their heavy equipment made it difficult for the Axis force to move through the forests and mountains. Their numbers were insufficient to occupy the entire country effectively so there was, therefore, always some area where the partisans could install themselves; there they could remain for as long as it took the enemy to mount a fresh offensive, which usually took some time. When the offensive came the partisans were quick to decamp.

The Italian capitulation opened the way to victory and expansion for the partisans. They had captured enough equipment to arm 250,000 men and all at once they found themselves in control of 50,000 square miles. At the same time the Allies decided to provide assistance and this they could do on a large scale from airfields in Italy. The partisans occupied the Dalmatian coast and islands and, though driven back, retained an air and naval base on the island of Vis. This became a staging post for continuous transport of men and equipment; twenty-seven boats flew the new Yugoslav flag with its red star; more than 1,000 tons of equipment were stocked there; Yugoslav prisoners of war were released in Italy and armed by the British; aircraft and tank crews were sent to train in Cairo. During 1944, in addition to vast quantities of food and medical stores, the partisans received: 100,000 rifles, 50,000 machineguns and sub-machineguns, 1,380 mortars, 600,000 grenades, 700 radio sets and 175,000 uniforms.

In November 1943 the second session of the Consultative Assembly was held in Jalce. It disowned the authority of the London government and decided that on liberation Yugoslavia should be a federal democracy. All danger was not past, however; in May 1944 an airborne operation against Tito's headquarters at Dvar almost succeeded and Tito and some of his troops had to be evacuated to Vis. By September 1944, however, the Army of Liberation was in control of most of Serbia; it was still on the defensive against the German troops holding on in Italy and those retreating from Greece. Elsewhere, however, it could lay down the law and Yugoslavs of all shades of belief joined it. Tito could dictate his terms to the London government and dealt with Churchill and Stalin as equals. He had indeed come far!

The French maquis

In western Europe no one, not even the communists, thought action by armed units to be possible on any major scale before liberation, apart from a few 'freelance groups' (*groupes francs*). The call-up of young men and workers for the compulsory labour service, however, presented the as yet undeveloped resistance, with a large problem. The call-up must be sabotaged since its object was to increase the enemy's war potential; moreover it would deprive the Resistance of its most pugnacious recruits – by the end of 1942 there were already 220,000 Frenchmen in Germany.

A vast effort was made in Belgium and Holland as well as France. The clandestine press never ceased reminding people that it was their patriotic duty not to comply with the call-up. Words were not enough, however; evaders had to have material assistance – papers, hide-outs, money. In France Jean Moulin set up an 'Action Committee against deportation', the main business of which was the production of false papers; more than half a million forged work permits were issued; some were distributed in working-class areas by Red Cross trucks; files were destroyed and fake registration certificates issued; in Holland raids on the printing works were organised, and collections made all over the country to meet the vast financial requirements. In Belgium a complete organisation named 'Socrates' dealt with nothing else. The Dutch government in London announced that it would authorise loans and undertake to repay them.

Under these conditions evaders were numerous; to escape the house-searches they left their homes for the more secure wooded and mountainous areas of the country. At first they were merely fugitives, but clearly they were going to have to fight one day. The Resistance, therefore, found itself faced with the problem of arming and training the *maquis*.

In France[1] all the resistance movements quickly realised the potential advantages of a *maquis*. The MUR set up a '*maquis* service' visualising direct action, as distinct from the 'Secret Army' which was a 'wait-and-see' organisation. The FTPF looked on the evaders as a reserve for their strong-arm groups and canvassed these

---

[1] The country being flat, guerrilla warfare was not possible in Holland. In Belgium *maquis* were formed in the Ardennes but, owing to the course of the war, they never played the role for which they were intended.

spontaneously formed *maquis* in order to take control of them; at the head of their organisation was a 'National Military Committee'. Though little disposed to this type of warfare the leaders of ORA [*Organisation de Résistance de l'Armée*] realised the importance of the development; from Algiers they received orders and resources so that they too could form *maquis* to act as the advanced guard of the army being trained and equipped in North Africa.[1]

Under these conditions *maquis* sprouted in all the mountainous areas of France, primarily in the south where the terrain was more rugged and where, even after occupation, the Germans, who were not very numerous, allowed more freedom to the local administration. There were never many *maquis* in the Pyrenees since they were too far from the main areas of fighting, although there was a spontaneous resurgence of the Spanish guerrilla movement. In the mountains of Limousin, the Auvergne, Vivarais, the Cevennes, Morvan, the Jura, Dauphine, Savoie, Provence and the Montagne Noire, however, groups ranging from under fifty to several hundreds were to be found. In the north *maquis* were fewer and formed later; they were located principally in the Ardennes, the Vosges and Sologne.

All this was a spontaneous rather than an organised development; the longevity, location and activities of the *maquis* varied considerably, as did their views and feeling of commitment. The FTP, for instance, advocated the formation of numerous small highly mobile groups which should 'act like a mercury bubble', splitting in one area to regroup in another but always giving proof of their presence and pugnacity. The MUR was more afraid of the unfortunate consequences for the population which such action might entail. The ORA preferred large-scale 'mobilisation *maquis*', located in natural fortresses and if possible in uniform; they would receive from outside the heavy equipment necessary to form semi-regular units which would liberate areas of national territory and so prepare the way for the invading forces.

In fact, enemy attacks forced all the *maquis* to place themselves on a war footing. The first to move were the Italians who made several drives into the Alps in the summer of 1943. In March 1944 the Germans decided to mount a spectacular operation; several thousand soldiers dressed in white were launched through the

---

[1] It should be emphasised that many young officers, particularly the final term at Saint-Cyr (which had been evacuated to Aix-en-Provence), proved themselves good guerrilla leaders.

snow against the great *maquis* of Glières in Savoie; it was 500 men strong but had already suffered from two months of fighting against Vichy forces. Other battles took place around Amberieu, Bellegarde and Oyonnax.

The landing of June 1944 created general activity which attempted to deceive the enemy as to the true objectives of the Allied armies and impose the greatest possible delay on the movement of his reinforcements to the main theatre of operations, Normandy.

The Italian partisans

In Italy the Allied landings took place without any support from the Resistance except in Rome and Naples, where a spontaneous popular revolt broke out against enforcement of the compulsory labour service; there a number of civilians joined groups of soldiers attempting to oppose the German occupation of the city. From autumn 1943 Italy south of the front was administered by the Allies, the Badoglio government attempting to obtain for itself some vestige of power and eventually being recognised as a co-belligerent. The whole of northern Italy, on the other hand, was occupied by the Germans, assisted by the last remnants of fascism grouped around Mussolini in the Republic of Salo. The anti-fascist parties had plenty of supporters, particularly in the towns; it was from them that the more important groups of partisans were formed.

The first groups appeared in the Abruzzi, then in Tuscany, along the Apennines and in the Marches; they were the result of spontaneous reactions to German requisitioning and they included disbanded soldiers hoping to evade captivity. The situation was different in the Po plain and in the Alps where the communists (the 'Garibaldi' formations), the socialists (the 'Matteoti' formations) and the Action Party ('Justice and Liberty' formations) were both influential and active. In Lombardy and Venetia the terrain was not very favourable and the Germans kept a firm grip on the lines of communication which were of vital importance to them. In Liguria and Piedmont, however, the partisans were numbered in thousands; they included city workers who had fled to the country, demobilised soldiers, members of the intelligentsia and of the middle and peasant classes. The struggle developed on two fronts – against the Germans and the neo-fascists; among the latter the 'black shirts' were given the thankless task of dealing with the partisans.

An original feature of the Italian partisan movement was that, in the areas which it liberated, it set up 'republics' where it decreed the overthrow of fascism; the most noteworthy examples were in the Val d'Ossola, the Cuneo region and the area around Ampezzano – which comprised over forty parishes. Unfortunately the partisans felt themselves obliged to defend these areas and turn them into fortresses; field fortifications were constructed, behind which the partisans were sometimes massacred.

From summer 1944 the Rome government, in competition with the 'Liberation Committee for Northern Italy', attempted to put some semblance of order into the welter of *maquis*. They nominated regional military commanders who regrouped the partisans into brigades and divisions, intending to launch them against the German rear when the final Allied offensive came.

The Allies, however, looked askance at the revolutionary explosion in northern Italy. They were conserving their men and material; Churchill, in particular, was anxious first to consolidate the authority of the King which was very shaky. During the summer of 1944 partisans in the western Alps fraternised with the French *maquis* but later encountered the hostility of the French Provisional Government for whom Italy was still the enemy; partisans who crossed the frontier were treated as prisoners of war and in the Val d'Aosta the French government encouraged local autonomist tendencies or even attachment of the area to France.

The Allies had decided that Italy should remain a secondary theatre of war. With the onset of winter in 1944–45 Alexander halted his troops at the threshold to the Po plain, at the northern end of the Apennines. He warned the partisan leaders that they would have to rely on their own resources, advising them to 'demobilise' their men. They did this as best they could, and at the price of severe losses, the partisans continued to exist, hiding in the valleys; they used their enforced vigil to expand their clandestine recruiting. By the spring of 1945 over 200,000 partisans were ready for the final assault, both in the towns and in the countryside.

Counter-guerrilla action

The size and violence of the guerrilla movement took the Germans by surprise. Until 1942 its quiesence lulled them into a sense of security in the west. In the east the object of the internment of Jews and the massacre of potential leaders in Poland and the USSR was not so much the prevention of possible reactions as the enforcement of vast post-war plans for a thousand-year Reich built on racial principles and maintained by the 'warrior-peasant'. In his directive for 'Barbarossa' Hitler had ordered that 'partisans are to be pitilessly liquidated in battle or when trying to escape'; no quarter was to be given and no prisoners taken. The object of these brutal tactics was to nip revolt in the bud; when it proved unsuccessful the Führer's first reaction was one of pleasure, since his most determined opponents had made the error of coming out into the open – 'the partisan war has the advantage of eliminating all those who oppose the National-Socialists'.

By 1942, however, OKW was becoming less optimistic; one report spoke of real danger. In an order of September 1942 Hitler admitted the fact: 'During recent months these gangs have exerted a very serious threat in the east and are seriously imperilling our supply lines.' But how to stop them? The Wehrmacht had gladly accepted a division of responsibilities which left to Himmler's men the somewhat unglamorous task of 'keeping order' in the rear areas; but this was now no mere question of police operations. Initially it was agreed that the SD would continue to deal with 'small groups', but at what level did the numbers and activity of a partisan group mean that it was no longer 'small'? The authority of the army and its counter-espionage resources had to be extended; then a special staff had to be set up and an increasing number of units withdrawn from the front to act as security forces. Satisfactory methods still had to be found – formation of 'strong points' in the villages, organisation of mobile units, evacuation of large areas so that the partisans might dig themselves in giving the security forces a chance to return in force, drive them out and destroy them.

In fact the Germans never got the better of the partisans, who were supplied by the collective farms. General Officers commanding areas were authorised to act as they saw fit, but hunting guerrillas through the woods ended in failure and large-scale

cordon-and-search operations yielded little since the major preparations involved enabled the alarm to be given long before. Certain
commanders, however, produced some answer. In spring 1942,
General Schmidt, commanding 11 Panzer Army in the Briansk
sector, hit on the idea of nominating a Russian civilian, Kaminsky,
as Sector Governor with power to appoint officials uncontrolled
by the Germans except through the Army Commander. Kaminsky
appointed mayors, did away with the collective farms, distributed
the stocks of goods and tools among the people and formed a
militia of several thousand men equipped with light tanks which
engaged the guerrillas in a merciless war, whilst the Germans
remained as spectators. The idea was to give the inhabitants the
feeling that they were fighting to defend their own possessions.
When the Germans withdrew, however, the militia degenerated
into groups of highway robbers and had to be disbanded. On a
smaller scale one battalion commander trained some of his sections in ambush tactics; they registered one or two successes,
taking sabotage teams by surprise in the act of laying mines. The
resulting feeling of insecurity led to a reduction of partisan activity
in the area; the capture of a few prisoners enabled the Germans to
discover and destroy some of the partisan camps, but success of
this sort was rare.

To retain their best troops at the front the German General
Staff decided to use 'satellite' units in the rear areas, the volunteers
of the anti-bolshevik crusade such as the Hungarians and Italians.
Prisoners of war and Lithuanian or Ukrainian nationalists no
longer came forward owing to the relentlessly severe policy
adopted by the Germans; when an attempt had been made to send
them into action against their fellow-countrymen at Kursk, many
had deserted. There was no alternative but to send them to
Western Europe where Tartars, Croats, Bosnian moslems and
other 'Mongols' were responsible for various atrocities until
eventually some of them, sensing a change in the wind, went over
to the *maquis*. From the German point of view the best solution
was to exploit the fanaticism of the collaborators in a sort of civil
war; all the 'quislings' – Flemings, Ustashi, neo-fascists, Mussert's
nazis, Darnand's militia – were commissioned to 'maintain order',
each in their own country. Darnand even became a Minister in the
Vichy government with authority over the regular police; the
Militia set up summary 'courts martial' for men captured from the
maquis.

These methods were fairly successful in the west but in the east the Red Army's offensive forced the Germans to restrict the anti-partisan struggle to the protection of vital strategic points and punitive expeditions.

Great hopes were placed on the latter and for this reason 'an example was to be made'. The instruction came from on high. Following a directive from Hitler, Keitel ordered: 'Use of the severest methods. ... In the occupied countries human life is worth less than nothing and an intimidation effect can only be obtained by extraordinary severity. ... As reprisal for one German soldier killed the rule should be sentence of death for 50–100 partisans. ... The method of execution should contribute to the intimidation effect.' In October 1944 Field Marshal Kesselring in Italy observed that 'sabotage was becoming more and more frequent and transport increasingly handicapped'; he accordingly decreed that 'this scourge must disappear. ... As an initial measure I hereby order an anti-partisan week ... which should demonstrate our strength to these gangs; repression will be pitiless'.

It was indeed. In addition to the ss, the Wehrmacht initiated seizure of hostages, mass executions, burning of farms and villages. On the slightest pretext the entire population of a locality would be murdered, as at Kragujevac in Yugoslavia, where 7,300 people were massacred including all the school-children with their teachers. These frightful scenes might spread fear in a certain area, but they aroused hatred elsewhere; as the communists had predicted, fresh legions sprang from the blood of the martyrs. In any case what can anyone do when an entire population is hostile? It cannot be totally exterminated. This type of 'repression' is not merely horrible; it proved to be both stupid and ineffective.

The dividends and price of guerrilla warfare

The defeats suffered by the occupiers at the hands of the guerrillas were certainly more numerous than the successes they scored; locally they might destroy the guerrilla movement but always it rose from its ashes. The enemy were forced to commit increasingly large forces against it – in Russia in the summer of 1942 there were fifteen divisions, of which ten were German. By denuding the front the Soviet partisans played a strategic as well as a tactical

10

role; the same applied to the *maquis* of the Vercors, Mont Mouchet and Limousin when they held two German divisions away from the Normandy landing beaches.

It is equally certain that nowhere – and this is a constant in military history – did the guerrillas score a decisive success. In the Peoples Democracies the importance of guerrilla warfare during the second world war is consistently emphasised as part of the propaganda supporting certain political views; the object is to prove that, when organised by the communist party, popular masses possess irresistible strength. In fact guerrilla warfare can only wear the enemy down, demoralise him and make him easier meat for the regular armies. The vast majority of German units never came in direct contact with the guerrillas.

In any case the country in which guerrilla warfare takes place pays a high price. Through the suffering it causes and the mistakes it makes, for which the population pays the bill, guerrilla warfare creates lasting divisions and persistent hatreds; in addition it is always accompanied by internecine struggles, not only between resisters and collaborators but also between partisans of differing ideologies. Yugoslavia was not the only place where *chetniks* fought communists; in France too many a clash occurred, and accounts were squared by assassination.

Nevertheless, guerrilla warfare was an essential stage on the road to national liberation. In the crucible of the partisan group resolution ripened, characters were formed and the conviction grew that the occupier was at the mercy of a well-led rising; in France the *maquis* formed the core of the 'French Forces of the Interior'. Conversely, thanks to the *maquis*, political parties were able to acquire armed militias and to keep them after liberation for purposes which were anything but patriotic. Finally after the war the 'pseudo *maquis*' took advantage of the resulting anarchy for their own ends, as did the 'real *maquis*' on occasions until the rule of law was re-established.

In any case, if the partisan groups were to co-operate with the invading armies effectively, two conditions had to be fulfilled. The first was that they should discipline themselves, conform to the requirements of a common strategy and restrict themselves to their allotted role. This meant that they must renounce some of the spontaneous urge which had hitherto constituted their strength and be prepared to receive both the cadres and the weapons which only the Allies could give them, if they were to become a genuine

'Army of the Interior'. Without the assistance of Allied armies, in this case of the Allies, guerrillas may keep an endemic focus of revolt alive – but they are also its prisoners.[1]

The second proviso is that, within the country which it intends to liberate, guerrilla warfare must not be an end in itself but must become a factor in an overall policy. The guerrillas may reduce to impotence the administrative machine installed by the occupier but, having done this, the partisans will not be fulfilling their true role unless they become the army of a clandestine state, issuing its own laws, levying taxes, consulting with its allies and even instituting its own judicial system.

Because these conditions did not apply in the USSR, the army and regular authorities were able to assume direction of partisan action with great rapidity. Elsewhere this 'regularisation' was achieved by various methods and with differing degrees of success. The lesson to be drawn from guerrilla warfare during the second world war is that apparently primitive methods of warfare can be combined with the most modern techniques. If the regular armies are initially defeated, guerrillas can play a major part in defensive strategy; once these same regular armies have been reconstituted, guerrillas can assist their offensive operations. In no case, however, can they be a substitute.

[1] Clausewitz said: 'If you wish to avoid pursuing a shadow, popular warfare must always be considered as combined with war waged by a standing army, both working on a single plan.'

CHAPTER 17

The Clandestine State

The political situation in the occupied countries was usually a complex one. Except in the USSR there existed side by side governments-in-exile and clandestine forces which recognised their legitimacy to a greater or lesser degree; there were constant clashes within the underground; as the war situation swung in favour of the Allies collaborator leaders looked for a loophole and made discreet preparations for a 'reversal of alliances'. Finally the Allies were primarily interested in ensuring the success of the assault on Fortress Europe but, particularly in the case of the Soviet Union, they were not entirely without ulterior motives of a political and social nature.

Nevertheless, it was clear to all that a divided Resistance would remain weak and doomed to wither away. The Allies were the first to wish to see it coalesce so that they might genuinely count upon it when the time came but meanwhile did not run the risk of wasting their resources in men and equipment. The governments-in-exile wished to see the resistance forces unite and then gain control of them for they feared the disorder caused by unruly forces might become an obstacle to their return to power. Some of these governments, particularly the Polish and Provisional French Government in Algiers, were anxious to assert themselves against the Allies and ensure that they did not play fast and loose with the rights and liberties of the liberated countries. From their point of view, therefore, it was important that, when they returned home, they should find a solidly organised authority, well installed and capable of speaking in the nation's name. All were thinking of the wounds to be healed, the reforms to be initiated and the preservation of order, all the time wondering what sort of world would emerge from the war.

The resisters themselves were convinced that strength lay in unity; on their own initiative they had frequently regrouped, arranged to co-operate or carried out mergers. The compartmentation necessitated by underground work, however, did not make for closer relations. Above all, group leaders, justifiably proud of their achievements, were extremely touchy on the subject of their personal authority and autonomy. Outside the USSR the communists kept themselves to themselves, both from habit and as a matter of tactics, but when orders arrived from Moscow to extend a hand to anyone who would grasp it, they were often first to make advances to their companions in the struggle.

'National fronts' and genuine clandestine states were set up with more or less extensive ramifications all over Europe. In eastern and central Europe, backed by the advance of the Red Army, the communists were in the lead. In western Europe they had to come to terms with other shades of opinion. In most cases the legitimacy of the governments-in-exile was not disputed, though sometimes they had to assert themselves vis-à-vis their allies. Finally in Poland, Yugoslavia and Greece a dramatic dichotomy of authority led to convulsions, destruction and death.

The USSR and the national fronts

In the USSR Stalin, who had become both Alexander Nevsky and Ivan the Terrible, had welded together all the nation's forces without worrying too much about those Soviet citizens who had hitherto been no friends of the bolshevik régime. In the areas occupied by the Germans, however, preparations were made to return to the pre-war state of affairs with the minimum of change. The only new feature was the infusion of some new blood from the partisans.

In countries adjacent to the USSR whose armies were fighting and whose leaders were hostile, the communists attempted, even before the Red Army had reversed the fortunes of war, to rally the nationalist anti-German sections of the population to their side. For a long time, because of the German victories and the persecution to which these people were subjected, their prospects of success were nil but with the victorious advance of the Red Army they reopened. They spread their net wide, including not only their pre-war enemies who had thrown them into prison but even leaders as compromised as Admiral Horthy's son and King

Michael of Rumania. They drew the line only at unrepentant hard-core 'fascists', even accepting the military, though with reservations as regards those who had actually fought against the USSR.

Accordingly the Rumanian communists, with more persistence than success, approached the leaders of the Social-democrat Party, also the National Peasants (Manin) and National Liberals (Bratianu). In June 1943 they formed the 'Anti-Hitler Patriotic Front' but only a few small groups joined them. In April 1944 they were more fortunate and set up a 'United Workers' Front' together with the socialists; in May 1944 they reached agreement with Tatarescu's Liberal Party. A month later the army and the Palace were turning to them.

In May 1944 the Hungarian communists contacted other illegal political associations such as the Smallholders Party, the Social-democrat Party and the National Peasant Party. Two months later these four decided to set up a 'Hungarian Liberation Committee'. Underestimating their strength, however, Admiral Horthy, the Regent, could not bring himself to join them. The first Hungarian resistance government was formed in 'liberated' territory at Debrecen in December 1944; it called for revolt by the inhabitants of all areas still containing Germans on whose side, part of the Hungarian army were still fighting.

As early as the end of 1942 the communist party in Bulgaria had set up a 'Fatherland Front' in firms, factories and city areas; they were joined by certain intellectuals, 'military patriots' and liberal leaders. In May 1943 four parties formed the 'National Committee of the Fatherland Front'; this was not a total success since only a minority of socialists joined; on 'the Right' only a few individuals were contacted.

The object of these agreements was clear: it was to disperse anti-Soviet forces and prepare the way for the Red Army. The manoeuvre failed in Hungary but was successful in Rumania and Bulgaria. Within these 'National Fronts' communists were in a minority; they calculated that, under cover of national union, opinion would be favourable to their arrival in power. They knew that subsequently they could, if necessary, call in the assistance of Soviet forces. They were determined, however, to leave nothing of the previous political and social structures in existence. The situation in Czechoslovakia was very different.

Beneš and Russo-Czechoslovak friendship

In Czechoslovakia non-communist resistance had been directed by a Committee of Six ever since January 1940; it took its orders without question from the Beneš government in London. After June 1941 the communists made proposals for co-operation, which the others rejected. After the assassination of Heydrich, however, the non-communist resistance was annihilated and the communists renewed their approaches to the survivors. They found certain of the communist proposals somewhat disquieting but decided to accept, primarily at the instigation of Beneš.

Beneš decided, drawing his lesson from the 'Munich Agreement', that henceforth Czechoslovakia would be powerless in face of a German threat unless assured of Soviet support. He also had to take account of the fact that the Red Army would certainly be the first to enter Czechoslovakia and would do so via Slovakia where there was a ferment of anti-Czech nationalism; the fate of Czechoslovak unity would be in the hands of the Russians.[1] The Czechoslovak President, therefore, decided to conclude twin agreements: on the international level with the USSR, on the national level with the communists.

In December 1943 he went to Moscow and returned with a treaty under which the USSR and Czechoslovakia promised each other mutual assistance during and after the war for a term of twenty years. One clause guaranteed 'reciprocal respect for independence and sovereignty' and included a commitment to 'non-interference in the affairs of the other State'. The Czechs considered that this eliminated the possibility of a communist government imposed on Prague from Moscow, particularly seeing that the communists, Gottwald and Slansky, had taken part in the treaty negotiations.

The pre-war state of affairs was not to be entirely re-established, however. In the first place the Russians had hinted that they wished to take over sub-Carpathian Ruthenia and Beneš had given his agreement in principle. Secondly he had approved a vast plan of economic and social reform put forward by the

---

[1] Their intentions were neither clear nor entirely disinterested; the Moscow radio station beamed on Slovakia was called 'Free Slovakia' and not 'Free Czechoslovakia' as Beneš had requested.

communists and had agreed to accept a communist Prime Minister over the government of national union to be formed on liberation. He had described the liberation as 'a national revolution combined with a social revolution'.

On 8 May 1944 a further agreement laid down that the USSR would return to Czechoslovak authority responsibility for administration of territories liberated by the Red Army; with some foresight the two parties also agreed on the use to be made of wartime acquisitions, distribution of captured equipment, feeding of the population, etc. So – and the event was a landmark – London emigrés, Moscow emigrés and clandestine resisters had succeeded in reaching agreement both for the present and the future. One ticklish problem was left pending – Slovakia's place in the Czechoslovak State; even the Slovak communists showed some trace of separatist tendencies and were consequently suspected of 'bourgeois nationalism' by their Czech comrades. After all, some of them had given vent to the idea of setting up a soviet republic in Slovakia rather than reintegrating into the Czechoslovak State.

To guard against this possible danger but even more to ensure that he was on the spot at the crucial moment, Benès established his government in Kosice in January 1945. As the Germans withdrew, 'national committees' were set up everywhere to re-establish Czechoslovak administration under the umbrella of so widespread and confident a national union that the future seemed guaranteed. Nevertheless, the communists inside and the Russians outside held the reins of power and exerted extraordinary pressure on the Czechoslovak government.

Communist triumph in Yugoslavia

In Yugoslavia, as areas of national territory were liberated and while the partisans were still battling, a new state with a new social and administrative structure had been established. This was no clandestine organisation. The new post-war Yugoslavia emerged fully armed from the war – a war which had been both patriotic and revolutionary.

In every parish under their control the communists set up a 'Popular Committee' to exercise political and administrative authority in place of the titular officials; their real or supposed enemies were either 'retired', interned or ruthlessly executed. In the 'regions' 'Provincial anti-fascist Councils' were formed, with communists in all positions of power. Above these provisional institutions the 'political commissars' were the real masters of the new régime; they formed the connecting link between the 'Liberation Army' and the civil authorities; they took the economic decisions – on requisitioning or expropriation, for instance; they subjected both partisans and inhabitants to an intense propaganda campaign as part of their 'political education'.

Tito, who was a Croat, understood and shared the wishes of the inhabitants of the various provinces which went to make up Yugoslavia, differing though they were in race, language, religion, customs and standard of living. Though the teachings of marxism were perhaps somewhat above their heads, the promise of self-administration made good sense to them. But to decide to organise Yugoslavia on a 'federal and democratic' basis without the agreement of the King or his government, was tantamount to disowning both one and the other. The direction in which the country was evolving was clear. Partisans made no secret of the fact that they looked upon the USSR as their ideological home.

The London government had to give way. It divested Mihailovich of his titles and functions and invited the *chetniks* to place themselves under Tito's orders. Tito was promoted Marshal, Commander-in-Chief of the Peoples Army and President of the National Liberation Committee, on which all provinces were represented; he thus became the real master of the country. Despite the fact that the partisans had forbidden King Peter to return until the people had pronounced on his future, the London government recognised the new revolutionary institutions. The British brought heavy pressure to bear on the young king, forbidding him to fly to Yugoslavia, and in February 1945 he commissioned Tito to form the first government of liberated Yugoslavia – Shubachich, Prime Minister of the London government, was to be no more than Vice-President.

Among European resistance movements Yugoslavia was a special case. Terminology, ideology and structure all changed completely. This development had been assisted by the Churchill-Stalin agreement of October 1944 guaranteeing the USSR and Great Britain equal influence in the country, but in fact none of his allies had made any real attempt to impose their wishes on

10*

Tito. Henceforth he was free to conduct the affairs of his country as he wished.[1] Events followed a very different course in Poland.

The dramatic Polish dichotomy

The Polish government in London had no large forces at its disposal, although several thousand men had succeeded in leaving France and the Middle East at the time of the French armistice. No one, however, among the Allies or in Poland itself, doubted its legitimacy. The four main non-communist parties (Peasant, Socialist, Christian Workers and National Party) had formed a 'Council of National Union'. The clandestine organisations were supported by the entire population – communists were few and since the Russo-German Pact no one listened to them; resistance was, therefore, spread throughout the country in a tight-knit network with no missing links.

A Delegate-General of the London government was in charge of the underground administration; he was assisted by heads of services, analogous to ministries, and by regional representatives; the latter had recruited full-scale staffs in the towns and local public services. Instructions to boycott the orders of the occupation authorities, therefore, penetrated down to the lowest level. Para-military groups had formed spontaneously and had merged into the 'Home Army' (A K); this had a C-in-C and regional commanders; it had even been laid down that service in the Home Army would count double for pension and retirement age. The Home Army was responsible for all warlike actions, such as sabotage, assassinations and partisan operations. The four political parties had kept their independence; each had its own press, recruited its own supporters and broadcast its programme; their representatives formed a sort of parliament which theoretically exercised control over both the London government and the directing agencies of the underground. Clandestine resistance, therefore, represented nothing less than the Polish nation in existence as a national entity as in pre-war days. But it was

---

[1] Albania developed along similar lines. Advised by the Yugoslav communists, Enver Hodja fought the Italians and then the Germans and their collaborators, at the same time successfully expelling anti-communist resisters from the National Front. Communist solidarity proved stronger than nationalism – the Italians had given Albania the Yugoslav region of Kossovo, which was populated primarily by Albanians, and the Germans had raised several battalions there to fight against the Yugoslav partisans.

something else as well – an emergent democracy; in occupied Poland political parties were more powerful, more emancipated and more active than in independent Poland which had been a dictatorship. Polish resistance, therefore, had cohesion and strength unparalleled in Europe.

Only a few ultra right wing groups and the communists remained outside this overall organisation, but even they were not without links to the Home Army which was the provider of weapons and money. The communists had taken heart again after June 1941; in 1942 they reappeared in the guise of the 'Polish Workers' Party' with a 'Popular Guard'. From this time dichotomy existed. Nevertheless, realising their comparative weakness and being, in fact, patriotic Poles, the communists had made certain approaches to the Home Army which its leaders rejected.

The vast majority of the Polish nation and the London government regarded the USSR as an enemy equivalent to Germany. General Sikorski, however, realised that some agreement with the Kremlin was an absolute necessity and, although criticised rather than supported by most of his colleagues, went to Moscow to meet Stalin. He visualised negotiations on a basis of equality but Stalin did not make his task easier. After all, at the height of the battle for Moscow Stalin had told Eden that he had no intention of relinquishing the Polish territories which Hitler had allowed him to annex. Nevertheless, unwillingly Stalin agreed to release the Polish prisoners of war so that they might form a Polish army in the USSR. The Soviet authorities, however, placed obstacles in the way of its recruitment and refused to use it on the Soviet front as Sikorski wanted. His object was that it should enter Poland with the Red Army, though remaining dependent on the London government. Eventually it was decided that it should be sent to train in Iran whence it would take part in operations in the Middle East under the command of General Anders; it was to be equipped by the British and would have the benefit of American 'lease-lend'.[1]

In the month of April 1943, however, the German authorities in Poland discovered a mass grave of several thousand Polish officers in the forest of Katyn and this wrecked the precarious agreement between the Polish government in London and the

[1] As a comparable situation, think of the French army being reconstituted in Algiers but refused participation in the Normandy or Mediterranean landings and fighting in Lithuania and Bessarabia.

USSR. When the Poles accepted an inquiry by the International Red Cross as suggested by the Germans, the USSR severed diplomatic relations with them. From this time on the USSR took numerous steps to form a Polish political authority and a Polish army, both divorced from the London government. It was not yet clear whether Russia intended to use these as pawns in later negotiations or whether she proposed to carry them along in the baggage train of the Red Army and hand over complete power to them.

An 'Association of Polish patriots' was formed in Moscow which turned into the 'Polish National Committee' in January 1944; it was controlled by communist exiles and proceeded to raise an army corps, commanded by General Berling, from the few Poles remaining in the USSR. When the Red Army entered Poland in July 1944 it installed the Committee in Lublin. In the liberated areas the 'Lublin Committee' mobilised the young conscript classes and these recruits increased the 'Berling Corps' to army size. At the same time the Committee acted like a government, promulgating reforms and distributing land to the peasants; in the name of self-determination of peoples it agreed to cede to the USSR Polish Ukraine and Byelorussia. Relations between the 'Home Army' and the 'Popular Army' became embittered. Contact between the 'Lublin Committee' and the London government was non-existent, the former treating the latter as usurpers. The Poles were not to know that at Teheran in October 1943 the British and Americans had implicitly accepted the Russian demands; both in London and in Poland itself they remained as hostile to the Soviet 'liberator' as to the German occupier. The Home Army even set up an anti-communist committee; all four political parties warned the Allies against 'any form of totalitarianism', stipulated that Poland must regain her pre-war frontiers in the east and rejected 'any attempt to impose on Poland a type of government of eastern manufacture'.

Admittedly violent clashes were avoided; as it entered Poland the Red Army merely incorporated into the 'Berling Corps' any members of the Home Army who came forward; although sometimes it disarmed and interned them. From then on there were two Polish resistance movements, two governments and two armies. Left to themselves the Poles would undoubtedly have reached agreement or at least a non-communist majority would have emerged. In fact Poland was sacrificed to the uneasy alliance between the major Allies; once more the Polish nation was torn between its western inclinations and the pressure of its geographical situation in the east. Stalin's determination and the presence of the Red Army drew it irresistibly eastward. But before that the ghastly drama of the Warsaw rising was to occur.

'Untroubled resistance' in north-west Europe

Except in France the resisters of western Europe united without difficulty. No one in any of the countries concerned doubted the authority of the heads of state or governments in power in 1940, whether they had remained on the spot as in Denmark or taken refuge in London. All, including the USSR, admitted that this part of Europe was a British zone of influence; no sense of nationalist pride prevented the resistance from working with SOE and carrying out its orders. Everywhere resistance united under the direction of legitimate authorities.

In Denmark the king and the government had gradually moved from an attitude of resignation to one of almost open hostility to the Germans; the administration kept in step with them. In 1944 the various resistance groups formed a 'Free Danish Council' to co-ordinate their activities and they found it quite natural that the head of SOE should be a member. The only difficulty came from the USSR which cold-shouldered the Council because Denmark had despatched some volunteers to fight with the Wehrmacht. The Danes had to make amends and to avoid any clash between the 'Free Council' and the government, the King recognised the Council as a *de facto* authority and certain members of the government joined it.

In Norway only two resistance movements had ever existed. The stronger was that formed and controlled by the military, known as *Milorg*; it had not invariably been in agreement with SOE on the advisability of certain acts of sabotage, but it was loyal to King Haakon and obediently carried out its government's orders.

In Holland Queen Wilhelmina's prestige had remained extremely high. Though certain members of the Dutch government-in-exile had at times given proof of failing determination, she had never wavered in her resolve to fight. The leaders of the various resistance groups were neutral; they had played no political role prior to the war and the majority of them did not aspire to power. Not until June 1944 did the Queen and Prime Minister suggest that the Resistance unite on the broadest possible basis so as to form a Committee representative of public opinion which could advise the liberation government during the period preceding the election of an assembly. A 'Superior Consultative Committee of the Underground' was therefore formed; at its first meeting the majority decided that after liberation resistance would have no further part to play.

In Belgium the situation was different. King Leopold had remained in the country but held aloof from the Resistance. The communist minority was the driving force behind a most active movement, the 'Independence Front'; it had a widely circulated press, included 'action groups' and had raised a 'Belgian partisan army' backed by a 'Patriotic Militia'. No one, however, cast doubt on the authority of the government-in-exile; it controlled the Resistance through two separate agencies, the *Sûreté de l'Etat* [State Security] co-ordinating civil resistance, and the Ministry of National Defence working with SOE which controlled military resistance. It seemed logical to extend this dual system of control into Belgium; the Secret Army was responsible for all 'military action' and the 'Independence Front' for 'civil action'. On the spot it was not always easy to differentiate, but the system did simplify and assist both the organisation and unification of the Resistance. The major problem of the attitude and future of King Leopold remained, however; many of the resisters, and particularly the 'Independence Front', were extremely hostile to him.

Difficulties in consolidating Italian resistance

In Italy the Resistance had had nothing to do with the major events such as the Allied landings, the fall of Mussolini or the signature of the armistice and it was still weak even at the end of 1943. On communist initiative the clandestine political parties had formed a 'Liaison Committee' including communists, socialists, Action Party, Christian democrats, Liberals and Labour Democrats. But the exiles who returned to lead them found it difficult to re-establish contact with the new generation. They had little support from public opinion and their possibilities of action were limited. They formed a political coalition of the most varied shades of opinion but, to remain in being, it was forced to postpone indefinitely the solving of the problems which divided it. It was agreed only on the subject of its opposition to fascism and its consequences.

Moreover, the King and the Badoglio government kept the Resistance at arms length with the approval of the Allies, particularly the British; Churchill could see no defence against the rise of communism in Italy other than the monarchy, the army and the Catholic Church. In occupied Rome the anti-fascist parties formed a 'Committee of National Liberation' under the chairmanship of Bonomi; he set himself up in the capital and claimed control of the war and of all Resistance activities throughout the country. The administration, prominent personalities, the army and the Church remained loyal to the Badoglio government, whereas the Committee was divided in its attitude. To the astonishment of all Togliatti, the communist leader, returned from Moscow with orders to 'recognise' Badoglio – a striking illustration of Stalin's political strategy of 'National Fronts' which aimed to unite all those fighting nazi Germany on the broadest possible basis. Grudgingly the other parties followed the communist lead.

The anti-fascist parties tried various tactics. They first attempted to obtain a place in the government and gain 'recognition' from the Allies. They achieved this when Bonomi replaced Badoglio as head of government after the liberation of Rome. They also planned to co-ordinate all the varied and chaotic activities of the 'Liberation Committees' throughout occupied Italy, of the short-lived 'republics' which they controlled and of the partisan bands which remained for all practical purposes independent, though some claimed allegiance to the Communist or Action parties.

The existence of an anti-fascist government in Rome, recognised by the Allies, obviously made matters simpler, but it was difficult for it to assert its authority in the north. Through the fortunes of war Italy had reverted to her traditional regionalism which her comparatively new-found unity had not altogether obliterated. The South, poor, illiterate and politically uncomprehending, remained subject to its dignitaries, its obsolete customs and a conservative Church; Rome was the capital only in the eyes of the Romans and the Vatican was as influential there as the government; the North was a conglomerate of great industrial cities, mountainous areas where the family was the most important unit, and the Po plain with its great estates and intensive farming.

The parties set up a 'Liberation Committee for Upper Italy' located in Milan and constituted on the lines of that of Rome, but it differed in that a major part was played by the socialists and communists in view of their hold on the working classes. The Committee accepted the authority of the Rome Committee in principle but in practice remained separate. The Allies were disturbed by its revolutionary tendencies and preferred to have nothing to do with it.

At the end of 1944, however, military considerations forced them to pocket their pride; on the eve of their final offensive they were unwilling to forgo any form of assistance, but they provided weapons and equipment somewhat grudgingly. Their main object was to ensure that the partisans were properly commanded and disciplined and for this purpose a 'General Headquarters of volunteers for occupied Italy' was set up in June 1944 under a regular officer, General Cadorna. The Liberation Committee, however, was unwilling to relinquish its authority over the partisans and regarded Cadorna merely as an adviser; it attached to him two of its members, Longo of the Communist Party and F. Parri from the Action Party. Decisions were to be taken in concert. The object was to ensure that the forces which had previously supported fascism, did not retain power under cover of wartime unity.

By the beginning of 1945, therefore, Italian resistance was winning through slowly; it had overcome its differences, asserted itself vis-à-vis the Allies and raised its troops. Meanwhile, in the midst of the German debacle, fascism was finally disintegrating. The Resistance carried out a widespread purge of the administration in liberated Italy. It remained to be seen, however, how far Italian public opinion, anaesthetised by twenty years of fascist dictatorship, would support it and how long it could remain united in view of its internal disagreements.

The initial regroupings in France

After her defeat France had been dismembered, occupied and exploited. The population was apathetic and many of the early resisters had placed their confidence in the Vichy government;

even more owed allegiance to Free France in London; some, primarily the 'movements' and the communists, remained unattached.

The Allies could not disregard French resistance. The British and Americans had selected France as the theatre for three of their most important strategic operations; Stalin was still supported by the French Communist Party which, though put to a severe test, still obeyed his orders and had managed to survive its vicissitudes. Everyone was wondering what role France would play in liberated Europe; she was, after all, a great power and the defeat of Germany and Italy would leave an immense vacuum. The outstanding problem was who would muster the French to bring France back into the war and how would he do it?

Free France, despite its setbacks, had gradually acquired supporters of such varied backgrounds that it had become a miniature reflection of French public opinion. General de Gaulle was regarded as the leader or symbol of resistance by socialists, radicals, trade unionists (both of the CGT and CFTC), moderates, leaders of the main clandestine 'movements' and outstanding personalities such as Mandel, Jeanneney, Massigli, Louis Gillet, General Cochet and R. Dautry. This was almost a plebiscite. Yet, although Free France covered almost the whole range of the ideological spectrum and could boast so many great names, its impact on public opinion and its true strength remained to be seen.

The communists, in particular, had struck out on their own. As early as May 1941 they had set up a 'National Front' which only gained real strength in 1942 in the northern zone and in 1943 in the south; its purpose was to achieve the broadest possible unity of Frenchmen of all backgrounds willing to fight the Germans. This was the only movement with a foot in both zones; the communists were the driving force but they had been joined by socialists, radicals, clericals, moderates and even some semifascists. In short it was a replica of Free France inside the country. It made no secret of its intention to 'head up' the entire resistance movement; thus the *Francs Tireurs Partisans français*, the most active clandestine military formation, in theory belonged to the 'National Front'; the communists said that they had drafted their own paramilitary groups into it and proposed that other resistance 'movements' do likewise. The latter were not invariably willing to conform. Many other resisters, particularly the socialists, were worried by the somewhat secretive attitude of the communists;

they had kept their own organisation and had placed only 'secondary figures' at the head of their resistance formations. The socialists especially were irritated by the communist slogan that they were the 'sole party of resistance'.

In view of this atmosphere of dissension and its inevitable accompaniment of overall weakness, the achievments of Jean Moulin were of first-rate importance. He persuaded the three big movements in the southern zone to merge and the five most important in the north to co-ordinate their efforts. He provided them all with unified services, already in existence in embryo but which he consolidated; others he created from the start. His organisation assisted and strengthened all resistance activities – the clandestine press, the welfare service, the 'reception committee' organisation, the anti-deportation committee, the planning committee. His aim was to unify all resistance without imposing too rigid a hierarchy or uniformity. His crowning achievement, and also his swansong, was the formation in May 1943 of the 'National Resistance Council' [*Conseil National de la Résistance* – CNR]; this included representatives of all eight major resistance movements, both the trades union federations and six political parties, some of which had been more or less reconstituted. The first act of the CNR was unanimously to recognise the authority of General de Gaulle and accept his political guidance, since 'from the darkest days he had never despaired of the country'.

Unification of French resistance

The French resistance would have been among the first to achieve unity of direction, had not the Americans upset matters – President Roosevelt loathed General de Gaulle, sometimes for rather petty reasons. In North Africa, first through Darlan and then through Giraud, the Americans were instrumental in prolonging, almost resurrecting, the Vichy régime just when it was sinking into disrepute and impotence in France as a result of its policy of collaboration and its loss of all attributes of sovereignty.

This is not the place to tell the story of the month-long rivalry between the two French resistance movements, that of London headed by General de Gaulle and supported by the Resistance at home and that of Algiers headed by General Giraud, supported by the Americans and backed by the African empire and the remnants of the French army and navy. The remarkable fact was that the weaker side won; its victory was undoubtedly partly due to the personality of General de Gaulle but equally to the clandestine resistance. From the moment when he could prove that he was speaking in the name of French resistance, combined under the 'National Resistance Council' (which proposed to give Giraud command of the troops and de Gaulle political control), General de Gaulle could present himself to the major Allies as the mouthpiece, indeed the leader, of a French nation united in battle.

Subsequently, in June 1943 the 'French Committee of National Liberation' was formed, first together with General Giraud and then under the sole leadership of de Gaulle. In May 1944 it became the 'Provisional Government of the French Republic' and it was this which finally put an end to the Vichy régime and its pretences.

On a smaller scale France was now in a somewhat similar position to the USSR. In the first place she was once more a co-belligerent member of the great anti-German coalition and her object was to become an Ally in her own right – particularly in the settlement of the Italian question. Secondly resistance was continuously gaining in strength throughout the occupied areas. From Algiers the new French government's authority now covered the entire colonial empire with the exception of Indo-China and Corsica. It had raised a modern army, equipped by the Americans, in which it had fused, not without difficulty, the Free French Forces, the Armistice Army, 'escapers' from France and new recruits both coloured and 'colonist'. This army had fought in Tunisia and then in Italy where it had covered itself with glory, erasing the disaster of 1940; it was preparing to take part in landing operations on the soil of France. At the same time General de Gaulle was claiming for France a place in inter-allied councils; he made his voice heard during the discussions preceding the Mediterranean landing. As elections were impossible, the French government revived local government institutions in Algeria; it formed an embryo parliament including representatives of the Resistance; among the ministers were leaders of 'movements' and clandestine parties, including the communist – which led to some friction between the President of the Provisional Government and the Party.

Preparations for liberation

France now began to receive the equipment demanded by the Resistance, both from Algiers and from London, delivered by American aircraft. To direct and staff the Resistance the government made use of a twin-headed 'delegation' – civil and military; the latter was subdivided into regional delegations in charge of the distribution of weapons to the resistance. In each department Liberation Committees were set up on the lines of the National Resistance Council; henceforth they were the co-ordinating agencies for the Resistance and on liberation they functioned as local councils.

Careful preparations were made for liberation. It was decided to cancel all Vichy laws and bring both Vichy Ministers and collaborators to justice; Pucheu, who arrived in Algiers, for instance, was promptly condemned to death and executed. Ordinances were drafted providing for nomination of 'commissars of the Republic', a purge of the administration, the provisional exercise of authority pending the organisation of elections and control of the press.

On 1 February 1944 the 'French Forces of the Interior' (FFI) officially came into being, in principle absorbing all military resistance formations – the Gaullist Secret Army, the communist *Francs-Tireurs et Partisans* and the Army Resistance Organisation (ORA) which owed allegiance to Giraud. France was divided into twelve military regions and an FFI leader was nominated for each region and department, not without some difficulty. The ORA in particular wished to be directly subordinate to Algiers and its leaders only grudgingly accepted the authority of the civil heads of the regions.

On the national, regional and departmental levels the French 'Home Army' had a staff on regular army lines consisting of the usual four sections. For security reasons and also to gain time, however, the organisation was decentralised. In theory at least, the intelligence circuits remained completely separate from the FFI, merely sending to the FFI Intelligence Sections at regional or departmental level such information as they collected.

To co-ordinate all this and ensure that the directives of the Allied staff were followed, in March 1944 General Koenig was appointed Military Representative in Great Britain of the Provisional Government's 'Committee for Action in France'; General Cochet occupied a similar position in Algiers dealing with the southern zone. After much negotiation all Allied intelligence and action agencies dealing with France were placed under the orders of Koenig's staff – BCRA of course, but also, at least theoretically the 'French Sections' of SOE and OSS. By April 1944 a plan for the use of the FFI on D Day and thereafter had been drawn up with the Allies. Vast sabotage plans were worked out and issued to those responsible for implementing them.

On the eve of the Allied landings, therefore, French resistance concentrated all the national energies and was also unified on the broadest and most complete basis. It had achieved the widest degree of unity France had ever known in history – communists working with moderates or even with ex-Vichyites. The main architect of this veritable miracle was General de Gaulle; in the autumn of 1940 no one would have thought it possible. He had become the undisputed leader of the country, and some felt that his role should not end with liberation. So, in the spectrum of the traditional French political forces destined to re-emerge on liberation, appeared a new factor – Gaullism.

The black spots

Nevertheless, certain black spots remained. In the first place, despite the strength and support it had acquired, the Provisional Government was not yet 'recognised' by the Allies as the government of France. They proposed to administer the liberated areas through a system of military government as in Italy and to issue 'occupation francs' – which General de Gaulle described as 'fake money'; they reserved the right to call in non-Gaullist personalities, perhaps even including the flotsam of Vichy, to form a government in Paris. When liberated, France would still be dependent on her allies, particularly the Americans for armaments, food, finance and help towards economic recovery. No one could tell whether the Vichy puppets would not try to cling to their posts or whether the Allies would not keep them there against the wishes of the Resistance.

More important still, beneath the apparent general wave of patriotism, differences persisted and ulterior motives were still at work. The various partners had come a long way in a short time to meet each other and mistrust had not entirely vanished.

Taking resistance as a whole, the communists had been playing an increasingly important role ever since 1943, and as a result, they occupied an increasingly important, sometimes leading, place in the co-ordinating and directing agencies. Their clandestine press had the largest circulation; they were responsible for the most numerous and most spectacular acts of sabotage and assassinations; though less well armed than the others, their *maquis* were the most mobile and active. Moreover, they had in effect seized the reins of power in the reunited *Conféderation Générale du Travail* (CGT) at the expense of Léon Jouhaux's 'federated' section which had formed the majority before the war. Though in a minority on the 'National Resistance Council', they succeeded in retaining two of the five seats on its Standing Committee, the 'active core', and they were subsequently equally successful in the 'Departmental Liberation Committees'; they filled two out of the three places on 'Comac' (the 'Action Committee') which was responsible for all armed action. The 'National Front' subterfuge gave them pride of place over the non-communists, sometimes even over the reactionaries, who had joined them out of patriotism and then found themselves submerged by communist drive and authority.[1] Nevertheless, though preaching unity, participating in unified organisations and even urging their formation, the communist party kept itself to itself; its groups of armed men, the *Francs-Tireurs et Partisans français* (FTPF), did not integrate into the FFI except on paper. In its propaganda, moreover, the party claimed to have hurled itself into the Resistance as soon as General de Gaulle had issued his call – erasing with a stroke of the pen the entire period when it had been supporting the Russo-German pact. It co-operated with the Provisional Government but took no part in it; it complained that it was not given enough weapons; it attacked the BCRA – and so forth. Its other partners found this attitude disquieting; the communist party seemed to have concluded a marriage of convenience with the Resistance, but to be keeping its real purposes in the dark. At the end of the war, they feared it might try to organise a sort of French 'Red October' and seize power by means of political and social revolution. Beneath the apparent harmony there were violent clashes

[1] As we shall see, the 'reactionary' General Giraud was taken in by the phrase 'National Front' and in fact distributed weapons to communists only.

inside the resistance organisations – particularly between socialists and communists. Even if there was no concerted plan for the seizure of power by force there certainly seemed to be large-scale penetration of the resistance authorities from within, and the end result might be the same.

A parallel cleavage appeared between the external Resistance represented by the Algiers government and the clandestine Resistance, primarily the 'National Resistance Council'; the Government distrusted the Council, proposed to 'relegate it to history' as soon as possible and meanwhile to direct and control it. But the underground could boast its sufferings and its martyrs; it was thirsting for decorations, recognition and responsibility; it was bursting with vast plans for reform in all fields. It was inspired by a desire for retribution and purification; it was determined to punish the traitors who had placed themselves at the service of the enemy and had been responsible for the death of so many of its members. Even though the term meant different things to different people, this force, bubbling with ideas and long-stifled energy, carried on its banners the word Revolution.

On the eve of the Allied landings French resistance had not solved all its problems – they were, after all, the fruit of four years of oppression, misery, humiliation and struggle. However, it had taken the necessary steps towards the two final stages which would lead it to the summit of victory: the national rising and the seizure of power.

All over Europe, therefore, as the long-awaited moment of Liberation approached, the Resistance looked for strength in unity. Even in Austria a 'Provisional National Committee' was formed in December 1944; its composition was Catholic at first, but contact was made with socialists and even with a communist. The Committee was supported by Austrian anti-fascists exiled in Switzerland and eventually made contact with the Allies. Only the German anti-nazi movement did not survive the setback of 20 July 1944 but that had been a demonstration of resolve by a few men rather than a genuine national clandestine movement.

Nevertheless, this essential unity was split down the middle by the yawning gap between the Anglo-Americans and the Soviets, which began to grow as Hitler's defeat became inevitable. In Greece the communists in Elas and other resisters in Edes did not succeed in bridging their differences; admittedly a 'Provisional

Committee of National Liberation', approved by the King, had been formed in the mountains, but it remained a paper exercise. The Polish drama proved that this duality in the Resistance could even bring the victors up against each other. A third world war was looming even before the second was finished; because they were determined to avoid this the British and Americans, led by Roosevelt, sacrificed Poland to maintain their fragile agreement with the USSR. So the country which had been first in the war, which had suffered most from occupation and whose people had fought the most valiantly was rewarded for its agonising struggle by the bitter fruits of subjection to a foreigner, yesterday's enemy. History's sense of equity was indeed peculiar.

Not all the occupied peoples were to meet so tragic a fate. All were not equally successful, however, in staging a national rising, the final phase of resistance and the essential preliminary to liberation.

Comments on the chart opposite

This chart illustrates the extreme complexity of the organisation of French resistance. At one and the same time it was attempting to co-ordinate forces inside and outside France, to unite the clandestine forces, to concentrate all national shades of political and intellectual opinion, to prepare for the seizure and exercise of power on liberation, to take over the official administrative machine from Vichy, to guarantee a minimum of democratic representation and still preserve that unity of direction necessary for the prosecution of the war.

This last object, one of vital importance, was in fact achieved. Nevertheless, the chart reminds us that throughout the organisation two parallel authorities existed, a fact which led to some friction, but did not degenerate into violent clashes. On the one hand was the 'National Resistance Council' and on the other the Algiers government. They more or less shared some of their services. The government attempted to control the Resistance, cutting out the Council and with the liberation of Paris it succeeded thanks to the personality and popularity of General de Gaulle.

It will also be noted that the secret services always remained divorced from the remainder of the Resistance and directly under

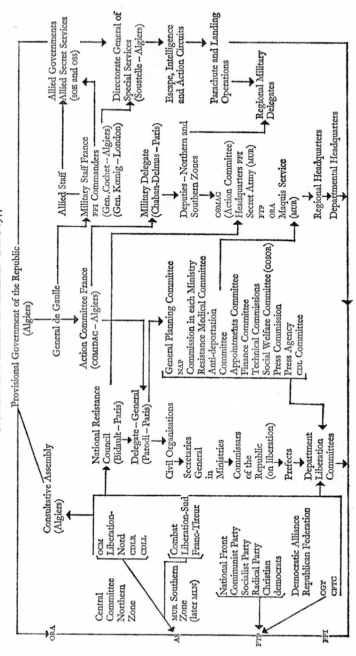

ORGANISATION OF THE FRENCH RESISTANCE – SPRING 1944

the Algiers government. The same applied to the Army Resistance Organisation (ORA) which was somewhat suspect to other resisters because of its Vichyite origin and which was willing to take direct orders only from the army staff in Algiers.

What the chart does not show adequately is the strength of the communist party and the extent of its infiltration. In the first place it controlled the National Front, the FTP and much of the CGT; it had a hand in certain resistance movements such as *Libération-Sud*. Secondly, although not always in control, it was the driving force behind the National Resistance Council, Comac, headquarters FFI and many departmental Liberation Committees, particularly that of Paris. Several of its members became prefects; it was represented in the Provisional Government and the Consultative Assembly. Finally it had formed certain organisations entirely under its control which are not shown here, such as the 'Patriotic Militia', the 'Union of French Women' and the 'United Forces of Patriotic Youth'. It had no influence, however, over the Army of Africa or 'Secret Services'. Clearly, however, the communist party was adept at discovering, pursuing and delineating the channels which might lead it to control over clandestine resistance.

CHAPTER 18

The National Rising

No one on either side was in any doubt that the resistance struggle would culminate in a national rising. The general plan depended on four factors: the political and strategic objectives of the Allies, the intentions and influence of the governments-in-exile, the unity and vitality of the resisters, the violence of the fighting or the Germans' relative lack of interest in the area. In fact there was a fifth factor: like the anti-nazi coalition, the 'shadow army' was divided into two opposing wings, the communist and non-communist. If conditions dependent on these factors were favourable, success was likely to be complete, as in Paris; if one of them was absent, drama and failure would ensue, as in Warsaw.

The general rising as seen from outside

In many respects the views of the three major Allies on the subject of national risings were identical: they had assisted the Resistance to form and grow and they intended to make use of it at the decisive moment in their great offensives when it would have reached its maximum efficiency. They would, therefore, approve of risings, even instigate them, but on two conditions, that they retain control and that the risings fitted into their military and political plans.

The British and Americans expected the Resistance to assist them in four ways: to provide precise information on the enemy and his movements; to provoke disorder behind the lines and to immobilise the maximum number of his units; to act as an advanced guard scouting in front of the main body of the invading forces or as a rearguard keeping order after they had moved on and the enemy had gone; finally to protect certain vulnerable points (bridges, ports, railways, etc.). With these aims in view, before the arrival of their armies they despatched to occupied territory a certain number of specialist teams known as 'Jed-burghs'; they consisted of three men and their purpose was to provide information on the real strength of the resisters, their needs and the services they could render. In addition 'operational groups' were sent to direct and control the larger existing *maquis* or form the core of new ones; parachute battalions (SAS) were dropped to harass and mislead the enemy and compel him to disperse his forces. The 'Jedburgh' teams consisted of volunteers from the forces under the governments-in-exile, escaped resisters from occupied territory and British or American officers or NCOs who had been given suitable training. The British and Americans had no territorial claims and few political objectives in post-war Europe, but they did have ulterior motives in some cases. In Greece, for instance, Churchill was primarily interested in ensuring the return of a pro-British King in order to guarantee British predominance in the Mediterranean.

The Soviet attitude was not very different. As it advanced the Red Army did its best to spread disorder behind the enemy lines by parachuting instructors individually or in groups to the partisans; they were recruited either from communist refugees in Moscow or from prisoners of war or deserters from the satellite armies – Slovaks, Hungarians or Rumanians. As the advance proceeded the Russians pressed into their service, in the name of an anti-German crusade, the forces which the Wehrmacht had used against them in the anti-communist crusade. But, particularly from the summer of 1944 onwards, Stalin was more ruthless than either Churchill or Roosevelt in subordinating immediate military objectives to vast long-term political plans. In all countries he wished to impose governments favourable to the USSR, directed or activated by communists, and he was prepared to trample on anything which stood in the way of his plans. He indicated to Eisenhower, who gave way, that it was the Red Army's prerogative to take Vienna and Prague. Thus the boundary of Russia's zone of influence in Europe and the potential dividing line between the two worlds was pushed very far west.

The governments-in-exile had little say on the subject of these vast plans. As a matter of expediency the Allies generally only revealed them either at the last moment or not at all and never in their entirety. The exiled governments had no means of changing or opposing them. Nevertheless, they had not lived through their country's defeat and then fought relentlessly in order to be

deprived of their authority at the last moment even by their protectors and friends. They did their best to assist the Allies and
reduce destruction and casualties in their country as far as possible; consequently they had no wish to see the national rising
take place on too large a scale or risk leading to some catastrophe.
When they knew or suspected that the Allies had in mind some
idea unfavourable to them, they were determined to assert themselves, and present them with the *fait accompli* of the nation, or at
least the capital, in revolt, and liberating itself. This is what happened, with very differing results, in the case of the French in
Paris, the Poles in Warsaw and the Czechs in Prague.

As far as the Germans were concerned, although the Resistance
was a nuisance to them, it was not their main enemy. Putting first
things first, in some cases they simply evacuated, as in Corsica or
Rumania. In general terms, as their defeat became more certain,
they fought harder in the east against the Soviets than in the west
against the British and Americans to whom they surrendered in
thousands. This difference in attitude towards their enemies partially explains the savagery with which they crushed the insurgents
in Slovakia and Warsaw.

The general rising as seen from inside

In the towns, lack of space hindered the guerrillas; barricades
were of little use if tanks were available. On the other hand, even
a small number of determined men could hold up a superior and
better armed enemy – as had been seen during the ghetto rising
in Warsaw. Every house could become a stronghold and the
defenders could move to the adjoining house when their situation
became untenable. Removal or rearrangement of street nameplates or house numbering could turn a town into a jungle; areas
could be isolated by destruction of the telephone system; cellars
were available as shelters or ready-made bunkers. In close-
quarter fighting the besieged were not entirely helpless even in
the face of tanks, thanks to the 'Molotov cocktail'. From the point
of view of the inhabitants, on the other hand, if a rising took
place in a town it became a battlefield and a heap of ruins; they
were doomed to such ghastly suffering as starvation, bombing,
mass shootings and epidemics. Complete cities, however
famous, might be destroyed by the nazis – after all they had

subjected Warsaw, Rotterdam, Belgrade and London to blind bombing.

The communists refused to recognise these problems; they minimised them, emphasising solely the reduced numbers of the occupation forces – 'we are twenty million Frenchmen; faced with this army of patriots, of what account are a few *Boche* divisions scattered all over France and a few thousand militiamen?' They pointed out that people who did not fight would be left with a choice between internment and being shot; the rising was the 'sole means of self-defence'. Moreover, it would seize the initiative from the occupation forces and put them on to the defensive, resulting in a sensational and triumphant reversal of the situation. Faced with a national rising involving the entire country, the occupier would be besieged in the midst of his conquests.

But, according to the communists, the national rising must not be an old-style *levée en masse*. There could be no question of shouting 'Everyone to the barricades' as in June 1848 or calling for a 'breakthrough' by the National Guard as in 1871; the only result of such anachronisms would be bloody defeat. In communist eyes the national rising was the crowning phase of 'direct action' – when the mass of people would be controlled and guided by the communist party. Every man would be placed according to his fighting capacity, but also according to his 'political level' or 'class-consciousness', in other words his degree of devotion to the Party.

Viewed in this light, the national rising was no affair of small units such as parachute commandos. It was 'action by everybody, men, women and even children, young people, workers, managers, peasants, intellectuals, employees, officials, officers, NCOS, priests, teachers, traders'.[1] For the majority their place of work would be their battle station. Officials should refuse to obey orders and sabotage them; women should incite the population by protesting against inadequate rations; workers should call a general strike. This should not be a mere stoppage of work; factories, railway junctions and telephone exchanges should be occupied and workers' militia formed to defend them. Sabotage should be so widespread that not a single train would run for the enemy's benefit; roads should be blocked by felled trees, bridges blown up as convoys crossed them. At the same time armed

[1] 'Call to the people of all Paris' – notice by the 'Paris Liberation Committee'.

groups should attack enemy posts or isolated vehicles; every village and every town should become a base for raiding parties. Not least among the results would be the 'recovery' of weapons captured from the enemy.

A national rising on these lines could hardly fit into Allied strategy. From the point of view even of the Resistance authorities there was considerable risk that it would rapidly get out of hand, for it would amount to the creation of a large number of independent battlefields and, once launched, developments would be largely in the hands of those on the spot. Once on the move the 'masses' were a formidable force, like a force of nature, a social avalanche carrying all before it and not knowing when to stop. The communists were fully aware of this; they accepted the risk because they made no distinction between the military objective and the political aim. On 1 June 1966 *France d'abord*, the FTP newspaper, wrote: 'The task does not begin on D Day nor finish with it; it will continue after victory.'

The communists were not the only people to plan and prepare so complete and militant a form of rising; in Poland, for instance, the members of the Home Army were just as determined. In general, however, the communist propaganda and example had eventually convinced the others.[1] Moreover, as the enemy's defeat drew nearer, people climbed on the bandwagon, hoping to counteract years of indecision by a few days of dynamic action. In the 'National Liberation Movement' in France, and among certain groups of officers in Bohemia, there were reservations. The rising should only be initiated, they said, in full agreement with the inter-allied high command and should only be ordered by the highest resistance authorities; otherwise it would only result in useless bloodshed. They expressed their fears of competitive destruction and 'terrorist' excesses with resulting damage to the good name of the Resistance. Not everyone thought the general strike the perfect solution – the enemy, after all, still had formidable methods of coercion – was there not a risk of starvation in the towns? – might not a partial immobilisation of transport be more effective than a total stoppage?

In the Algiers Consultative Assembly Claudius Petit said: 'We have always been on the side of action but we do not wish to see a number of French cities destroyed to no good purpose; people should be dissuaded from the useless and the spectacular.' The

[1] See article entitled '*Il n'a pas d'heure H*' in *La Marseillaise* of May 1944.

other parties feared that the communists had ulterior motives and had no wish to fight in order to put them in power; they also feared the violence and disorder created by an uncontrolled mass of human beings; after all everyone could remember the futile excesses of the Commune of 1871. Instead of mass action, which would necessarily be undisciplined, they preferred the use of military or paramilitary forces such as the police, gendarmes or fire brigades. They could be closely controlled by their leaders; they could act against certain defined points to destroy or protect them, on the orders of the Allies and only when their arrival was imminent.

In most occupied countries, therefore, when the final phase of the resistance war arrived, two trains of thought, two sets of ideas and methods existed side by side or in opposition – and each side knew that the future of the country might depend on its action. In France, for instance, both sides had given much thought to the precedent set by the liberation of Corsica.

The auspicious precedent of Corsica

In Corsica the whole affair was over extremely quickly and easily. The fall of Mussolini and the capitulation of Italy had left the 80,000 Italians occupying the island completely bewildered. Public opinion was unanimously hostile to the Italians, whose presence seemed to presage annexation to Italy which not a single Corsican would have accepted; the few collaborators had discreetly remained in Italy. There were many resistance groups, both 'Gaullist' and 'National Front', but their enthusiasm for action was greater than their resources. As a matter of personal policy, General Giraud had provided the 'National Front' with arms, at the same time asking its leaders to await orders from him before taking action.

On 9 September 1943 the 'National Front', realising the extent of the Italian débâcle, hastened to establish a 'Liberation Committee' in Ajaccio. The Germans were evacuating their forces from Sardinia and moving them northwards through Corsica; as early as 15 September convoys were attacked. Except at Levie, wherever the *maquis* came in contact with the enemy it proved to be the weaker side despite occasional armed assistance from the Italians. But, like a magnet, the rising attracted help from outside;

the Americans refused to provide ships or aircraft but on 14 September, with considerable difficulty, the French submarine *Casabianca* and two French torpedo boats landed the 'shock battalion'; it was followed by a further 4,000 men on the 23rd – but the Germans still had 30,000 men and 100 tanks. Nevertheless, they continued to withdraw, attacked from the ridges of the central mountain range, and by early October they had evacuated the island.

The liberation of Corsica made a considerable stir. In the first place it was a purely French operation and a symbolic one too, for troops from North Africa and the Resistance had worked closely together. The Allies had taken no part except for their belated and clumsy action in bombing Bastia – after the last German had left.[1] This brilliant success was achieved with only 70 killed and 250 wounded and there had been numerous deeds of heroism.

The communists claimed this success as justification for their tactics of the permanent offensive. 'The Corsicans,' the 'National Front' proclaimed, 'have confirmed the accuracy of Stendhal's dictum: "Audacity makes good sense." ... Organisation is only a method of rousing the people to action.' In fact, had the Germans not been withdrawing, the Resistance would have been sadly disillusioned.

No sooner was the island liberated than the 'National Front' called upon the people to demonstrate at town halls and in village squares. It denounced and punished the 'traitors'; it expelled municipal authorities and held elections by show of hands in public places. The island, therefore, became covered by 'National Front' municipal councils, of which communists formed the nucleus – whereas before the war the communist party had been insignificant. Moreover, in Algiers F. Billoux advocated an infusion of young blood into the regular army by turning at least a thousand Corsican partisans into officers – the Hoches and Marceaus of the Resistance. The communists did not, of course, question the authority of the Algiers government in which they were represented, but they did strengthen their position in the French political game. What were they up to?

---

[1] In Vol. IX of his *History of United States Naval Operations in World War Two* Admiral Morison considers that the French vessels would have been better employed watching the approaches to Bastia in order to hamper the enemy's evacuation.

Success in Bucharest and Sofia

The arrival of the Red Army on the Dniester in the spring of 1944 greatly alarmed the Rumanian leaders, and with good reason. On 20 August their two armies were crushed fighting the Germans; invasion of the country was imminent. On 23 August the young King Michael, without great difficulty, persuaded General Antonescu to resign; as a precaution he had the General arrested – probably thinking of the example of King Victor-Emmanuel in Italy. The King proclaimed that Rumania had broken off relations with the Axis and joined the Allies. As in Rome, the Resistance, represented by the 'National Democratic Front', played little part in this upheaval but its mere existence had helped and it benefited from the change. Four of its leaders, one of whom was communist, were included in the new government which consisted mainly of technicians obedient to the King. This bold stroke took the Germans by surprise, but they were too weak to react other than by bombing the city. The King was hoping to negotiate their withdrawal, but the communists, together with units of the Rumanian army, attacked enemy detachments and occupied vital points in the capital; revolt spread all over Rumania and several thousand German soldiers were made prisoner. The Russians arrived in Bucharest on 28 August, and the city was officially liberated. At first they behaved as enemies; the armistice which they granted on 12 September stipulated the return to Russia of the Bukovina and Bessarabia.[1] It was clear that Russia did not intend to forgive Rumania too quickly for her participation in the 'anti-bolshevik crusade' and the looting of Odessa. For the moment, however, even Stalin himself congratulated King Michael.

In Bulgaria the Bagrianov government withdrew its troops from Greece and Yugoslavia; on 5 September its successor under Muravief decided to ask the Soviet Union for an armistice. It thought that it could keep the Russians out of Bulgaria and the communists out of the government. On 26 August, however, the 'Fatherland Front' had decided to initiate a rising which began in Sofia on 6 September with strikes in the factories and public

---

[1] The British and Americans had assured the King that, like them, the Russians would have no objection to the return of Transylvania to Rumania.

transport and the release of political prisoners. During the night 8/9 September a 'Fatherland Front' government, which included two communists, was formed. On learning of these developments the Russians suspended military operations. They entered Sofia on 16 September and Bulgaria declared war on Germany – she had never been at war with the USSR.[1]

Both in Rumania and Bulgaria seizure of power by the Resistance undoubtedly saved the people from the wrath of the Red Army. In both countries it took place without difficulty and almost without internal opposition. These developments, particularly that in Rumania, were of major importance to the Allies since at a stroke the Germans had lost vital resources, particularly in oil, and the way into central Europe south of the Carpathians now lay wide open to the Red Army. In both cases power changed hands as the result of a *putsch* rather than a rising and clearly the approach of the Red Army and its tacit approval had paralysed the 'collaborators'. In both cases too resistance unity had proved valuable, but the communists had also shown how adept they were at taking advantage of popular upheavals; they were only a tiny minority, but nevertheless they controlled the government in Sofia and were represented in it in Bucharest. The real winners were the Russians; almost without fighting they had eliminated two of their enemies and kept the British and Americans away from this part of Europe. The question was: how long would they be content with only a partial political victory in Bucharest and how long would they tolerate King Michael and his régime?

Setbacks in Slovakia and the Vercors

Slovakia, though a German protectorate, was an independent state, unoccupied, clerical rather than fascist despite its single party. The people accepted the régime since unlike the Bohemians they were not anti-German by tradition. The government began to lose some of its moral support when it sent troops to fight in Russia – not that the Slovaks, who were conservative and Catholic, had any leanings towards communism but because they felt themselves racially akin to the Russians. Desertions were numerous and Slovaks formed the majority of the Czechoslovak army corps which fought with the Russians under the command of General

[1] An armistice was nevertheless signed in Moscow on 28 October.

Svoboda. When the Red Army approached Slovakia in the spring of 1944 the leaders of the Slovak state were wondering how to extricate themselves from the impasse in which they were entangled. Like the Rumanians they hoped to do so by a simple about-turn which was ostensibly without great danger since German troops were located no nearer than the borders of Moravia and Slovakia.

On their side, in accordance with agreements concluded with the government-in-exile, the communists contacted the anti-German 'bourgeois elements' and at the end of 1943 a 'Slovak National Council' was formed with local committees in the country; in principle the Council accepted political and military direction from the London government. The Prime Minister was Srobar, a friend of Benès, and command of the forces was given to Colonel Golian, commandant of the Banska-Bystrica garrison. By the end of 1943 the Russians had dropped instructions by parachute and *maquis* were fighting in the woods and mountains.[1]

The Red Army was now approaching the barrier of the Carpathians, the summit of which was held by two Slovak divisions interspersed between German units. If the Slovaks rose, there was a good chance that the Slovak units would distintegrate and the enemy front collapse; in addition the German army's rail communications from the northern Carpathians to Hungary would be cut. Accordingly in July the Red Army parachuted no fewer than twenty-four staff groups to the partisans.

The rising took place in August, but the Slovak troops at the front did not revolt; General Malar, their commander, spoke over the radio to other disaffected units -- which were the majority, even including the gendarmes – and some of them lost their will to fight. The Germans advanced into central Slovakia; they seized the initiative and so stifled any offensive by the insurgents. After a few weeks fighting, on 19 October 1944 they entered Banska-Bystrica where the 'Slovak National Council' was sitting. Some of the insurgent forces were made prisoner and the rest dispersed into the mountains. The rising cost the Slovaks nearly 25,000 men.

This clear defeat raised a certain number of problems. The communists accused Golian (who was shot by the Germans) of having given the signal for the rising too early, saying that he

[1] The *maquis* also included French and Yugoslav escaped prisoners of war and some labour service conscripts.

wished to confirm the authority of the Czechoslovak government before the arrival of the Red Army – as the Poles did in Warsaw. On his side Benès complained to Moscow about the activity of 'communist traitors'. Apparently, harmony did not invariably reign within the 'Slovak National Council'.

Moreover, the Slovak rising was isolated – the Czechs made no move to support it;[1] it could only have succeeded had the Germans decided to withdraw, as in Rumania. Himmler himself, however, had moved to Vienna and decided to send reinforcements, since Slovakia commanded the approaches to the Hungarian plain, Vienna and Upper Silesia.

Finally, the revolt broke out because the arrival of the Red Army appeared imminent, but in fact it did not move. It only advanced on 8 September when the rising had been crushed; it was then held up at the Dukla pass and did not press its attack home; not until 18 October did it cross the frontier; until that time its offensive was concentrated north and south of the Carpathians. It looks, therefore, as if the Red Army merely wanted to create a diversion for the Germans in Slovakia in order to assist its advance elsewhere. It may also be that the flood of nationalism on the part of the insurgents – even including communists like Husak who had little in common with the Moscow refugees – was unwelcome to Stalin; if this is so, his attitude towards Slovakia was very similar to that he adopted in the case of Warsaw, despite his agreement with Benès.

Though there was no connection between the two, the Slovak rising had much in common with that of the Vercors in France. The country was similarly mountainous; *maquis* had formed, spontaneously at first but later encouraged and supported by the Resistance authorities, both Jean Moulin in France and the 'National Liberation Committee' in Algiers. The Vercors was a natural fortress, a central plateau surrounded by rocky mountain crests. A vast plan was worked out to turn it into a redoubt, against which enemy attacks would beat in vain and which, by its example, would summon the entire Alpine resistance to the colours; from it raiding parties would descend into the plain and it would perhaps even form a corner of liberated France, the 'Vercors Republic'.[2] Fighting went on for over a month, from 15 June to

---

[1] The Hungarians somewhat half-heartedly fought the insurgents to the end.
[2] The civilian head of the Vercors even believed that General de Gaulle would arrive and address the nation over the radio.

23 July; the *maquis* had not been given the necessary heavy equipment and their numbers were inadequate to defend the entire rocky perimeter; they were attacked by enemy artillery and aircraft and taken by surprise in their rear when gliders landed with a cargo of ss.

In both cases defeat was bloody and reprisals monumental – 700 people were massacred in the Vercors. In both cases the same initial error was made – belief that prolonged defence was possible in mountains, which were in fact riddled with roads and broad valleys. More important still, by concentrating their forces in a redoubt, both partisans and *maquis* forfeited their mobility, the secret of the guerrilla's success. Both in Slovakia and the Vercors the risings were directed by professional soldiers. It is surprising, however, that the communists, who were very few in the Vercors, did not make better use of guerrilla tactics in Slovakia.

Most important of all, in both cases the essential aid from outside was totally lacking; the Vercors *maquis* complained bitterly that they had been 'betrayed'. Nevertheless, despite their disastrous consequences, the risings were not in vain; enemy forces were tied down far from the decisive theatres of war, Normandy and the Ukrainian and Rumanian plains. In August fighting was resumed in the Vercors, when the *maquis* were better supported. In Slovakia one of the aims of the rising was achieved, recognition by all concerned of a greater degree of autonomy for the country within a liberated Czechoslovakia; from then on, moreover, the Germans could place no confidence in the Slovaks.

The Warsaw drama

In view of the attitude of the Red Army as it entered Poland and the measures decided upon by the Lublin Committee,[1] the Polish government in London was faced with a cruel dilemma: if it did nothing, it would forfeit all authority in Poland; on the other hand the clandestine parties which supported it had protested against 'this fresh Soviet aggression' and announced themselves opposed to 'any cession of territory'. The Poles had long since prepared plans for a general rising and had communicated them to the British, but it had been agreed that they would not be put into force unless German defeat was imminent and the western

[1] See preceding chapter.

Allies were in a position to provide the necessary assistance. In July 1944 neither of these conditions applied.

General Bor-Komorovski, commander of the Home Army, emphasised the danger of remaining inactive as the Red Army approached Warsaw, as this would leave the initiative for the rising to the communists. The Polish government in London agreed and on 25 July Bor was given plenary powers to take such measures as events might dictate. On 29 July when Radio Moscow issued an appeal to the people of Warsaw – 'let the million Poles become a million soldiers' – Bor was afraid of being forestalled and fixed 1 August for the start of the rising. He was sure of the enthusiasm of his men but, to demonstrate that they were acting in their own right, the Polish government had warned neither the British and Americans nor the Russians. Mikolajczyk, the Prime Minister, went to talk to Stalin, thinking that the rising would place him in a stronger position vis-à-vis his formidable opposite number, Stalin. He was bitterly disappointed.

The Polish decision was, in fact, a grave one; it risked depriving the insurgents of all Allied assistance since no promises had been made and nothing had been prepared. In the event, the British indicated at once that they were in no position to drop parachute troops or carry out bombing; they did, nevertheless, try to drop equipment but of the first fifteen aircraft despatched six were lost; of the 56 operations attempted between 3 and 14 August, only 23 were successful, 11 aircraft were shot down and 11 others badly damaged. British assistance to the insurgents was, therefore, both costly and inadequate.

Clearly assistance could only come from the Red Army. On 1 August Rokossovsky was only six miles from Warsaw and he had covered 375 miles in six weeks; he seemed only to have to keep up his momentum for a day or two and the Polish insurgents had paved the way better than those in Bucharest and Sofia. But, to the stupefaction of all, the Red Army remained immobile on the right bank of the Vistula until 10 September. Admittedly it was in need of regrouping, its lines of communication were inordinately long, the crossing of the Vistula could not be improvised and the Germans had sent in fresh troops. Nevertheless, the Red Army had encountered similar difficulties in many other places and nowhere had it remained inactive for so long. Probably Stalin was unpleasantly surprised by the scope of the Polish national rising – the Warsaw communists had placed themselves

under Bor's orders – and he would have been aware of the anti-
Soviet aspect of the operation. At the risk, therefore, of delaying
his offensive into Reich territory, he took a cold decision to allow
the rising to burn itself out; he did not even dispute the Luftwaffe's air superiority; worse still he described the leaders of the
rising as 'criminals' and 'provocateurs'.

So the injudicious timing of the insurrection became clear.
Faced with the attitude of their Soviet ally, the British and
Americans did not come forward with aid. The Americans, whom
the Poles besought to send aircraft, would not do so without
Stalin's agreement, and the British offloaded these hazardous
operations on to Polish crews. The aircraft had to fly low, in the
full glare of the anti-aircraft searchlights; the dropping zone was
a wood where much equipment was lost; half the aircraft did not
return. On 27 August all assistance was stopped. The British then
asked the Russians to allow their aircraft to land and refuel on
their airfields since they were closer to the target. Stalin refused.

Of 46,000 insurgents only 20,000 were armed with a rifle or
sub-machinegun; they had ammunition for only seven days –
some had been manufactured in small underground factories; they
had no anti-aircraft defence. For sixty-three days they fought
unaided. Not until the forty-first day did the Russians – or rather
the Poles of the 'Berling Corps' – attempt to cross the Vistula to
establish bridgeheads on the left bank; on 23 September they were
forced to cross back again. From 13 September the Russians began
to send in ammunition, but in what quantities and with what
results? Soviet historians and Poles in exile argue fiercely on the
subject – 156 mortars, 500 anti-tank guns, 22,000 automatic
weapons and 113 tons of food, say the Russians; 50 tons, of which
15 were food, says General Bor; he adds that many containers
were smashed on landing since they had no parachutes.

On 18 September the Americans finally despatched 100 Flying
Fortresses having obtained agreement for them to land on Red
Army airfields. But by that time Warsaw was blanketed in smoke;
it was impossible to tell which parts of the city were still held by
the insurgents and the majority of the 1,800 containers were lost.
Moreover it was too late; although resistance continued until 2
October, the insurgents were crushed by German tanks. When Bor
surrendered, the Home Army had lost 10,000 killed and 7,000
wounded; 50,000 inhabitants of Warsaw had died and 300,000
were deported. Those parts of the city which had not been

destroyed in the fighting were systematically demolished when it was over.

For the Resistance the lesson was a bitter one. It proved that, without Allied assistance, the partisans, however heroic – and the Poles had fought heroically – must inevitably succumb to enemy superiority. At the same time it revealed Stalin's implacable determination to destroy anything in the way of his plans – which visualised, not the liberation of occupied territory but the imposition of Soviet domination and the Soviet order of society. On 27 December 1944 Stalin wrote to Roosevelt that 'the elements under orders of the London Poles had committed the worst transgressions'; he was not content merely to abandon the Poles to their miserable fate; he denigrated and vilified them, like his opponents during the 'great trials'.

'Self-liberation' in Paris

In France careful preparations had been made to support the Allied troops as they landed. Manifold sabotage was to take place in the 'communications zone', where the boundaries would change as the Allies advanced; the *maquis* were to act in the 'nonoperational zone' immediately ahead of the 'combat zone'. Several plans had been prepared: the 'Green Plan' designed to paralyse rail transport in France for a fortnight, the period required to establish a bridgehead and concentrate the forces landed (as annexes there were plans for the destruction of inland waterways and blockage of the road network); 'Plan Blue' dealt with sabotage of the electricity system; 'Plan Tortoise' set out guerrilla action required to delay the enemy concentration.

But, if these plans were to be implemented, the FFI should have been properly equipped and reinforced by airborne troops. Their equipment required 60 tons per day; yet in March 1944, the most favourable month, only 20 tons were delivered. Consequently only half the FFI were more or less armed on D Day and even they had no artillery, tanks, anti-aircraft, anti-tank guns, aircraft or supply service.

Nevertheless, acts of sabotage were numerous and frequently spectacular – 52 locomotives were destroyed in the Bellegarde depot on the night of 6 June 1944. All the *maquis* went into action and the desired result was achieved – the German troops did not

11*

know which way to face and were kept totally in the dark about the real intentions of the Allies. At the same time members of the FFI, most of whom were unarmed, reached their assembly points – there were several thousand men at Mont Mouchet in the Auvergne. A general action order was issued from London and everywhere armed groups attacked the enemy. But this general rising received only meagre support from the Allies; several 'liberated' towns were recaptured by the Germans, and unarmed *maquis* were massacred in many places. London then issued an order, difficult to enforce, to restrict guerrilla warfare.

Things went better in August after Brittany had shown the Americans how widespread and violent the rising was and how much assistance it could give them. It gathered momentum once more with the 15 August landing on the Mediterranean coast, the main centre of revolt being in the Alps. What would the Parisians do? From the end of July retreating German troops were moving through the city daily, but the garrison was still 17,000 strong with some one hundred tanks. Were they simply to await the Allies?

Neither the Algiers government nor the Paris Liberation Committee, whose chairman was Tollet, a communist, while Rol-Tanguy, another communist, commanded the FFI, had any intention of doing so. The government intended to show the Americans that in Paris as in the liberated areas of France it was the government expected and acclaimed by the French. The Liberation Committee proposed to prove that, far from being passive, French resistance was the first to fight for the liberation of its country. But between these two authorities areas of mistrust still existed. Parodi and Chaban-Delmas, the civil and military delegates of the government, had been ordered to canalise the rising, but the communists had both the resources and the will to act.

On 14 July, following a communist appeal, marches headed by French flags had taken place at various points. The railwaymen went on strike on 10 August, the metro, the police and the gendarmerie on the 15th and the post and telephone services on the 18th. After that the strike was general. On 16 August the Paris Liberation Committee issued notices calling officers and NCOs to arms; on the 18th the communist party called the population to arms. French flags were hoisted on public buildings, several municipal buildings were occupied by the FFI and skirmishes took place near the Luxembourg, in the 18th and 19th *arrondissements* and in the suburbs. Police resisters took over the Prefecture of Police and, in the revolutionary tradition of Paris, the National Resistance Council set itself up in the Hotel de Ville. But the Allies were not due to arrive for another fortnight since the Americans intended to by-pass Paris in order to maintain pressure on the enemy and avoid having to feed the vast population. There was a risk of the rising being crushed.

On 19 August, Nordling, the Swedish Consul, negotiated a suspension of hostilities; it was observed by some of the resisters but not the communists. On 22 August the Liberation press began to appear; resisters had taken possession of the radio station and of the Ministries, in which Secretaries-General were installed; barricades appeared in many places. Tanks attacked the Prefecture of Police and brief street battles occurred at various points. There was a risk that Paris might be destroyed.

A mission from Paris went to see Generals de Gaulle and Koenig and on their insistence the Americans authorised General Leclerc's division to move on the capital. Captain Dronne's detachment reached the Hotel de Ville on the evening of 24 August. On the 25th troops of two French Armoured Divisions drove into the city by the southern and western gates; their advance was greatly assisted by the FFI who pinpointed centres of enemy resistance. During the afternoon General von Choltitz signed the surrender of the German garrison. On 26 August, while men of the militia fired on the crowd from the roofs and interior of Notre Dame, General de Gaulle drove down the Champs Elysées in triumph.

The Germans could undoubtedly have done a great deal of damage to Paris, as they did to Warsaw. A number of factors, however, weighed in favour of the rising. In the first place the Wehrmacht had decided to evacuate France and dig in in the Vosges and Ardennes to shorten its front and gain time; thus General von Choltitz, the garrison commander, could hardly be very bellicose; his troops remained on the defensive, enclosed in a series of strongholds which surrendered one after the other. Above all the Americans gave way to French entreaties and changed their plans to suit the French. Henri Bernard thinks they were wrong: 'Had Eisenhower by-passed the capital as he intended, one wonders how far the Allied forces might not have advanced if they had had available the supplies and transport resources diverted to Paris.'[1] Militarily the question is worth

[1] Henri Bernard: *Histoire de le Résistance europénne*, p. 187.

asking, but in total war moral factors must be taken into account. Throughout the world, and in Germany in particular, the moral effect of the capture of Paris was enormous; it was well worth a few million gallons of petrol and the loss of a few miles. In any case Eisenhower had already turned down Montgomery's out-flanking plan. For the French it was clear that the rising had to be attempted. As had been the case eleven months earlier in Corsica, the political repercussions of a meeting in the capital between fighting men from outside and those from inside were immeasurable. It signified the rebirth of France through the unity of Frenchmen in battle.

The liberation of Prague

The same factors, backed by the same determination, worked in favour of the rising in Prague.[1] After the setback of the Slovak rising and the resulting delay in the arrival of the Red Army in Czechoslovakia, Czech resistance had gone to some extent into cold storage. Not until late April 1945 was a 'Czech National Coun-cil' formed in Prague; it included delegates from all parties but the Benès government was represented only by a captain, dropped by parachute; the officers' clandestine organisations, which had remained loyal to Benès, were kept at arms length. Benès was installed in Kosice in full agreement with the USSR but, though recognising his authority, the 'National Council' remained some-what aloof from him and at cross purposes also – like the French CNR and the Algiers government.

There was no compelling reason for a rising in Prague except the communist desire to put themselves in the limelight. The Czech officer groups would have preferred to await the Allies, preferably the Americans; the latter, however, having reached Pilsen, halted and then withdrew because of their agreement with the Russians. Nevertheless, when the revolt did break out, prob-ably as a spontaneous reaction 'from below', everybody fought. The 'Protectorate' authorities – Hacha was dying – had lost all

---

[1] Earlier, on 7 April, Austrian flags had been hoisted on certain buildings in Vienna and skirmishes had taken place in the working-class quarter. A resistance emissary crossed the German lines and was a valuable adviser to Marshal Tolbukhin during his entry into Vienna. Plans for a rising had been brought to nought by treachery and the resulting arrests.

influence. The Germans knew of the existence of the National Council and were willing, if necessary, to negotiate with it.

The rising began in small ways on 5 May – burning of German books, tearing down notices, putting up portraits of Mazaryk. Police seized the central radio station, taking the Germans by surprise and disarming them; barricades appeared, nearly 1,600 in all. On 6 and 7 May, German attacks gradually reduced the centres of revolt. An American offer of help to the National Council was refused through the mouth of Smrkovsky.[1]

Prague appealed for help and thousands of volunteers from the surrounding countryside came to its aid, all determined to wipe out the years of humiliation by fighting. Nevertheless, faced with the enemy's superiority, the insurgents were in process of giving way when, on the evening of the 7th, Germans carrying white flags announced the capitulation of the Wehrmacht. The troops, who were already in retreat from the whole of Bohemia to escape the Red Army, proposed a cessation of hostilities provided they could withdraw with their weapons. On the evening of the 8th the National Council accepted. The Russians did not enter the city until next day.

The rising did not, therefore, have the benefit of outside assistance as did that in Paris. On the other hand it was unable to force the occupation forces to surrender. The communists' political aims became plain for all to see when, on the 8th, they asked the insurgents to remain on the barricades saying: 'The new Republic will belong to the workers.' Czech resistance was forced to conform to an inter-allied agreement which left Bohemia in the Soviet occupation zone; it had had no freedom of choice. Undoubtedly, however, the Czechs were swayed towards the Russians by strong feelings of friendship and gratitude.

[1] Czechoslovak historians subsequently upbraided the Americans for not having done what they were asked not to do, even accusing them of having deliberately allowed the Germans to suppress the revolt – a curious interpretation of the facts, stemming from the cold war.

ANALYSIS OF PRINCIPAL NATIONAL RISINGS

	Timing[1]	Insurgents' Unity[1]	Support from Governments-in-exile[1]	Allied Support[1]	German Resistance[3]	Military Result[4]	Political Result[4]
Corsica	+	+ C[2]	+	−	−	S	S C[2]
Bucharest	+	+ C		−	−	S	S C
Sofia	+	+ C		−	−		S C
Slovakia	+	+ C	+	−	+	F	F
Vercors	−	+	−	−	+	F	F
Paris	+	+ C	+	+	−	S	S
Warsaw	−	+	+	−	+	F	F
Prague	−	+ C	+	−	−		S C

[1] + = good; − = unfavourable
[2] C = major communist role
[3] + = strong; − = weak
[4] S = successful; F = failure

CHAPTER 19

Seizure of Power, Restoration, Renovation or Revolution?

It now remains to evaluate the part played by each resistance movement in the liberation of its country and describe the changes it was able to bring about when it came to power. In most cases its victory meant the end of the underground, at least in the form in which it had existed under occupation. Even when acclaimed by the majority of public opinion as its successes came to light, the Resistance remained a heterogeneous minority linked by a fragile unity. Liberation brought to the surface once more the mass of fence-sitters, anxious to return to their pre-war mode of life. Norway, Denmark, Holland and Belgium, for instance, more or less returned to their old ways. In the totalitarian dictatorships the evils of fascism were not all swept away at once by the defeat of the Axis; in Italy the Resistance continued to struggle to turn the country back into a democracy; when the war ended no one could say when or how Germany would be purged of nazism, whose memory was linked both to frightful crimes and brilliant victories.

Most important of all, the Allied coalition which had more or less held together until the end of the struggle, began to show cracks which heralded a break-up. The Resistance, which was only part of this coalition, inevitably reflected and suffered from the great new division between the liberal capitalist democracies and the socialist totalitarian democracies – the split was to be seen even among the inmates of concentration camps. The whole of central and eastern Europe 'liberated' by the Red Army was subjected to Soviet tutelage externally and communist party rule internally – Poland, Hungary, Rumania, Bulgaria, Albania and Czechoslovakia. In Greece a terrible civil war, which had begun in the underground, continued to tear the country apart; failure there was complete.

In only two cases did the national Resistance really achieve its objectives. In Yugoslavia, while fighting was still in progress, the partisans formed and imposed a new régime of national communism, but at the price of internecine warfare, the results of which are still cruelly felt today. France, on the other hand, regained her soul in a new-found national unity; she narrowly avoided a bloody revolution but then made a fresh start by instituting the major reforms planned in the underground.

In all the liberated countries national freedom was only regained at the price of heavy sacrifices both in manpower and material wealth. A lasting germanophobia is imprinted in many minds.

North-west Europe: Return to the status quo

In the smaller countries of north-west Europe occupation had not uncovered any major flaws in the constitution nor had resistance brought in new men or new groupings. On the contrary, four or five years of subjection had merely made the old institutions and the return of the familiar authorities seem more desirable.

Norway had not been the scene of another round of fighting, although *Milorg* was prepared for it. On 6 May 1945 the Resistance seized the main strategic points without much difficulty. Seventeen German divisions, which would have been of much more use elsewhere, were still in the country and they allowed themselves to be disarmed without argument. On 10 May, Norwegian parachute troops from Great Britain together with clandestine resisters made a peaceful entry into Oslo; King Haakon and his government soon followed them in similar fashion. By its dual struggle against indigenous fascism and the occupying power, the Resistance had increased Norwegian devotion to democracy and consolidated a national unity which was hardly assisted by the great distances and differences of language.

In Denmark the secret army had reached 10,000 men by the end of 1944; it was armed with British and Swedish weapons but never had cause to use them. The Danes brought their war to an end by means of a major strike; to prevent the withdrawal of troops from Norway to Germany all pilots stopped work in April 1945 and so immobilised 450 German ships; 19 tugs successfully escaped to Sweden. On 5 May a British mission landed near Copenhagen while the Germans were evacuating the country. Although the King and his government had followed rather than guided the development of public opinion, they had lost nothing; the King was still popular and his government regarded as legitimate. The underground was thanked for its loyal services and with that its role ended. Nevertheless, there was one profound change; the people felt themselves less dependent on their mighty German neighbour and more closely tied to Great Britain.

Holland had not the good fortune to be liberated quickly or completely. After the failure of the Arnhem airborne operation a sizeable part of the country remained subject to particularly severe occupation – the deportation of all men from 16 to 40 years of age had been decided upon; a terrible famine claimed thousands of victims. The London government administered the liberated areas through the channel of certain resistance personalities. The 'Royal Brigade' arrived from England to take part in the fighting; 5,000 volunteers were armed and placed under the command of Prince Bernhard. In the occupied area resistance was more 'activist' than before – on 7 March 1945 Rauter, the German Commissar-General, was assassinated. The 'College of trustworthy persons' prepared the various measures which would be necessary on liberation and when Seyss-Inquart, the 'Protector', was driven to surrender, this was the body to which he turned; two of its members carried the good news to London and, with this information, the Allies were enabled to save many lives. Queen Wilhelmina returned from London more revered than ever. Nevertheless, although the men of the Resistance willingly took a back seat, the underground had changed certain aspects of political life; parties had lost some of their religious affiliations; the working class, which had played a major role, was henceforth represented by a non-confessional 'labour party'; the communists, though numerically few, were more prominent.

In Belgium sabotage was widespread from 8 June 1944 primarily on the main Brussels–Paris and Aix-la-Chapelle–Liège lines to delay movement to Normandy of German troops stationed in Holland. It was resumed on 1 September but the Germans were only moving through the country and the Ardennes *maquis* had no time to harass them. Belgian SAS were the first Allied troops to enter the country and Brussels was liberated by a Belgian brigade. The main resistance exploit, however, was the prevention of the destruction of Antwerp and the help given to the Allies in seizing the port installations intact; the Allied supply situation was then considerably eased. Belgium was threatened by a grave political crisis, however. Most of the Resistance – primarily the communists and socialists, the former having emerged stronger and more active – called upon King Leopold to abdicate. He refused to recognise the authority of the Resistance and made his decision dependent upon that of the nation; meanwhile his brother Charles was commissioned to act as regent. More important still, occupation had exacerbated the differences between the Fleming and Walloon racial groups; the Walloons accused the Flemings of having been too susceptible to the temptations of collaboration and even of having visualised partition of the country by attaching Flanders to the 'State of Thiel' planned by the nazis. Belgian unity, a fragile thing anyway but held together by the monarchy, was therefore doubly threatened.

Central and eastern Europe: a communist monopoly

Although no 'division of the world' had ever been made between the Allies, at Yalta or anywhere else, a *de facto* situation had arisen in Europe, recognised in the 'gentlemen's agreement' between Churchill and Stalin of October 1944; subsequently it was substantiated by the ambition of Stalin, the defeat of Churchill and the relative weakness of Great Britain, the death of Roosevelt and the withdrawal of the Americans. In fact each of the major Allies dealt as it wished with the sphere of influence conquered by its armies. The USSR's share, acquired for it by the Red Army, was three million square miles and seventy million people represented in 1945 by Czechoslovakia, Poland, Rumania, Hungary, Bulgaria and Albania. Both history and geography dictated that these Slav, Magyar and Dacian tribes, hopelessly divided among themselves by frontier disputes, should rotate between their powerful German and Russian neighbours. This was the Russians' hour.

Before the war the communist party in all these countries with the exception of Czechoslovakia had been weak, proscribed and hounded by the police forces of authoritarian governments. But the ground was well prepared for communist penetration, except in Bohemia which was more inclined to pan-slavism. The urban proletariat was miserable, the agricultural proletariat slaves of great landed proprietors; the ruling classes had compromised themselves with the German occupation régime and cared little about improvements in the people's standard of living; the masses were illiterate and so immune to the attractions of freedom of thought; the intellectual minority had succumbed to the doctrine of revolution despite the fact that Hitler's racial policy had deprived it of its Jewish catalyst.[1] There were plenty of seeds to ensure a vigorous growth when the Red Army arrived with its 'political education' cadres.

Soviet procedure was approximately the same everywhere. In the first place the forces which had lately been fighting against the Red Army were turned against Germany; 450,000 Bulgars and as many Rumanians were sent to fight in Transylvania, Hungary, Slovakia and Yugoslavia; by the end of the war Svoboda's Czechoslovak corps, 18,000 men strong at the end of 1944, numbered 60,000.

Then the communist refugees in Moscow returned to their countries, taking with them the orders of the Kremlin. In many cases they were rough uneducated beings who had spent much of their time in prison and for whom loyalty to the USSR compensated for lack of a past history in their own country. The collapse of the ruling classes resulting from their collaboration with Hitler, however, opened the doors of power to them. At first they were careful not to seize it completely, as they could have done with the Red Army present; while the war was still in progress it was important not to alarm other resisters – victory required the co-operation of everybody. Through the medium of the 'National Fronts', therefore, governments stemming from the Resistance were formed; communists were in a minority, but they generally took care to retain one key post, such as Minister of the Interior in charge of the police. Agreement was easily reached on a short-term programme such as economic recovery and punishment of collaborators. In many cases the old institutions and personalities were retained – King Michael in Rumania, King Simeon in Bulgaria and President Benès in Czechoslovakia, for instance. Only in Poland were the real or supposed opponents of the communists faced with the brutal dilemma: submit or vanish.

But the communists were quick to expand and strengthen their influence and authority. Punishment of collaborators enabled them to break the old ruling classes, many of whom had, in fact,

[1] On Poland see the remarkable appreciation by Léon Noel, the French Ambassador, dated 25 May 1936, in *Documents diplomatiques français*, Series 2, Vol. II, 1964.

accepted rather than supported fascism. At the same time they infiltrated into the new machinery of State, simultaneously maintaining, controlling and directing popular agitation in accordance with a well-constructed plan.

In Slovakia the communists were assured of a majority in eight out of the thirteen 'National Committees'. In general they chose as partners people representing intellectual trends rather than delegates of organised political parties. Still confining itself to Slovakia, the communist party merged with – in other words absorbed – the socialist party. The formation of trades unions, an entirely new development, brought with it a further degree of regimentation. The 'National Committees' seized power 'spontaneously'; they reduced the Beneš government delegates to the status of mere errand boys to the Red Army; realising that this development was irreversible Beneš dissolved the government-in-exile. Claims were made for vast and immediate social change; the trades unions demanded collectivisation of business enterprises and workers' control of production. The communists emphasised the urgency of 'agrarian reform', certain that this would strike a chord with the Slovaks, who were mostly peasants. The result was the nomination of the communist Gottwald to presidency of the 'National Front' in March 1945 and seizure of power by street demonstrations on the part of the Prague communists two months later.

In Rumania the 'National Democratic Front' published a draft programme on 25 September 1944. In principle it was supported by all parties in the Front. Its main themes were expropriation, confiscation and nationalisation; the old political leaders Maniu and Bratianu thereupon left the Front. It could rely for support, however, on the trades unions – which both officials and workers were more or less forced to join – and on the new 'workers party' combining communists and socialists. The great estates were 'spontaneously' divided; large areas of the country were administered direct by the Red Army. Vishinsky arrived from Moscow to force on King Michael the formation of a new government in which there would be more communists; 'bourgeois' Ministers were double-banked by communist State Secretaries. By February 1945 to all intents and purposes the communists and their fellow-travellers were in power.

Thus in each liberated country a new state was gradually set up, drawing on the Resistance and constituted with patriotism as its motto; the communists chequered the country with their close-knit organisation; the official state became nothing but a framework and the traditional parties supporting it mere office organisations without genuine popular backing; as these shells were gradually emptied, they became easy to break when the moment arrived. In principle the USSR had no hand in these internal metamorphoses; Molotov even arrived in Bucharest – before Vishinsky – to promise that Rumania's political and social order would not be changed. In fact, however, the Red Army and its 'political instructors' had much to do with the new state of affairs although officially it was created according to the wishes and by the action of the 'popular masses'. Nevertheless, the USSR kept an eye on its own interests; it was the legatee of German property; it demanded a high level of reparations from its ex-enemies even though they were now its friends; it achieved its territorial objectives in Polish Byelorussia and the Ukraine, in Czechoslovak Ruthenia and in Rumanian Bessarabia and Buko-vina; it compensated these mutilated countries by large-scale cessions of territory from the vanquished Hungarians and Ger-mans. Even more important, the USSR hastened to 'integrate' the economy of the 'liberated' countries into its own; it removed machine tools, material and stocks; it set up 'mixed companies' in which it took the place of the western capitalist companies – Rumanian oil was an outstanding example; in commercial deals it fixed prices of goods at rates favourable to itself.

In short, while assisting the formation and growth in the satel-lite states of political régimes and social structures modelled on its own, the USSR behaved as if the primary object of the advance of communism was to serve its own politico-military aims. A new imperialism began to appear, born of the revival of Russian nationalism. For the 'liberated' peoples the evil memories of occupation were too close for them to worry about this or even perceive it; moreover they gained certain advantages from the new order and their leaders were staunchly loyal to Moscow. Nevertheless, certain signs, indicative of a new attitude, were to be seen; in some cases communists returning from exile and com-munists from the underground did not automatically agree, as in Slovakia. Like those of the USSR the communists of the occupied countries had not deployed their conviction and their energy in the liberation of their country without rediscovering the virtues of patriotism or even of nationalism. In the long run national communism was the Resistance's legacy to the Third International. Nowhere did it assert itself so forcefully as in Yugoslavia.

National communism by the Yugoslavs

No resistance movement had made so great a contribution to the cleansing of its country from the stain of foreign occupation as the Yugoslav partisans. At the beginning of 1945 they were organised in four armies comprising fifty-three divisions averaging 8,000 men each. Transformation of the partisan bands into a people's army had been successfully completed; the necessary minimum of ranks, insignia and command structure had been reintroduced; decorations had been awarded. But each commander remained first and foremost a communist.

In the autumn of 1944 the partisans had co-operated with the Red Army in Serbia. They had cleared the country areas of the occupying forces – reduced by the defection of the Bulgars and Hungarians – as also of the *chetniks* under Nedich and Mihailovich; the latter had ultimately taken refuge in Bosnia. They had failed in front of the larger towns owing to lack of heavy equipment. On 14 October these ragged soldiers with their mixture of weapons, still fiercely aggressive, entered Belgrade with the leading Soviet tanks. Subsequently they completed the liberation of Serbia on their own, recapturing Uzice in November.

They were frequently supported by the Anglo-American air forces based in Italy. It was the Red Army, however, which provided them with the experts, the instructors and the staffs to complete the transformation of the partisan bands into a powerful army able to use the various weapons arriving from all sides and to play its part in the more static warfare now necessary.[1]

In March 1945, therefore, the Yugoslav people's army, the only one among its clandestine counterparts capable of doing so, took the offensive on its own against the German strongholds in Bosnia, Croatia and Slovenia. Tito worked on a broad strategy visualising combined attacks against Sarajevo in the centre, along the Adriatic and between the Drave and Save rivers on the flanks.

---

[1] The entry of the Red Army was greeted with delirious enthusiasm. A partisan leader such as Djilas stated that for him 'Stalin in 1944 was more than a war leader . . . he was the embodiment of an infallible and impeccable ideal . . . the brotherhood of the men of tomorrow'.

After some delay due to the construction of new defence lines by the enemy, Sarajevo was captured on 6 April; the advance reached Trieste on 1 May and contact was established with the British Eighth Army coming up from Italy; on 7 May a German unit was surrounded and annihilated at Ilir-Bistrica; Zagreb was captured on the 8th and the last Ustashi strongholds in Slovenia liquidated between 9 and 15 May. In two months the people's army had taken 200,000 prisoners. Yugoslavia had been liberated by the Yugoslavs.

No other national resistance movement had been so close to the people or understood and expressed their hopes and desires so well. The words of the partisan 'educators' to the peasant masses were simple and beckoning, they promised an end to illiteracy, emancipation of women, distribution of land, a higher standard of living, direct control of business enterprises and public affairs. The communist party thus appeared as the big brother, the guardian of the people. The population felt that it was making progress both nationally and socially.

This new Yugoslavia had been bought at the price of the sufferings of an entire people and the blood of hundreds of thousands of victims of the national and civil wars. Its creators had no intention of allowing it to be governed by anyone but themselves. Consequently King Peter came under Tito's axe and Mihailovich was condemned for 'treason'. When Churchill met Tito in Capri he found himself facing an equal, not a protégé. Tito subsequently blocked any Anglo-American operations in Yugoslavia; what was more, he demanded Trieste which the British and Americans had promised to Italy. In the government formed by Tito in March 1945 twenty-three out of twenty-eight portfolios were held by communists. All the key ministries were in the hands of partisans.

When Tito went to Moscow in September 1944 to meet Stalin and the partisans joyfully linked up with the Red Army, Churchill bitterly regretted the aid which he had given Tito. He was not to know that the Moscow meeting had been stormy and that it had followed a polite but acrid exchange of correspondence in which Tito had requested Stalin to keep his advice to himself if he was not in a position to provide assistance. Of course this was not a break; Yugoslavia had broken only with her capitalist, feudal and pro-fascist past. But this unprecedented heretical refusal by a communist party to conform to the ukase from the master of the

Kremlin heralded the emergence, by and through the Resistance, of Yugoslav national communism.

France recovers her unity and greatness

After a crushing defeat and four years of suffering and exploitation France provided forces for her liberation which were better equipped and possessed of an incomparably better fighting spirit than they had in 1939; this was one of the results of the new spirit born in the Resistance. General Leclerc's armoured division had landed in Normandy with the Americans, had spearheaded them into Paris and Strasbourg and had finished in Berchtesgaden. The First French Army under de Lattre de Tassigny had landed more divisions in Provence than the American Seventh Army; it had liberated Haute-Alsace and had not halted until it reached the Danube. As for the FFI, they had done all that the Allies asked, frequently with heavy casualties; the major intelligence circuits, particularly 'F2' and 'Alliance', had kept ahead of the Allies throughout the German retreat; the *maquis* had expended themselves blocking the Wehrmacht's routes through the Vosges and in the Ardennes. The FFI had liberated towns, guarded prisoners, protected the flanks of the Allied armies, safeguarded their communications and kept order. From October 1944, 60,000 unsupported FFI were besieging the 'German pockets' at La Rochelle, Royan and Verdon; a further 140,000 had been 'amalgamated' into the First Army.

Fighting was carried on with enthusiasm, almost light-heartedly. Gradually, as hope returned and victory approached, wide national unity emerged. Everywhere the Vichy administration handed over its powers to the Resistance authorities without demur, often of its own volition; Marshal Pétain and Pierre Laval, who had been removed to Sigmaringen against their will, considered that they represented no one but themselves; only a few thousand collaborators had followed their German masters.

Many people had been worried about the attitude of the communist party. Yet, although in many cases it had the larger forces, it made no attempt to seize power by force, not even in the southwest where there were no Allied troops and the resistance organisations – Liberation Committees and Courts Martial – were wielding power in a somewhat revolutionary manner. Probably following directives from Stalin, the party resigned itself to an important but secondary role; it lined up behind General de Gaulle and took its place in the united resistance; it played the democratic game; more important still, it made efforts to restrain the revolutionary tendencies resulting from occupation – it advised the workers against striking and, on his return from the USSR, Maurice Thorez himself disarmed the 'patriotic militia'.[1]

In France, as in Czechoslovakia, the exiles from London and Moscow worked with the Resistance and they proved to be the people who took over direction of public affairs. Nevertheless, compared to its pre-war position and despite the temporary setback of the Russo-German pact, the communist party emerged from the resistance far more powerful, refurbished and ostensibly fitted to take the lead through the legal machinery of universal suffrage.

Gaullism

A new political force emerged from the confusion; it was full of promise, but also of ambiguities; it was called 'Gaullism'. It had its mythology – 'the call of 18 June', its 'companions' and its symbol, the 'Cross of Lorraine'. It was composed primarily of new-comers to politics, but it had also made inroads into the older parties – socialists, radicals, Christian democrats and moderates; many of those with communist leanings were sympathetic towards it.

Its basis was the determination of those who looked to General de Gaulle to keep France in the war. Though ideologically its message of a 'sacred union' was somewhat limited, its framework was wide enough to draw recruits from the most varied backgrounds. Frenchmen outside France, who had retained their freedom of action, and Frenchmen inside France, who tested the walls of the prison their country had become as they tapped round them in order to bring them down, were all marching blindly one in front of the other; their goal and final meeting

---

[1] According to A. Lecoeur, Jacques Duclos was highly offended because he was not invited to drive down the Champs Elysées at General de Gaulle's side. After hearing him speak at Grenoble in the winter of 1944–5, however, A Gobetti noted in his diary: 'Much nationalism, but where is the communism?'

point, was General de Gaulle. In principle there were no politics in this movement; more accurately, there was a sort of truce. Rising above their past and present differences, the resisters searched for that which united them and concluded that, under the circumstances, their common denominator was expressed in the person and voice of General de Gaulle.

The question was: would the unity which had formed around General de Gaulle, disappear with the causes which had brought it about? He was the champion of a France brought back to life by the sword; he had given back the country its honour and at the same time endowed it with renewed strength. What, precisely, should be his role in a liberated France? Would his task be completed at the very moment of victory? Or were his country's misfortunes the stimulus for a regeneration which only he could control and which he must be allowed to finish?

The political parties and in particular the communists were the main forces trying to reduce the General's image which legend was in process of magnifying to more than life-size. With the approach of victory they claimed that he was no more than the President of the Provisional Government of the French Republic; admittedly he was in charge of public affairs; he was even in command. In their view, however, alongside him, and in opposition to him, stood the 'National Resistance Council' which spoke for all sections of the underground and had, therefore, acquired a representative democratic character.[1]

This notion of de Gaulle developing from a 'Symbol' into a sort of King Log and then a Cincinnatus returning to his plough was counterbalanced by another concept born of a real 'leader mystique'. This mystique originated in London, in Free France. It went further than the obedience and respect which the soldier owes his superior officer and became a commitment of loyalty to the person of General de Gaulle, the liegman's contract with his sovereign. Most of the militants in the clandestine 'movements' felt its pull. Inspired by dangers surmounted and victories won, aware of the extraordinary nature of their Iliad, the resisters were frequently inclined to regard General de Gaulle as a real superman who had raised them above themselves. One of them wrote: 'We asked for nothing better than to place our faith in this voice rising

[1] In two proclamations to the people in August 1944 the 'Liberation Committee' of the Department of Allier referred solely to the 'National Resistance Council' without a single word about General de Gaulle.

from the abyss'.[1] His person was enveloped in spell-binding mystery.

Viewed from this angle de Gaulle was far more than a symbol or a figure in history who, at the dictate of circumstances, had had some definite task to perform. He became an exceptional personality, a man of such stature that he towered over his era, a man who merited feelings of admiration, confidence and devotion. His mission had no limit in time; he was the figurehead of his country, a prime mover in history; he would emerge from the shadows or from his retreat when the time came to make his mark on events and to save his country from the direst peril. Among the resisters of France, therefore, the expectation grew, in hazy outline, that, should Armageddon return, the 'saviour' of June 1940 would reappear.

At the end of the war, therefore, it was impossible to say whether, through the Resistance, France would renovate her political institutions or whether she would return to the 'rut' of the Third Republic – there was no question of a 'popular democracy'. On the economic side, however, far-reaching and immediate reforms, worked out by the Resistance, were introduced.[2] The mines, the Renault works and the airlines were nationalised, press and radio placed in the hands of public corporations. Planned economy was instituted with currency control, import licences and nationalisation of the main discount banks; freedom of trade union association was re-established and a social security system set up, all as part of a 'modernisation and equipment plan' worked out by Jean Monnet and designed to turn France into a great industrial power.

In foreign policy General de Gaulle continuously reaffirmed France's determination to be independent. In his eyes the British and Americans were allies worthy of affection and respect but they should not consider themselves as protectors. To avoid being tied too closely to them de Gaulle went to Moscow to balance the situation; he paved the way for *rapprochement* with Italy; he approached Belgium, Holland and Luxemburg proposing formation of a western Entente, of which the Rhine would be the 'artery'. He did not, of course, forget the colonial empire which had proved loyal in the darkest hours; though there could be no question of granting independence to its peoples, at least

[1] Auguste Dupouy: *Mémorial,* date and publisher unknown.
[2] See the author's *Courants de pensée de la Résistance.*

the Brazzaville conference offered them the possibility of self-administration within a 'French Union' and the prospect of an improvement in their standard of living.

Through the Resistance France had recovered her unity and her national and individual freedom. There was nothing to show that she could not once again have pretensions to greatness.

A hard task for Italian resistance

After the hard winter of 1944–45 during which the Italian partisans were left to themselves and survived as best they could, the struggle resumed in the spring under the guidance of Allied missions. In April, when the German front cracked, general strikes broke out in the great industrial towns of the Po plain, Turin, Biella, Vercelli, Novara and Milan; they were directed by 'Agitation Committees' mainly communist-inspired. The strikes were accompanied by fighting, the workers having hidden arms in their factories. Under the double pressure of attacks from the partisans coming down from the mountains and strikes in the cities the Germans evacuated several towns before the arrival of the Allied armies. Mussolini, trying to escape into Switzerland, was recognised at Dongo on 27 April, arrested and executed.

Everywhere power was wielded by 'Liberation Committees'. Their internal differences immediately exploded and their inadequacy became evident. The communists, who styled themselves the 'Resistance Party' and whose ranks were swollen by very many last-minute supporters, wished to turn the Committees into revolutionary Assemblies using 'National Front' tactics and so seize control of the new State from within. The Action Party had the same idea but it consisted primarily of intellectuals and had no solid backing in public opinion. The socialists were divided on the direction to take; one half, following Nenni, wished to go some of the way with the communists, the other under Saragat refused to do so. The moderates, led by the Christian democrats, wished to re-establish the full authority of the Rome government as soon as possible. They were supported by the Allies who, warned by events in Yugoslavia and Greece, clearly would not have allowed the communists to seize power in Italy. Consequently the latter did not try.

These differences of view with their latent frictions prevented

Italian resistance from working out any real political programme. Its first, if not its only, objective was the fall of fascism. It had confined itself to promising 'democracy freed from fascist paternalism and drawing its strength and unity from the people alone'. In somewhat more precise terms it had visualised the formation of 'management councils' for businesses which, it said, were justified by the 'high standard of political and national consciousness' of which the workers had given proof. These general phrases were developed into definite plans which could be implemented when needed as was done in France; in particular no attention had been paid to rural problems, a serious omission in a country inhabited mostly by peasants.[1]

The Resistance was united only on the 'royal question'; it forced King Victor-Emmanuel to abdicate, thinking to condemn fascism a second time over. A referendum was held on whether or not the monarchy should be retained. In fact fascism was still deep-rooted and had not been eradicated by the administrative purge, which would have risked depriving Italy of all experienced officials had it been taken as far as the Action Party wished. Early in 1945 a peculiar newspaper appeared, 'L'Uomo qualunche' edited by G. Giannini; from the tone of its attacks on the new men and organisations and the success it gained it was evidently expressiong the nostalgia felt by many Italians for the Mussolini era. Italian resistance was, therefore, in no way prepared to solve the grave problems from which Italy was suffering – underdevelopment of the Mezzogiorno, excessive social inequality, over-population, inadequate education, shortage of power and raw materials. Nevertheless, it had played a vital role; it had largely contributed to the renewed taste on the part of the masses for freedom and politics; it had turned Italy back into a democracy; it had extricated her from the position of beaten enemy; finally it had to all intents and purposes maintained her territorial integrity. In many respects it had been tantamount to a new Risorgimento but, compared to the first, had been more widely based and had roused the entire nation.

The Greek drama

Everywhere in Europe the Resistance had achieved all or some

[1] See Catalano: *L'Italia della dittatura alla democrazia,* Milan 1965.

of its aims – everywhere except in Greece and Germany. In Greece some co-ordination was laboriously worked out when the Papandreou government was installed in Athens in September 1944; it ended, however, when the government tried to disarm the clandestine groups. Elas refused. Perhaps its leaders had been deceived into thinking that Tolbukhin's army was heading for the frontiers of Greece. This time Stalin was loyal to his horse-trading agreement with Churchill – which he had not been in the case of Rumania – and did nothing to help the insurgents. It may, therefore, be assumed that he had not instigated the revolt. The case of Greece exposed the vast difference between the great successes of the USSR and those of international communism: when Stalin judged that the interests of the USSR as a State were involved, he deliberately sacrificed those of communism.

Although Elas was inspired and directed by communists, its members also included anti-fascists who were horrified by these events. The government's sole object seemed to be the return of the King to Athens without a plebiscite and the re-establishment of the *status quo ante,* in other words a dictatorship on the Metaxas model but without Metaxas and supported by the 'collaborators'. Nowhere was it more obvious than in Greece how little reliance the Allies could place on the Resistance and how impotent the latter was when facing them. Churchill decided to send British troops to Athens and they fired on the insurgents – on resisters. On their side the resisters had undoubtedly embarrassed Allied strategy with their ill-timed revolt. It was a paradox and the result was an impasse and the utter failure of the Resistance.

The German vacuum

With the defeat of the Wehrmacht and the death of Hitler Germany became a total political vacuum, a situation aggravated by material destruction, the stern presence of the victors, the stoppage of production and transport, the flight of some and the apathy of the majority. Nazism's sole achievement was the creation of widespread chaos in central Europe – 'Germany Year o'. Revelation of the nazis' gigantic crimes flabbergasted many Germans and filled them with shame; it also increased the victors' hatred of the vanquished.

German resistance had disappeared from the scene after the

suppression of the 20 July 1944 coup. Only in Munich did the Americans discover a few anti-nazis who helped them to occupy the city on 28 April, a few days before the Wehrmacht's capitulation. What could be built in this political desert? For the moment the Allies were concerned primarily to mete out punishment to the nazis and so they behaved as stern occupiers settling the Germans' fate, either in concert or each in their own zone without asking German advice. But subsequently what would happen? No one could say. What could anti-nazism do for the Germans?

In the east exiled communists returned with the Red Army, took over the main posts in the administration and directed the reconstituted trades unions. At the same time, however, the Soviet occupation forces took their revenge for their country's sufferings; thousands of prisoners of war lived miserably in captivity; factories were dismantled and machine tools removed to the USSR. Communism made an even less auspicious start in Germany than in Poland.

Though some non-communist resisters such as von Stauffenberg or Arvid Harnack had dreamt of Germany as the go-between between East and West, midway between communism and western democracy, the majority placed their hopes in total rejection of totalitarianism and the advent of a liberal régime. The 'Kreisau Circle' inspired by von Moltke regarded Christianity as one of the historic pillars of the German nation and the family as the kernel of society; restoration of the rule of law, guarantees of individual liberties and worker participation in the management of businesses seemed to him to provide the foundations on which a new Germany might be built.[1] Before his execution von Moltke wrote to his sons: 'All my life I have fought that narrowness of view, violence, arrogance and intolerance . . . which have reached their paroxysm in the National-Socialist State'. But who had listened or would listen to such a doctrine?

Henri Bernard was quite right when he said that these German resisters 'though few in number because they were an élite, provided an immortal example. Every European resister should solemnly bow his head to their memory with respect and gratitude'.[2] The fact remains that in May 1945 no one could say

[1] See Collenot: 'L'Opposition allemande contre Hitler' in Revue d'Histoire de la Deuxième Guerre mondiale, October 1959.
[2] Henri Bernard: Histoire de la Résistance européenne, p. 81.

whether the Germans would be fired by this example, whether the martyrs had shed their blood in vain, whether future generations of Germans would believe in honour, liberty, justice and the dignity of man and be prepared to fight for them.

The price of resistance

Everywhere resistance made its mark on the second world war; it even imparted to the war its own significance, that of the resurrection of subject nations through recovery of their independence, of a struggle against nazi oppression and hope of a better world. Poorly armed though it was, the Resistance had frequently been the advance guard of the Allied armies; it was closer to the enemy and more vulnerable to his counterstrokes. It suffered terribly as a result.

In all countries numerous examples can be cited of heavy casualties from enemy reprisals. In Norway 1,100 officers were arrested during the night of 16 August 1943 and 1,200 students on 30 November of the same year. In Belgium the entire male population of the village of Menseel-Kiesegem was deported because a Canadian airman was found there; 64 people lost their lives. In Rome on 30 March 1944, 355 hostages aged between 14 and 75 were shot at the Ardeatine pits; a few months later the entire population, 532 people, of Sant'Anna in Tuscany was massacred and the village burnt to the ground. In Yugoslavia, in addition to the 7,000 shot in Kragujevac, 1,766 people were shot in a day at Kraljevo and 6,750 in ten days in Belgrade – all in October 1941.

After the assassination of Heydrich, Hitler gave orders that 30,000 Czechs should be put to death at once. Frank, Heydrich's successor, decided on 'a special repressive action to give the Czechs a lesson in propriety'. His choice fell upon the little town of Lidice because two of its inhabitants had left the country in 1939 and were serving in the RAF. The day after the 'Protector's' funeral a convoy of trucks arrived; the town was cordoned off and all exits barred. The inhabitants were then assembled in the square and lined up, men on one side, women on the other. The men were shot in groups of ten, while the houses were blown up – the same 'technique' was later to be used at Oradour-sur-Glane. The dreadful scene was filmed to lend weight to the lesson. Then bulldozers moved in to flatten the ruins and tear up the trees; the whole area was then surrounded by barbed wire with a notice 'Anyone approaching this fence and failing to answer a challenge will be shot'. Such were the 'lessons' which the occupying power wished to give the occupied peoples; numerous similar examples could be quoted; no country was spared these atrocities.

Under these conditions losses in the struggle against occupation were high. In Holland 2,000 people were executed, 10,000 resisters killed and over 100,000 deportees did not return. In Greece 60,000 were executed, 50,000 resisters killed and 200,000 people deported; in addition nearly 200,000 houses were destroyed. In Yugoslavia over 1½ million people were 'missing', 20 per cent of the houses were destroyed, 50 per cent of the cattle and 64 per cent of the industrial potential. Poland headed the miserable 'bled to death' record – over 5 million deaths or 15 per cent of the population and in material destruction 80 per cent of the transport facilities and industrial equipment. Warsaw was destroyed as to 11 per cent in September 1939, by a further 25 per cent during the ghetto rising and yet another 25 per cent in the rising of August 1944; thereupon, the Germans demolished the remaining 30 per cent of the houses. The only part of the city to escape was Praga where the Red Army was installed.

What conclusion can be drawn from this tale of suffering, destruction and sacrifice other than to say that the bestiality and cruelty of the nazis in occupation surpassed anything previously known to history ? The Resistance cannot be held responsible for these horrors – millions of Jews were massacred though they had never lifted a little finger against their torturers. Plans for the future Warsaw, drawn up before the risings, have been found; the city was to be reduced to a population of 15,000, all German, and a Polish settlement constructed at a respectful distance to provide the slave labour. A plan to annihilate their real or supposed enemies was inherent in nazi ideology even before the war; it had been worked into concrete plans in the early days of occupation. These plans were to be implemented whether the occupied people acquiesced or refused, whether they were submissive or rebellious.

The fact remains that action by the Resistance did, on occasions, draw down the wrath of the nazis on areas or groups of human beings otherwise temporarily spared. There was no concealing the fact, which resisters quickly learnt to their cost, that people who embark on resistance pay a high price. But resisters all over Europe were agreed on one point, that freedom is without price, whether for its preservation or its recovery.

Conclusion

There was not a single occupied country which did not give birth to its clandestine resistance – this is the first and most important conclusion to be drawn from this study. Everywhere one finds the same root causes, the same initial procedures and similar phases of development; the differences lay in scope, timing and the varying combinations of parties which depended on area and tempo of conflict – in one place collection of information was the main feature, in another guerrilla warfare. Nevertheless, there was no such thing as a 'European Resistance'.

Despite their periodic 'summit meetings' the Anglo-Americans and the Soviets seldom agreed on strategy and never co-ordinated their campaigns. It is hard to see, therefore, how the Resistance could have co-ordinated its action all over Europe; it was working in the dark; by its very nature it was no more than the sum total of a multitude of tiny operations, the continuous breakdown of a constantly renewed struggle. Even within each nation, resistance was only administered and directed at a late stage, with considerable difficulty and somewhat imperfectly – in France many acts of sabotage were carried out by the light of nature in the summer of 1944 despite the fact that great 'plans' had been worked out and numerous directives issued; the Prague insurgents were not wholly under control of the Kosice government; order was not immediately re-established in liberated Turin. Except perhaps in the USSR (and this is not certain), resistance consisted of a large number of movements existing side by side rather than an intermingling of forces. When unity was achieved, it was invariably temporary and local resulting from the pressure of some exceptional event such as the attempted assassination of Hitler, the Warsaw rising or the Piedmont *maquis*. Security and the difficulty of communication dictated the general rule that resisters, even though geographically and ideologically allied, should know nothing of each other; on liberation many were completely taken aback to discover fellow-resisters in people whom they had never suspected. The various activities took place in watertight compartments – the 'partisan's' life and his war, for instance, had nothing in common with those of the guide for 'escapers'. Even in the summer of 1944 French Resistance in the northern zone did not altogether regard that in the south as its counterpart. Communists and nationalists might smile at each other and make statements about brotherhood in arms but in fact their purposes were quite different.

In this tangle of situations, national interests, ideologies, human relations, mentalities, dormant conflicts and emergent rivalries what explanation can be given for the astonishing similarity which eventually emerged? The fact that all were fighting one and the same enemy and were similarly in touch with the major Allies had much to do with it; even more important, however, was the collective urge, springing from the very bowels of the nation – the determination to survive. Stirring calls by great personalities such as de Gaulle, Stalin or Tito could shake the peoples out of their natural lethargy; false starts were avoided and some organisation was introduced by the military secret services and international communism. But the Resistance only reached its full stature when, by raising the country to revolt, it became the embodiment of the nation, with all its diversity and all its contradictions. Viewed overall, clandestine action resembled the apparently aimless hurrying and scurrying of the anthill, each insect busy with its tiny task, none apparently concerned with any other, paths crossing and their efforts apparently vain and disorderly. Yet some ultimate purpose ruled this apparent fragmentation, the solidarity and permanence of the community.

One can, therefore, see why the enemy did not always suspect the mines which the underground moles were digging beneath him and why the Allies, intent upon striking the enemy's vitals, saw in the Resistance an apparent dispersion of effort rather than an exhaustible source of strength. Today once more, in the age of the computer and the hydrogen bomb, the politicians and the military are ignoring or belittling the apparent throw-backs to an obsolete past, recently in Algeria, in Vietnam now and in Czechoslovakia perhaps tomorrow – the protests, the agitation, the strivings of vanquished peoples seemingly condemned to irretrievable impotence.

This contrast between modern technique and the throw-back

to more ancient times constituted by guerrilla warfare makes it difficult to evaluate the part played by the Resistance in the second world war. The criteria by which victory in conventional warfare is judged are not applicable to resistance warfare; a soldier without a rifle is no longer a soldier but a typewriter is one of the main weapons of the underground fighter; the pamphlet is the forerunner of the 'Molotov cocktail'. When an army dissolves its war is over, for it will take years to reconstitute and can only be of use if the situation takes a favourable turn – this was what the men of Vichy thought and it was the tragedy of the French Armistice Army. The 'shadow army', on the other hand, can melt away if the enemy offensive becomes too hot; it will do so only to recover its strength through contact with its country and its people – in Slovakia, in the Italian Alps, in Brittany and in many other mountain areas. An offensive by a tank army necessitates months of preparation, the assembly of vast stocks and large-scale static logistic resources; a rising cannot be improvised, but it must be spontaneous. This difference in character is one of the objective explanations for the drama of Warsaw; it might have led to a drama of Paris.

The Resistance suffered its defeats of course – what great commander has not? But its mistakes were no greater than those of the Allied airmen who bombed towns of no military importance or the artillerymen who shelled their own infantry. It can justifiably be accused of excesses in the so-called 'purge' of the liberation, but it should be remembered that this was no more than revenge for the crimes of the nazis and the collaborators, an inevitable explosion after four years of suffering and rage; as soon as the authority of the Resistance was recognised, it put a stop to these things.[1] The Resistance can at least put forward the excuse that it had had to improvise its methods day by day and that it had taken up the torch which others had let fall. Side by side with its heroes it had its cowards, its braggarts, its adventurers and even its traitors – what collection of human beings has not? It was no band of supermen; many of its members talked under torture – who can be sure that he would not have done the same? Some deserted their post even before being arrested; their physical strength had let them down. Their nerves would have been subjected to a far less severe test had they stayed quietly at home

---

[1] Not to mention the massacres of prisoners which are a normal feature of so-called 'regular' wars but over which historians draw a discreet veil.

and waited for a better future. There are many books today telling of sensational exploits; others justly praise the martyrs who have been set up as symbols. The Resistance of course included these, but it was something else as well – the anthill of the nation, seething with millions of little acts, obscure, humble, sometimes ineffective, but unfortunately invariably dangerous. Resistance was the will to do something, but not necessarily the success of that something; it gathered together the every-day men, who did not necessarily emerge from their mediocrity; it was a force of all-comers. Some, raised to heights of which they did not know themselves capable, became involuntary heroes, but all had heard the call to heroism.

It hardly seems necessary to repeat that the Resistance did not win the war; for the major Allies it was only a bonus, though in passing it should be noted that it produced less destruction than the 'bomb carpet'. Without Allied support it would frequently have been ineffective or have remained a mere flash in the pan, but the task of the Allies would have been far more arduous without its assistance. Imagine the Allies landing or advancing in the dark, without the eyes and ears of an entire population of accomplices, without its advice or its guides, still worse facing its hostility; all the Allied armies found to their cost the difference between advancing through friendly country and entering German territory where every stone might conceal a trap. How many opportunities did the Allies squander by failing to make the best use of resistance, by arming it too little and too late, this volunteer force which owed them nothing – think of the Algiers *putsch*, Slovakia or the Vercors, to say nothing of Warsaw.

There can be no doubt that, had the Resistance met with less prejudice, had it been better understood, had its armament been more generous, had it been wisely used, it could have saved human lives and prevented material destruction and political imbroglios and hastened victory. Such as it was, with its weaknesses, its divisions and its limitations, it was more than a 'fourth service'; in fact it developed into a *second conflict* parallel to or rather a substratum of that of the great coalitions and conventional armies; its progress was more uncertain and its aims less immediate, for it did not invariably end when the guns stopped firing and some of its results have been far-reaching.

Once demobilised the soldier returns home, puts on his ordinary clothes and goes about his business; for him the war is no more than a series of memories, good or bad. But when does the battle end for the volunteer resistance soldier? One thing is certain: when his term of service ostensibly ends with the departure of the occupier, he is not the same man as when it began, and sometimes the change is a profound one. Because he is an ordinary citizen, as he goes along the resister discovers other purposes for his volunteer service; many considered the liberation of their country as no more than a prelude to renewal or even revolution. Some, both socialists and communists, rediscovered the country they thought they had forgotten; others had become aware of the flaws in their society, of the defects in their institutions, of the imperfections in their economic structure, all of which weakened their country; remedies seemed both necessary and urgent and the result was a change of heart for many nationalists.

Resistance was initially a violent defensive reaction to protect the territory and possessions of the nation and it accentuated xenophobia and disputes between peoples. Conversely, because all were fighting the same enemy and the unification of Europe under his iron heel, or in response to the call of some deeper sense of a common destiny, many resisters became aware of the bonds uniting them across the barriers of language, conflicting interests and frontiers. Von Moltke advocated the union of the churches; French *maquis* and Italian partisans, the one rejecting the Vichy régime and the other fascism, met high in the Alps and signed a pact of friendship. Gradually foreigners arrived to join the national fighting groups – deserters from the Wehrmacht, emigrés, prisoners of war, runaways from the labour service – and so each national resistance took on an international character. As early as December 1942 Henri Frenay wrote: 'The men of the European resistance movement will be tomorrow's builders of the new Europe . . . organised on a basis of law, liberty, equality and fraternity.' Here were the outlines of a process of reconciliation between men who had been thus transformed by the Resistance, and it was a process full of promise for new national and European structures.

The masses of the people had been shaken to their foundations by great upheavals. In coping with this situation the marxists were undoubtedly the best trained and the most adroit; they knew how to address the people in their own language; as a result theirs were the most notable successes. The main beneficiary was the USSR despite the Russo-German pact and principally owing to the successes of the Red Army. Nevertheless, from the depths of history occupation had brought to the surface another catalyst for revolt, national sentiment. The general strikes in Turin, Paris, Copenhagen, Amsterdam or Prague were no strikes for higher wages or better conditions; they were patriotic risings. From two points of view, therefore, there was proof that subversive warfare could spring from the most diverse motives and that it was the preserve of no party and no class. In any case a perceptible change in political and social relationships within the liberated countries was not the only outcome of that combination of nationalist emotion and the wind of revolutionary change which was the background to resistance; it soon proved to be one of the most powerful explosive mixtures ever produced by history – after all the French Revolution had set light to all Europe. The colonial peoples, or in more general terms the under-developed peoples, soon learnt to recognise and make use of it. This may explain why, when the liberation of Paris was announced, people danced in the streets of Montevideo and also why, on the very day the war in Europe ended, revolt broke out in Sétif. Viewed from this wider angle, it may not be an exaggeration to claim that the Resistance to Hitler was a foretaste of the epoch in which we are living, pregnant with significance for the present, if not also for the future.

Chronology

Date[1]	The War	Occupation (including satellites)	French Resistance	Resistance other than France
1939 September	End of hostilities in Poland	Formation of Reich Central Security Department (the RSHA). Numerous arrests in Prague. Decision to confine Polish Jews to ghettos.		Thousands of Czechoslovaks cross into Poland to fight. Boycott of trams in Prague (30).
October		Start of executions in Poland (107 in first batch). Polish universities closed. Forced labour announced for Polish Jews.		Throughout the 'phoney war' Czech intelligence circuits keep the Allies and USSR informed (Stations Sparta I and II). Czech military form UVOD.
1940 June (25)	Entry into force of Franco-Italian and Franco-German armistice.	Opening of Auschwitz and Neuengamme concentration camps.	General de Gaulle's broadcasts from London. Three batches of men leave Ile de Sein.	Arrival in London of Queen Wilhelmina of Holland, King Haakon of Norway, President Benès, the Grand Duchess of Luxemburg, Presidents Pierlot and Sikorski.
July	Action of Mers el-Kebir	Confiscation of French possessions in Alsace. National Assembly grants plenary powers to Marshal Pétain (10).	Formation of 'Free French Forces' in London.	Demonstrations in Holland. Publication of Libre Belgique. Formation of 'Special Operations Executive' (SOE).

August	Battle of Britain. Vienna 'award' between Rumania and Hungary, Rumania and Bulgaria.	Appointment of a German administrator in Luxembourg and Gauleiters in Alsace-Lorraine.	Formation of *Musée de l'homme* group. French Cameroons and French Equatorial Africa join Free France.	First agent dropped in Holland.
September	Italian offensive in Libya. Signature of Tripartite Pact (Germany, Italy, Japan). Formation of 'America First' Committee in United States.	French occupation indemnity fixed at 400 million frs per day. General Antonescu becomes *Conducator* of Rumania.	Failure of Anglo-Gaullist operation at Dakar.	Louvain University refuses exchanges with German universities.
October	Italian attack on Greece (28). Hitler abandons plan for landing in Great Britain.	Hitler-Pétain meeting in Montoire. Deportations from Alsace-Lorraine. Occupation of Rumania by the Wehrmacht. Construction of wall round Warsaw ghetto.	Publication of first issues of *Pantagruel* and *Arc*.	Greek government rejects Italian ultimatum. Assassination of German police commandant in Katowice.
November	British attack on Italian fleet in Taranto.	First arrests in Holland.	Student demonstrations at Arc de Triomphe (11). Formation of *Confrérie Notre Dame* circuit.	Belgian government in London reconstitutes the *Sûreté d'Etat* responsible for clandestine action in Belgium.

¹ Basically for the war in Europe.   Figures in brackets indicate day of month.   (This is applicable throughout.)

Date	The War	Occupation (including satellites)	French Resistance	Resistance other than France
December	Roosevelt initiates 'Lease-Lend' British offensive in Libya. Formation of combined Anglo-American staff. Decision to give priority to war in Europe.	Institution of 'racial list' in Poland. Punishment camp set up in Colditz for prisoners of war.	Saboteur shot in Bordeaux (2). Formation of 'OCM'. First issues of Libération-Nord.	Formation of 'Association for armed struggle' in Poland.
1941 January	Italian forces capitulate at Tobruk.	Pogroms in Rumania.	Formation of 'Valmy' and 'Pat O'Leary' circuits. 'Blind' drops of Free French agents.	Greek troops enter Albania and approach Valona. Brussels University closed.
February	Front stabilises in Libya. Arrival of the Afrika Korps.	Pogroms and deportations of Jews in Holland; the 'Gueux' trial. Arrests in the Musée de l'homme group. Admiral Darlan becomes Prime Minister in Vichy.	Leclerc attacks Kufra oasis. 'Alliance' circuit formed.	Strike in Holland out of sympathy with the Jews.
March	Italian defeats in Eritrea and at Cape Matapan.	The Germans enter Bulgaria. Dutch Jews concentrated in Amsterdam.	Capture of Kub-Kub in Abyssinia and victory of Keren in Eritrea by Free French Forces.	Coup d'état in Belgrade (27). Raid on Lofoten islands. Formation of 'Independence Front' in Belgium.

April	The Germans invade Yugoslavia and Greece (6). Capture of Addis Ababa by the British (10). Athens falls to the Wehrmacht (27).	Dismemberment of Yugoslavia and formation of 'Ustashi' state. Dismemberment of Greece.	Coal strike in the departments of Nord and Pas de Calais. First issue of *Voix du Nord*.	Dutch government in London underwrites resistance 'loans'.
May	Capture of Crete. The *Bismarck* torpedoed. Flight of Rudolf Hess to Britain.	Introduction of compulsory labour service in Alsace. Opening of Struthof camp.	First SOE parachute drop. First radio message passed to London.	First 'Comet' escape line begins to function. German flag torn down from Acropolis.
June	The Wehrmacht invades Russia.	Death penalty for Polish Jews found outside the ghettos. Massacres of Jews at Jassy and Kovno. Agreements between Vichy and the Germans known as the 'Protocols of Paris'.	Free French enter Damascus. First 'National Front' pamphlets. First parachute drop of equipment.	'Mill', organiser of the 'Mill Service', dropped into Belgium.
July	Battle of Smolensk.	Himmler 'keeps order' in Russia; the *Einsatzgruppen* in action. Several thousand Poles, primarily Jews, shot in Bialystock area. Vichy forms 'special sections' for 'anti-communist repression'. Formation of Volunteer Legion to fight bolshevism. Deportations of Jews from Bukovina and Bessarabia.	First issues of *Libération-Sud* and *Défense de la France*.	Revolt in Montenegro against Italian occupation. Polish-Soviet agreement. Stalin orders 'scorched earth' policy. Surrounded Soviet units carry on guerrilla warfare at Polotsk, Oulla, Minsk and elsewhere.

Date	The War	Occupation (including satellites)	French Resistance	Resistance other than France
August	Capture of Odessa and Krivoi-Rog. Battle of Kiev. Signature of 'Atlantic Charter'.	Introduction of 'hostage system' in occupied France. First executions of communists. Opening of Drancy camp.	German soldiers killed in Paris and Lille. Armistice of Saint-Jean-d'Acre ends operations in Syria. Attempted assassination of Laval and Déat.	Yugoslav partisans capture Uzice. Sabotage of petrol depots in Czechoslovakia. Partisan units fighting behind the German lines in Russia, particularly at Moghilev.
September	Beginning of siege of Leningrad. Capture of Kiev (19).	30,000 people executed in Kiev. Heydrich becomes 'deputy' to von Neurath in Bohemia, where the Germans ban all higher education. Exhibition: "The Jew and France" in Paris. Construction of Birkenau camp.	Formation of 'National Committee' in London. First Lysander landing. Formation of FTP. The 'Ronsard Mission' organises communications.	Formation of *Milorg* in Norway. Boycott of the entire official press in Prague (28). Formation of 'National Liberation Front' in Greece.
October	Wehrmacht arrives before Moscow which is evacuated. Capture of Kharkov.	Massacres of Kragujevac, Belgrade and Kraljevo in Yugoslavia. Attacks on synagogues in Paris. Execution of hostages in Chateaubriant, Nantes and Bordeaux (22). Installation of gas chambers in several ghettos.	Assassination of German Commandant of Nantes (21). Conversations between Resistance movements and Americans in Switzerland.	Fighting between *Chetniks* and Partisans.

November	Battle of Moscow. Siege of Sebastopol.	Thousands of Jews murdered in Riga. On Himmler's orders all escaped and recaptured prisoners of war to be handed over to the Gestapo. Thousands of German and Czech Jews deported to Russia. Opening of a German university in Strasbourg. General Weygand recalled from North Africa on German orders.	*École pratique des hautes études* [Senior Staff College] set up in New York. First issue of *Combat*.	Sabotage of Ploesti oil wells. Student demonstrations in Prague.
December	Japanese attack on Pearl Harbour (7); entry into war of United States. Red Army counter-offensive before Moscow.	Pétain-Göring meeting at Saint-Florentin (1); first convoy of French deportees; imposition of 1 milliard Fr fine on Jews of Paris. Keitel issues 'Night and Fog' order. Chelmno extermination camp set up in Poland. Serious famine in Greece.	First issue of *Cahiers du Témoignage chrétien* and publication of *Socialisme et liberté*. 220 acts of sabotage in the Paris area during the month. Free French landing on Saint-Pierre-et-Miquelon.	Stalin founds the 'Union of Polish Patriots'. German attack on Leningrad partisans. Tito forms the first 'Proletarian Brigade'. Raid on Vaagso in Norway.
1942 January	Signature of 'United Nations' declaration in Washington. Rommel's offensive in Libya.	Decision to initiate the 'Final Solution of the Jewish Problem'. Arrest of 100 Jews in Paris.	Free French Intelligence Section in London becomes the B C R A (*Bureau central de renseignement et d'action*).	Establishment of an American Secret Service Section in Switzerland. Hungarian units attack the partisans at Poutivl.

Date	The War	Occupation (including satellites)	French Resistance	Resistance other than France
February	The *Scharnhorst* and *Gneisenau* pass up the Channel.	Creation of 'Law and Order Service Legion' (SOL). Opening of Riom trial. Quisling in power in Norway.	Bruneval raid (27). Start of conquest of the Fezzan by Leclerc.	Sixteen villages under partisan administration in the Viasma area. Partisans liberate Dorogobouyi in Smolensk area.
March	British operation against Diego-Suarez.	Hitler places Sauckel in charge of the compulsory labour service in occupied Europe. First convoy of French deportees to Auschwitz. Thousands of Jews murdered in Minsk.	Raid on Saint-Nazaire (27). The 'Alsace' Fighter Wing in action in Libya.	Beginning of the 'England-spiel' in Holland. Partisans destroy the locks of the Dnieper-Bug canal at Pinsk.
April	American surrender in the Philippines. Tokyo bombed by US aircraft.	Oberg appointed head of the SS and Police in Paris; 500 hostages arrested in Paris. Laval returns to power in Vichy. Destruction of Televaag in Norway. Punishment stalag opened at Rava Russka. Appearance of mobile gas chambers in Russia.	General Giraud escapes from Koenigstein and refuses to give himself up. Formation of the 'General Committee of Experts' (CGE) and the 'Information and Propaganda Office' (BIP) by Jean Moulin.	Strike in Holland in sympathy with officers re-interned as prisoners of war. SOE sends back to Denmark the conservative leader, Christian Moeller. Student detachments from Leningrad carry out 24 raids on German airfields.

May	Red Army offensive in Kharkov area.	Wearing of yellow star obligatory for Jews in the occupied zone. Punishment oflag opened in Lübeck.	General Koenig's brigade defends Bir-Hakeim. First issues of *Populaire* and *Lettres françaises*.	Assassination of Heydrich in Prague (27). *Maquis* appear in Greece.
June	Rommel at El Alamein, 80 miles from Alexandria.	Decision to deport all Jews from France; beginning of the 'changing of the guard'. Destruction of Lidice in Bohemia. Punishment stalag for NCOs set up at Kolberjercyn.	Appearance of first 'dossier' from OCM. Statement by General de Gaulle finally concludes agreement between Free France and the resistance movements.	Formation of OSS (Office of Strategic Services) in US. Formation of partisan headquarters in the Ukraine. Sabotage of Tirgoviste arsenal in Rumania.
July	Wehrmacht captures Sebastopol.	5,000 Jews murdered at Kovno. First deportation of French 'politicians' from Compiègne; large scale arrests of Jews in France; *Vélodrome d'Hiver* manhunt; introduction of direction-finding vehicles into the southern zone; 'hostage system' extended to include families.	Free France becomes 'Fighting France'. Numerous demonstrations all over France on 14 July. First BCRA escape line working.	The Gestapo breaks up the Schulze-Boysen-Harnack group.

Date	The War	Occupation (including satellites)	French Resistance	Resistance other than France
August	Wehrmacht reaches the Volga and Mount Elbruz.	Introduction of military service in Alsace-Lorraine. Luxembourg annexed to Germany.	Raid on Dieppe in which French commandos take part (18).	British take over Polish corps under General Anders in Iran. Strikes in Luxembourg against military service for Germany. The *Rote Kapelle* circuit broken up. Partisans from Chernigov carry out 100 acts of railway sabotage.
September	Beginning of Battle of Stalingrad. Allies enter Tananarive.	Initiation of *Action Reinhard*.[1] Vichy law calling up Frenchmen between the ages of 21 and 35 into compulsory labour service. Execution of 113 'terrorists' in France.	Formation of NAP [*Noyautage des administrations publiques* – penetration of public services]. Sabotage of German transmitting station at Sainte-Assise.	Formation of 'German Officers League' in USSR.
October	Eighth Army offensive in Libya.	Murder of 15,000 Jews in Minsk. 50 members of 'Polish Workers Party' hung. Ribbentrop orders all German missions abroad to hasten deportation of Jews.	Strike against compulsory labour service in Lyon. General Delestraint appointed Commander of Secret Army. Meeting between Generals Clark and Mast at Cherchell.	British mission parachuted into Greece. Numerous acts of railway sabotage in Warsaw area. Bomb explodes in German dance hall in Warsaw.

[1] Deportation of Jews and seizure of their possessions as punishment for assassination of Heydrich for which the Jews were in no way responsible.

November	Rommel's retreat from El Alamein. American landing in North Africa (8).	Invasion of unoccupied France. Occupation indemnity raised to 500 million Frs per day. Armistice Army disbanded. Polish Jews sole concern of SS. German report registers extermination of 360,000 Jews in USSR in two months.	Putsch in Algiers and Rabat; Clark-Darlan agreement in Algiers. French West Africa supports Darlan and Réunion joins Free France. Action by General de Lattre de Tassigny at Montpellier. Meeting of steering committee of MUR at Lyon. Fleet scuttled in Toulon (27).	Sabotage of Gorgopotamos viaduct in Greece (25). Meeting of National Anti-fascist Liberation Council in Bihac. 'Revolutionary Liberation Army' formed in Yugoslavia.
December	Germans withdraw from the bend of the Don.	Admiral Derrien capitulates at Bizerta. Keitel orders 'use of all methods against Soviet partisans including women and children'.	Formation of 'Army Resistance Organisation' (ORA). First voyage of the *Casabianca* to Corsica. Murder of Darlan in Algiers. Giraud becomes 'Civil and Military Commander-in-Chief'.	Arrival of French 'Normandie-Niemen' Air Regiment in USSR. Formation of 'National Action Front' in northern Italy; first SOE missions parachuted into Italy and to Mihailovich. By end of winter 1942 area 165 × 25 miles near Briansk liberated by partisans.
1943 January	Interallied conference at Anfa (14–27).	Destruction of old port in Marseilles. First convoy of French women sent to Auschwitz. Formation of Militia under command of Darnand. Kaltenbrunner becomes head of RSHA.	Giraud–de Gaulle meeting in Anfa. Leclerc completes conquest of Fezzan. Leclerc and de Larminat meet in Tripoli. Grenier arrives in London to report adherence of communist party to Fighting France.	Partisans in area of Kalinin attacked by over 12,000 men.

Date	The War	Occupation (including satellites)	French Resistance	Resistance other than France
February	Paulus capitulates at Stalingrad.	All Frenchmen liable for compulsory labour service. German report emphasises that the 'Ustashi' government does not enjoy people's confidence.	Formation of 'Air and sea operations Service'.	Sabotage of heavy water installation in Norway. Execution of a Dutch collaborationist General. Battle of Neretva in Yugoslavia. Soviet partisans liberate Pavlograd and are attacked by 20,000 men at Osveya; communist party holds clandestine conference at Zhitomir. Execution of members of 'White Rose' circuit in Germany.
March	Capture of Gabes. Wehrmacht recaptures Kharkov.		French Guiana joins Fighting France. First *maquis* in the Vercors and Savoie. Formation of 'Co-ordination Committee' in occupied zone.	Workers strikes in Turin, Milan and Genoa. Czechoslovak corps fighting with the Red Army. A thousand partisans destroy the main bridge over the Desna.
April	Allied forces from east and west meet in Tunisia.	Sauckel–Laval agreement on release of prisoners of war for work. Oberg-Bousquet agreement on police co-operation. Discovery of mass grave in Katyn.	Reconstitution of the CGT (Perreux agreements). Formation of '*maquis* Service'. The corvette *Aconit* sinks two German submarines.	Rising in Warsaw ghetto (19). Fighting between Elas and Edes in Greece. German report estimates 80,000 partisans in Byelorussia; partisan unit destroys a bridge over the Besed on German lateral communications road.

May	von Arnim capitulates at Cape Bon. Dissolution of Comintern. Rupture of Polish-Soviet relations.	Despatch to Germany of French 1941 and 1942 classes of conscripts.	Numerous demonstrations all over France on May Day. Formation of 'United Youth Forces'. First meeting of 'National Resistance Council' (CNR). French naval squadron in Alexandria joins Giraud.	British mission despatched to Tito. Demonstrations in Bulgaria in support of Jews. Major partisan raid in Gomel-Kiev area; partisans in Byelo-russia attacked by 80,000 men. Partisans in control of one-third of Greece and under heavy Italian attack.
June	Surrender of Pantelleria. Battle of Kursk.	Creation of 'anti-terrorist section' in every Appeal Court of France. Arrest of General Delestraint, Jean Moulin and General Frère.	Formation of 'French National Liberation Committee' (CFLN) in Algiers. First Italian attacks on the *maquis* in Savoie.	Numerous attacks by partisans co-operating with the Red Army in the Kursk sector. Formation of 'Anti-Hitler Patriotic Front' in Rumania.
July	Allied landing in Sicily. Bombing of Peenemunde.	Numerous internments of French 'Night and Fog' prisoners in Struthof. By order of Bormann all Jews at mercy of Gestapo with no right of appeal.	French Antilles join the CFLN. Formation of 'Anti-deportation Committee'. Election of Georges Bidault to presidency of CNR.	Death of General Sikorsk (4). Formation of 'Army of Belgium'. Fall of Mussolini (25). Numerous co-ordinated attacks by Greek partisans. Formation of 'Free Germany Committee' in Moscow. Several areas in Ukraine liberated by partisans; units of Vlassov's Army go over to Red Army in Byelorussia.

Date	The War	Occupation (including satellites)	French Resistance	Resistance other than France
August	Capture of Kharkov by Red Army.	Arrest of a thousand Norwegian officers (16).	Steering committee of MUR sets itself up in Paris.	Despatch of SOE mission to Rumania. Numerous strikes in northern Italy. Revolt in Bialystock ghetto. 'Recovery' of assets of Warsaw issue bank. Numerous acts of railway sabotage in Byelorussia; partisans in control of 80,000 square miles of USSR.
September	Italian capitulation. Allied landing at Salerno. Russians recapture Smolensk.	Germans occupy Italy as far south as Rome.	Liberation of Corsica. *Maquis* battles in Corrèze. Nomination of 'Regional Military Delegates'. The CFLN demands a voice in working out the 'Italian settlement'.	The Italian fleet joins the Allies Cephalonia garrison holds out. SOE section set up in Bari. Internecine conflict between Elas and Edes; the British suspend equipment deliveries to Elas. Admiral Horthy undertakes to surrender as soon as Allied troops approach Hungary. Over 100,000 partisans active on railway sabotage in the USSR (Operation Concert).

October	Russians cross the Dnieper.	Arrest of General Bastin in Belgium. Deportation of Jews to Denmark. Special tribunals, manned by the Gestapo, set up in Poland. Mussolini forms the 'Italian Social Republic' in Salo.	The BCRA and military secret service merged into the *Direction generale des services spéciaux* in Algiers. 'Action Committees' set up in France.	Rescue of Danish Jews. SOE organises departure of Bohr, the atomic scientist. Popular revolt in Naples; Italian partisans fighting near Brescia. Revolt in ghetto of Sobibor.
November	Red Army captures Kiev. Heavy water installations in Norway bombed.	Arrest of Count Ciano. Arrests among professors and students of Strasbourg University, evacuated to Clermont-Ferrand.	Occupation of Oyonnax by *maquis* of department of Ain (11). First session of Consultative Assembly in Algiers.	In Brussels a fake *Soir* substituted for the real one. Tito proclaims himself Marshal of Yugoslavia; the anti-fascist Council in Jalce decides that Yugoslavia shall be a federal state. Ukrainian partisans carry out raid over 1,250 miles of enemy rear areas.
December	Teheran conference.	Darlan nominated Secretary of State for the 'Maintenance of order'.	Formation of 'National Liberation Movement (MLN). 'French Expeditionary corps' arrives in Italy.	Beneš signs agreement with Stalin. Tito announces deposition of King's government; British withdraw their mission from Mihailovich. Despatch of second SOE mission to Rumania. Half Byelorussia under partisan control; they destroy large vehicle convoy near Moghilev.

Date	The War	Occupation (including satellites)	French Resistance	Resistance other than France
1944 January	Opening of Red Army offensive at Leningrad. Landing at Anzio.	Convoys of French women deported to Ravensbruck. Count Ciano executed at Verona.	Opening of Brazzaville conference. Churchill–de Gaulle conversations in Marrakesh on arming French Resistance.	Many instances of sabotage of high tension lines in Belgium (15–16). The four main Polish parties form a 'National Union'; overall sabotage plan initiated in Poland. Formation of Polish 'National Committee' in Moscow.
February	Battle of Cassino	The Abwehr taken over by the nazi party security service (the SD). 140 hostages shot in Warsaw.	Formation of 'French Forces the Interior' (FFI). German attacks on the *maquis* in Ain. Revolt in Eysses prison.	The ferry transporting heavy water sunk by Norwegian resisters. Churchill announces British aid for Tito only. Assassination of Kutschera in Warsaw. Admiral Horthy requests withdrawal of Hungarian troops from the front.
March	Red Army reaches Polish frontier.	Massacre of 'Ardeatine Pits'. Hungary occupied by the Germans.	Pucheu condemned to death in Algiers. CNR programme adopted. 'Departmental Liberation Committees' set up. Attack on the *maquis* in Glières.	Workers strikes in northern Italy. USSR 'recognises' the Badoglio government.

April	Red Army captures Odessa and liberates Crimea. Bombing of Ploesti.	Massacre of Ascq. Deportation of Hungarian Jews.	Edict by CFLN organising public authorities on liberation. Communists join CFLN. Generals Koenig and Cochet appointed to command the FFI. Vercors *maquis* attacked by the Militia.	Members of the Liberation Committee join Badoglio government. Greek fleet mutinies in Egypt. Formation of 'United Workers Front' in Rumania.
May	Capture of Cassino and Sebastopol.	Numerous arrests at Figeac. Large French convoys to Auschwitz. Hungarian economy integrated into that of the Reich.	German report records 500 'Terrorists' shot and 4,000 arrested during preceding month.	Declarations of Franco-Italian friendship by French resisters and Italian partisans in the Alps. Airborne operation against Tito's headquarters at Dvar. Formation of a headquarters for Polish partisans in the Ukraine.
June	Capture of Rome (4). Allied landing in Normandy (6). Red Army crosses the Beresina.	Massacre of Oradour-sur-Glane. Hangings in Tulle. Massacres at Distomos in Greece.	The CFLN proclaims itself the 'Provisional Government of the French Republic'. French First Army captures Elba. Philippe Henriot executed. Bourgoin's battalion parachuted at Saint-Marcel; general rising and main battles in Limousin, the Vercors, Auvergne and Brittany.	General strike in Copenhagen. Conference in Lebanon for formation of Greek government of national union. Numerous partisan attacks in Bobruisk-Vitebsk area.

Date	The War	Occupation (including satellites)	French Resistance	Resistance other than France
July	Capture of Minsk and Brest-Litovsk. Opening of Bretton Woods conference.	Massacre of the Vercors. Keitel orders all escaped and recaptured prisoners of war to be handed over to the Gestapo.	Allies accord *de facto* recognition to French Provisional Government. French enter Sienna.	Formation of Belgian Secret Army. Formation of 'College of Trustworthy Persons' in Holland. Attempted assassination of Hitler. Removal of a V1 from Poland (20). Formation and recognition of the 'Lublin Committee' by the USSR.
August	Rumania and Finland ask for an armistice. Allied landing in Provence (15).	Last convoy of deportees leaves from Compiégne. Massacre of Sant'Anna in Tuscany. Thousands shot in Warsaw.	Rising and liberation of Paris. Provisional Government moves from Algiers to Paris.	General Cadorna appointed Commandant of Volunteer Liberation Corps in Italy; partisan fighting in Modena area. King Peter disowns Mihailovich. Removal of Antonescu, coup d'état, Red Army enters Bucharest. Rising in Warsaw. Rising in Slovakia.

September	Allies cross the Belgian frontier. Airborne operation at Arnhem.	Village of Marcour in Luxembourg set on fire. Massacre of Bassano. Germans evacuate Greece. Last convoy of deportees leaves from Lille-Loos area.	French First Army and 2 French Armoured Division meet at Dijon. The 'Elster column' surrenders to the FFI. The FFI absorbed into the French Army. *Maquis* fighting in the Vosges.	Belgian Resistance saves the installations of the port of Antwerp. All Dutch clandestine forces united under command of Prince Bernhard; large-scale strikes in Holland. The Papandreou government returns to Athens. Italian partisans form the 'Republic of Val d'Ossola'. Coup d'état in Sofia and entry of Red Army.
October	Red Army captures Riga and Cluj. Churchill-Stalin agreement on 'zones of influence'.	Kesselring orders 'pitiless repression' of partisans in Italy. Seizure of power by the 'Arrow Cross' in Budapest and deportation of Admiral Horthy.	The FFI made responsible for clearing the 'Atlantic pockets'. *de jure* recognition of the Provisional Government. Opening of judicial inquiry on Marshal Pétain.	General Alexander asks Italian partisans to suspend action. Liberation of Belgrade with partisan assistance (20). Enver Hodja's partisans in control of Albania. Athens occupied by the British. End of Warsaw rising. Revolt by Auschwitz guard unit.
November	Capture of Ravenna.	Famine in occupied Holland. Deportation of thousands from Rotterdam.	Strasbourg liberated by Leclerc. French First Army reaches the Rhine. Nationalisation of the coal mines. Institution of High Court of Justice.	Mission from 'Upper Italy Liberation Committee' arrives in Rome. Sabotage of Aalborg airfield.

Date	The War	Occupation (including satellites)	French Resistance	Resistance other than France
December	German offensive in the Ardennes.		Edict instituting 'national indignity'.	Allies recognise 'Upper Italy Liberation Committee'. Outbreak of Greek civil war. Hungarian 'Liberation Committee' formed at Debrecen. The Lublin Committee proclaims itself the Provisional Government of Poland.
1945 January	Russians enter Warsaw and Upper Silesia.		French offensive in Haute-Alsace.	The Beneš government instals itself at Kosice. Liberation of Auschwitz. Truce in Greek civil war.
February	Yalta conference. End of German resistance in Budapest. Bombing of Dresden.		Capture of Colmar. First French Army along the Rhine from Basle to Strasbourg.	Tito commissioned to form a coalition government. Yugoslav attacks towards Trieste and Sarajevo.
March	Rhine crossing.		Formation of French military administration for occupied Germany.	Rauter, the German Commissar-General, assassinated in Holland. Gestapo building in Copenhagen bombed (21). 1,000 railway cuts in Norway in a single night (14). Unification of Italian partisans.

April	FFI offensive in the Alps and Val d'Aosta.	Russians capture Vienna.	Execution of Mussolini (28); general strike in northern Italy.
	Pétain claims prisoner of war status.	Airborne operation in Holland.	Strikes in Denmark.
	Reduction of the 'Royan pocket' by the Army of the Atlantic.	Red Army enters Berlin. Hitler commits suicide. Americans and Russians meet at Torgau.	Yugoslav partisans enter Trieste. Liberation of Belsen, Dachau and Ravensbruck.
May	Liberation of island of Oleron. Leclerc enters Berchtesgaden.	German capitulation.	Milorg units disarm German troops in Norway. Rising in Prague. Liberation of Zagreb (8); final battles in Slovenia.

Abbreviations

AK	The Polish Home Army.
BCRA	*Bureau Central de Renseignements et d'Action* – the Free French agency for intelligence and resistance.
CFLN	*Comité Français de Libération Nationale* – Co-ordinating Committee for French resistance, SOE/Free France.
CFTC	*Confederation Française de Travailleurs Chrétiens* – French Christian Trades Union Federation.
CGT	*Confederation Générale du Travail* – principle French Trades Union Federation.
CNR	*Conseil National de la Résistance* – French National Resistance Council formed in France by Jean Moulin in 1943.
DGSS	*Direction Générale des Services Spéciaux* – French co-ordinating agency for all underground movements in final stages of liberation.
Edes	Right wing monarchist Greek resistance movement.
Elas	Left wing, communist-inspired Greek resistance movement.
FFI	*Forces Françaises de l'Interieur* – French Forces of the Interior combining all resistance movements, SOE and OSS for final phase of liberation.
FTP(F)	*Francs-Tireurs et Partisans (Français)* – communist-inspired resistance organisation in France.
MNB	*Mouvement National Belge* – combined Belgian resistance movement during final phases before liberation.
MUR	*Mouvements Unis de Résistance* – United Resistance Movements. One of the principal French resistance movements.
NAP	*Noyautage des Administrations publiques* – penetration of the public services. A French resistance organisation designed to infiltrate the official hierarchy.
OKW	*Oberkommando der Wehrmacht* – the High Command of the (German) armed forces.
ON	*Obrada Naroda* – National Defence. A Czech resistance organisation.
ORA	*Organisation de Résistance de l'Armée* – Army Resistance Organisation. The resistance organisation of the French Armistice Army.

OSS   Office of Strategic Services. The United States agency dealing with secret intelligence and resistance.

RSHA   *Reichssicherheitshauptamt* – Reich Central Security Department. The German combined security organisation manned by the SS and including the Gestapo.

SD   *Sicherheitsdienst* – Security Service. The SS Security Service.

SOE   Special Operations Executive – the British organisation formed for the direction and support of resistance.

SOL   *Service d'ordre de la légion* – law and order service. A Vichy collaboration organisation.

UVOD   The Czech military resistance organisation.

VNV   *Vlaams national Verbond* – the Flemish nationalist organisation.

Bibliography

GENERAL

Books and Documents

Bernard, Henri: *Histoire de la Résistance Européenne*, Marabout Université, Brussels 1968.

European Resistance Movements: Vol. 1 – First International Conference on the History of the Resistance Movements (Liège Conference) 1960; Vol. 2 – Proceedings of the second International Conference on the History of the Resistance Movements (Milan Conference) 1964, Pergamon Press, London; *Britain and European Resistance Movements 1939–1945* (Oxford Conference) 1962 – roneoed.

Michel, Henri: *Les Mouvements clandestins en Europe*, Presses Universitaires de France, Paris 1965.

Miksche, F. O.: *Secret Forces, the technique of underground movements*, Faber & Faber, London 1950.

Kriegstagebuch des Oberkommandos der Wehrmacht (OKW War Diary), edited by H. A. Jacobsen, A. Hillgruber, W. Hubatsch and P. E. Schramm, Bernard & Graefe, Frankfurt, 1961–4.

Warlimont, W.: *Im Hauptquartier der deutschen Wehrmacht*, Bernard & Graefe, Frankfurt 1962; *Inside Hitler's Headquarters*, translated Richard Barry, Weidenfeld & Nicolson, London 1964.

Periodicals

'*Aspects de la Résistance Européenne*' in *Cahiers d'Histoire de la Guerre*, Imprimerie Nationale, No. 3 of 1950.

Cahiers internationaux de la Résistance, 35 Castellsgasse, Vienna – quarterly publication by Fedération internationale de la Résistance; ten issues had appeared by 1963 when publication ceased.

Revue d'Histoire de la Deuxième Guerre mondiale, Presses Universitaires, Paris (quarterly – full bibliography – reports and comments – issues specially devoted to the history of resistance).

13

CHAPTER I

Fascism and Nazism

Bullock, A.: *Hitler – A Study in Tyranny*, Odhams Press, London, Harper, New York 1964.
Gallo, Max: *L'Italie de Mussolini*, Perrin, Paris 1964.
Hofer, W.: *Le national-socialisme par les textes*, Plon, Paris 1963.
Salvatorelli, L. and Mira, G.: *Storia del Fascismo, l'Italia dal 1919 al 1945*, Edizioni di novissima, Rome 1953.
Shirer, W.: *The Rise and Fall of the Third Reich*, Secker & Warburg, London 1960.

Nazi Racism

Ardent, H.: *The Origins of Totalitarianism*, Allen & Unwin, London 1958.
Delarue, J.: *Histoire de la Gestapo*, Fayard, Paris 1962; *The History of the Gestapo*, translated Mervyn Savill, Macdonald, London 1964.
Manvell, R. and Fraenkel, H.: *Heinrich Himmler*, Wm Heinemann, London, Melbourne, Toronto, Cape Town, Auckland 1965.
Poliakov, L.: *Harvest of Hate*, P. Elek 1956.
Poliakov, L. and Wulf, J.: *Das Dritte Reich und die Juden*, Arani Verlag, Berlin 1955.
Reitlinger, G.: *The Final Solution*, Valentine Mitchell, London 1953.
Tenenbaum, J.: *Race and Reich, the story of an epoch*, Twaine, New York 1956.

The Exploitation of Europe

Arnoult, P.: *Les Finances françaises sous l'occupation allemande*, Presses Universitaires, Paris 1951.
Brandt, K. and others: *Management of agriculture and food in the German-occupied and other areas of Fortress Europe*, Stanford University Press, 1953.
Broszat, M.: *Nationalsozialistische Polen-Politik*, Deutsche Verlagsanstalt, Stuttgart 1961.
Cepede, M.: *Agriculture et Alimentation en France pendant la Deuxième Guerre mondiale*, Genin, Paris 1961.
Collotti: *L'Occupatione nazista in Europa*, Editori Riuniti, Rome 1964.
Milward, A.: *The German economy at war*, Athlone Press, London 1965.
Sawicka, St: '*Un pillage scientifiquement organisé*' in *Cahiers Pologne-Allemagne*, July 1960.

CHAPTER 2
The Collaborators

Cotta, M.: *La Collaboration*, Colin, Paris 1964; *Procès de la Collaboration*, Albin Michel, Paris 1948.
Hayes, P.: *'Bref aperçu de l'histoire de Quisling'* in *Revue d'Histoire de la deuxième Guerre mondiale*, No. 66, April 1967.
'International Fascism' in *Journal of Contemporary History*, Wiener Library, London, No. 1, 1966.
de Jong, L.: *The German fifth column and the Second World War*, Routledge & Kegan Paul, London 1956.
Paape: *'Le Mouvement national-socialiste en Hollande'* in *Revue d'Histoire de la deuxième Guerre mondiale*, No. 66, April 1967.
Soucy, R.: *'Le Fascisme de Drieu la Rochelle'*, ibid.
Willequet, J.: *'Les Fascismes belges et la deuxième Guerre mondiale'*, ibid.

The Satellites

Barbul, G.: *Mémorial Antonescu*, Editions de la couronne, Paris 1950.
Dincic: *'L'Etat oustacha'* in *Revue d'Histoire de la deuxième Guerre mondiale*, April 1969.
Lacko, M.: *'Les Croix Flechées'*, ibid, April 1966.
Lettrich, J.: *History of modern Slovakia*, Praeger, New York 1957.
Mourin, M.: *Le Drame des Etats satellites de l'Axe*, Berger-Levrault, Paris 1957.
Victor: *'Evolution de l'Etat slovaque'* in *Revue d'Histoire de la deuxième Guerre mondiale*, October 1963.

The Vichy Régime

Aron, R.: *The Vichy Régime*, translated Humphrey Hare, Pitman, London 1958.
Farmer, P.: *Vichy, political dilemma*, Oxford University Press, London 1955.
Hytier, A.: *Two years of French foreign policy*, Droz, Geneva 1958.
Jäckel, E.: *La France dans l'Europe d'Hitler*, Fayard, Paris 1969.
Michel, H.: *La France sous l'occupation*, Presses Universitaires de France, 1959; *Vichy, année 40*, Laffont, Paris 1966.

Collaboration in USSR

Armstrong, J. A.: *Ukrainian nationalism 1939–1945*, Columbia University Press, New York 1955.
Fischer, G.: *Soviet opposition to Stalin*, Harvard University Press, 1948.
Junin, A.: *'La Défaite psychologique allemande sur le front de l'Est'* in *Revue d'Histoire de la deuxième Guerre mondiale*, April 1962.

CHAPTER 3

The Allies

Baudot, M.: '*La Résistance française et les alliés*' in *European Resistance Movements*, Pergamon Press, London 1964.
Boltine, E.: '*L'Union soviétique et la Résistance en Europe*', ibid.
Deakin, F. W.: 'Great Britain and European Resistance', ibid.
Duroselle, J. B.: '*Les Grands Alliés et la Résistance extérieure française*', ibid.
Haestrup, J.: 'Denmark's connection with the Allied powers during the occupation', ibid.
de Jong, L.: 'The Dutch Resistance movement and the Allies', ibid.
Kogan, N.: 'American Policies towards European Resistance Movements', ibid.
Michel, H.: '*Les Alliés et la Résistance en Europe*' (general report at Milan conference 1961), ibid.
Parri, F. and Venturi, F.: 'The Italian Resistance and the Allies', ibid.

The Exiles

Benès, E.: *From Munich to new war and new victory*, Allen & Unwin, London 1954.
Delperrie de Bayac, Y.: *Les Brigades internationales*, Fayard, Paris 1968.
Delzell, C. F.: *Mussolini's enemies*, Princeton University Press, 1961.
de Gaulle, Gen. C.: *Memoirs*, Vols 1 and 2 – *Call to Honour*, translated Jonathan Griffin, Collins, London 1955; *Unity*, translated Richard Howard, Weidenfeld & Nicolson, London 1955.
Michel, H.: *Histoire de la France Libre*, Presses Universitaires de France, Paris 1963.
Passy, Col.: *Mémoires*, Vols 1 and 2, Solar, Monaco 1947 and 1948.
Rothfels, H.: *Die deutsche Opposition gegen Hitler*, Fischer Bücherei, Frankfurt 1958; *The German Opposition to Hitler*, translated L. Wilson, Wolff 1961; '*L'Opposition allemande à Hitler*' in *Revue d'Histoire de la deuxième Guerre mondiale*, October 1959.
Tempel, Dr: *Nederland in London*, Tjeenk Willink, Haarlem 1946.

CHAPTER 4

Baudot, M.: *L'Opinion publique sous l'occupation*, Presses Universitaires de France, Paris 1960.
Bosseler and Steichen: *Livre d'or de la résistance luxembourgeoise*, Ney-Eicher, Esch sur Alzette 1952.
Krajina, W.: '*La Résistance tchechoslovaque*' in *Cahiers d'histoire de la guerre*, Imprimerie nationale, Paris, February 1950.

Lecoeur, A.: *Le Partisan*, Flammarion, Paris 1963.

L'Herbier-Montagnon: *Cap sans retour* (Air Force escapers to London), Solar, Monaco 1948.

Lejeune, F.: *Livre d'or de la résistance belge*, Leclercq, Brussels 1948.

Noguères, H.: *Histoire de la Résistance française*, Vol. 1, Laffont, Paris 1967.

Rémy, Col.: *La Ligne de demarcation* (ten vols), Presses de la Cité, Paris 1960–1969.

Vaccarino, G.: '*La Résistance au fascisme de 1923 à 1945*' in *European Resistance Movements*, Pergamon Press, Vol. 1, pp. 69–96.

(For works dealing with the early days of resistance in France the reader is referred to the author's *Bibliographie critique de la Résistance*, SEVPEN, Paris, 1964.)

CHAPTER 5

Radio

Bramstedt, E.: *Goebbels and national-socialist propaganda*, Michigan State University Press, 1965.

Frazer, L.: *Propaganda*, Home University Library, London 1957.

Gillois, A.: *De la Résistance à l'Insurrection*, Steve, Lyon (no date).

Lockhart, R.: *Comes the reckoning*, Putnam, London 1947.

Schumann, M.: *Honneur et Patrie*, Edition du Livre français, Paris 1945 (BBC Free French spokesman).

Wittek, B.: *Der britische Atherkrieg gegen das Dritte Reich*, Fahle, Munster 1962.

Zeman, Z. A. B.: *Nazi Propaganda*, Oxford University Press, London 1964.

Clandestine Press

Bellanger, Col.: *La Presse clandestine*, Armand Colin, Paris 1961.

Conti, L.: *La Resistenza in Italia*, Feltrinelli, Milan 1961.

Demany, F.: '*La Presse clandestine en Belgique*' in *European Resistance Movements*, Vol. 1, pp. 163–70, Pergamon Press.

Inventaire de la presse clandestine conservée en Belgique, Archives Générales du Royaume, Brussels 1966.

List of the Polish undergound collection, Standford University 1948.

Roux-Fouilliée: *Catalogue des périodiques clandestins conservés à la bibliothèque nationale*, Paris 1954.

Ugeux, W.: '*Quelques considérations techniques et morales sur l'expérience de guerre menée en Belgique occupée*' in *European Resistance Movements*, Vol. 1, pp. 170–81, Pergamon Press.

Winkel, L.: *De Onkergrondse pers 1940–1945*, Mart-Nijhoff, The Hague 1954.

CHAPTER 6

Movements

Calmette, A.: '*L'Organisation civile et militaire*' in *Combat*, Presses Universitaires de France, Paris 1957 (Series '*Esprit de la Résistance*').
Demany, F.: *Histoire de la Résistance belge et du Front de l'Indépendence*, Presse de la Résistance, Brussels 1944.
Granet, M. and Michel, H.: *Combat*, Presses Universitaires de France, 1957 (Series '*Esprit de la Résistance*').
Granet, M.: *Défense de la France*, ibid. 1960.
Scholl, I.: *Six against Tyranny*, translated Cyrus Brooks, John Murray, London 1955.

Escape Lines

Brome, V.: *The Way Back*, Cassell, London 1957.
Ippécourt, P.: *Chemins d'Espagne*, Gaucher, Paris 1948.
Nouveau, H.: *Des capitaines par milliers*, Calmann-Lévy, Paris 1958.
Ramonaxto, H.: *Ils ont franchi les Pyrenées*, Éditions de la Plume d'Or, Paris 1955.
Rémy, Col.: *Réseau Comète*, Perrin, Paris 1966.

Intelligence Circuits

Bergier, J.: *Secret Weapons – Secret Agents*, translated Edward Fitzgerald, Hurst & Blackett, 1956.
'F 2' in *Revue historique de l'Armée*, No. 4 of 1952.
Fourcade, M. M.: *L'Arche de Noé*, Fayard, Paris 1968.
Hillarion (V. Adm. Philippon, J. A.): *Le Blocus du Scharnhorst et Gueisenau*, France-Empire, Paris 1967.
Leclère, F.: '*La Composition d'un réseau, "Zéro-France"*' in *Revue d'Histoire de la deuxième Guerre mondiale*, January 1966.
Martelli, G.: *The Man who Saved London*, Collins, London 1963.
Michel, H.: '*La Source K*' in *Revue des PTT*, 1957.
Rémy, Col.: *Mémoires d'un agent secret de la France Libre*, (four vols) France-Empire, Paris 1959–1962; *The Silent Company, Courage and Fear, Portrait of a Spy, May Morning*, Arthur Barker, London 1948–57.
Ugeux, W.: *Le Passage de l'Iraty*, Henneuse, Lyon 1961.

Soviet Circuits

Bourgart, J.: *L'Espionnage soviétique*, Fayard, Paris 1962.
Flicke, W. F.: *Agenten funken nach Moskau*, Neptun Verlag, Munich-Wels 1954.

Heilbrunn, O.: *The Soviet Secret Services*, Allen & Unwin, London 1956.
Perrault, G.: *The Red Orchestra*, translated P. Wiles and L. Ortzen, A Barker, 1969.

CHAPTER 7

External Agencies

Dalton, H.: *The Fateful Years*, Muller, London 1957.
Floege, E. F.: *Un petit bateau tout blanc*, Imprimerie commerciale, Le Mans 1962.
Foot, M.: *SOE in France*, HMSO, London 1966.
Fuller, J. O. *Madeleine*, Correa, Paris 1953; Gollancz, London 1952.
Gubbins, Sir Colin: 'Resistance movements in the war' in *RUSI Journal*, May 1948.
Langelaan, G.: *Un nommé Langdon*, Laffont, Paris 1950.
Morgan, J. W.: *The OSS and I*, Norton, New York 1957.
Pijade: *La Fable de l'aide soviétique à l'insurrection nationale yugoslav*, Borbon, Belgrade 1950.
SOE in general – see record of Oxford Conference in *European Resistance Movements*, Pergamon Press, 1962.
Sweet-Escott, B.: *Baker Street irregular*, Methuen, London 1965.

Air and Sea Operations

Lherminier, Cdt: *Casabianca*, translated Edward Fitzgerald, Muller, London, 1953
Livre d'or de l'Amicale Action, O.R.I., Paris 1953.
Lombard, M.: *Parachutages, l'organisation du B.O.A. en Côte-d'Or*, Imprimerie Bernigaud et Privas, Dijon 1945.
Réseaux d'action des Forces françaises libres in *Revue de la France Libre*, January 1958.

CHAPTER 8

Antherieu, E.: *Le Drame de l'Armée de l'Armistice*, Editions des Quatre Vents, Paris 1946.
d'Argenson, Marquis: *Pétain et le Pétainisme*, Creator, Paris 1953.
Danan, Y.: *La Vie politique à Alger de 1940 à 1944*, Librairie générale de droit et de jurisprudence 1963.
Delarue, J.: *Trafics et crimes sous l'occupation*, Fayard, Paris 1968.
Ehrmann, H. W.: *La Politique du patronat français*, Armand Colin, Paris 1959.
Kammerer, A.: *La Passion de la flotte française*, Fayard, Paris 1951.
Michel, H.: 'Le Giraudisme' in *Revue d'Histoire de la deuxième Guerre mondiale*, July 1959.
Remond, R.: *La Droite en France de la Ire Restauration à la Ve République*, Aubier, Paris 1963.

Sereau, R.: *L'Armée de l'Armistice*, Nouvelles Editions françaises, Paris 1961.

Siegfried, A.: *De la IIIᵉ à la IVᵉ Republique*, Grasset, Paris 1957.

Wheeler-Bennett, Sir J.: *The Nemesis of Power*, Macmillan, London; St Martin's Press, New York 1953.

Wright, G.: *Rural Revolution in France*, Oxford University Press, Stanford Uiversity Press, 1964.

'X . . .': '*Le marché noir allemand en France*' in *Cahiers d'histoire de la guerre*, no. 4 of 1950.

CHAPTER 9

Parties

Auriol, V.: *Hier, demain*, Charlot, Paris 1945 (two vols).

Blum, L.: *Oeuvres complètes*, Vol. 1, Albin-Michel, Paris 1955.

Chabod, F.: *L'Italie contemporaine*, Domat-Montchrestien, Paris 1950.

Choiseul-Praslin, Duc de: *Cinq Années de Résistance*, Le Roux, Strasbourg 1949.

Fiat: '*L'Insurgé*' in *Revue d'Histoire de la deuxième Guerre mondiale*, July 1962.

Groussard, Col.: *Chemins secrets*, Bader-Dufour, Paris 1948.

'*La CGT dans la Résistance*' in *La Voix du Peuple*, Paris 1946.

Ligou, D.: *Histoire du socialisme*, Presses Universitaires de France, Paris 1962.

Loustaunau-Lacau, G. A.: *Mémoires d'un Français rebelle*, Laffont, Paris 1948.

Mayer, D.: *Les Socialistes dans la Résistance*, Presses Universitaires de France, Paris 1968.

Machefer: '*Aspects de l'activité du Progrès social français*' in *Revue d'Histoire de la Deuxième Guerre mondiale*, April 1965.

Pyromaglou: *La Résistance grecque, introduction à sa formation*, Athens 1948.

Safaris, General: *Greek Resistance Army*, Borch Books, London 1951.

Verdier, R.: *La Vie clandestine du parti socialiste*, Éditions de la Liberté, Paris 1944.

Weber, E.: *Royalism and Reaction in 20th century France*, Stanford University Press, 1962.

Churches

Bedarida, F.: *Aus origines du témoignage chrétien*,
Les *Eglises protestantes pendant la guerre et l'occupation*, Messageries évangeliques, Paris 1946; *Les Clandestins de Dieu, la Cimade*, Fayard, Paris 1968.

Dincic: '*L'Etat oustacha*', op. cit. (see Chap. 2).

Duquesne, J.: *Les Catholiques français sous l'occupation*, Grasset, Paris 1966.

Friedlander, S.: *Pie XII et le IIIe Reich*, Le Seuil, Paris 1964, translated Chas. Fullman, *Pius XII and the Third Reich*, Chatto & Windus 1966.

Lewy, G.: *The Catholic Church and Nazi Germany*, Weidenfeld & Nicolson, London 1964.

L'Huillier: '*La Politique du Vatican dans la crise mondiale*' in *Revue d'Histoire de la deuxième Guerre mondiale*, July 1966.

Poulat, E.: *La Naissance des prêtres ouvriers*, Casterman, Paris 1955.

Zahn, G.: *German catholics and Hitler's war*, Sheed & Ward, London and New York 1963.

CHAPTER 10

Prisoners of War

Ambrière, F.: *Les Grandes Vacances*, Éditions du Seuil, Paris 1956.

Blackman, M.: *By the Hunter's Moon, the fine story of a very exciting escape*, Hodder & Stoughton, London 1956.

Brilhac, J.: *Retour par l'URSS*, Calmann-Lévy, Paris 1945.

Congar, J.: *Leur résistance, mémorial des officiers évadés de Colditz et Lübeck*, Renault, Avesnes 1949.

Eggers, E. R.: *Colditz, the German Story*, translated Howard Gee, Pan Books, London 1963.

Hautecler, G.: *Evasions réussies*, Soledi, Liège 1966.

Hertens and Poindessault: *Rawa-Ruska*, Editions du Cep, Bagneux 1945.

Le Brigand, Gen.: *Les Indomptables*, Berger-Levrault, Paris 1948.

Picard, R.: *L'ennemi retrouvé*, L'auteur, Macon 1953.

Silbert: '*Le Camp des Aspirants*' in *Revue d'Histoire de la deuxième Guerre mondiale*, October 1947, January 1958.

Deportees

Bayle, F.: *Croix gammée contre caducée*, Neustadt, Paris 1950.

Berben, P.: *Dachau*, Imprimerie Wellens, Brussels 1968.

Michelet, E.: *Rue de la Liberté*, Editions du Seuil, Paris 1955.

Modin, J. G.: *Le Bataillon d'Eysses*, Amicale des anciens détenus, Paris 1962.

Morse, A. D.: *While Six Million Died*, Secker & Warburg, London 1968.

Wormser-Migot, O.: *Le Système concentrationnaire nazi*, Presses Universitaires de France, Paris 1968.

Wormser, O. and Michel, H.: *Tragédie de la Déportation 1940–1945*, Hachette, Paris 1954.

Jewish Resistance

Borwicz, M.: *L'Insurrection du ghetto de Varsovie*, Julliard, Paris 1966.
Friedman, Ph.: 'Jewish resistance to Nazism' in *European Resistance Movements*, Vol. 1, pp. 195–214, Pergamon.
Knout, D.: *Contribution à l'histoire de la Résistance juive en France*, Editions du Centre, Paris 1947.
Mark, B.: *The Extermination and the Resistance of the Polish Jews during the period 1939–1944*, Jewish Historical Institute, Warsaw 1955.
Mazor, M.: *La Cité engloutie*, Editions du Centre, Paris 1955.
Michel, H.: 'Jewish Resistance and the European Resistance Movement' in *Yad Vashem Studies*, Jerusalem 1968.
Wellers, G.: '*Sur la Résistance collective dans les camps de concentration des Juifs*' in *Le Monde juif*, October–December 1966.

CHAPTER 11
The Communists

Bagoorn, F.: *Soviet Russian nationalism*, Oxford University Press, London and New York 1956.
Bonte, F.: *Le Chemin d'honneur*, Editions d'hier et aujord'hui, Paris 1949.
Autour du parti communiste français, Editions Sociales, Paris 1964; *Histoire du PC de l'Union soviétique*, Moscow 1960/1964.
Degras, J.: *The communist International*, Vol. 3, Oxford University Press, 1965.
Fabry, Ph.: *Hitler-Stalin Pakt*, Fundus Verlag, Darmstdat 1962.
Fauvet, J. and Duhamel, A.: *Histoire du parti communiste français*, Vol. 2, Fayard, Paris 1965.
Kriegel, A.: '*La Dissolution du Komintern*' in *Revue d'Histoire de la deuxième Guerre mondiale*, October 1967.
Laran, M.: '*Le Folklore soviétique*', ibid.; *Histoire du parti communiste français*, Vol. 2, Unir, Paris 1962.

Free Germany Committee

Einsiedel, H. Graf von: *Tagebuch der Versuchung*, Pontes Verlag, Stuttgart 1950.
von Puttkamer: *Irrtum und Schuld. Geschichte des Nationalkomitees Freies Deutschland*, Michael-Verlag, Berlin 1948.
Scheurig, B.: *Freies Deutschland*, Nymphenburger Verlag, Munich 1960.
Weinert, E.: *Das Nationalkomitee Freies Deutschland*, Rütten & Loening, Berlin 1957.

Appendix (Women in the Resistance)

Baudoin, M.: *Histoire des Groupes Francs MUR des Bouches-du-Rhône*, Presses Universitaires de France, Paris 1962.
Bloch-Serazin, F.: *Héroines d'hier et d'aujourd'hui*, Presses Universitaires de France, Paris.
Fuller, J. O.: *Madeleine*, op. cit.
Minney, R. J.: *Carve her name with pride*, Collins, London 1956.

CHAPTER 12

Cattin, E.: *Trains en détresse*, Julliard, Paris 1954.
Cremieux, R.: *Trois Etapes*, Nouvelle Societé d'édition, Paris 1946.
Durand, P.: *La SNCF pendant la guerre*, Presses Universitaires de France, Paris 1968.
Ereliska, M.: 'Le Mouvement de Résistance Bulgare' in *Revue d'Histoire de la deuxième Guerre mondiale*, October 1968.
Garnier, E.: 'Le NAP' in *Annuaire de la Résistance*, Editions de l'OGEPT, Paris (no date).
Gosse, L.: *René Gosse*, Plon, Paris 1963.
Michel, H.: *Courants de Pensée de la Résistance*, Presses Universitaires de France, Paris 1962, pp. 300–6; 'La Source K', op. cit. (Chap. 6).
Valland, R.: *Le Front de l'Art*, Plon, Paris 1961.

CHAPTER 13

Battaglia, R.: *Storia della Resistenza italiana*, Einaudi, Turin 1953.
Burgess, A.: *Seven men at daybreak*, Evans Bros, London 1960.
Grenier, F.: *Francs-Tireurs and Guerillas of France*, translated W. G. Corp, Cobbett, London 1943; *C'était ainsi*, Editions Sociales, Paris 1959; *Les Carnets de Ch. Debarge*, Editions Sociales, Paris 1951.
Luraghi, R.: *Il movimento operaio torinese durante la Resistenza*, Einaudi, Turin 1958.
Pajetta, G.: *Douce France*, Editori Riuniti, Rome 1956.
Okecki: 'La Résistance polonaise et les Alliés' in *European Resistance Movements*, Vol. 2, pp. 419–64, Pergamon.
Woodhouse, C. M.: *Apple of Discord, a survey of recent Greek politics*, Hutchinson, London 1948.
Zamojski: 'Recherches sur la Résistance polonaise' in *Cahiers Intérnationaux de la Résistance*, November 1959.

CHAPTER 14

Baumont, M.: *La Grande Conspiration contre Hitler*, Del Duca, Paris 1963.

Berben, P.: *L'Attentat contre Hitler*, Laffont, Paris 1961.

Buchheit, G.: *Soldatentum und Rebellion*, Grote, Rastatt 1962.

Danan, Y.: *La Vie politique à Alger de 1940 à 1944*, op. cit. (Chap. 8).

Deakin, F. W.: *The Brutal Friendship*, Weidenfeld & Nicolson, London 1962.

Debyser, F.: '*La chute du régime fasciste*' in *Revue d'Histoire de la deuxième Guerre mondiale*, April 1957.

Dhers, P.: *Regards nouveaux sur les années 40* (telegrams exchanged between Vichy and Algiers), Flammarion, Paris 1958.

Esquer, G.: *8 Novembre, premier jour de la libération*, Charlot, Algiers 1946.

Fabry, Ph.: *Balkan Wirren 1940–1941*, Wehr u. Wissen Verlagsgesellschaft, Darmstadt 1966.

Giraud, Gen.: *Un seul but, la victoire*, Julliard, Paris 1949.

Horthy, N., Admiral: *Memoirs*, Hutchinson, 1956.

Kammerer, A.: *Du débarquement americain au meutre de Darlan*, Flammarion, Paris 1949.

Michel, H.: '*Darlan et le débarquement allié en Afrique du Nord*' in *Cahiers de l'histoire de la guerre*, January 1949.

Pendar, K.: *Le Dilemme France-Etats-Unis, une aventure diplomatique*, Editions Beauchemin, Montreal 1946.

Peter II, ex-King of Yugoslavia: *A King's Heritage*, Cassell, London 1955.

Ranki, G.: '*L'Occupation de la Hongrie*' in *Revue d'Histoire de la deuxième Guerre mondiale*, No. 2, April 1966.

Ritter, G.: *The German Resistance: Carl Goerdeler's Struggle against Tyranny*, translated R. T. Clark, Allen & Unwin, London, 1958.

Vaussard, M.: *La Conjuration du grand conseil fasciste contre Mussolini*, Del Duca, Paris 1965.

CHAPTER 15

Bertrand, L.: *Faux Papiers*, Nathan, Paris 1945.

Borwicz, A.: *Vies interdites*, Castermann, Paris 1968.

de Bouard, M.: '*La Répression allemande*' in *Revue d'Histoire de la deuxième Guerre mondiale*, September 1963).

Delarue, J.: *History of the Gestapo*, op. cit. (Chap. 1).

Farge, Y.: *Rebelles, soldats et citoyens*, Grasset, Paris 1946.

Granet, M.: *Défense de la France*, Presses Universitaires de France, Paris 1960.

Marshall, Bruce: *The White Rabbit*, Evans Bros, London 1952.

Note: Many resisters have told their stories and given an account of their lives; the principal books of reminiscences of Frenchmen will be found in the author's *Bibliographie critique de la Résistance*, SEVPEN, Paris 1962.

CHAPTER 16

Raids

Kjelstald, S.: 'The Resistance Movement in Norway and the Allies' in *European Resistance Movements*, Vol. 2, pp. 324–40, Pergamon.

Philips, C. E. L.: *The greatest raid of all*, Heinemann, London 1958.

Rémy, Col.: *L'Opération Jericho*, France-Empire, Paris 1954; *Bruneval*, *Opération 'coup de croc'*, France-Empire, Paris 1968.

Robertson, T.: *Dieppe, The Shame and the Glory*, Hutchinsons, London 1963.

Guerrilla Warfare

Adler-Bresse: *'Témoignages allemands sur la guerre des partisans'* in *Revue d'Histoire de la deuxième Guerre mondiale*, January 1964.

Brajuskovie-Dimitrye: *'La Guerre de Libération nationale en Yougoslavie'* in *European Resistance Movements*, Vol. 1, pp. 298–347, Pergamon.

Dedijer, W.: *Tito Speaks*, Weidenfeld & Nicolson, London 1953.

Dincic: *'Tito et Mihailovich'* in *Revue d'Histoire de la deuxième Guerre mondiale*, April 1959, April 1960, April 1961.

Dixon, A. and Heilbrunn, O.: *Communist guerrilla warfare*, Allen & Unwin, London 1954.

von Dohnanyi, E.: 'Combatting Soviet guerrillas' in *Marine Corps Gazette*, February 1955.

Federov, A.: *L'Obkom clandestin au travail*, two vols, Editeurs français réunis, Paris 1951.

Fournier: *'La Guerilla communiste'* in *Revue d'Histoire de la deuxième Guerre mondiale*, July 1956.

Kennedy: *German anti-guerilla operations in the Balkans*, Washington 1954.

Kizia, C.: *'La Lutte du peuple ukrainien'* in *Revue d'Histoire de la deuxième Guerre mondiale*, July 1961.

Lombard: *'Le financement d'un maquis'*, ibid., January 1963.

MacLean, Sir F.: *Eastern Approaches*, Jonathan Cape, London 1949.

Redelis, V.: *Partisanenkrieg*, Vowinckel, Heidelberg 1959.

Rogers, L. S.: *Guerrilla Surgeon*, Collins, London 1953.

The Maquis

Blum, J.: *Un Groupe sanitaire dans le maquis*, Marmande, Paris 1954.

Dati sulla lotta partiziana, Rome, April 1954.

Legnani, M.: *Documenti della guerra partiziana*, Studi storici, October and December 1965; *La Résistance Italienne*, Corpo Volontari della Liberta, Milan 1947.

Quazza, G.: *La Resistenza italiana*, Turin 1966.

Revue d'Histoire de deuxième Guerre mondiale: Special number January 1963; 'Les Maquis dans la libération de la France', July 1964.
Tanant, P.: *Vercors*, Athaud, Grenoble 1948.

CHAPTER 17

Anders, Gen.: *Mémoires 1939–1946*, La Jeune Parque, Paris 1948.
Benès, E.: *Memoirs*, Allen & Unwin, London 1954.
Bobrowski, C.: *La Yougoslavie socialiste*, Armand Colin, Paris 1950.
Bojinov: *La Libération de la Bulgarie du fascisme et de la domination capitaliste*, Etudes historiques, Sofia 1960.
Catalano, F.: *Storia del CLNAI*, Laterza, Bari 1956.
Constantinescu-Jasy: *'L'Insurrection d'août 1944 (Roumanie)'* in *Revue d'Histoire de la deuxième Guerre mondiale*, April 1968.
Ereliska: op. cit. (Chap. 12).
Feyto, F.: *Histoire des democraties populaires*, Le Seuil, Paris 1952.
de Gaulle, C.: *Memoirs*, Vols 2 and 3 – *Unity* (op. cit.), *Salvation*, translated Richard Howard, Weidenfeld & Nicolson, London 1960.
Haestrup, J.: *From occupied to ally*, translated Reginald Spink, Udenrigsministeriet – Pressebureaumet, Copenhagen 1963.
Hostache, R.: *Le Conseil national de la Résistance*, Presse Universitaires de France, Paris 1958.
Mikolajczyk, S.: *Pattern of Soviet Domination*, Slow 1948.
Michel, H.: *Jean Moulin l'unificateur*, Hachette, Paris 1964.
Schmitt, Gen.: *Toute le verité sur le procès Pucheu*, Plon, Paris 1963.
Soustelle, J.: *Envers et contre tout*, Vol. 2, Laffont, Paris 1947.

CHAPTER 18

Aron, R.: *Histoire de la Libération de la France*, Fayard, Paris 1959.
Bartosek: *The Prague Uprising*, Artia, Prague 1965.
Boltine, Gen.: Statement at the Oxford Conference (see under Chap. 3).
Bor-Komorovsky, Gen.: *The Secret Army*, Gollancz, London 1950.
Calmette, A.: *'Les Equipes Jedburgh dans la Libération de la France'* in *Revue d'Histoire de la deuxième Guerre mondiale*, January 1966.
Choury, M.: *Tous bandits d'honneur*, Editions Sociales, Paris 1956.
Dansette, A.: *Histoire de la Libération de Paris*, Fayard, Paris 1959.
Denis, H.: *Le comité parisien de libération*, Presses Universitaires de France, Paris 1963.
de Lattre de Tassigny, Gen.: *Histoire de la 1re Armée Française*, Plon, Paris 1949; *The History of the First French Army*, translated Malcolm Barnes, Allen & Unwin, London 1952.
Leroux, R.: *'Les combats de Saint-Marcel'* in *Revue d'Histoire de la deuxième Guerre mondiale*, July 1964.

Martin, Gen.: *'Aspects militaires de la libération de la Corse'* in *Revue Historique de l'Armée*, No. 2, 1959.

Mathis, Capt.: *'Comment furent actionnées par l'Etat-Major de Londres les Forces Françaises de l'Intérieur'*, ibid.

Michel, H.: *'L'Aide apportée aux Alliés par la Résistance française'* in *Academie des Sciences Morales et Politiques*, 2nd half-year 1962.

Popesco-Puturi: *'L'Importance historique de l'insurrection armée d'août 1944'* in *Nouvelles Etudes Historiques*, Bucharest 1965.

Sereau, R.: *La Libération de la Corse*, Peyronnet, Paris 1955.

Solc, J.: *'Le Mouvement slovaque des Partisans'* in *Revue d'Histoire de la deuxième Guerre mondiale*, October 1963.

Tapie, V.: Long report in *Revue d'Histoire de la deuxième Guerre mondiale*, April 1962.

Index

Abetz, Otto, 37, 141
Aboulker, Dr, 234
Abwehr (German military intelligence), 117, 242, 243, 257–8, 260–1
Abyssinia, 61, 68
Action Committee against deportation (France), 283, 306
Action française, 151, 164
agents, 118–32, 249; training, 119–21; SOE operations, 121–5; land and sea transit, 125–7; parachute and air landings, 127–30; radio communications, 130–2; in occupied Russia, 185; double agents, 260–1
AK *see* Polish Home Army
Albania, 91, 124, 298n, 335, 338
Alexander, General, 215, 286
Algeria, 35, 108, 147, 148, 226, 306, 308, 309; Algiers *putsch*, 178, 231, 233–7, 358; *see also* French Provisional Government
Alsace, 143, 162, 246; Nazi germanisation of, 21, 40–1; non-acceptance of occuptaion, 77, 78, 79, 80; and mysticism, 80
AMGOT (Allied Military Government in Occupied Territories), in Italy, 240
anarchists, 65, 66, 155
Anders, General, 299
'Anti-Hitler Patriotic Front' (Rumania), 294
Antonescu, General Ion, 40, 43, 72, 124, 135, 143, 152, 230, 322
Aragon, Louis, 97
Armistice Army (Vichy France),

7, 13, 45, 82, 146, 147–9, 307, 357
Arrow Cross (Hungary), 41, 136, 219, 239
Arthuys, 104–5
assassinations, 195, 217–19, 310; of collaborators, 219–20, 278; of nazis, 221–4, 337
Association for Armed Conflict *see* Polish Home Army
Association for Polish patriots (Moscow), 300
d'Astier de la Vigerie, Henri, 233
Atlantic Wall, 33, 112–13
Auriol, Vincent, 110
Auschwitz concentration camp, 175, 176
Austria, 21, 35, 38, 63, 91, 311, 332n
Aveline, Cl., 97

Badoglio, Marshal Pietro, 123, 152, 240, 285, 303
Barth, Karl, 163
Bastid, Paul, 153
Baudot, M., 160, 164
BBC, 27, 58, 68, 81, 89–91, 93, 99, 175
BCRA, 70, 116n, 131, 251, 309, 310
Beck, Colonel Joseph, 47
Beck, General Ludwig, 242, 243
Belgian National Movement *see* MNB
Belgian Secret Army (originally: Belgian Legion), 146, 151, 302
Belgium, 28, 29, 54, 135, 192, 347; Walloons v, Flemings, 37, 41, 338; anti-nazi demonstra-

tions, 84; allied propaganda, 89, 90, 91, 99; clandestine press, 95; political parties, 103, 151, 152; escape lines, 109–10, 125; intelligence circuits, 113, 115; Allied agents sent to, 121; university's opposition, 143; government-in-exile (London), 154, 207; trade unionism, 155; churches, 160, 163; communists, 182–3; law courts' protest, 198; Jews, 201–2; compulsory labour service, 283; co-ordination of resistance, 302; liberation, 335, 337–8; nazi reprisals, 352

Belin, R., 156

Benès, Edvard, 43, 67, 183, 212, 223, 224n, 295–6, 324, 325, 332, 339, 340

Benouville, Guillain de, 250

Bergrav, Bishop, 162

Beria, Lavrenti, 183

Berling Corps, 300, 328

Bernard, Henri, 143, 212, 214, 273n, 331, 351

Bernhard, Prince (Holland), 83, 337

Bernstein, H., 66

Bessarabia, 43, 322, 341

Béthouart, General, 234, 235

betrayals and arrests, 257–62

Bidault, Georges, 162

Billotte, Captain, 171

Billoux, F., 321

Birkenau death camp, 26, 192

Bismarck, sinking of, 113

Bloch, Marcel, 142

Blocq-Mascart, 104, 105

Blum, Léon, 71, 76, 154

Bogucki, Roman, 221

Bohemia, 'Protectorate' of, 22, 35, 73, 222, 223, 333, 338

Bohr, Niels, 122

Bois, E., 67

Bonomi, 303

Bopp, J. M., 80

Borghesa, Prince, 136

Boris, King (of Bulgaria), 43

Bor-Komorovski, General, 327, 328

Bourdan, Pierre, 90

Brandt, Willi, 66

Bratianu, 152, 294, 340

British Intelligence Services see SIS

Brossolette, Pierre, 151, 154, 260

Bruneau, F., 94

Buchenwald concentration camp, 175, 176

Bulgaria, 22, 182; support for nazis by, 43; Allied broadcasts, 91, 92; clandestine press, 96; failure of SOE mission, 124; Jews, 202; sabotage, 214; assassination of traitors, 220; Fatherland Front, 294; liberation, 322–3, 334; Soviet tutelage, 335, 338, 341

Burgers, G., 212

Byelorussia, 11, 24, 278, 279, 300, 341; see also Soviet Union

Bytnar, Janek, 221

Cadorna, General, 304

Canaris, Admiral Wilhelm, 243

Capitant, Professor, 234

Casabianca, 127, 321

Cassou, Jean, 97

Catholic Church, 156, 157–62

Catroux, General Georges, 68n

Cavailles, J., 142

Ceux de la Résistance, 220

CFTC, 156, 162, 305

CGT, 156, 226, 305, 310, 314

Chaban-Delmas, Jacques, 330

Chamberlain, Neville, 61

Chamson, André, 97

Channel Islands, 11

'Chantiers de la Jeunesse' (Vichy para-military organisation), 205, 233

Chapelle, Bonnier de la, 220

Charles, Prince (Regent of Belgium), 338

Chautemps, Camille, 59

chetniks, 280, 290, 297, 342

China, 7, 50

Cholitz, General von, 331

churches *see* Catholic Church; Jews; Moslems; Orthodox Church

Churchill, Winston, 36n, 57, 83, 286 attitude to resistance movement, 51, 52, 53, 54, 123; French policy, 69, 230; Tito and, 280, 282, 297, 343; gentlemen's agreement with Stalin, 297, 338, 350; Greek policy, 316, 350

Ciano, Count Galeazzo, 157n

circuits, 103–4, 107–17, 264; *see also* clandestine movements

Civil and Military Organisation (France), 105

Clair, René, 67

clandestine movements, 102–3, 104–7, 264

clandestine press *see* newspapers

Clark, General Mark, 234, 236

Claudel, Paul, 141

Clausen, 41

Clausewitz, Karl von, 272, 291n

Clercq, de, 37, 41

CNR *see* French National Resistance Council

Cochet, General, 246, 205, 309

Colditz prison camp, 168, 169

Colette, Paul, 219

collaborators, 34, 35–48, 275; pre-war, 35–8; Hitler's policy towards, 38–9, 42; 'racial Germans', 39–41; organisation into groupings, 41–2; satellite states, 43–4; Vichy régime, 44–6; Polish, 46–7; Soviet, 47–8; execution of, 219–20, 278; in North Africa, 233

Comac (French Action Committee), 310, 313, 314

Combat, 97, 105, 106, 151, 162, 205, 219, 255n

Comintern, 88, 186

Comité France-Allemagne, 37

Committee for Action in France *see* Comac

Committee for the Defence of the State (USSR), 278, 279

Committee of National Liberation (Rome Committee), 303–4

communists, 154, 181–91, 199; high percentage in International Brigades, 65–6; 'National Front' as cover name for, 103; in Germany, 172–3, 188–90, 351; resisters in concentration camps, 175, 176; effect of Russo-German Pact on, 181–3; in USSR, 183–5; loyalty to USSR of, 186–8; view of sabotage, 211–12; and assassinations, 217–18; and strikes, 224–8; and guerrilla warfare, 267–9; support for national fronts, 293–4; attitudes to national risings, 318–20, 321; post-war monopoly in Central and Eastern Europe, 338–42; *see also* French Communist Party; Soviet Union Yugoslavia

compulsory labour service, 32–3, 63, 160, 166, 171–3, 198, 224, 264, 276, 283

Confrérie Notre Dame, 112

concentration (and death) camps, 63, 134, 165, 166, 176; Jews in, 26, 177–8; resistance in, 173–6; Frenchmen sent to, 190–1

conspiracies, 196, 230–44; attempted assassination of Hitler, 145, 189, 196, 240–4; Belgrade *coup d'état*, 231–2; Algiers *putsch*, 233–7; Admiral Horthy, 238–9; fall of Mussolini, 239–40

Corsica, 7, 19, 20, 307; liberation of, 127, 317, 320–1, 332, 334

Cot, Pierre, 66

cover names, 249, 255

Crémieux, Benjamin, 142

Crémieux decree, 233

Croatia, 19, 22, 35, 39–40, 41, 158–9n; *see also* Yugoslavia

Croce, Benedetto, 60, 123

Croix de Feu, 151

Curie, Eve, 67

Cvetkovish (Prime Minister of Yugoslavia), 231–2
Cyrankiewicz, Josef, 175
Czechoslovakia, 11, 22, 31, 43, 55, 72, 182, 247; anti-nazi demonstrations, 83–4; BBC broadcasts to 91; clandestine press, 96; intelligence circuits, 113; SOE operations, 124; 'National Defence', 146; communists, 182, 183; assassination of Heydrich, 222, 223, 224, 295, 352–3; relations between USSR and, 295–6, 335, 338; liberation of Prague, 332–3; see also Slovakia; UVOD
Czechoslovak government-in-exile, 154, 212, 223, 295, 324

Dachau concentration camp, 158, 173–4, 176
Daladier, Edouard, 152
Damaskinos, Dimitrios (patriarch of Greece), 163
Darlan, Admiral François, 46, 57, 220, 233, 234, 236–7, 238, 306
Darnand, J., 42, 46, 288
Dautry, R., 305
Déat, Marcel, 41, 219
Debré, Michel, 252–3
Decour, Jacques, 142
Défense de la France, 97, 106, 143, 171, 193, 207, 257
Degrelle, Léon, 37, 160n
Delestraint, General, 148
demonstrations, anti-nazi, 82–4, 193, 199
Denmark, 31, 40, 41, 126; nazi plans for, 21–2; anti-nazi propaganda, 91, 96; SOE operations, 121–2; military resistance 146; socialist government, 153, 154; communists, 182; Jews, 202; general strike, 227; Free Danish Council, 301; liberation, 335, 336–7
DGSS (France), 108
Dimitrov, Georges, 88, 92, 186n
Dittmar, General, 279

Donovan, General, 58
Doriot, 37, 38, 41
Dronne, Captain, 331
Druon, Marcel, 142
Duclos, Jacques, 345n
Durand, P., 227
Dutch East Indies, 67

Edes (Greece), 215, 311
Einstein, Albert, 64
Eisenhower, General Dwight, 59, 234, 236, 331, 332
Elas (Greece), 215, 311, 350
Elizabeth, Queen (of Belgium), 201
Eluard, Paul, 97
Engels, Friedrich, 268
Enver Hodja, 124, 299n
escape lines, escapers, 52–3, 73–6, 106, 108–10, 123, 170–1, 175–9, 192, 199, 260, 307
exiles (émigrés), 60–4, 66–7, 90, 109, 153–4, 178, 345; see also governments-in-exile
external resistance, 49–70, 118–32; attitude of major allies, 50–2; Great Britain, 52–4; USSR, 54–6; United States, 56–9; political exiles, 60–4, 66–7 Spanish Civil War, 64–6; governments-in-exile (London), 66–8; Free France, 68–70; training of agents, 119–21; SOE missions, 121–5; land and sea communications, 125–7; parachute and air landings, 127–30; radio communications, 130–2

Falkenhausen, General von, 163
false papers, 255–7, 258–9, 283
fascism, 31, 35–8, 133, 150; see also collaborators
Fatherland Front (Bulgaria), 294, 322–3
Faulhaber, Cardinal, 157
Faure, Paul, 154
Fédération républicaine (French), 152

FFI (French Forces of the Interior), 148, 178, 220, 291, 308, 309, 310, 314, 329, 330, 331, 344
Fighting Legion (Vichy France), 151, 159
Finland, 22, 91
Focillon, H., 67
France, 7, 11, 12, 19, 20, 22, 55, 81, 102, 133, 247, 265; invasion of unoccupied zone, 22; nazi plundering, 28–9, 31, 32; and monetary control, 29–30; labour conscription, 33, 171–2; collaborators, 41, 42, 43–4, 219; armistice (1940), 44, 45; Jews in, 45, 178, 201; us relations with resistance, 58, 59; non-intervention in Spanish Civil War, 65, 153; refugees to USA from, 66–7; growing support for de Gaulle, 70; escapes, 74, 75, 109, 110; non-acceptance of occupation, 76–7, 78; and malicious humour, 79; arms caches, 82; demonstrations, 83, 84; sabotage, 85–6, 212, 355; allied propaganda, 88, 90, 91, 99; clandestine press, 96, 97; movements and circuits, 104–8, 112, 113, 115, 116; allied communications and operations, 122–3, 125–6, 127, 129, 212, 263; Corsica liberated by, 127, 320–1; clandestine radio communications, 130–1; social classes, 135–6, 138, 139, 140; teachers/students opposition, 143; political parties, 151, 152–3, 154–5; and churches, 159–60, 161–2, 163; Freemasons, 164; deportees to concentration camps from, 173–4, 190–1; administrative resistance, 198–9; immediate action controversy, 207–11; assassinations, 217–18, 222, 223; punishment of traitors, 219–20; raiding parties, 220; strikes, 225, 226; Allied manoeuvres over resistance leadership, 230; Algiers *putsch*, 233–7; rationing, 248; initial regroupings of resistance, 304–6; and unification, 306–7; preparation for liberation, 308–9; underlying conflicts in resistance, 309–11; and complex organisation, 312–14; attitude to national rising, 318–20; failure of Vercors rising, 325–6; liberation, 329–32, 336, 344–5; gaullism, 345–8; *see also* Free France; Vichy régime

Franco, General Francisco, 65, 66
Francs-Tireurs et Partisans (Français) (FTP(F)), 13, 116n, 217, 218, 226, 272, 276, 283–4, 305, 308, 310, 314, 319
Franc-Tireur, 97, 207
Frank, Hans, 214, 352
Free Danish Council, 301
Free France (French government-in-exile), 53, 67, 68–70, 90, 108, 122, 132, 147, 154, 159n, 178, 230, 233, 235, 305, 346
Free French Forces, 68–70, 123, 147, 207, 233n, 307
Free Germany Committee, 93n, 188–90, 242
Free Slovakia radio, 295n
Free Yugoslavia radio, 92
'freelance' groups, 283
Freemasons, 105–6, 164–5
Fries Deutschland, 188
Frenay, Henri, 105, 106, 255, 359
French Army of Africa, 50, 110, 148, 149, 164, 284, 307, 314; *see also* Armistice Army, Free French Forces; ORA; Secret Army
French Committee for Action in France, 308–9, 313
French Committee of National Liberation (Algiers), 159n, 307, 325
French Communist Party, 182–3, 186–7, 207, 210–11, 305–6, 309, 310–11, 314, 330, 344–5, 346;

French Communist Party—*cont.*
see also CGT; *Francs-Tireurs et Partisans*
French Consultative Assembly, 156, 313, 314, 319
French Departmental Liberation Committees, 156, 308, 310, 314, 330
French Forces of the Interior *see* FFI
French National Committee, 69
French National Front, 97, 162, 271, 272, 305, 310, 313, 314
French National Popular Rally *see Rassenblement National Populaire*
French National Resistance Council (CNR), 13, 152n, 153, 155, 156, 162, 306, 307, 308, 310, 311, 312, 313, 314, 346
French Overseas Territories (Empire), 31, 45, 67, 68–9, 306, 347–8
French Popular Party *see Parti Populaire Français*
French Provisional Government (Algiers), 148, 286, 292, 307, 308–9, 310, 311, 312, 313, 314, 321, 330
French Social Party, 37, 151
Fromm, General, 243
'Front-line Soldiers' Legion' (Holland), 146

Galen, Bishop von, 157
Garibaldi units (Italian resistance), 158, 285
Gascar, P., 145, 167
de Gaulle, General Charles, 51, 55, 67, 73, 90, 123n, 155, 159, 178, 183, 218, 230, 310, 312; Roosevelt's dislike of, 57, 306; forms Free French movement, 68–70; rivalry between Giraud and, 92n, 108, 306–7; popularity, 99; communists and, 136n, 183; Algiers *putsch* and, 233, 235, 237; unification of resistance forces under, 305,

306–7, 309, 345; liberation of Paris and, 331
Gaullism, 309, 345–8
George, King (of Greece), 67
German 'Officers League', 189
Germany, Hitler's plans for Europe, 20–2; systematisation of terror in Eastern Europe by, 22–5; 'final solution' of Jewish question, 25–7; economic exploitation of Europe, 27–32; compulsory labour service initiated, 32–3; attack on USSR (1941), 55, 113, 117; antifascists in, 60, 62–4; Spanish Civil War and, 65; allied propaganda, 89, 91; resistance movements, 103; V1 and V2 launched by, 114–16; social classes, 135, 136, 138; attempted assassination of Hitler, 145, 189, 196, 231, 240–4; Catholics in, 157–8, 161; labour camps, 171–3; communists in, 172–3, 182; and Free German Committee, 188–9, 351; UVOD terrorism, 221; Yugoslavia attacked by, 232; repressive methods of police forces of, 257–62; counter-guerilla action 287–9; tougher attitude towards Soviets of, 317; evacuation of Corsica, 320–1; defeat, 350–2; *see also* collaborators; Russo-German Pact
Gestapo, 12, 42, 189, 193, 219, 221, 254, 258–60, 263
Giannini, G., 349
Gibraltar, 109, 126
Gillet, Louis, 305
Giraud, General Henri, 46, 92n, 108, 148, 152, 168, 230, 234–6, 306–7, 308, 310n, 320
Glières *maquis*, 276, 285
Gobetti, Piero, 61
Goebbels, Joseph, 20, 87, 91, 99, 141, 182
Goerdeler, Carl, 242
Golian, Colonel, 324–5

Göring, Hermann, 28–9, 32, 79, 158
Gottwald, Klement, 186n, 295, 340
Gouin, F., 154
governments-in-exile, 26, 51, 66–8, 118, 152, 154, 207, 212, 218, 262, 264, 276, 292, 293, 315, 316–17; see also Free France; French Provisional Government
Gramsci, Antonio, 61, 186
Grand Mufti of Jerusalem, 41, 163
Great Britain, 11, 27, 45, 46, 55, 137, 234, 239, 242, 336, 337, 338; resistance role of, 51, 52–4, 108, 111, 113; political exiles in, 60, 153–4; non-intervention in Spain, 65; escape routes to, 74–5; propaganda by, 87–91, 100; V1 and V2 rockets and, 114–16; training of agents by, 119–21; and SOE operations, 121–5; landing in Italy, 124, 215, 285; land and sea communications, 125–7; parachute and air landings, 127–30; Jewish policy, 179–80; communists in, 187; French policy, 230, 305, 309; Balkans policy, 231, 232, 237; bombing raids by, 212, 216–17, 226, 263–4, 321; support for Tito, 280, 282, 297, 342, 343; Polish policy, 299, 300, 327, 328; Italian policy, 286, 303, 304; political gap between USSR and, 311–12, 355; political objectives, 315–16
Greece, 36, 43, 83, 126, 190, 199n, 230, 265, 322; Italian occupation, 19, 20; communists, 51, 311–12, 350; British armed intervention, 54; government-in-exile, 67, 68; arms caches, 82; BBC broadcasts to, 91; SOE operation, 123; 'Six Colonels' organisation, 146; orthodox

church, 163; sabotage, 214, 215; civil war, 335, 349–50
Greek Provisional Committee of National Liberation, 311–12
Grenier, Fernand, 210, 217–18
Groeber, Mgr, 157
'Group of Five' (Algiers putsch), 233–7
guerrilla warfare, 267–91; marxist views on, 267–9; rules and conditions, 269–73; life in maquis, 273–7; in Russia, 277–9; in Yugoslavia, 279–82; in French maquis, 283–5; Italian partisans, 285–6; counter-guerrilla action, 287–9; dividends and price of, 289–91

Haakon, King (of Norway), 67, 301, 336
Hacha, Emil, 72, 183, 230, 333
Haenicke, General, 214
Hammerstein, General, 242
Hamon, Leo, 220
Harnack, Arvid, 351
heavy water, 75n, 212, 215–16
Heimwehr (Austrian fascists), 38
Henriot, Philippe, 220
Herriot, Edouard, 59, 153
Heydrich,   Reinhard,   124; assassination of, 222, 223, 295, 352
Himmler, Heinrich, 20, 23, 24, 91, 145, 163, 222, 241, 257, 287, 325
Hitler, Adolf, 12, 35, 37, 38, 76, 84, 93n, 136, 352; great European Reich of, 20–2; his view of Slavs, 23, 47–8; Jewish policy, 25, 26, 339; his view of collaborators, 38, 40; French policy, 44, 196; opposition to, 63–4; V1 and V2 rockets and, 114, 116; attempted assassination of, 145, 189, 196, 231-240–4, 355; Horthy collabora, tion with, 238–9; Operation Barbarossa of, 287; death, 350
Hoepner, General, 242

Holland, 11, 135, 145, 347; nazi plundering, 28–9, 31; and monetary control, 29; collaborators, 36–7, 41, 220; resistance, 53, 54, 77, 83; Allied propaganda, 89, 90, 91, 99; clandestine press, 96; political parties, 103, 152; escape lines, 109, 125; allied missions to, 122, 130; liberal professions' opposition, 142, 143; Army in, 145, 146; government-in-exile, 154, 207, 212; communists, 182; Jews, 202; assassinations, 222, 223; general strike, 227; 'Englandspiel' destroys resistance in, 261; compulsory labour service, 283; resistance groups unit, 301–2; liberation, 335, 337; resistance casualties, 353

D'Hoop, J. M., 166–7

Horthy, Admiral N., 12, 43, 72, 135, 203, 231, 238–9, 240, 294; son of, 293

hostages, 195, 217–18, 223, 289, 352

Hotz, Colonel, 222, 223

Hudal, Bishop, 157

L'Humanité, 65, 97, 99, 183, 210

Hungarian Liberation Committee, 294

Hungary, 31, 35, 40, 53, 100, 135, 139, 153, 182, 325; Horthy puppet régime, 12, 22, 43, 231, 238–9; and collaborators, 41, 219; escapes, 74, 75–6, 171; national front in, 294; Soviet tutelage over, 335, 338, 341

Ibarrubi, Dolores (La Passionaria), 186n

Independence Front (Belgium), 302

Indo-China, 307

Innitzer, Cardinal, 35n

intelligence circuits, 110–14; 'rocket affair', 114–16; Soviet, 116–17

intelligentsia, 141–4

International Brigades (Spain), 65–6

Ippécourt France 255–6

Ireland 22

Iron Guard (Rumania), 41, 136

Italian Action Party, 285, 302, 304, 348, 349

Italian Armistice Commission, 74

Italian Liaison Committee, 302–3

Italy, 22, 31n, 35, 36, 45, 54, 91, 100, 130, 133, 136, 138, 140, 182, 247, 280, 285; occupation in Europe of, 19–20; antifascist opposition in, 60–1, 96; Spanish Civil War, 65, 66; political parties, 103, 152; escape lines, 109; SOE operations, 123; Allied landings, 124, 215, 285, 302; Army, 145; Catholics, 157, 158, 161; communists, 158, 285, 302–4, 348; strikes, 227–8; fall of Mussolini 231, 239–40, 302; capitulation, 282, 302, 321; partisans, 285–6; conflicts within resistance movement, 302–4; liberation 335, 348–9; nazi reprisals, 352

Japan, 19, 50, 117

Jeanneney, 153, 205

'Jedburghs', 120, 316

Jewish Council (Judenrath), 177

Jewish National Home, 163, 179–80

Jews, 19, 24, 42, 63, 64, 97, 107, 109, 134, 154, 163, 166, 169, 190, 199, 246, 258, 339, 353; nazi 'final solution', 25–7, 287; aryanisation of businesses, 31; forced labour camps for, 32; anti-semitic laws in France, 45; Catholics' attitude to, 157, 158, 159, 162; resistance by, 177–80; rescue of, 201–2; in North Africa, 233, 235

Jouhaux, Léon, 310

Jousse, General, 234

Juin, General Alphonse, 234, 236

'Justice and Liberty' (Italian resistance movement), 62, 103, 285

Kallay (Prime Minister of Hungary), 238n
Kaminsky, 288
Karski, 74, 75, 193
Katyn mass grave, 187, 199
Keitel, General Wilhelm, 289
Keller, R., 201, 204–5
Kerillis, H. de, 66
Kessel, J., 142
Kesselring, Field Marshal, 289
Kluge, Hans von, 242
Koeltz, General, 236
Koenig, General Marie Pierre, 69, 308–9, 331
Koenigstein fortress, 168, 234
Kogon, Eugen, 176
Kragujevac massacre, 289
Krayevsky, Miroslav, 221
Kreisau Circle (Germany), 103, 136, 161, 351
Kursk, battle of (1943), 278–9, 288
Kutschera, General Franz, 222, 223
Kuusinen, 186n

labour camps see compulsory labour service
Lattre de Tassigny, General Jean de, 344
Laveleye, de, 83
Laval, Pierre, 59, 61, 171, 219, 230, 233, 344
Law and Order Service (Holland), 146
Lawrence, T. E., 269, 273
Leahy, Admiral William Daniel, 57, 58n
Leclerc, Marshal Philippe, 69, 331, 344
Lecoeur, Auguste, 65, 183n, 345n
Légion des combattants (Vichy), 136, 233, 235
Léger, Alexis (Saint-John Perse), 66
Lejeune, F., 94, 160

Lemaigre-Dubreuil, 233
Lenin, V. I., 268, 272, 276, 279
Leopold, King (of Belgium), 201, 302, 338
liaison officers, 193
Libération, 97, 162
Liberation Committee for Upper Italy (Milan), 286, 304
Libération-Nord, 106, 156, 219
Libération-Sud, 106, 156, 314
Lidice, nazi annihilation of, 223, 352–3
Liénart, Cardinal, 159–60
Lithuania, 24, 26, 180, 288
Longo, 65, 304
Lorraine, 21, 31; see also Alsace
Lübeck prison camp, 168
Lublin Committee, 300, 326
Luxemburg, 21, 91, 227, 347

Malar, General, 324
malicious humour, 78–9
Malraux, André, 65
Mandel, Georges, 305
Maniu, Iuliu, 152, 294, 340
Mann, Thomas, 64, 90
Manouchian, 222
Manoussakis, General, 199n
Manteuffel, Professor, 143
Mao Tse-tung, 7, 268–9, 271
maquis see guerrilla warfare
Marin, Louis, 152
Marty, André, 65, 186n
Marty, A., 142
Marx, Karl, 268, 272
Massigli, 110, 305
Mast, General, 233, 234, 236
'Master Plan East' (nazi colonisation plan), 21–2, 24
Matchek, 232
Matteoti brigades (Italian socialists), 96, 285
Mauriac, François, 97, 141
Maurras, Charles, 46, 151
Maurois, André, 66
Mauthausen concentration camp, 176 &n, 223
Mazaryk, Thomas, 43, 333
Megret, Maurice, 87

Mendès-France, Pierre, 153
Mendigal, Admiral, 236
Metexas, General Ioánnis, 36, 230, 350
MI9 (British intelligence), 52
Michael, King (of Rumania), 294 322, 323, 339, 340
Midol, Lucien, 226
Mihailovich, Colonel Draza, 124, 146, 211, 280, 297, 342, 343
Mikolajczyk (Polish Prime Minister), 327
Milorg (Norwegian resistance), 301, 336
Miranda internment camp, 109
Mirkovich, General, 232
MNB (Belgian National Movement), 105, 107
Molotov, V. M., 55, 181, 341
Moltke, Helmuth von, 136, 351, 359
Mont Mouchet maquis (Auvergne), 9, 274, 290, 330
Montsabert, General de, 234
Moravec, Colonel Frantisek, 73
Morocco, 233, 234
Moslems, 163-4
Moulin, Jean, 78, 94, 97n, 106, 121n, 129, 249, 252, 253n, 254, 258, 259, 260, 283, 306, 325
MRP (French Catholic party), 162
Munich Agreements, 83, 182, 238, 295
Munich, Ferenc, 65
Munk, Pastor Kaj, 96
MUR (French United Resistance Movement), 104, 216, 220, 255n, 258, 275n, 283, 284
Muravief, 322
Mussert, 36-7, 38, 41, 43, 288
Mussolini, Benito, 12, 20, 21n, 35, 36n, 38, 44, 136, 145, 158, 197, 285; opposition to, 60-1; fall of, 123, 227-8, 231, 239-40, 241, 320, 348
mysticism, 80-1

NAP (French Penetration of public services), 204-6

Napoleon Bonaparte, 267, 270
Nasjonal Samling (Quisling nazis), 162
national fronts (in Eastern Europe), 293-4, 339; see also French National Front
national risings, 264, 315-34; as seen from outside, 315-17; and from inside, 317-20; in Corsica, 320-1; in Bucharest and Sofia, 322-3; in Slovakia, 323-5; Vercors, 325-6; in Warsaw, 326-9; self-liberation in Paris, 329-32; in Prague, 332-3
Nazi-Soviet Pact see Russo-German Pact
Nedich, General, 43, 72, 230, 280, 342
Nenni, Pietro, 61, 66, 348
von Neurath, 83
newspapers and pamphlets, Allied, 88-9; clandestine press, 93-9, 100, 246, 283, 306, 310
Nitti, Francesco Saverio, 61
Noguès, General, 234, 235
non-acceptance of occupation, 76-8
Normandy landings, 8, 113, 238, 241, 285, 309, 311, 326, 329, 344
North Africa, 92n, 127, 147, 230, 306, 321; Italian control of, 19, 74; Allied landing, 58, 92, 231, 234; Arab nationalists, 163-4; see also Algeria; French Army of Africa
Norway, 31, 54, 247; nazi plans for, 21-2; fascist régime, 36, 41; allied propaganda, 89, 91, 99; resistance movements and circuits, 105, 113, 301; escape lines from, 109, 110; British operations, 122, 263-4; and 'Shetland bus' to, 126; lawyers and teachers' opposition, 142-3; army, 146; political parties, 152; government-in-exile, 154, 207; Protestant church, 162; allied bombing, 212; sabotage,

214, 215–16; liberation, 335, 336; Nazi reprisals, 352
nuclear research, scientists, 67n, 122, 215; *see also* heavy water

OCM (French 'Civil and Military Organisation'), 104, 106
Okecki, General, 171
OKW (High Command of Nazi Armed Forces), 23, 287
Olbricht, General, 242
ON (Czech 'National Defence'), 146
Operation 'Torch' *see* North Africa, allied landing
ORA (French 'Army Resistance Organisation'), 148, 284, 308, 314
Oranienburg concentration camp, 243
Orthodox Church, 163, 184
OSS, 57, 58 &n, 309
'Ostland', 24
Ouenza, 31
OVRA (Italian secret police), 62

Papandreou, George, 110, 350
parachute and air landings, 52, 53, 56, 119, 121, 122, 125, 127–30, 185, 192, 275, 336; SAS battalions, 316
Paris rising (August 1944), 206, 207, 264, 317, 329–32, 334
Parodi, A., 330
Parri, Ferrucio, 61, 304
Parti Populaire Français 37, 41
passive and administrative resistance, 197–206
Passy, Colonel, 119, 128n, 251–2
'Patrian recuperare' (Freemasons), 106
Patriotic Militia (Belgium), 302
Patriotic Militia (France), 314, 345
Patriotic School (Britain), 123
Patton, General George, 8
Pauker, Anna, 186n
Paul, Prince (Yugoslav Regent), 231, 232
Paulus, Field Marshal Friedrich von, 9, 198

Pavelich, 38, 41, 158
Peenemunde, rocket establishment at, 115
Peri, Gabriel, 182
Pétain, Marshal Philippe, 45, 68, 69, 72, 73, 88, 135–6, 147, 151, 153, 154, 159, 164, 230, 233, 235, 236, 344
Peter, King (of Yugoslavia), 67, 84, 232, 297, 343
Petit, Claudius, 319
Philip, A., 154
Pieck, Wilhelm, 186n
Pierlot, M., 67
Pillot, R. P., 80
Piludski, Joseph, 95
Pineau, Christian, 111
Pius, XIII, Pope, 157, 158
plundering, Nazi, 28–9, 30–2, 42, 48
Poitau, Captain, 272, 275
Poliakov, L., 174–5
Poland, 11, 30, 31, 41n, 60, 171, 190, 211, 224, 265; 'Government General' in, 21, 22, 24, 119; nazi systematisation of terror, 22–3, 287; extermination of Jews, 26–7, 179; labour camps, 32, 171; defeat of collaboration in, 46–7; escapes from, 73, 74, 75, 171; non-acceptance of occupation, 77, 78, 79; allied broadcasts to, 90, 91, 93, 99; clandestine press, 94–5, 96–7; political parties, 103, 105, 150, 153, 154; intelligence circuits, 113, 114–15; SOE and, 123; parachute and air landings, 129–30; social classes, 135, 138, 139, 140; clandestine university, 143–4; and military resisters, 146; trade unionists, 156; Catholics, 157, 158n; concentration camps, 175; Jewish resistance, 179, 180; sabotage, 214; raiding parties, 220–1; assassination of Kutschera, 222, 223; partisans, 274; communists v. non-communists, 298–

Poland—*cont.*
301; subject to USSR, 312, 335, 338, 341
Polish Council of National Union, 298
Polish government-in-exile (London), 26, 51, 67, 68, 108, 150, 154, 175, 264, 292, 298–300, 326, 327
Polish Home Army (AK), 51, 97, 105, 114–15, 130, 220–1, 222, 223, 224n, 298, 299, 319, 327, 328
Polish National Committee, 300
Polish Peoples Guard, 221
Polish War Crimes Study Group, 221n
Polish Workers Party, 221
political parties, 134, 150–5; clandestine movements and, 103; extreme right, 150–1; moderates, 152–3; socialists, 153–5, 305–6, 311, 348; Christian democrats, 153, 157, 162; radicals, 152–3; *see also* communists
Political Warfare Executive (PWE: Britain), 52, 90
Politzer, 141–2
Ponomarenko, General, 277
Portugal, 22, 53, 91, 125
'post-boxes', 250, 252, 243, 259
postal workers, 200–1, 204–5
Prague rising, 317, 332–3, 334, 355; *see also* Czechoslovakia
Prevost, J., 142
prisoners-of-war, 24–5, 74, 109, 134, 166–71, 188, 299
propaganda, Allied, 52, 87–101, 213, 278; rules of psychological warfare, 87–8; pamphlets and newspapers from outside, 88–9; radio broadcasts, 89–93; clandestine press, 93–9, effect and limitations, 99–101
Protestant Church, 162–3
'Protocols of Paris', 237
'Psychological Warfare Division' (Anglo-American), 87
Pucheu, 308

Pyromaglou, M., 82

Queuille, 153
Quisling, Vidkun, 36, 38, 41, 43, 142

radio, 58; system of 'personal messages', 53; clandestine, 81, 113, 130–2; allied broadcasts, 87, 89–93, 99, 100; training of operators, 120
Radio Moscow, 184, 189, 219, 295n, 327
Radio Orange, 90
Rado, 117
raiding parties, 220–1, 275–6; Soviet long-distance, 278
railwaymen, 200, 204, 227
Rakosi, 186n
Rassemblement National Populaire, 41
rationing, 248
Rauter, (Commissar-General in Holland), 222, 337
Rava-Russka prison camp, 168, 169
Ravensbrück concentration camp, 192
'reception committees', 252, 262, 306
Red Army, 11, 24, 47, 54, 56, 92, 100, 113, 116, 117, 184, 185, 187, 189, 229, 289, 293, 294, 316, 333, 339, 360; attitude to partisans, 50, 145; co-operation between resistance and, 214, 216; liberation of E. European countries by, 239, 296, 322–3, 332, 335, 338; in Poland, 299, 300, 301; and Warsaw rising, 326, 327–8
regular officers *see* social classes
Rémy, Colonel, 112, 206, 218n, 250–1
Renner, Karl, 35n
Renoir, Jean, 67
Renouvin, Jacques, 143, 219
resistance, 245–62; motives, 245–7; daily existence, 247–53; un-

derground mentality, 253–4; false papers, 255–7; betrayals and arrests, 257–62; nazi reprisals, 352–4

Revolutionary Army of National Liberation (Yugoslav partisans), 281–2, 297

Rexists (Belgium fascists), 37, 41, 105, 160

Reynaud, Paul, 68

Rhineland, remilitarisation of, 63

Ribbentrop, Joachim von, 20, 141

Riom trial, 154

Ritter (aide to Sauckel), 222

La Rocque, Colonel de, 37, 38, 151

Roey, Cardinal Van, 160, 201–2

Rokossovsky, Marshal Konstantine, 7, 327

Rol-Tanguy, 330

Romains, Jules, 66

Rommel, Field Marshal Erwin, 69, 242

Roosevelt, Franklyn Delano, 51, 53, 57, 59, 69, 237, 306, 312, 316, 338

Rosenberg, Alfred, 20, 23–4, 47, 141, 158

Rosselli brothers, 61, 62

Rote Kapelle (Soviet circuit in Germany), 116

RSHA (Nazi Security Department), 258

Ruge, General, 146

Rumania, 22, 31, 100, 143, 152, 153, 182, 230, 317; fascist régime, 35, 41, 43, 135; SOE missions, 124; sabotage, 214; miners' strike, 227; Bucharest rising, 264, 322–3, 325, 334; National Front, 294, 340; Soviet tutelage over, 335, 338, 340, 341

Russo-German non-aggression Pact, 47, 55, 56, 97, 138, 154, 158, 181–3, 186, 219, 298, 310, 345, 359

sabotage, 52, 84–6, 170, 172, 176, 195, 206, 211–17, 264, 278–9, 289, 309, 310, 318, 329, 337, 355

'safe houses', 245, 251–2

Saint-Hardouin, Tarbe de, 233

Saint-Pierre-et-Miquelon, 69, 159n

Salo Republic, 21n, 145, 158, 228, 285

Sangnier, Mari, 161n

Saragat, Giuseppe, 61, 348

SAS parachute battalions, 316, 337

satellite states, 43–4

'satellite units' (German), 288

Sauckel, Gauleiter, 33, 171, 222

Schaumburg, General, 222

Schirmeck internment camp, 41

Schmidt, General, 288

Schumann, Maurice, 90

Schuster, Cardinal, 158

SD (SS Security Service), 287

Secret Army (Gaullist), 13, 283, 308

Seyss-Inquart, Arthur, 142, 337

Sforza, Count, 61

Shubachich, 297

Sikorski, General Wladyslav, 67, 299

Sima, Horia, 41, 43

Simeon, King (of Bulgaria), 339

Simovich, General, 231–2

SIS (British Intelligence), 52, 261

Slovak National Council, 324, 325

Slansky, 295

Slovakia, 135, 171, 238, 274, 295; fascist régime, 22, 35, 39, 43; escape routes through, 74, 75; Soviet propaganda, 92–3, 100; failure of rising, 264, 317, 323–5, 332, 334, 358; separatist demands, 295, 296; communists in, 324, 325, 326, 340, 341; *see also* Czechoslovakia

social classes and groups, 135–49; aristocracy, 135–6; upper middle class, 136–7; middle class, 137–8; working-class, 138–9; agricultural workers, 139–40; intelligentsia, 141–4; regular officers, 144–6; Armistice Army, 147–9

Socialist Action Committee (French), 154

Socrates (Belgian resistance), 283

SOE (British Special Operations Executive), 52, 121–5, 212, 213, 215, 247, 251, 261, 263n, 301, 302, 309

'Song of the Partisans', 142

Sorge, Richard, 117

Soviet Union, 7, 11, 27, 28, 31, 40, 43, 60, 62, 70, 87, 136–7, 155, 242, 243, 292, 301; nazi occupied zone of, 23–5, 29; prisoners of war, 24–5; extermination of Jews in, 26; collaboration, 47–8; attitude to resistance, 51, 53, 54–6; nazi attack on (1941), 55, 113, 117, 139, 168; role in Spanish Civil War, 65; propaganda by, 87, 92–3, 96, 100; resistance circuits organised by, 108, 116–17; escape lines, 109; agents, 118, 121; peasants, 139, 140; Orthodox Church, 163; nazi labour conscription, 171; Jewish resistance, 179, 180; Communist Party, 183–5; foreign communists loyalty to, 181, 186–8, 210; Free Germany Committee, 188–90; Hungary and, 239; guerrilla warfare in, 263, 274, 277–9, 288, 289, 291; national fronts and, 293–4, 303; relations between Czechoslovakia and, 295–6, 332, 333; and Poland, 299–301, 327–8, 329; political gap between allies and, 311–12, 355; long-term plans of, 316; liberation of Rumania and Bulgaria, 322–3; and Slovak rising, 323–5; tutelage over Eastern and Central Europe of, 335, 338–42; Greek policy, 350; see also Russo-German Pact

Spain, 22, 45, 53, 109, 110, 136, 155, 284

Spanish Civil War, 50, 62, 64–6, 153, 182, 206, 280

Srobar (Czech prime minister), 324

SS, 12, 24, 26, 32, 174–5, 176n, 185, 198, 221, 289; see also Waffen-ss

Stalin, Josef, 40, 47, 51, 55, 57, 64, 92, 113, 154, 163, 185, 188, 228, 282, 303, 305, 345; signs Russo-German Pact, 181; forms 'national front', 184; abolishes Comintern, 186; Free Germany Committee and, 188, 189–90; gentlemen's agreement with Church in Balkans, 297, 338, 350; Polish policy, 299, 301, 327–8, 329; political objectives, 316; meeting with Tito, 343–4

Stalingrad, battle of, 9, 55, 56, 117, 185, 188, 241

Starhemberg, Prince, 38

Stauffenberg, Colonel Claus Schenk von, 242–3, 351

Stein, Karl, 267

Stepinac, Archbishop, 158

Stoyadinovich government, 36

strikes, 224–8, 264, 336, 348, 360

Stroop, ss General, 179

Stulpnagel, General von, 242

Stwosz, Witt, 32

Sudentanland, 21, 35, 39, 64

Suhard, Cardinal, 159

Superior Consultative Committee of the Underground (Holland), 302

Svoboda, General, 324, 339

Sweden, 22, 91, 109, 110, 125, 126, 171, 202, 336

Switzerland, 22, 75, 109, 111, 117, 125, 171

Szalassy, 41, 203, 239

'Szare Szeregi' (Polish resistance), 221

Sztojay, 238, 239

Szyr, Vice-President, 65

Tabouis, Geneviève, 66–7

Tatarescu, 294
Teheran Conference, 116, 300
Teske, Colonel, 279
Texcier, Jean, 'Advice to the Occupied' by, 77
Thorez, Maurice, 186n, 345
Thyssen, Baron von, 64
Tillion, Germaine, 104
Tillon, Charles, 218, 269n, 272
Tiso, Mgr, 43
Tisserant, Cardinal Eugène, 158
Tito, Josip Broz, 65, 92, 124, 276, 280–2, 297–8, 342, 343
Todt Organisation, 33, 115
Togliatti, Palmiro, 61, 186, 303
Tolbukhin, Fedor, 351
torture of prisoners, 259–60
trade unions, 134, 153, 154, 155–7
Transylvania, 22, 35, 40, 43, 238, 339
Tresckow, General von, 242
Treves, Claudio, 61
Triolet, Elsa, 97
Tripartite Pact, 231–2, 238
Trotskyists, 65, 66
Tunisia, 31, 35, 233, 234, 237, 307
Turati, 61
Turkey, 22, 126
Tyrol, 21n, 35

Ukraine, 24, 31, 180, 185, 278–9, 300, 341
Ulbricht, Walter, 65, 186n
Union of French Women, 314
United Forces of Patriotic Youth (France), 314
United States, 40n, 137, 233, 239, 242, 299, 320, 343; resistance role of, 51, 53, 56–9, 108, 115, 118, 121; political exiles in, 66–7, 153–4, 178; propaganda of, 87, 92; invasion of Italy, 124, 215, 285; communists in, 187–8; bombing raids by, 212, 216–17, 226, 263–4, 321; French policy, 230, 305, 306, 309; Algiers putsch and, 233–7; AMGOT set up by, 240; support for Vichy régime, 306; military and economic aid to French, 307, 308, 309; political gap between USSR and, 311–12, 355; objectives, 315–16; Polish rising and, 327, 328; and liberation of Paris, 330, 331; and Prague rising, 332, 333; Normandy landings, 344
United Workers Front (Rumania), 294
Ustashis, 19, 38, 39, 41, 158, 258n, 279, 280, 280, 343
UVOD (Czech resistance), 96, 221

V1 and V2 rockets, 114–16
Vallin Charles, 151
Van Hecke, 233
Van Severen, 151
Vayo, Alvarez del, 65
Vercors, Le Silence de la Mer by, 97
Vercors maquis, 9, 178, 274, 276, 290; failure of rising, 264, 325–6, 334, 358
Vichy régime, 12, 22, 47, 58, 105, 106, 141, 143, 172, 183, 288, 305, 309; equivocal situation of, 43–6; hunting of resisters by, 45, 258; Allied relations with, 52, 122, 230, 306; de Gaulle's view of, 69; aristocracy's support for, 135–6; political parties under, 151, 152, 153, 154; and Work Charter, 155–6; Algiers putsch against, 233–7; end of, 307, 308, 344; see also France
Victor Emmanuel, King (of Italy), 133, 152, 238, 239–40, 286, 303, 322, 349
Vildé, Boris, 142, 247
Vishinsky, A. I., 340, 341
Vistel, Alban, 247
Vlakhovich, 186n
Vlassov, General Andrei, 47, 168, 189
VNV (Flemish Nationalists), 160
Voice of the Vatican, 81, 157

Waffen-SS, 145, 163

War Crimes Commission, 32
Warsaw, Jewish (ghetto) revolt (1943), 179, 317; rising (1944), 7, 90, 97, 222, 264, 317, 325, 326-9, 334, 355, 357, 358; destruction of, 353; *see also* Poland
Wehrmacht (German Armed Forces), 20, 22, 24, 25, 29, 37, 39, 46, 63, 96, 116, 144, 166, 186; casualties, 32; invasion and occupation of USSR, 40, 56, 92, 184, 270, 279-80, 289; in Spain, 65; foreign units, 98, 100; prisoners of war captured by, 66; loyalty to Hitler, 145; in Hungary, 238; defeat in Rumania, 239; plot against life of Hitler, 189, 240-4; counter-guerrilla action by, 287-9; evacuation of France, 331, 344; defeat, 350, 351
Weinert, E., 188
Weygand, General Maxime, 69, 147, 203, 230
White Rose (German student group), 161
Wilhelmina, Queen (of Holland), 67, 301-2, 337

Wittek, B., 99
Witzleben, Field Marshal von, 242, 243
women resisters, 192-4
works of art, German plundering of, 32, 198-9
WRN (Polish socialists), 154
Wurm, Bishop, 162

Yugoslavia, 31, 60, 140, 153, 182, 190, 238, 265, 322; Italian occupation, 19, 20; support for fascism, 35, 36, 38, 43; government-in-exile, 67, 68, 280, 297; Allied broadcasts, 91, 92; clandestine news sheets, 96; escape lines from, 109; SOE operations, 123-4, 127n; Mihailovich's *chetniks*, 146, 280, 342; women partisans, 192; sabotage, 215; Belgrade *putsch*, 231-2, 237; guerrilla warfare, 274, 279-82; Kragujevac massacre, 289; communist triumph in, 296-7, 335-6, 342-4; resistance casualties, 352, 353

Zéro-France (resistance circuit), 112